MY YEARS WITH GORBACHEV AND SHEVARDNADZE

MY YEARS WITH
GORBACHEV AND
SHEVARDNADZE

The Memoir of a Soviet Interpreter

Pavel Palazchenko

With a Foreword by
Don Oberdorfer

The Pennsylvania State University Press
University Park, Pennsylvania

DK290.3
.P35
A3
1997

Library of Congress Cataloging-in-Publication Data

Palazchenko, Pavel.
    My years with Gorbachev and Shevardnadze : the memoir of a Soviet
interpreter / Pavel Palazchenko ; with a foreword by Don Oberdorfer.
        p.   cm.
    Includes index.
    ISBN 0-271-01603-5 (alk. paper)
    1. Palazchenko, Pavel.   2. Soviet Union—History—1985–1991.
3.   Translators—Soviet Union—Biography.   4. Gorbachev, Mikhail
Sergeyevich, 1931–   —Friends and associates.   5. Schevardnadze,
Eduard Amvrosievich—Friends and associates.   I. Oberdorfer, Don.
II. Title.
DK290.3.P35A3—1997
947.085′4—dc20   96–25686
                                                                              CIP

The great things of life are what they seem to be, and for that reason . . . are often difficult to interpret.

—Oscar Wilde

Contents

Foreword by Don Oberdorfer

Much has been written about the foreign policy of the Soviet Union in the Gorbachev era, which ended the Cold War and changed the world even before the collapse of the system that Mikhail Gorbachev headed and sought to reform. In the West, Secretaries of State George Shultz and James Baker, Ambassador Jack Matlock, and a host of historians and journalists, including this writer, have described at length the episodes and crises in the six years of Gorbachev's diplomatic leadership. In Moscow, Gorbachev himself and his foreign policy adviser Anatoly Chernyaev, among many others, have had their say in books. For all this, Pavel Palazchenko adds a new dimension from an intimate vantage point.

As the principal English interpreter for Gorbachev and his friend and foreign minister, Eduard Shevardnadze, Palazchenko was a participant in nearly all of their negotiations with the United States from 1985 to the end of the Soviet Union in December 1991. As this memoir shows clearly, Palazchenko was more than a mere diplomatic functionary. His was a keen intelligence and a remarkably open mind, which, as he worked, assessed what he saw and heard, and explored in his own head the future of the historic changes he was witnessing.

We journalists who watched the drama unfold between the United States and the Soviet Union in the Gorbachev-Shevardnadze era became accustomed to the sight of this bald, mustached figure at the side of the Soviet leaders, whether at the bargaining tables in summit meetings or on informal occasions, as when Gorbachev gave a Red Square walking tour to Ronald Reagan, or James Baker took Shevardnadze fishing at Jackson Hole, Wyoming.

Because both Gorbachev and Shevardnadze relied on him so completely in their respective meetings with Americans, and because he remained constant while U.S. presidents, secretaries of state, and negotiators changed with the turn of administrations, Palazchenko witnessed more of the diplomatic interaction of the two most important states than any other individual. Somehow the gleam in his eyes conveyed the impression to us that his interests were much deeper than linguistic, that he was thinking while he was talking—and we were right. Until the end of the Soviet Union, it was not possible for him to express his own ideas and observations. Finally, in this memoir, this prime eyewitness to history provides his own unique view of a memorable period in international politics.

A fluent English speaker, who sharpened his skills on the interpreting staff of the United Nations and later at the Soviet foreign ministry, Palazchenko developed in time well-reasoned convictions on the national and international issues that were subjects of the meetings he interpreted. In 1987 he became an official of the arms control section of the foreign ministry, as well as continuing to be the top English interpreter for Soviet leaders. In 1991, following the resignation of Shevardnadze, he became a member of the foreign policy development staff in Gorbachev's presidential office.

The position of interpreter is a sensitive and highly confidential one. Palazchenko recounts that it appealed to him in part because he was regarded as "not quite a government official but more one's own person." At the same time, it imposes obligations of confidentiality that he continues to recognize even though the government he worked for no longer exists. In keeping with this, Palazchenko forthrightly informs his readers that his account, while frank, is incomplete because he is not at liberty to disclose everything he saw and heard. Palazchenko continues to be closely associated with Gorbachev at the International Foundation for Socio-Economic and Political Studies (the Gorbachev Institute) in Moscow. Even so, he is candid about Gorbachev's failings in office, as well as informative about the courage and determination that led to Gorbachev's many accomplishments.

What is most impressive about this book is the personal and human dimension of Palazchenko's observations about the people who made history from 1985 to the end of 1991. From his first important interpreting job for Gorbachev—a one-on-one conversation with Indian Prime Minister Rajiv Gandhi—the author managed to observe far more than the formal exchanges of words. From body language, nuance, and personal expressions of the kind that never show up in government memoranda of conversations or other official documents, Palazchenko acquired insights into the character and personality of great figures of the day as they interacted with one another.

Here are his firsthand impressions of Ronald Reagan, George Bush, George Shultz, James Baker, Margaret Thatcher, and many others in action at moments of tension or triumph and episodes of personal camaraderie with Soviet leaders.

Palazchenko provides a new dimension of insight and understanding to his portraits of those on the Soviet side, especially Gorbachev and his remarkable foreign minister, Eduard Shevardnadze. Palazchenko worked for both men and, more than that, came to have a relationship of trust with each of them. His account tells us more than we knew before about how and why these two old friends drifted apart as the final crises of the Soviet Union erupted.

Palazchenko depicts a Gorbachev who was pulled in opposite directions by his dual position as the initiator and leader of reforms but also the head of a powerful state with institutions, traditions, and personnel inherited from the totalitarian past. He writes that it would have been "suicidal" for Gorbachev to declare war on the Communist establishment that had brought him to office, or to ignore it or dissociate himself from it, even as he was maneuvering to replace it with new, more democratic institutions and a new breed of more flexible people. "Like the symbol of the old Russia, the two-headed eagle, [Gorbachev] had to be ambivalent, at least in some situations," Palazchenko observed.

Shevardnadze, on the other hand, had rapidly evolved from Communist Party boss in Georgia to a realistic, bold, and imaginative leader of the country's international affairs. Until late in 1989, when revolutionary developments in Eastern Europe, the breaching of the Berlin Wall, and the impending integration of East Germany into the West made Soviet foreign policy highly controversial at home, Shevardnadze enjoyed a relatively free hand from domestic constraints. As Palazchenko analyzes the problem, domestic issues, especially the use of Soviet military power against the people in Shevardnadze's native Georgia and its impending use elsewhere in the country, were at the root of Shevardnadze's little-known attempt to resign at the end of 1989 and his sudden and sensational resignation a year later, warning of a coming "dictatorship." The breakup of the Gorbachev-Shevardnadze team just as conservatives in Moscow were becoming much stronger had dire consequences, as Palazchenko feared at the time.

While he does not shrink from criticizing their failures and shortcomings, Palazchenko depicts with sympathy the conflicting interests and pressures that limited the maneuvering room of Gorbachev, Shevardnadze, and likeminded associates in this dramatic period. "Revolutionary times are cruel to decent people," he observes at one point. Both the drama of the times and the humanness of the main actors are sharply etched in Palazchenko's account.

During the abortive coup of August 1991, a move that failed to topple Gorbachev but in fact robbed him of most of his power, Palazchenko resolved to take a menial job, saying that he was ready to work as a night watchman rather than cooperate with the new regime. His true grit was a symbol of loyalty to Gorbachev and the reforms he instituted and of disdain for the coup-plotters who sought to return the country to the policies of earlier times. Palazchenko's combination of modesty and intellectual strength, and his keen powers of observation, make his firsthand account of the last years of the Soviet Union illuminating to today's readers and valuable to future scholars and historians. It is an important contribution to our understanding of one of the great turning points of the twentieth century.

By Way of Introduction

The nights of late December are the longest of the year. Certainly the night of December 20, 1990, was the longest for me in many years. It was the day when Eduard Shevardnadze, foreign minister of the Soviet Union, announced his resignation. It is not easy to disturb me, but I had a sleepless night. I did not know yet that there would be other sleepless nights later—the night after the killings in Vilnius in January, the nights during the coup in August, and again the long nights in December 1991, culminating in President Mikhail Gorbachev's resignation statement on December 25.

My life changed after that. I no longer have to rise early and rush to my office, which during the last four months of my work with President Gorbachev was in the Kremlin. I no longer have to spend hours reading cables from embassies around the world, including places like Gaborone or La Paz, from which ambassadors have to remind Moscow of their existence. My working days no longer end at 9 or 11 o'clock at night. It is a different life for me now. I have time to think about the years (1985–1991) I spent working closely with those two men—Gorbachev and Shevardnadze—who did so much to change my country and the world.

Those years also changed me. My position as interpreter for Gorbachev and Shevardnadze gave me a unique view of what was happening, though some things may be too difficult to see and understand at close range.

I have great respect for Mikhail Gorbachev and Eduard Shevardnadze. I also respect their many partners in the talks and negotiations in which I took part as the interpreter, and I am bound by the trust of those men and women. This has to affect the book that I write. There are things—human things and secrets of governments—that I will not mention.

Thus, this book will be frank, but it must be incomplete. It is mostly a personal memoir and an equally personal commentary. As a student of English at the Moscow Institute of Foreign Languages more than twenty years ago, I never dreamed that I would ever be doing this kind of work. I did not think that I would be working in the Soviet government. I was preparing for a career in teaching, or maybe publishing. But most of all I, like all of us, never thought it possible that my country would go through such a radical transformation in my lifetime.

My life has turned out to be much more interesting than I expected.

And my country's history continues to amaze and fascinate the world. It all came together in the years after 1985, and particularly in 1991. I am sure many people will write about their personal experiences of that time. I feel I must.

One
FORMATIVE YEARS
1949 – 1985

Early Influences

I was born in 1949, the year when the first Soviet nuclear weapon was tested. Many other things happened that year: another splendidly decorated line of Moscow Metro—the subway—was commissioned, Joseph Stalin wrote articles on Marxism and linguistics, and Nikita Khrushchev was transferred from the Ukraine to Moscow. The year 1949 saw another of Stalin purges that destroyed the lives of many thousands and their families.

In August 1949 my grandmother was arrested as a former member of the "Trotsky-Zinoviev opposition." It happened in our apartment in the little town near Moscow where we then lived. My mother later told me in some detail how it happened. The group of secret police who came to make the arrest searched the rooms thoroughly, going through every book and all the clothing. They even ordered Mother to take me from the bed in which I was sleeping and searched the bed for God-knows-what.

Grandma returned "from the North" in 1955. She was not among the first people released when Khrushchev opened the prison camps and exonerated most political prisoners. Many officials were in no hurry to review the fabricated cases of the 1930s and 1940s.

I remember Grandma's return vividly. Mother and I went to Moscow to

Yaroslavl Station to meet her. We came early—or maybe the train was late—so we spent an hour or so riding the circle line of the Moscow Metro. The stations seemed huge and overbearing to me. They still do.

We returned to the room in the communal apartment where Mother and I lived after being expelled from Grandma's comfortable, old apartment following the arrest. Later we moved several times, and I remember all those rooms and apartments. Whenever I return to the little town where my mother still lives, I like sometimes to approach the houses in which our family lived in different times, more or less comfortably or in hardship.

Grandma was "rehabilitated," which means that the accusations against her were dropped, but she did not resume her membership in the Communist Party. She did not speak of the reasons, but I suspect she was not particularly happy about the country's development and its government. When Alexander Solzhenitsyn's *One Day in the Life of Ivan Denisovich* was published in 1962, she began to talk to me and my mother about camps and how people survived there.

She kept the faith in the ideals of her Communist youth, but she openly scoffed at the propaganda line that, despite the purges and years of imprisonment, most people continued to be staunch Communists and believed in the correctness of the party's policies. "You have to be stupid to believe that everything was basically all right while your own life and the lives of millions of people were ruined," she used to say. She died in 1962—vaguely socialist in her heart but very unhappy about the party bureaucracy, strongly anti-Stalinist but also constantly exasperated at Khrushchev's boorishness and his numerous mistakes.

By the time Khrushchev was stripped of his posts and retired to his dacha after a party coup on October 14, 1964, I had developed an interest in politics—or what was called politics in the Soviet Union of that time. I read the newspapers regularly. I also read *Novy Mir*—the literary magazine edited by Alexander Tvardovsky that published not only Solzhenitsyn and other writers but also excellent articles on history, philosophy, and literary criticism, in which, mostly in veiled form, many Soviet dogmas and clichés were mercilessly destroyed.

I admired Khrushchev for what he did in breaking with the Stalinist past, even though only partially, and releasing millions from the prison camps. For that I was ready to forgive him his numerous mistakes and stupidities. But most people were not. So while I considered his removal an unfortunate setback for the country and a sign of an impending return to some form of Stalinism, most people around me were either indifferent or quite pleased.

They expected that there would now be "greater order." They went about their business unaware that hope for change and for making the Soviet Union a normal country was being taken away from them.

Novy Mir continued to be published under Tvardovsky. It had numerous problems with the censors—sometimes the issues came several months too late—but it kept alive the flame of good writing and clear thinking until 1970. I was an avid reader. For me and many of my contemporaries it was a mind-forming experience. The magazine's closure, as well as the invasion of Czechoslovakia, was the definitive expression of the victory of Neo-Stalinism.

Millions of people who had breathed the air of intellectual freedom in the early 1960s had to make a choice as the last signs of that freedom disappeared. The great majority chose to conform. I don't think it was a difficult choice. The regime was not very harsh to those who did not fight it openly. And people had to go on living. They earned their bread, raised their children, and despised the party bureaucracy. For many, that was enough.

I was then a student at the Institute of Foreign Languages in Moscow. The tightening of ideological screws went on throughout the five years that I studied there, and the stupidity of the official ideology was not even funny. The mood in our discussions of political events and the country's prospects was mostly somber. Still, those were the good years of my life. I and my friends were young. We studied with genuine interest. We did not have much money, but we scraped enough together for parties with girls and a lot of drinking (vodka was cheap in those days). And we had the Beatles.

I am sure that the impact of the Beatles on the generation of young Soviets in the 1960s will one day be the object of studies. We knew their songs by heart. A typical group of young people would have someone playing the guitar surrounded by a group listening or singing along with varying proficiency. To the Beatles, even more than to my teacher of phonetics, I owe my accent. But I and my friends and contemporaries owe them something else too.

In the dusky years of the Brezhnev regime they were not only a source of musical relief. They helped us create a world of our own, a world different from the dull and senseless ideological liturgy that increasingly reminded one of Stalinism. Our generation chose their melodies—and also their freedom, their mistakes, their crises. I believe that only some of us in those years drew inspiration from Andrey Sakharov, for we had not yet matured enough to understand his vision. But the Beatles were our quiet way of rejecting "the system" while conforming to most of its demands.

In 1968 I decided that I would not be able to work for the government. I took the invasion of Czechoslovakia hard. I liked that country, I had friends there, and I was even learning the Czech language for fun and information from the lively Czech newspapers. I remember how I was struck by the cartoons of the country's leaders in those newspapers. I regarded such cartoons as a healthy thing, and yet I understood that in the Soviet Union of that time nothing of the kind was even conceivable. Of course, it was only one small example of how incompatible the evolution of Czechoslovakia was with the regime then existing in my country.

So the evolution was broken off. I soon understood that it was inevitable, but I could not accept it. Because I had decided not to try to enter government service, I made no effort to conceal my views, and that was probably noted by "competent bodies." Some friends cautioned me against being too frank, but the frankness had no serious consequences—the rejection of the invasion was so widespread among students and the intelligentsia that only open protests were suppressed. But I was not the kind of person to demonstrate against the invasion in Red Square. In fact, I was developing an ambivalent attitude toward the dissident movement, which was just then beginning to gather momentum. I thought their effort was perhaps valiant but useless—it was only embittering the regime and helping the conservatives to justify any move to the right. I argued about it fiercely with some of my friends.

There was another matter on which I and my friends—and most of the dissidents and most Soviet citizens generally, including the country's leaders—differed. They all were afraid of China, while I thought the threat was exaggerated. The "Chinese danger" was then on everyone's mind. It is difficult to imagine today how much people were scared by the prospect of war with China. That fear was shared by Brezhnev, Solzhenitsyn and the man in the street. I thought it was enormously exaggerated. In terms of its military might or of its political or economic attractiveness, I did not see China as a dangerous adversary to my country. But most people disagreed with me. Fear of China often reached the point of hysteria. In retrospect I see only one positive by-product of that fear: it helped to push the leaders of the Soviet Union toward détente with the United States.

Détente was welcomed by everyone I knew. People had great hopes, which turned out to be naive. But the beginning was promising. The "enemy image" of the United States was gradually receding, and a kind of ideological thaw seemed to begin in 1972 or 1973. To many people it was barely perceptible, and in fact it never amounted to much. Still, many people began to believe then that a "convergence of the two systems" was possible, or that at least a less rigid and less harsh Soviet system could result from détente abroad.

Career Decisions

In 1972 I graduated from the Institute. During my last year I had to start thinking about what I intended to do with my life—something I had avoided doing in the preceding years. There was not much choice. The "good careers" in my field were all in government, more precisely in the foreign ministry or the KGB. I was not attracted by those careers, and I do not think I would have had much chance if I had been. Those were really closed clubs that rarely admitted people who came out of nowhere. Family ties meant everything. I thought so then, and I later found that it was generally true.

I was a good student, not because I worked particularly hard but because I liked my studies, enjoyed reading, and learned quickly and easily. Only a couple of times did I have to make a real effort to pass an exam. On one occasion it was "economic geography of the United States," another time it was something called "scientific atheism"—in fact, as taught by our professors, it was a brief course in the history of religions, which I enjoyed. My main interest continued to be languages. Both English and French fascinated me in endless ways. Translating, particularly good prose, was an adventure and often, when I felt I had hit on the best word or phrase, a real joy. I also started to work as a simultaneous interpreter, which at the time was regarded as something enormously difficult and almost mysterious. It also paid good money.

So I thought the best thing for me to do after graduating would be to stay in the Institute as a teacher. I knew that my own teachers would welcome me as a colleague. The job was, frankly, not particularly demanding. After all, you can teach successfully if your student is capable and interested; if not, no amount of effort will help. Most teachers were therefore a little cynical, but the atmosphere was good, and I was looking forward to joining the faculty. I knew that my salary would be low, but I would have time to work on the side and earn quite enough as a translator or interpreter.

Things turned out differently. Sometime during my last term at the Institute I was invited to the United Nations language-training course, where entrance exams were in progress. The exams consisted of translations from English and French and an interview with a group of U.N. officials who came for that purpose from New York. Passing the exams was no problem. It was the first year when a large group of students from my Institute became trainees at the U.N. course. Before that, few had been invited, and preference was given to students from the Institute of International Relations, an altogether different kind of place. Of the students at the Institute, few were "unconnected," and the emphasis was on subjects that for lack of a better word we called ideological, not on languages.

The small group of aspiring simultaneous interpreters at the U.N. course in my year consisted entirely of graduates of my Institute. I soon found out that there was nothing mysterious about interpretation. It took a combination of three things: a good command of languages, some knowledge of the subject being discussed, and boldness—some would say, panache. At the time I did not know that many people in the business of interpretation relied on such boldness as the principal ingredient in their success.

After passing the final exams, most of us began to prepare to leave for New York or Geneva—most, but not me. I was not married, which made me not quite reliable in the eyes of "the system." Signing the contract with the United Nations had to wait—the Soviet government would approve my appointment only after I married. The U.N. Secretariat was willing to wait, and I did not want to make such an important decision as marriage hastily. So I spent a year teaching and interpreting. By that time I had gained a rather good reputation. I also learned that competition among interpreters can sometimes be fierce and that, as in other professions, there are a lot of loose and often unfair talk, many inflated reputations, and a great deal that is focused on solely money.

For a person who entered the field as a well-trained but rather naive young man, finding out such things was something of a shock. I tried to stay away from the infighting and concentrate on professional improvement. When I came to New York in November 1974 I was confident that I could succeed in my field and that I would enjoy my work.

U.N. Interpreter

I spent five years at the United Nations. Those years—from 1974 to the end of 1979—were not the best for the organization. The member states regarded it as mostly irrelevant and sometimes harmful to their interests. Morale among the staff was low, and the spirit of international civil service seemed gone forever. The prestige of the Soviet Union was not high. The Soviets working in the Secretariat were bound by numerous constraints. We often felt that our dignity was affected but that we could not do much about it.

Still, I do not recall those years as bad. And it is not just that memory always selects the better parts of the past. I remember that time as the years when I grew as a professional. I lived and worked in a city that many find difficult to understand and impossible to like.

And I became a family man. Having married Lyudmila a few months before coming to New York, I went through all the problems and joys of building a family in a foreign environment. It was not easy, and the marriage eventually ended in divorce. But I still keep—like old snapshots—the memories of our good moments. In August 1978 my son Nikolay was born at Lenox Hill Hospital on Lexington Avenue.

I made quite a few friends among my countrymen and among New Yorkers and co-workers at the United Nations. I watched the world of international diplomacy. I thought about my country, wondering about its future.

The workload at the United Nations seemed light to me, and the meetings that I interpreted were often boring and even appeared silly. But I did not complain. First, there were quite a few meetings of the Security Council, and some of the General Assembly, that were exciting and professionally challenging. Second, I tried to handle even dull assignments as jobs to be done properly. Many of my colleagues disagreed and were openly cynical about most of the work they were doing.

Interpreters are a funny lot. Most are talented people with a good mind, an ability to grasp things quickly, and a broad knowledge of many subjects and issues. One really must know a great deal, at least superficially, to pass muster as a U.N. interpreter. Very soon one begins to feel that, knowing and understanding so much, one could do more important things. Much of what must be interpreted begins to sound silly, and one develops a condescending attitude to diplomats, government ministers, and even heads of state.

I quickly saw that this attitude was a trap. Interpretation is, after all, a craft, and wide-ranging knowledge is not a great merit in and of itself. I saw that my colleagues who were frozen in the attitude of cynical condescension toward just about everything were not interesting persons themselves, and indeed suffered from a kind of superiority complex sometimes bordering on a psychological disorder. Anyway, the United Nations of the time was easy to dismiss, and even to hate, for its bloated bureaucracy and seemingly pointless rituals, but I found it more interesting to watch and to learn.

The U.N. Diplomatic Scene

The diplomats who headed the U.N. missions in those years were a diverse group. I remember some of them as very colorful and strong individuals. Daniel Patrick Moynihan was one of the most intelligent and probably the most colorful of all. He liked to take a swipe at Soviet ideology, and most of the time he had a point. Of course, he was not much of a conciliator and therefore not much of a diplomat, but that skill was not in great demand at a time when the United Nations was regarded as above all an ideological battleground.

When I came to New York the Soviet ambassador was Yakov Malik, a veteran in a seemingly perpetual state of anger and bitterness evenly distributed toward friend and foe alike. Listening to his U.N. speeches, and particularly to him talking to the Soviet community at some gathering, one would find it difficult to believe that détente had replaced the Cold War. China was the number one enemy, but the United States was no friend, to say the least, and don't expect anything good from France, Britain, Japan, etc. I wondered how our country expected to survive in a world like that—with no real friends, and enemies practically everywhere.

In 1976 Malik was replaced by Oleg Troyanovsky, a very different kind of man. He was the son of the first Soviet ambassador to the United States, and he was a diplomat in everything he did and said. Everyone admired his manners, his English, and the spirit of conciliation and consensus that he exuded. He was extremely cautious, and I don't think he ever tried to make waves, to significantly affect the policies of the country he represented. But he certainly represented the Soviet Union with dignity and probably never did anything to embarrass it or to aggravate the problems it frequently inflicted on itself. Compared with Malik, Troyanovsky was a man of a different generation, and I was beginning to think that simple generational change could perhaps save my country.

Between Anger and Indifference

We were all worried about the country's future. Returning to the Soviet Union on home leave, I was struck not even by the obvious inferiority of the standard of living compared with America (that I could explain away in many ways, and I did) but by the fact that there were no obvious sources of growth and social energy. People were cynically looking for ways to earn as much money as they could with as little effort as possible. Nothing worked. No one cared. General Secretary Brezhnev, whom I tried to respect for being less of a Stalinist and apparently more humane than some of his Politburo colleagues, was passing into senility and quickly becoming the laughingstock for everyone. Most people thought it great fun; I found it quite demoralizing.

I was smart enough to understand that the root of all our problems was in the economy. The economic system of "developed socialism" was so obviously inefficient that even its short-term viability seemed doubtful to me. In my youth I read in *Novy Mir* some excellent articles on economic reform that openly called for creating a market economy in the Soviet Union. I knew enough about Lenin's "new economic policy" (NEP) to see the similarity between those market economy models and the NEP, and between them and the economic systems in the "normal" countries of the West. But the economic reform of 1965, which I thought could be the beginning of slow movement toward some form of market economy, was dead and buried by the mid-1970s. The country's malaise and the people's pervasive cynicism, which were even more evident on my short trips home, stemmed from the inability of Brezhnev's leadership to contemplate any economic reform. But the windfall of the oil money saved the system. It dragged on and on even in its senility—ugly, unpleasant, not too dangerous for the world or for its own people, but lacking a rationale and a future.

I saw what was happening to the people as a result of that. Most were trapped in a narrow corridor between anger and indifference. Many lost all hope. Some could not grasp what was happening. Others were cynically making a career in the system while hating it (those were the people I found difficult to understand). All often went through crises and shocks.

The defection of Arkady Shevchenko, who was a senior Soviet official in the U.N. Secretariat with the rank of under-secretary general, was a real shock to most of us. I don't know what happened to him and why. He presented himself in interviews and books as an ideologically committed opponent of the Soviet leaders and then of the Soviet system itself. Recently he talked to some reporters from our country, putting out the same line. I think that this is quite unlikely. He was not respected among the Soviet community in New York for any intellectual or diplomatic achievements. He was known as a heavy drinker, and most people believed that his meteoric career was due to his connections and his friendship with the son of Foreign Minister Andrey Gromyko. He probably compromised himself in some way

(I don't think he knew many secrets he could pass on), and then, suspecting the KGB had found out, thought it best to defect.

Whatever the explanation, the impact of Shevchenko's defection on the morale of Soviets in New York—and I suspect in other places too—was severe. People saw it as a sign of how rotten things were, and they were right.

In the 1970s many Soviet writers and artists left the country for the West. Some went quietly and legally, others defected. However they did it, the country was losing much of its creative talent. They too were losing a great deal, for in those years emigrating from the Soviet Union in most cases meant leaving it forever—the authorities closed the door to former Soviet citizens. Some of them made statements full of bitterness not only against the regime but also, it seemed to me, against their country. I disliked that. But in our discussions of the new wave of emigration with my friends and family, I never condemned those who were leaving. It is natural for people to seek a better and freer life. How they do it is their own business. This was the view of many of my friends too.

Seeking a Challenge

My five years in New York flew by rapidly. For a man in his twenties the city is a great adventure. I did not think much about my own future—I felt that somehow everything would work out fine. I thought vaguely of continuing for some time as a teacher at the Institute of Foreign Languages, working on the side as interpreter and one day maybe returning to the United Nations for another five-year contract. The system worked in an odd way: it accepted that you can go to work there on long-term assignments again and again, but it did not accept the idea of a lifetime contract. You had to return to the Soviet Union, work there for some time, and apply again. Maybe I should be thankful for that, for if lifetime appointments had been permitted for Soviet citizens then as they were later, in the years of perestroika, I probably would have decided to stay on in New York, worked quietly for many years in the Secretariat, raised my family and saved money for a nice house in the suburbs. It was not a bad prospect, but what actually happened to me was much more interesting and rewarding—morally if not financially.

My last General Assembly session was coming to an end, and we were packing in preparation for leaving. I cannot say we had much to pack. We spent a lot on theaters and entertainment, and we liked to offer guests some

Russian hospitality and a table full of food. I put together quite a good library and was proud of my stereo system. That was about all.

My colleagues who were also leaving and I threw a party for our friends at the Secretariat. The occasion was somewhat sad, but everyone seemed to be in good spirits. We were discussing political events, and all agreed that there was a feeling of unease in the air. No one, of course, knew what was in store, and we wanted to believe that some good things would be happening too. The life ahead looked like a continuation, not a totally new experience.

On the plane to Moscow my one-year-old son slept most of the time. I was finally beginning to think seriously about my future. We were returning to a country where I had never worked for a long time and did not even have an apartment of my own. I had no doubt that I would be able to earn a comfortable living, but I suspected that my work would not be challenging enough, and that worried me. The prospects looked so-so. But I was willing to set aside those worries for some time in order first to take a rest and settle down.

Soviet Troops Enter Afghanistan

I arrived home in the Soviet Union on December 20, 1979. A few days later Soviet troops entered Afghanistan. I learned of the invasion from an announcement on television—which was, as always in such cases, cryptic and buried deep in the news program. The next day, I turned on the radio to listen to shortwave Western stations. The Voice of America was broadcasting live the U.N. Security Council meeting at which Afghanistan was being discussed. I heard the voice of one of my friends interpreting someone's sharply worded statement denouncing the invasion. From that and from the editorial commentaries, I quickly understood that things had just taken a bad turn.

I want to give a frank and unvarnished account of my feelings at the time of the invasion. Today everyone is portraying himself as a "principled opponent" of that action from the very outset, but I believe that they are less than sincere. As I remember, many people in the Soviet Union, including some of my friends, reacted at best with indifference. Some believed nothing terrible was happening, and some, for no particular reason, even supported the invasion. Few accepted the government's arguments; most thought that no explanation was needed, that if something was necessary, let them do it.

As I recall my own reaction and the reaction of most of the people I knew, one thing stands out: I and many others believed that because this invasion was not in Europe the consequences would not be too severe and that the world would sooner or later "forgive" or just forget the whole thing. It was, of course, wishful thinking. We worried about the reaction of the West and about the implications of Afghanistan for U.S.-Soviet relations, but we did not think too much about the death and devastation this war would bring. We did not think much about the sufferings of the Afghan people. And it is this, rather than any other mistaken view or erroneous assessment, that I regret today.

Of course, I felt that the Soviet Union had been dragged by one of its satellites into something pointless and dangerous. After similar events in Angola and Cambodia, one had to wonder whether the country was in control of its own behavior or being manipulated by others. It seemed downright humiliating. Whose bidding would we have to do next? Where would the next crisis be—Western Sahara, Chad, or Sri Lanka—and when would it all end?

I wanted to rationalize the events for myself. Unlike eleven years earlier in Czechoslovakia, the government of Afghanistan had indeed asked for Soviet troops to come in—but it did not ask to be overthrown in the process. So the rationalizations were not convincing. I had one hope: that the whole thing might end quickly. After all, it is always possible "to declare victory and go." Years later, when I knew much more about the Afghan war, I became convinced that even in 1982 or 1983 that was a real possibility. The war was of low intensity at the time, and a couple of sharp words to the Afghan leaders—"We have done what we could to help you, now it's up to you to sink or swim"—would have quickly made them talk to the opposition and reach some agreement. Of course, Yury Andropov, Dmitry Ustinov, and Andrey Gromyko, who made the decision to send the troops in and easily sold it to the almost senile Brezhnev, were committed to going all the way and probably never even thought of just withdrawing. It fell to Gorbachev to undo their mistake in much more difficult circumstances, when the United States was giving enormous assistance to the mujaheddin and the war was at its most intense point.

There was another angle on the Afghan events, which emerged in my discussions with colleagues in 1981 when I was working in the foreign ministry. It was the time of the crisis in Poland, which was in some respects similar to the preinvasion developments in Czechoslovakia. The possibility of another Soviet invasion was therefore very much in the air and much debated. Soviet diplomats in Vienna, where I was working in the summer of that year at conventional arms reduction talks, discussed it too. Most concluded it would not happen because we were bogged down in Afghanistan and, some said, because Afghanistan had made it quite clear how pointless invasions were. All agreed that "without that thing in Afghanistan" the decision to send troops to Poland would have been made without much hesitation.

I was told later that in 1980 and 1981 the same group in the Politburo was considering the possibility of invading Poland and "setting things in order" there. I cannot imagine how they hoped to accomplish such an impossible feat, but they indicated to Wojciech Jaruzelski, the Polish leader, in no uncertain terms that they were ready to do it, which practically forced him to declare the state of siege and ban Solidarity. By doing that, he saved his country from something much worse.

In January 1980 I did not know many things and understood very little. I found what was happening distasteful, but I have to admit that I did not react to Afghanistan as emotionally as I had reacted eleven years before to the suppression of the Prague spring. I had become much more of a conformist, and I was thinking more about other things.

A Job at the Foreign Ministry

Soon after the New Year holiday, I got a call from a former colleague with whom I had studied at the U.N. course and who was now working in the foreign ministry. He told me that the translation department of the foreign ministry was expanding and that I would be offered an appointment there. He strongly recommended that I jump at the opportunity, and he did not have to spend much time persuading me. By then I knew that practical work as translator and interpreter attracted me much more than teaching. There was, of course, the moral problem. I was beginning work for the government, and I knew that would mean sacrificing some of my freedom and independence. But in a way, in the Soviet Union of the time everyone was working for the government or for some state organization—the state monopoly was total. I believed I was doing it not as a party official or a propaganda hack but as a professional working in a field that was inherently dedicated to reaching mutual understanding rather than fomenting conflict. So for me it was an acceptable compromise.

In March 1980 I for the first time entered the forbidding building at Smolenskaya Square as an employee of the Ministry of Foreign Affairs. I did not feel particularly important. I did not have any far-reaching plans. I intended to take it from day to day, settling down in my new position and gradually taking care of my personal problems, of which housing seemed to be the principal one. I was ready to accept for some time a rather dull and uneventful life. Indeed, lowering one's expectations can be a useful tactic, for in those first years my life indeed turned out to be quite dull and uneventful.

The translation department of the foreign ministry was taking on people with U.N. experience. Until then it used to be a small operation catering to the high-ranking officials of the ministry and of the Soviet government in general. When I joined the department, providing translators and interpreters for short-term and long-term assignments at the United Nations was a new task, only just beginning. The group I joined was small, close-knit, and a little supercilious about everyone and everything, in the way longtime interpreters can be—skeptical but most of the time not arrogant or aggressive. All the stories, anecdotes, and jokes were about the big bosses of the past and present. In most of those stories, the big shots did not look very good. They were depicted as haughty, often ill-informed, and sometimes downright incompetent. The leaders of foreign countries did not fare much better. In all the stories, the interpreter stood out as a towering presence—always calm, ingenious, and ready to smooth things over and correct the mistakes and stupidities of others. I heard those stories many times and saw how new dramatic details would be added, but I believe the stories were basically true. Nevertheless, I soon lost interest in that kind of talk—you can only take so much of it without yawning.

My first assignments were not too challenging, and I had plenty of time to do other things. I tried to understand how the foreign ministry worked and to develop my own views of the issues. Following the invasion of Afghanistan, international relations were in a deep freeze, and no one knew how long that would continue. And that is just about all I remember of the year 1980.

Geneva Arms Control Talks

In 1981 I had several interesting assignments, including the conventional arms reduction talks in Vienna and what were later called the INF (intermediate-range nuclear forces) talks in Geneva. The INF negotiations left a profound imprint on my mind—I was there from day one until they broke off in December 1983. Working in the Soviet delegation was a new experience for me, quite different from anything I had gone through before. I was able to get an inside view of how things worked at arms control negotiations. I met and sometimes developed relationships with people of the kind I rarely associated with before—Soviet and U.S. diplomats, military and intelligence officials, and my colleagues, the interpreters working on the U.S. delegation. I also took serious interest in the abstruse and often frustrating details of arms control.

The story of the INF talks is well known, and there is no need to tell it here. When the talks started, most of us believed that the Soviet position was quite defensible. After all, we had to face all those intermediate-range weapons of NATO countries, including British and French missiles and the so-called forward-based systems—that is, U.S. aircraft with nuclear weapons deployed in Europe, which were not counted against the strategic arms ceilings. Equality and equal security, as many on the Soviet side sincerely believed, required that we have a counterweight to all those nuclear weapons, and the SS-20 appeared to be an appropriate system for that purpose. It looked like a plausible position, and certainly in the first months of the negotiations I did not hear anyone in the delegation questioning it.

The delegation was headed by Yuly Kvitsinsky, a man of great charm and ability. His knowledge of the issues was broad and profound, and he was extremely intelligent and erudite, ready to discuss just about anything from classical music to outer space. He was different from most Soviet officials I had known, and everyone on the delegation admired and respected him. The Americans, led by Ambassador Paul Nitze, also seemed to like him and to be ready to do business with him. But the positions of the two sides were so far apart that it was not at all clear how they could be brought closer together without one side caving in.

Kvitsinsky had a sharp tongue. At one of the first meetings of the delegations he called the U.S. proposal for "a zero option" (the Soviet Union destroying its INF missiles and the United States forgoing the deployment of similar ones) a hole in the doughnut. I was lucky to be able to translate it without an embarrassing pause or without replacing the phrase with something only vaguely descriptive. Later he put me on the spot a few more times with proverbs or colloquial phrases that are unusual in diplomatic negotiations. I am grateful to him, because those lessons in inventive interpretation taught me never to panic. This is not the only thing an interpreter must learn, but it is one of the most important.

For two years I was the interpreter and note-taker at meetings between Kvitsinsky and Nitze. The negotiations, although doomed by the unwillingness of the Reagan and Brezhnev (later Andropov) administrations to consider seriously any alternative approaches that differed from their initial positions, were grinding on as a kind of ritual. It was often quite depressing—the same people facing each other, the same positions and arguments being recited for the umpteenth time, the same dull "working lunches" and cocktails.

Both chief negotiators, however, had class, and even though from time to time some irritation developed between members of their delegations, they never allowed it to degenerate into undiplomatic exchanges or mutually aggressive behavior. Because for reasons beyond the delegations' control the two countries were on the threshold of a resumed Cold War, preserving civility during the negotiations, and reasonably good contacts outside the formal talks, was quite an achievement.

I watched Paul Nitze with a mixture of wonder and respect. I wondered whether he was quite comfortable with the official U.S. position and its total rigidity (it later turned out that he was not), and I respected him for his competence, his grasp of every detail, and his precision in thought and language. He was always ready to tick off, say, "the seven arguments for the non-inclusion of sea-launched cruise missiles in the strategic arms ceilings" or the technical characteristics of the large phased-array radar. He indicated many times that he was unhappy about many provisions of the SALT-1 and SALT-2 treaties, considering them too much to the advantage of the Soviet Union. But he also found ways to indicate that he was willing to consider a compromise.

Like Kvitsinsky, Nitze also had a sharp tongue, and he knew how to use tough language. I remember how he said to Kvitsinsky, during the discussion of the Soviet demand that U.S. forward-based systems be included in the count of INF weapons on the U.S. side, "This horse has already been sold twice. You have already got much too high a price for it. You will not be able to do it again. Please convey that to Moscow." Nitze believed that not including U.S. medium-range aircraft based in Europe in the SALT ceilings had not been a Soviet concession but had been paid for in both SALT-1 and SALT-2 by U.S. concessions to the Soviet Union on such issues as Soviet heavy missiles and the Backfire bomber. It was a plausible though not totally convincing argument, but hearing it expressed in such stark terms was somewhat jolting. I felt that Nitze sometimes wanted to project a very tough image, suggesting that a deal cut with such a tough negotiator would stick and would have no problem with ratification in the U.S. Senate.

Nitze really wanted to cut a deal. He said to Kvitsinsky at one of their first meetings: "You are a young man. You will have other negotiations. But for me this is the last one. So I am not here to go through the motions. I want a fair agreement." I believed Nitze, and I think Kvitsinsky believed him too. Nitze wanted his career to culminate in a crowning achievement, and that was why in June 1982 he took that famous "walk in the woods" with Yuly Kvitsinsky near Saint-Cergue, a few miles from Geneva.

I was not present at that first behind-the-scenes talk and learned about its substance only in September, when the delegations returned to Geneva after the summer recess. The idea of the "walk in the woods" deal was simple. Nitze thought, and Kvitsinsky indicated that he agreed, that the Soviet Union's greatest concern was the ballistic Pershing-2 missiles, not the slow-flying cruise missiles. So, for nondeployment of the Pershing missiles the Soviet Union would have to agree to substantially cut the number of its SS-20s in Europe and freeze their deployment in Asia.

The Soviet leaders at that time should have understood that it was the best possible deal for them. Why they refused even to consider it I can only guess. Two possible explanations come to mind. First, they might have thought they would lose face; after all, the agreement would mean that the United States would still be deploying some missiles in Europe while the Soviet Union would be cutting the number of its SS-20s and actually destroying them. (I am sure, however, that our propaganda could have found a way to orchestrate such a deal properly.) Second, our leaders might have still hoped that the antimissile movement in Western Europe would make any U.S. deployment impossible and therefore that there would be no need for Soviet concessions. If that was the reason for rejecting the "walk in the woods" idea, it was the height of narrow-mindedness.

I have to admit that my own enthusiasm for the "walk in the woods" idea was not great, because by that time I was beginning to see the advantages of the "zero option" for my country. That realization did not come at once, but I was gradually allowing myself to be persuaded.

We in the Soviet delegation often discussed the progress of the talks and the merits of the positions of each side. That was rather unusual at the time, for people did not feel that they could do so frankly. But Kvitsinsky's delegation was different. The atmosphere was more relaxed than it was in Moscow at the time, as I remember, and people trusted one another more. My recollection is that this was true mostly of foreign ministry people in the delegation. We found it both difficult and not prudent to talk to the military, although there were different kinds of people among the military in our delegation.

In our group of interpreters we referred to the military generically as "the colonels." Most were quite competent in their field, with a good command of numbers, technical data, and details of previous negotiations. There were notable exceptions, though. Sometimes the mistakes of one colonel (soon promoted to the rank of general) were so obvious and embarrassing that we even had to change what he said in translation. He also tended to let his emotions get out of control—more in the company of Soviets than of Americans. But most of our military were not like that. They were basically normal and even nice people. Even so, something prevented me from trying to talk candidly to them, and whenever they spoke in an informal setting it was not about anything important.

But with the foreign ministry people—and particularly my colleagues, the interpreters—we could talk things out. We knew the arguments of both sides almost by heart. I can't say I was impressed by every American argument or totally turned off by the Soviet position. Far from that. But on one point the Americans were, I felt, 100 percent right: the Soviet INF position, at least initially, meant that the Soviet Union wanted equality with all its potential adversaries—the United States, Britain, France, and China—combined. I felt that, besides being wrong in principle, this was also totally unnecessary in the overkill world of nuclear weapons.

Another point I made to myself and to those of my friends with whom I talked frankly was that, unlike the United States, the Soviet Union was not able to place INF missiles anywhere close enough to U.S. territory. The United States had its allies in Europe, and the Soviet Union had already been burned trying to deploy a previous generation of its INF missiles in Cuba and would not try again. Thus, basically, a situation with zero INF missiles was desirable for my country. The trick was how to get there after all the financial, technological, and propaganda investment in the old position. Obviously, the Brezhnev and Andropov leadership was not willing even to contemplate this.

So the talks dragged on as the Americans prepared for bringing the first Pershing and cruise missiles to Europe. During the summer of 1983 it was decided in Moscow that once the United States began deployment in Europe we would break off the negotiations. The Europeans were worried about that prospect, so we believed that even talk of breaking off might make them push the United States to somehow modify its position, maybe returning to the "walk in the woods" idea, which, I heard then, had begun to look attractive to some people in Moscow, including the increasingly influential Marshal Sergey Akhromeyev. But the Americans and the Europeans were firm in their intention to begin the deployment.

The mood in our delegation was somber. I felt that at the last moment some dramatic move by the Soviet Union—such as deactivating a large number of SS-20s—could influence the European governments. But even if someone had proposed anything of the kind, it would have had no chance of being considered in the last months of the Andropov government. The general secretary himself was dying. Some knew and others suspected it. The intelligence people on the U.S. delegation were openly asking questions about his health. The overall atmosphere was a little bizarre.

In the end, things took the worst possible turn. The delegation had come up with what seemed to be an elegant way of withdrawing from the negotiations. Kvitsinsky prepared and cleared with Moscow a statement saying that because the Americans were beginning deployment of their missiles and the overall strategic situation was therefore changing radically, the Soviet Union would have to reconsider its position in a fundamental way. The Soviet delegation was thus declaring that the current round of talks was over and that it would not set a date for resumption of the talks.

At the last meeting, in December 1983, Ambassador Kvitsinsky read that statement to Nitze, and I dutifully translated it. Nitze expressed the appropriate regret. As we were leaving the U.S. delegation headquarters, Kvitsinsky and I were met by a throng of reporters, who knew that something dramatic was happening. The ambassador repeated what he had told Nitze. Without saying so, we felt that we had left the door open—just a little.

The next day we packed our bags. Kvitsinsky gave a party for his people. As we were having cocktails, we watched the evening news program from Moscow. The announcer read a blunt statement by Andropov regarding the deployment of American INF missiles in Europe: no diplomatic language, no openings left. U.S. deployment, the statement said, made it impossible for the Soviet side to continue the talks; talks could resume only when the U.S. missiles were withdrawn from Europe. It was, of course, a totally unrealistic demand—and a little later it was announced that the Soviet Union was breaking off START (Strategic Arms Reduction Talks) too, for the same reason.

As we listened to the Andropov statement, no one said a word. We left the room in almost total silence, and I felt that most of us were unpleasantly surprised, and some even appalled, by the statement's crudeness. Andropov seemed to be a reasonable man, and many people pinned great hopes on him as a leader. I wondered why he had signed such a statement. Did they bring the paper to him when he was in a bad mood, or was this new approach his own idea? Had he given the military a "carte blanche"? Was he so ill that he was unaware of what was happening? I did not know then, and I don't know now.

Apathy and Discontent After Andropov's Death

I returned to Moscow in early December. The mood in the city was gloomy, and apathy was in the air. The hope that many people felt in 1982 when Brezhnev died and Andropov became the country's leader had almost evaporated. The propaganda campaign against the deployment of U.S. missiles had created an almost prewar atmosphere in the country. People were depressed about the downing of a civilian Korean airliner by Soviet air defense a few months before and the worldwide condemnation of the government's behavior following that tragedy.

Yury Andropov died in February 1984. He was still well regarded by most people, and there was genuine sadness, punctuated by everyone's distaste for the man who was chosen to replace him as general secretary: Brezhnev's crony Konstantin Chernenko. There was nothing one could like about that man—he was boorish, colorless, and sometimes seemed almost illiterate because he read his speeches with great difficulty. But to me it did not make much difference, for I was no great fan of Andropov either.

My reservations were not so much about the man Andropov as about his policies. As a person, he was not unattractive. He seemed to have a good mind, and he was concerned about the country's future and willing to try to do something to change things for the better. And yet he belonged to the generation whose time had passed before he became the country's leader.

Andropov had hinted that there would be changes in the way the country was run, but he began by insisting on the need for order and discipline. The idea may not have been totally wrong to start with, but the way lower-ranking officials went about implementing it was crazy. For example, customers in stores during working hours were rounded up and had their documents checked, in an effort to combat employee absenteeism, and office workers in Moscow were punished for being ten minutes late for work. The government announced a campaign to fight corruption and bribery, but there was no indication that it understood that a nonmarket economy in which everything is distributed from above made large-scale corruption inevitable. The war in

Afghanistan continued and intensified. Sakharov was still in exile in Gorky, and dissidents were persecuted or forced to leave the country.

I was not enthusiastic about the dissidents. As a group they seemed too disparate. Some were Western-oriented and seemed genuinely committed to the ideas of human rights and democracy. But it seemed to me that they were too ready to appeal to the West for help, which was often counterproductive, strengthening the hand of conservatives in the Central Committee. I also disliked the nationalists, who were becoming increasingly numerous among the dissidents—both the Russian nationalists, like mathematician Igor Shafarevich, and the non-Russian nationalists, whose grievances were real but expressed in what I felt was a dangerously aggressive way.

The country seemed outwardly calm, but there was much discontent below the surface. In Moscow the intelligentsia—a curious mixture that included, among others, real intellectuals and rather simpleminded office workers— gathered in the kitchens of their small apartments to vent their feelings of malaise and discontent. I did not often go to such gatherings, for the endless discussions seemed unproductive and pointless to me. They went on and on in circles, and there was little that people really disagreed about, but everyone was making his point in a forceful and sometimes aggressive manner. They were often drinking vodka, and voices were soon raised; sometimes it nearly came to blows. It depressed me even more than the frustrating everyday life outside those kitchens. One thing was clear: the system under which the country was operating was outdated, and the ideology on which it was based not even worth discussing. It was a waste of time.

What could one do? My family had by that time fallen apart, victim to the numerous problems associated with our relocation from New York to Moscow and my frequent absences (lower-ranking staff of Soviet delegations were not then allowed to take their families to Geneva). My professional life had begun to bore me. I read a lot, went to theaters and concerts, and generally concentrated on myself. This is what the Russian middle class always does in times of reaction or social malaise. I never read as much Chekhov and Tolstoy, F. Scott Fitzgerald and Graham Greene, Simenon and Maurois, and I never listened to as much good music as at that time. It was not lost.

Stockholm Arms Control Talks, 1984

In the fall of 1984 I got a new assignment. I went to Stockholm as interpreter in the Soviet delegation to the negotiations on confidence- and security-building measures in Europe. It was then the only East-West arms-control negotiation still under way—not interrupted, for some curious reason, but with gloomy prospects all the same. The delegation was small, and I was the only interpreter.

The Soviet Union's initial position in these talks—which were among all European countries, the United States, and Canada—could only be described as bizarre. Having agreed earlier in Madrid on the mandate of the Stockholm talks, which included such confidence-building measures as advance notification of military exercises and troop movements, and inviting observers to the exercises, Foreign Minister Andrey Gromyko opened the talks in January 1984 with a position calling for, among other things, a treaty on the nonuse of force in Europe, a ban on the first use of nuclear weapons, and the prohibition of chemical weapons.

I was told by friends in the delegation that Gromyko had blasted the proposal foreign ministry officials had prepared based on the Madrid mandate as something completely "technical," not fit for political negotiations, and had insisted on throwing in some old proposals that had nothing to do with the agreed subject matter of the talks.

This position was difficult if not impossible to defend. The only argument that Oleg Grinevsky, the head of the Soviet delegation, could produce was that nothing in the Madrid mandate ruled out discussion of such questions. But he was evidently ill at ease repeating that argument, and he frequently complained to me and others that the whole thing was rotten. I often felt sorry for him. As a professional diplomat, he felt his mission was to seek agreement and to report honestly to Moscow that the position he was instructed to put forward made agreement impossible. But the mood in the Moscow leadership, we all felt, was one of irritation with the very idea of negotiations with the West.

As always, I studied the subject matter and the vocabulary of the talks carefully. That might seem pointless, a waste of time, since the negotiations were obviously going nowhere, but I had learned long ago to approach anything I did seriously, as if it actually mattered and something truly hinged on my understanding of the issues and my performance as interpreter. I discussed the talks with Grinevsky, who was surprisingly frank, and other people and came to some conclusions.

It was obvious that our position had to change, but no one knew whether doing so would become politically feasible any time soon. But the U.S. position too had some weak points, which were criticized not only by us but also by the Europeans, who were quite sympathetic to Grinevsky's plight.

They believed that the implausibility of the Soviet position only made it easier for the Americans to refuse, for example, to discuss any constraints on the scale of their European maneuvers, which every autumn brought tens of thousands of U.S. soldiers to Europe. These huge exercises of military power made the Europeans uncomfortable, and I suspected that even the American chief delegate at the talks, Ambassador James Goodby, a pleasant and reasonable man, was not happy about his government's refusal to discuss any limitation. In any case, no one expected a serious discussion, under the circumstances. The delegates were just going through the motions of negotiating.

Chernenko's Passing and Gorbachev's Election

The news from home was discouraging. In the embassy we could watch Soviet television, which often showed an increasingly ill Chernenko at some ceremony or meeting with a foreign official. It was clear that he would not live long. The U.S. delegation's interpreter, Bill Krimer, a veteran of U.S.-Soviet negotiations whom I had met at the INF talks, once asked me about Gorbachev, suggesting that he would be the next Soviet leader.

Gorbachev had impressed Western officials and public during his trip to London at the end of 1984. I could not tell Bill Krimer much about him—we did not know much about our leaders then. There was a vague feeling among many of us that it would be good if Gorbachev became general secretary. The country was tired of old leaders who kept dying. But what kind of leader would he be? And what kind of leader did the country want? Different people had different answers.

I remembered reading a speech by Gorbachev at some conference on "ideological work" in fall 1984. The subject was depressing. "Ideology" had become a dirty word for most people. But repetition of the same old dogmas and rhetorical clichés (which we called "the Talmud") that no one I knew believed was continuing in countless articles and reports. Thousands and thousands of people made their living in that field, and even now, when everything seems to have changed, many still do, in a chameleon-like way.

I would not say that Gorbachev's 1984 speech was that much different from the standard prevailing at the time, but many people saw it as at least an attempt to take a new look at some stereotypes, without undermining the foundations of ideological dogma, and welcomed the more lively language suggesting a somewhat different kind of Party man.

In early March 1985 television showed a totally disabled Chernenko being congratulated on his election to the Supreme Soviet and presented with a bouquet of flowers, which probably survived him. He died a few days later. This was not unexpected, and there was little mourning. Another state funeral would take place, and a new general secretary would be elected. No one in the delegation doubted that it would be Mikhail Gorbachev.

To mark Chernenko's passing, a meeting was held at the Soviet embassy. Boris Pankin, then ambassador to Sweden, presided. Grinevsky made an appropriate speech, mentioning Chernenko's contribution to the European security process. (In the mid-1970s Gromyko, who had a vested interest in the success of the Helsinki process, was able to get the increasingly influential Chernenko to support his position in the Politburo against Mikhail Suslov, who objected to many provisions in the Helsinki Final Act concerning human rights and information.)

The atmosphere at the meeting was one of complete indifference—so different from the meeting in Geneva in November 1982 a little more than two years earlier, when Brezhnev died. That death too had been expected, but he was the country's top leader for so long, and everyone, regardless of how they felt about him, was so used to the old man that there was at least a feeling of sadness in the air, as well as concern for what the future might bring. But Chernenko was the third leader of the country to die in less than thirty months.

This truly was the beginning of a new and unknown period for all of us. The current round of the Stockholm talks was to end soon, and I was returning to Moscow. At a reception in the embassy an American reporter I knew asked me whether I expected to return for the next round. I said that I didn't. I don't know why I said that. But indeed I did not return when the Stockholm talks resumed. The next few months changed my life.

TWO

A RATHER SPECIAL ASSIGNMENT: GORBACHEV AND SHEVARDNADZE

1985

From Gromyko to Gorbachev

On a Friday evening early in May 1985 I got a call from my boss at the translation department, who told me that Mikhail Gorbachev was giving an interview to an Indian reporter the next day and that I would be interpreting. He said it in an almost routine way, and I appreciated that. I kind of played along, refusing to consider it an earthshaking event. A neighbor sitting in my kitchen at the time I got the call asked what the call was about. I told him calmly, and he too, I thought, was not particularly astonished. Looking back on it today, I wonder why it seemed so routine. At that time a lot of importance and even a sense of mystery attached to the position of General Secretary of the Central Committee of the Communist Party. Interpreting for him was, to put it mildly, a rather special assignment.

I had never before interpreted for any top Soviet leader. A couple of times I had interpreted at Foreign Minister Andrey Gromyko's talks with foreign ministers of third world countries. Gromyko spoke some English and understood the translation. He corrected me once or twice—unnecessarily, I thought. I did not find interpreting for him challenging. Indeed, the arms control talks had been much more difficult and technically more complex. I could not say that the foreign minister had impressed me greatly.

Gromyko had an uncanny way of uttering simple phrases and platitudes that might come right from a *Pravda* editorial in such an important way that one had to think there was much more behind his words than was apparent. But I think many of his counterparts saw through that manner. Gromyko obviously had their respect, for he was much more knowledgeable, hard-working, and reliable than most of his Politburo colleagues, and many people tended to think of him as indispensable—though I am sure he could become that only in the Soviet Union.

Years later American television newsman Dan Rather asked Eduard Shevardnadze what he thought of his predecessor. Shevardnadze spoke of him with due respect and said that Gromyko knew how to make himself indispensable to Soviet leaders. I also remember how—in 1987, if I am not mistaken—at a lunch Shevardnadze gave for East European foreign ministers one of them began to speak of Gromyko in a disparaging way. Shevardnadze interrupted and said that Gromyko's two great achievements were the Helsinki Final Act and the two SALT treaties.

But Gromyko had not prepared me for Gorbachev. When on the next day I was in Gorbachev's office interpreting his remarks to a slightly dazed Indian reporter, I saw a lively and dynamic man, well-briefed, responding quickly and easily to questions and quite lacking the commanding, overbearing manner I had come to expect in our leaders. His answers did not contain any revelations and were more or less what one would expect. But it was impossible not to like the man.

Among other things, the reporter asked Gorbachev whether it was true that to some extent he owed his career to Andropov's support. Andropov was then still popular among most Soviets, and Gorbachev could have taken advantage of the question. But he didn't. He just said, yes, he had worked with Andropov and learned a lot from him, but that he had also crossed paths with other party leaders, such as Brezhnev and Suslov. Somehow I liked that answer. Later too, Gorbachev never tried to exploit people's attitudes toward his predecessors. That, as I learned later, is what French President François Mitterrand noted after his first meeting with Gorbachev in the fall of 1985. This man, Mitterrand said, does not take cheap shots at Brezhnev or Chernenko; he understands that it is the system that must be reformed.

Gorbachev's assistant for foreign affairs, Andrey Alexandrov, whom he inherited from his predecessors, said I had done well and even that we would be meeting again soon, but I did not think it very likely. Victor Sukhodrev, the English interpreter for all Soviet leaders from Khrushchev to Gorbachev, was number one, and rightly so, and although there were rumors that he would soon be appointed ambassador to a European country, I did not expect to become his successor.

Gorbachev-Gandhi Talks

A few weeks later Indian Prime Minister Rajiv Gandhi arrived on his first official visit to Moscow. It was also the first visit by a foreign leader to the Soviet Union under the new leadership. He was met at the airport by Soviet Prime Minister Nikolay Tikhonov, a man in his late seventies, and Foreign Minister Gromyko. Right after the official ceremony at the airport, a downpour started, and it was still raining when the motorcade entered the Kremlin. The open-air welcoming ceremony with the Gorbachevs had to be canceled, and after a hasty photo opportunity at the entrance to one of the Kremlin buildings, which was to be Gandhi's residence, the guests retired to rest before the start of the formal talks.

The talks were a set-piece affair. The two delegations were present in full, with Tikhonov, Gromyko, Defense Minister Marshal Sergey Sokolov, and a few others present on the Soviet side, and a large Indian contingent, of whom I recall V. P. Singh, then finance minister and a close ally of Gandhi, and later his opponent, defeating him in the 1990 election. Only Gorbachev and Gandhi spoke, both keeping close to their prepared notes and saying all the appropriate things. I was somewhat disappointed, though also pleased that my interpretation went well and without incident.

The next morning, Gorbachev and Gandhi met for a one-on-one talk that lasted more than three hours. I came close to being late for the meeting and had to run along what seemed an endless Kremlin corridor to arrive on time at Gorbachev's office on the third floor—which later I entered dozens of times, and fortunately never late for a meeting.

The two men hit it off immediately, talking freely and informally. This was the first of many meetings they had over subsequent years. I interpreted at almost all their one-on-ones. Gandhi was always either alone or with one assistant. I noticed that he did not trust many people around him, but he always seemed calm and in control. He spoke in a measured way, in clear and well-thought-out sentences. In that he was different from Gorbachev, who sometimes launched into long explanations, groping for the right word and, as it were, thinking aloud. But I felt that Gorbachev and Gandhi had a great deal in common on a much deeper level. They never said it in so many words, but I believe they felt mutual sympathy for each other as leaders of two extremely difficult countries, two men whose success was by no means ensured. Maybe Gandhi felt it more than Gorbachev, for I suspect that he had a more tragic sense of life.

Gandhi was, I think, an intensely moral man. As a statesman he was perhaps underrated, particularly in the West. When he was assassinated in 1991, it was clear from many commentaries and editorials that he had not been understood by many. The moral streak in him was much more obvious in direct contact, and it clearly appealed to Gorbachev. Gorbachev's idea of the primacy of universal human values over class or ideological struggles had not yet evolved into a full-scale concept, but it was probably already taking shape in his mind. Gandhi too said he wanted to bring morality and politics together, and I believe he was or soon became quite unhappy about many aspects of India's domestic and foreign policies that he had inherited.

Gandhi was a reluctant politician in more than one sense of the word. The resilience of the politics and policies that he instinctively disliked often left him frustrated, but he did not despair, and he wanted to continue his perhaps impossible crusade. The assassination stopped him. I remember how hard Gorbachev took the news of Rajiv's death, though at that time he was in the midst of an excruciatingly difficult period in his own career.

Gorbachev trusted Rajiv Gandhi. He shared with him his plans, his ideas, including some that had not yet taken final form, and even his doubts. They sometimes met at difficult times for one or the other, or for both, and their talks seemed to give them the strength to carry on, to persevere, in the face of problems, shocks, and betrayals. I shall tell about some of those meetings later in this book.

I regarded the Gandhi visit as a first for me. I had interpreted at a real summit, and I felt I did reasonably well—as well as could be expected of a person who had done little special preparation and had not expected to be trusted with something that important. I was not overly excited or particularly nervous. Maybe it was that same boldness that I felt we simultaneous interpreters had to have and that often saved us from panic or embarrassment. Anyway, as a result I now knew that summit-level interpretation was something I could do.

Gorbachev's Start

The first step the Gorbachev government took, which everyone remembers today, was to begin an antidrinking campaign. Almost everybody agrees it was also Gorbachev's first mistake, that he started out on the wrong foot with something that was not pressing, and ruined the budget base in the process. This may be true, and it is close to what I felt at the time, but I did not blame Gorbachev then and I don't think we should blame him now. He had inherited the campaign from the previous leaders—Andropov, Chernenko, and even Brezhnev, under whom the legislation to address the country's drinking problem began to be prepared.

Gorbachev had been part of that government too, but the idea that the problem needed to be addressed was not only the government's. Popular pressure was abundant. The media were full of demands for drastic measures and even for prohibition, and not all of them were orchestrated by the authorities. Prominent and respected writers, academics, and physicians were frightening the public with warnings of danger to the nation's genetic survival and urging that something be done. The measures finally announced in May 1985 were well short of prohibition, and in the atmosphere of those days even that seemed to be a victory for common sense.

The local bureaucracy started to carry out the orders from above—such as reducing the production of liquor and closing down liquor stores and bars— with a vengeance. There is no limit to what this country's bureaucracy can do to make even a well-intentioned effort a counterproductive travesty. And, of course, no one really thought about how to patch up the budgetary gap. But the press kept complaining that not enough was being done to fight alcohol.

Order or Reform?

No one, it seemed, was aware of the real issues and the real dangers. The word "perestroika" was not yet widely used. The country and its leaders were looking for goals and words that could energize the people, and the people were waiting for some gift from above—something that would change their lives for the better. Even a small improvement would have created enormous enthusiasm if it were tangible. But everyone seemed to understand change and improvement differently. And every institution—the party, the army, the numerous government ministries, for example—had its own idea of what should be done and its own demands to present to Gorbachev.

Reading in the press and talking to people, I felt as if two parties had formed in the country: "the party of order" and "the party of reform." There were sometimes strange bedfellows in those parties, and if you asked any one of them they would all say they were for change, that things "can't go on like this any longer." I don't think anyone—not Gorbachev, not Sakharov, not the party, not the dissidents, not the foreign observers—understood how many conflicts and contradictions had accumulated in the country and how difficult it would be to put it back on the road of normal development. Compared with the preceding years, it was an interesting time. More was happening, there were more news and more unexpected events than ever before, at least as far as I could remember.

Gromyko Is Replaced by Shevardnadze

The news of Eduard Shevardnadze's appointment as the Foreign Minister of the Soviet Union was a real shocker. Who could have expected a provincial party leader from Soviet Georgia to be chosen to replace Gromyko, the venerable and "reusable" old man who commanded almost universal respect among his countrymen, even those skeptical of the system as a whole? I learned of the appointment in Budapest, where I was with a Soviet delegation at an international conference. The reaction there was of surprise and almost disbelief.

When I returned to Moscow I found that few people at the foreign ministry welcomed the choice of Shevardnadze. The objections were what could be expected—that he had no foreign policy experience, that he was not even from Moscow, and that the appointment had not been explained properly to the diplomatic professionals. I also believed that Gromyko's prestige and experience in the world of Kremlin power politics had made the foreign ministry people feel secure and protected against any unpleasant surprises and that they feared Shevardnadze would not be able to stand up for them.

So, at best, Shevardnadze had some sympathy but not much support. Most of the talk was about how he would begin to fight nepotism and patronage at the foreign ministry. There was some of that indeed, although it was by far not the biggest problem at the foreign ministry. A little later Shevardnadze tried to do something about it, but he quickly saw that the effort to introduce greater fairness in the personnel policy and weed out nepotism was degenerating into another "campaign" with more losses than gains and ordered a stop.

What was lacking in discussion of the new appointment was any understanding that the Soviet Union's foreign policy had to change. The "war fever" that gripped the country in late 1983 as U.S. missiles began to arrive in Europe had subsided during 1984 and early 1985. Other things were on people's minds, and interest in foreign affairs was limited. I too thought that Shevardnadze's foreign policy would be mostly a continuation of Gromyko's. Even though some of its aspects seemed wrong or outdated, I felt it would be difficult to change much quickly. Also, our Western partners, particularly the United States, did not seem very cooperative. President Ronald Reagan's statements seemed calculated to rankle the Soviet leaders.

In the offices and corridors of the foreign ministry building at Smolenskaya Square, people continued to discuss Shevardnadze. Any news from the seventh floor, where the foreign minister's office was located, was avidly grasped and discussed again and again. It was said that Shevardnadze kept very long hours and that he was mostly listening to the department chiefs and leading experts and keeping his opinions to himself.

Simultaneous Interpretation Comes to Helsinki

Less than one month after his appointment, Shevardnadze was to make his first appearance abroad. It was a difficult one—the meeting in Helsinki of the foreign ministers of countries participating in the Conference on Security and Cooperation in Europe (CSCE) to commemorate the tenth anniversary of the first Helsinki Conference at which the CSCE Final Act was signed. It was, of course, more than a commemoration. In addition to the discussion of European issues, most ministers must have regarded it as an opportunity to take a first look at Shevardnadze. A meeting between him and U.S. Secretary of State George Shultz was scheduled, and it turned out to be more than just a get-acquainted meeting.

Through diplomatic channels, Shultz had proposed that most of the discussion be with simultaneous rather than consecutive interpretation, which would save time if it worked well but could be dropped if it didn't. Georgy Korniyenko, Shevardnadze's first deputy and left over from Gromyko's time, was said to have objected, but he was overruled by Shevardnadze, who said it should be tried. It did look like a risk at the time, particularly because Shevardnadze had so little time to prepare for the meeting and because simultaneous interpretation created greater pressure and required quicker reaction. So the decision to accept Shultz's suggestion was made almost at the last minute. It later became the rule that most of the full-scale meetings with delegation members and experts were interpreted simultaneously, while the one-on-one or small-group meetings had consecutive interpretation. The arrangement worked well, since both forms of interpretation had their advantages suited for particular settings or situations. But in Helsinki it was a first. Many things were for the first time then. At the last moment I was told that I would do the simultaneous interpretation at the Shultz-Shevardnadze meeting (the interpreter in the Soviet delegation could do only consecutive).

The decision to try simultaneous interpretation at a major bilateral diplomatic meeting echoed an old debate between the proponents of consecutive interpretation and simultaneous interpretation. Both have their advantages, but consecutive interpretation has a much longer tradition. It is sometimes said half-jokingly that it is one of the oldest professions.

But in the nineteenth century there was little need for interpretation, at least in European diplomacy, since French was the lingua franca of international relations and spoken by all diplomats and most heads of state and government. The change came after World War I. Harold Nicolson, in his famous book about the Paris Peace Conference, wrote that the reason interpretation became necessary—and appropriate—was that U.S. President Woodrow Wilson and British Prime Minister David Lloyd George "were no linguists." This, of course, was before IBM engineer Gordon Finley patented the idea and equipment for simultaneous interpretation in 1926. The period between the two world wars was the heyday of consecutive interpretation.

The best practitioners of consecutive interpretation—such as Antoine Wellemann, Jean Herbert, and the Kaminker brothers—became legendary. The requirements and standards were very high. The interpreter was expected never to interrupt the speaker, who might speak for as much as twenty or thirty minutes, and even more. Interpreters used an intricate system for notetaking that combined symbols, abbreviations, and acronyms with a heavy reliance on memory and intelligence to achieve results that were sometimes stunning. The world record is surely held by André Kaminker, who once interpreted a French diplomat's speech that lasted two and a half hours without interruption.

After the Second World War, although simultaneous interpretation began to be accepted and was used—for example, at the Nuremberg trial of Nazi war criminals—most of the veteran consecutive interpreters with League of Nations experience fiercely resisted the use of simultaneous interpretation at the United Nations. They argued that it was just not as good as the old way, that in addition to the problem of listening and speaking at the same time, the need to start interpreting before the end of a phrase or sentence—to say nothing of a full, meaningful passage—and the difference in the structure of various languages, meant that the simultaneous interpreter was condemned to produce a very flawed translation, in terms of content and particularly style.

There was some truth to that argument, especially during the initial years, when interpreters were just beginning to master the new method. But *amour propre* was probably also a factor in the debate. Almost every leading consecutive interpreter was something of a prima donna, a star used to shining in front of large and often powerful audiences. I suspect that such people resented the relative obscurity of quietly toiling in the interpreter's booth.

The debate went on until about 1951, with some proponents of "la noble consécutive" adamantly refusing to accept the inevitable. In the end, it was the expansion of the number of U.N. working languages, from two (English and French) to five, including Russian, Chinese, and Spanish, that proved decisive. Very simply, consecutive interpretation of a U.N. speech into four languages would take too much time. Given that ultimate argument, the last holdouts had to agree that simultaneous interpretation was the only way out. Most of them followed the principle "If you can't beat them, join them" and became masterful practitioners of simultaneous interpretation.

Despite an awkward moment here and there, simultaneous interpretation soon became the accepted method at large international gatherings. It does have some disadvantages, including a need for technical equipment. Consecutive interpretation is, of course, more intimate and its use in tête-à-tête discussions has never been seriously questioned. I believe that this pattern will hold for many years to come.

All Eyes on Shevardnadze

But back to the summer of 1985. The Helsinki meeting was basically a gathering of thirty-five foreign ministers, each with a prepared statement and a schedule of meetings with his counterparts. It would be no exaggeration to say that the eyes of everyone were on Shevardnadze. I watched from the gallery as he entered the huge auditorium of the Finlandia Hall accompanied by a security guard (I later became very friendly with the man, Dima Kazachkin, one of the few persons Shevardnadze had brought with him from Tbilisi) and a small group of foreign ministry officials. They sat down and put on the earphones to follow the speech of a foreign minister who was then speaking from the rostrum. Then the chairman gave the floor to the foreign minister of the Soviet Union.

Eduard Shevardnadze went resolutely to the podium and began to speak. He was, of course, reading from a prepared speech, the contents of which I more or less knew, so I watched rather than listened. He looked extremely uncomfortable—stiff, worried about something, unable to relax or concentrate. He was so nervous that he stressed the wrong syllables, had to begin some phrases twice, and could not find the right voice and the right pace. In the middle of his speech he seemed to regain his composure and ended fairly well, to much encouraging applause, but I still felt sorry for the man. It was not an impressive performance. I did not know I had just heard a man with whom I would work closely for more than five years, whom I would watch many times with genuine admiration and always with respect. All that was still to come.

Shevardnadze Meets with George Shultz

The meeting with Secretary of State Shultz was held on the next day. I was a little worried about possible technical hitches with the interpretation equipment. I was also worried about Shevardnadze. If he had been so nervous just reading his speech, how would he fare in a face-to-face meeting with the experienced George Shultz? I was to be pleasantly surprised. Shevardnadze seemed much more confident and relaxed than the day before, and he went through the meeting with Shultz with little apparent effort. I noticed he was sticking closely to his talking points—or as we liked to call them half-jokingly, the "phrase book," the prepared briefs on every issue likely to be raised. (Later, when I worked at the USA and Canada department of the foreign ministry, I took part in preparing those briefing papers. After the first few months in office Shevardnadze became less dependent on them.)

Shultz was watching Shevardnadze closely, in a sharply appraising way. One could see that he was keenly interested—there was none of that characteristic cool and even seemingly indifferent look of his. He spoke confidently, with the calm assurance of a pro but, I felt, without arrogance. The two men were to spend hundreds of hours together in the next few years. I don't know whether on that day in Helsinki they believed they would establish a personal and very human relationship, and whether they wanted such a relationship then. None of it was yet apparent; the beginning was quite formal. But neither was there any animosity or mutual anger. Shultz and Shevardnadze were not in the combative mood that had characterized U.S.-Soviet relations in the previous years. I was returning to Moscow with a feeling of relief.

Emerging Popular Interest in Gorbachev and Shevardnadze

At the time, people I worked with, and some of my friends, sometimes asked me about Gorbachev and Shevardnadze, but it did not happen often, for most people then were not in the habit of seriously discussing the country's leaders and their policies. The prevailing attitude used to be indifference or mild contempt. And there were jokes—the famous political jokes from the Khrushchev and Brezhnev periods. Everyone was telling those jokes. It was a clear sign that the fear that was so pervasive in the Stalin era was no more. But there was a different kind of fear, a fear that kept most people from engaging openly in dissident activity, and often even from thinking about the country's future in any serious way. There was also frustration. People did not expect much from the general secretary or the prime minister that would actually affect their lives. They certainly expected nothing good from them.

Thus the emerging popular interest in Gorbachev and Shevardnadze seemed to be a sign for some change. I had not yet glimpsed any of the universal enthusiasm and support for Mikhail Gorbachev that became so widespread a little later, but indifference was gradually giving way to curiosity and then to sympathy.

What answer could I give those who wondered what kind of people Gorbachev and Shevardnadze were? I could not say much. I knew them too little, and it is not my custom to put on a self-important air and make people believe that I know something they don't just because I sometimes sit next to high officials.

I responded to the questions cautiously, among other reasons because I was not always sure what was on the questioner's mind and whom he was going to talk to next. I said I did not know the two men very well yet but that they seemed to be good people, honest and hardworking, wanting to do something good for their country.

Their past was in the party, and I had always wondered about that organization. It seemed to assume responsibility for everything, and many of its officials were not the cynical and corrupt sort that was hated so much. They seemed to want to do something good, and many of them worked from morning to night like squirrels on a treadmill, but still the party seemed to be drifting with no apparent purpose or clear goal. No one believed in the utopian goals of Khrushchev, but a lot of phrases from his time, and even Stalin's, were still there, in everyday propaganda and in some of Gorbachev's speeches. I wished he could break out of that circle, but that possibility seemed remote to me. Anyway, I did not do much "profound thinking" at the time. There just seemed to be a breath of fresh air for all of us, and I liked the new general secretary and foreign minister.

At the United Nations with the Shevardnadze Team

In September 1985 I went to New York with the Soviet delegation to the 30th session of the U.N. General Assembly. I was returning to a city I liked and had enjoyed working in. This time I was looking forward to a different kind of work: not simultaneous interpretation at General Assembly meetings but interpreting for Shevardnadze, who was eagerly awaited there.

I recalled the atmosphere at the Soviet mission to the United Nations in previous years when Andrey Gromyko had come for his annual two-week stay. There seemed to be electricity in the air, with everyone tensely expecting something not very pleasant to happen at any time. This time the mood was similar, but it began to relax when Shevardnadze and his team actually arrived. It included a few people who had worked with Gromyko, but also some new faces. I later came to know well two of Shevardnadze's closest assistants, Teimuraz Stepanov and Sergey Tarasenko. Almost immediately, they seemed different from other officials on the team.

One could hardly imagine two men more different from each other. Stepanov was the only policy assistant Shevardnadze had brought with him from Tbilisi. Half-Georgian, Stepanov had a sometimes short temper and a tendency to lose heart in troubling situations. But beneath the somewhat inhospitable surface, he had a very good mind, great powers of observation, and sound judgment. He also had a way with words, and Shevardnadze relied on him both for speechwriting and for a candid and ingenuous assessment of problems from the standpoint of a man not burdened by years in the foreign ministry.

Tarasenko was a most extraordinary product of the foreign ministry. Always calm, cheerful, and ready to help, he was capable of taking a fresh view of things and explaining his thoughts in simple, man-in-the-street language. His knowledge of international affairs, particularly U.S.-Soviet relations and the Middle East, was wide-ranging. I saw many times how he destroyed his opponent with simple and coherent arguments, but he never humiliated anyone.

In the years when we worked together, I sometimes had my problems with the two men, particularly when I moved from the translation department to the U.S. desk and developed my own views on some issues, which could differ from theirs. But I regard my association with Stepanov and Tarasenko as a fortunate part of my life in those years. We are still friends.

Shevardnadze's speech at that session was the first—and cautious—attempt to chart his own course oriented toward what later became known to the world as "the new thinking." Written in prose that was a little too florid for my taste, it was unmistakably the speech of a new foreign minister. Many of the old positions were still there, but one felt that he was trying to reach out and eager to be understood. It was different from the stiff and imperious speeches of the recent past. It was also difficult to translate.

This was the first General Assembly session without Victor Sukhodrev as the Soviet delegation's chief interpreter. Our paths had not crossed very often, so I mostly admired him from afar. We sometimes talked, and we both agreed that the most difficult thing for the foreign minister's interpreter was translating his General Assembly speeches into English. It was difficult to combine the demands of great precision with the need to say it in clear and readily understandable English sentences. The Russian original simply made the latter impossible sometimes. But one had to try—and very often, we agreed, it was an ordeal.

So this time I had to do it without Victor's help and guidance. The speech was rewritten several times, and the final draft, containing about twenty-five typewritten pages, was given to me the afternoon of the day before Shevardnadze was due to speak. Small amendments were passed to me as late as 10:00 P.M. Every sentence seemed to present a problem.

No translation is perfect, but I tried to make it as close to satisfactory as I could, or at least to avoid egregious mistakes or oversights, which is often the most difficult thing—awful gaffes could crop up in the most masterful translation. I worked until the small hours of the morning, leaving the office after 5:00 A.M. I felt I had done a good job, and I was happy.

The Soviet foreign minister's speech was the big event of the day, and I went to the General Assembly hall to hear it. His delivery was much better than in Helsinki, although he always was more forceful speaking extemporaneously than reading a prepared text. He looked confident and relaxed and overall was a great success. His colleagues and observers of international affairs were beginning to like him.

The foreign minister's visit to New York in the fall is always an occasion for numerous meetings with counterparts from various countries, and I interpreted at many of them. The most important meetings were those with George Shultz.

The two countries' positions on most arms control, regional, and bilateral issues were still far apart. It seemed impossible to bring them closer together. Most diplomats and observers on both sides felt quite pessimistic about the prospects of U.S.-Soviet relations, at least while Ronald Reagan was in office.

For General Secretary Mikhail Gorbachev this created an uncomfortable situation. As a new leader, he was expected to deliver some foreign policy achievement, but prospects for that were not good. Under the circumstances, I believe it was the instinctive decision of the Gorbachev-Shevardnadze team to patiently study the issues to find any opening that would make an agreement possible and to try to develop a human relationship with their counterparts in other countries. In that regard, as in all others, relations with the United States seemed to be the toughest challenge.

Reagan-Shevardnadze Talks at the White House

Shultz and Shevardnadze had several meetings, and I gradually began to feel how they were cautiously moving toward understanding each other's problems and respecting each other, even occasionally with some warmth. A meeting with President Reagan was scheduled at the White House, and it was my impression that Shevardnadze was not exactly looking forward to it—he was worried about how the meeting would go.

A severe storm battered New York a couple of days before the White House meeting. It was caused by the fringes of Hurricane Gloria, which was then ravaging the U.S. Southeast. The rain and the winds were so bad that Shultz, who was in New York for the Security Council meeting to commemorate the fortieth anniversary of the United Nations, was not sure that we would be able to get to Washington by plane. As a fallback he suggested that we go there on a special train he had ordered in case the storm did not subside.

The next day, however, the storm seemed to blow over, and we went to the airport to fly to Andrews Air Force Base near Washington. At first it seemed the one-hour flight would be uneventful, but it soon got very bumpy. Some air pockets and jolts seemed to frighten even the flight attendants. Shevardnadze had invited a few people to his compartment to discuss the meeting with President Reagan. He was talking when the plane was land-ing—in pouring rain and against a high wind. A sudden gust of lateral wind threw the plane lurching to the left, and I thought we might either miss the runway or touch the ground with a wing. All of us were pale for a moment. The plane landed all right, but later we were told that Americans on the ground had been worried too. It rained all night, and I did not sleep well because of the combined effect of weather, nervousness, and jet lag. But the next morning the weather suddenly changed; indeed, I think it happened during Shevardnadze's meeting with Reagan, which gave both of them and the press good material for jokes and metaphors.

Shevardnadze was prepared for the meeting; he had studied the "phrase books" again and again and himself wrote out the main talking points on small pieces of paper. They were not unlike Reagan's famous "cards," but in the course of the conversation Shevardnadze digressed from his briefs signifi-cantly. Only in the first minutes of the talk was he tense.

Ronald Reagan was a mystery to us. No one could imagine then that in a few years his rhetorical anticommunism would be surpassed by our own orators, many of them members of the Communist Party for most of their lives. In 1985 his statements rankled not only the Soviet leaders but most of the ordinary Soviets too. They disturbed me, not so much because of their substance but mostly because I felt they were absolutely unnecessary and counterproductive in the dangerous world of nuclear missiles and explosive conflicts involving the superpowers. Why was he doing it? many of us asked. And we could find no answer.

In the conversation with Shevardnadze, Reagan's language was only a little milder, and sometimes the minister had to respond. I remember the foreign minister speaking of the "moral and political unity of the Soviet people," almost halfheartedly. He was probably more concerned about whether it was possible to find a way to deal with a U.S. president who seemed so close-minded. After the first White House talk, that was very much an open question.

But one could not help liking Ronald Reagan. He was affable, animated, and even, it sometimes seemed, eager to please. I was not then very close to the minister, and he did not invite me—as he later often did—to his postmeeting discussion with Anatoly Dobrynin, then still our Ambassador to Washington, and other diplomats. But I would not have been surprised to learn that Reagan's charm and affable manner was mentioned in that discussion. Here was a charismatic politician if there ever was one. He had the support of the American people, who had reelected him overwhelmingly a year before. Whether you liked him or not—and you would if you forgot about the issues dividing the two countries—you had to deal with him.

It may seem that I am using hindsight and adjusting my thoughts and feelings of the time. But I have checked with my family and friends. This is more or less what I was saying in 1985 and 1986. I believe that Eduard Shevardnadze must have had similar impressions and feelings—otherwise, meeting Ronald Reagan would have been pointless. And Shevardnadze is not a man who does things just because they have to be done.

Preparations for the Reagan-Gorbachev Summit

I stayed behind with the rest of the Soviet delegation in New York as Shevardnadze and his team left for Moscow. I had not yet become part of the minister's "inner circle," which left me with considerably more freedom but at the same time kept me out of the day-to-day work on the big issues. So when the preparations began for the first Reagan-Gorbachev summit which was to be held in November 1985 in Geneva, I was a spectator in New York, following the maneuverings of the two sides as they were reported in the media, and wondering whether I would be involved in the Geneva summit itself in any way. As I understood later, there was quite a competition for that in Moscow in the months preceding the summit, and I am happy I had an absolute "alibi" so far as that competition and anything unpleasant always associated with such things is concerned. I never liked office politics and have always tried to stay away from it.

It was decided that the summit talks would consist both of tête-à-têtes between the two leaders and of expanded delegation meetings. The latter were to be interpreted simultaneously. Four or five days before the summit, I was told that the Soviet mission had received a cable from Moscow instructing them to help me get to Geneva immediately. I was given a ticket and spent a few hours getting the Swiss visa. The next day I was on the plane flying to Geneva, having a pleasant chat with a chocolate salesman from Italy.

Before the summit, there had been a lot of debate among the Soviets in

New York over whether meeting at that time was wise from our standpoint. That seems odd today, but at the time summitry was at the center of diplomatic and political maneuverings in U.S.-Soviet relations. The focus in all the discussions was almost exclusively on the arms control issues.

By the time Gorbachev came to power, arms control talks between the Soviet Union and the United States had resumed. In late 1984, Shultz and Gromyko had worked out a face-saving formula that allowed the Soviet Union to return to the talks quietly, disregarding its demand for the withdrawal of U.S. missiles from Europe, made so imprudently in the Andropov statement of December 1983. As part of the negotiations, a special group was set up to deal with the questions of antiballistic missiles (ABM) and space weapons. Behind that action was, of course, the Reagan administration's plan for building a space defense system, which everyone called "Star Wars." The obsession of the Soviet military-scientific-industrial complex—and, I believe, of most Soviet policymakers and diplomats—with that problem was then absolute.

I remember my reaction in March 1983 when Reagan first launched the "Star Wars" idea in a major speech. I was in Geneva at the time, and the speech was a complete surprise not only to the Soviets but also to the Americans, who were at a loss to explain this departure from the generally accepted philosophy of strategic deterrence and arms control.

My own feeling was that it was something very personal and bizarre on the part of Reagan that might fizzle out if we did not react too harshly. But things took a different turn. The Soviet reaction was highly emotional, and although there was much that could be criticized in the Reagan plan, this was done not in a reasoned and careful way but in a tone approaching hysteria. In time I too was carried away by the anti–Star Wars feeling, and only later, in 1987, when I became more closely involved with the negotiations, did I go back to the initial "take it easy" approach. It is our first reactions that are often right, but we don't always have the courage to stick to them.

In 1985 the arms control talks were going nowhere. Both sides held firmly to their positions. When the United States proposed an early summit meeting, there was tremendous pressure on Gorbachev to try to use it as a lever to extract some arms control concessions, and in fact to make "progress on disarmament" a condition for holding the summit. There were also doubts on the Soviet side about whether anything useful could come out of the summit at all.

President Reagan was not held in high regard by most Soviet officials. Many were afraid that holding a meeting for the sake of meeting would appear to be a one-sided victory for the Americans and therefore hurt Gorbachev at home. And many were of the view that we could not usefully discuss anything with Ronald Reagan. He was too anti-Soviet, they said, and too superficial. It was rumored that a month before, at the French-Soviet summit in Paris, François Mitterrand had told Gorbachev he could not imagine what he would discuss with Reagan.

So accepting an early Soviet-American summit had been a courageous decision for Gorbachev and did not come easily, as we later learned. In hindsight, therefore, it is quite natural that I found the Soviet contingent in Geneva more than a little nervous. It was rather large, and it contained both old and new people. Of the old ones the most visible, as always, was Leonid Zamyatin, a loud and overbearing man who was then in charge of the Central Committee's international propaganda department. Among the new ones was Alexander Yakovlev, recently elected Secretary of the Central Committee, who seemed rather reserved and modest but nevertheless exuded an air of quiet authority.

The Americans clearly wanted the summit to be a success. They checked every detail of protocol, security, and interpretation arrangements. Working with them on the preparations, I could not help noticing that they seemed almost like Germans in their meticulousness. It was so unlike our "let's hope it turns out well" approach.

The Summit: "For Everything There Is a Season"

I shared the interpretation duties at the summit with Nikolay Uspensky, an official from the second European department of the foreign ministry who later became its chief and then the Soviet ambassador to Sweden, so my impressions are somewhat incomplete because I was not in on every play. I did mostly the simultaneous part.

I recall that the chemistry between Gorbachev and Reagan did not seem good at first. Reagan was working from the script, sticking closely to his note cards, which of course contained nothing but the well-known U.S. positions. At times Gorbachev seemed frustrated, but he did manage to drop here and there hints of flexibility on arms control and on some regional issues, particularly Afghanistan. So far as the latter is concerned, the Americans certainly took note, and Reagan said so at the second meeting of the delegations, which took place in the refurbished building of the Soviet mission. Between those full-scale meetings, the two leaders had a tête-à-tête (at which I was not present) where some rapport began to emerge between them.

The rapport was visible at a dinner in the Soviet mission to the United Nations, a sprawling compount of buildings that I remembered well from the time a few years back when I had been working in the Soviet INF delegation. I was asked to interpret at that dinner, hosted by Mr. and Mrs. Gorbachev, and I must admit I was quite excited about it, although interpreting at official dinners is not the kind of assignment most interpreters relish. As a rule, the interpreter is seated behind the host and must contend with the waiters (accidents can result from awkward movements of waiters, interpreters, or guests). You are not eating, it is often noisy, and you almost have to shout so you can be heard at the other end of the table. Later, when he was host at dinners, Gorbachev would ask that a place be reserved for me at the table, and I felt a lot better, whether I had the time to eat or not.

All this, however, was of little or no importance that night in November, when I had a chance to observe the first relatively informal encounter between Gorbachev and Reagan. It went quite well. Little or nothing was said about the issues discussed at the talks. Instead, the conversation was mostly about seemingly irrelevant or unimportant things, with the ladies taking active part. Some of it was funny, some was quite frank.

Mrs. Reagan told how after the assassination attempt, a couple of years before, President Reagan had to do a lot of "chest exercises." "His chest and shoulders have gotten so big that his old suits no longer fit," she said. "We have had to buy all new ones." She also spoke about her work in the antidrug campaign and asked whether drugs were a problem in the Soviet Union.

I do not remember whether it was Gorbachev or Raisa who answered the question, but the answer struck me as a good one, reasonably frank and certainly free of any ideological cliché like "it can't happen under socialism": "No, not really—or perhaps not yet. But drinking is a big problem, and if nothing is done its consequences can be as bad as anything for the nation."

Someone joked that, despite the antidrinking campaign in the Soviet Union, drinking in moderation was still a good idea, particularly for a toast for peace between the Soviet Union and the United States.

"Oh, yes, it is only drinking without a toast that is called alcoholism," Gorbachev responded with a laugh, and after everyone joined in the laughter following translation, he proposed a toast. He said that the two countries had had a complex relationship, with some good times, such as the years as allies during the Second World War, and some bad times—the Cold War era. "Both sides must probably bear some blame for the setbacks and reverses," he added. "But let us think more about the future, not about the past." He continued, "There is a time for everything," and quoted a passage from Ecclesiastes: "For every thing there is a season, and a time for every purpose under the heavens: A time to be born, and a time to die, . . . a time to break down, and a time to build up, . . . a time to throw away the stones, and a time to gather the stones together. . . ." That was a quite accurate quotation from the Bible, and it happened at a time when religion was still officially "suspect" in the eyes of most Soviet officials. Yet I do not recall being surprised by it, nor did any of those present later describe it as something extraordinary. It sounded quite natural and sincere coming from Gorbachev. The toast ended with an appropriate call for improved U.S.-Soviet cooperation, and the next day the hard work to build it resumed, amid the usual problems, obstacles, and misunderstandings.

As the Soviet and American diplomats prepared for the summit, the Americans firmly refused to entertain the idea of some concluding document or communiqué of the summit. They felt that such communiqués had been used by the Soviets in the past to insert language that reflected long-standing Soviet positions that they later invoked to the detriment of the less-than-vigilant U.S. side. During the summit, however, Reagan was persuaded that a joint statement might be a good idea, and work on it began between mid-level diplomats, with sometimes a push from the principals or the foreign ministers. It did not go without a hitch. In fact, sometimes the situation seemed hopeless. At one point, when lower-level officials were waiting for the two leaders, who were meeting one-on-one, Leonid Zamyatin yawned and said loudly, "Well, I know how it all is going to end." He did not elaborate.

A few minutes later something crazy happened: the lights went off in the Soviet mission's building. It was a total blackout, which lasted for less than a minute as the emergency generator on the grounds of the mission was switched on. There had apparently been some malfunction in Geneva's power system, and an entire block of buildings was without electricity. I don't know what thoughts and suspicions went through everybody's mind during those thirty seconds, and also afterward.

Work on the joint statement, which the two leaders were to sign in a public ceremony on the morning of November 21, went on throughout the night, but they finally succeeded in hammering out mutually acceptable language. As I read the statement, what struck me immediately was the sentence affirming that "nuclear war cannot be won and must never be fought." Compared with some of the previous statements of high U.S. officials and of Ronald Reagan himself, it seemed revolutionary. Indeed, in the first Reagan term there was a lot of talk about the need to have forces that would prevail in a nuclear war. And there was the famous statement by Alexander Haig: "There are things more important than peace." Soviet propaganda made much of that statement and, as always, greatly overdid it, but in the context of other statements and actions by the Americans, it did seem to suggest that a limited nuclear war was being considered as a realistic option. All kinds of war-fighting scenarios were being discussed in the media. So the sentence in the joint statement (it is interesting that the sequence of clauses was reversed in the Russian text: "must not be fought and cannot be won") was, in my view, genuinely meaningful.

As the summit was drawing to a close, I thought that both Reagan and Gorbachev could feel satisfied. The U.S. president had not retreated from any of the substantive positions on various arms control issues, which people like Caspar Weinberger were adamantly protecting. Gorbachev had scored what appeared at least to the ordinary people as a foreign policy success, projecting himself as a capable summiteer who was able to "charm the West" (though suspicions of the Soviet Union's intentions had not disappeared) and extracting from Reagan an important statement that nuclear war must never be fought.

For me, it was also a summit of crazy surprises. As I was preparing to go home I learned that the consular section of the Soviet mission could not locate my passport, which they had given to the U.S. consulate to obtain a visa for my return to New York for the remainder of the General Assembly. I kept trying to get them to find my passport until the moment the motorcade with the Soviet delegation left for the airport to take a special flight to Moscow. After hesitating a few minutes, I decided to join the team and asked the driver of a rented car I had used during the summit to rush me to the airport. We were not able to catch up with the motorcade, but we did get to the airport just barely before the plane's takeoff. I was going back to Moscow without my passport.

On the plane I told Ambassador Dobrynin about it. "The motherland will accept you," Dobrynin joked. And after I explained the situation to a passport control official at the airport, it did.

So 1985 seemed to be ending on a good note. The summit went down well with the people at home. Overall, too, things appeared all right. The new year, 1986, which would see Gorbachev's January 15 arms control statement, the 26th Party Congress, Chernobyl, and Reykjavik, was ahead.

NEW THINKING, OLD PROBLEMS

Three

1986

Gorbachev on Arms Control, Economic Reform, Peace, and Freedom

On a night in mid-January 1986 I was summoned back to the foreign ministry, from which I had just returned. I was asked to edit the translation of a lengthy text entitled "Statement by the General Secretary of the CPSU Central Committee M. S. Gorbachev." I looked through the statement first, as I usually do before starting a translation. The subject was disarmament ("disarmament" had become the accepted term in the Soviet Union, whereas "arms control" was used by the West). It was clear that Gorbachev wanted to combine the presentation of positions designed to advance the ongoing arms control negotiations with a vision that went beyond current events. The goal he spoke of was to abolish nuclear weapons by the year 2000.

As a person who had by that time formed his own—and I believed well-informed—view of arms control and disarmament, I read the statement with a dual feeling. I was not enthusiastic then about the objective of a nuclear-free world because it was not very realistic and perhaps even utopian. It was fashionable to say that you can't disinvent nuclear weapons. Would it not be better to concentrate on what practical steps could be taken to reduce the number of nuclear weapons, I wondered. I believed that quite a few such steps could be taken unilaterally, given the enormity of the arsenals that were sufficient to destroy the world many times over.

Later I thought about this many times, particularly after the summit at Reykjavik, where the objective of a nuclear-free world was seriously discussed. I now think that "the vision thing," so often criticized and even ridiculed, is necessary and important. Nuclear weapons will probably never be used, and sooner or later the world will rid itself of them, probably passing through the phase of minimum deterrence. It is good that this goal was put forward. Statesmen have limited lifetimes, and they should be remembered not only for managing current political affairs but also for being able to propose larger goals. It is Gorbachev's unique achievement that he set the agenda for his country and for the world.

The statement, on which I worked until 4:00 A.M., included some positions on current arms control issues that I thought had already been overtaken by events. But there were also some bold new proposals, including the willingness to consider an agreement providing for zero INF missiles in Europe for both the Soviet Union and the United States. I believed that, after years of propaganda aimed at proving that we should have in Europe enough INF missiles to counterbalance the nuclear forces of Britain and France, it took courage to propose something that clearly disregarded those forces and looked like acceptance of the original U.S. proposal. (There was, however, one difference: Gorbachev sought to retain the SS-20s deployed in Asia.) I had a clear feeling that this and some other points must not have pleased at least some of our generals who had become used to the total rigidity of Soviet arms control positions.

Another event of early 1986 was the somewhat delayed 26th Party Congress, held in February. The party was then the decision-maker on all issues, both foreign and domestic; the Congresses only ratified them after they had been prepared in caucuses, often following a great fight. But this Congress was eagerly awaited. People were anxious to see what the leadership had arrived at. The attitude was different from what it was before and during the previous two or three Congresses, which left people indifferent and amounted to a show of party unity and Brezhnev's ill health.

On the day the Congress opened, I took a day off and watched Gorbachev deliver his report on television. It was shown in full. Gorbachev looked vigorous and in control. The report was rather long, which was traditional, and contained quite a few equally traditional ideological and propaganda clichés. We were used to them and had a way of ignoring them, trying to read between lines. But there was no need to read between the lines this time to understand that the report contained some things that were really new.

Gorbachev spoke of the need for genuine reform of the economy, saying that just tinkering with it while changing nothing in a fundamental way was futile. He spoke of giving greater freedom to the peasants along the lines of Lenin's "new economic policy," specifically mentioning the policy that Lenin called state capitalism. And he spoke of the principle of reasonable sufficiency for defense. This meant a redefinition of military parity, which was then still interpreted, and not only by the military, as requiring strict equality in almost every category of weapons.

The Congress left a mixed impression. At the final meeting, Gorbachev spoke of socialism as a way to "peace and freedom," and just uttering the word "freedom" in such a setting was highly unusual. Most of the delegates, who represented the old apparat, seemed not to notice that charged word, but I did. On the other hand, the new version of the party program adopted at the Congress did not seem much different from the previous one, and it disregarded some bold proposals for change that had been discussed in the media before the Congress convened.

One exception was the section on international affairs, which included the concept of a basically indivisible and interdependent world with many common interests and values. But I had hoped for more and was disappointed when at the last meeting Alexander Yakovlev reported that the program commission regarded most of the proposed changes as merely editorial and suggested that no substantive changes be made. Clearly, Gorbachev was being cautious. The Politburo came out of the Congress practically unchanged.

I continued to work in the foreign ministry, often translating for Gorbachev or Shevardnadze. I recall Gorbachev's meeting with Senator Edward Kennedy, at which Anatoly Chernyaev was present for the first time as Gorbachev's new assistant for international affairs. Chernyaev was extremely reserved, and it took me some time to see what an extraordinary man he was. I later worked closely with him, and in the final months of Gorbachev's presidency he was my boss. He was a good boss and a strong man, and I think we both liked working together. There will be more about him later.

Chernobyl

No one writing about 1986 can avoid mentioning Chernobyl. Even writing about it is painful, but I have to do it because it had a significant effect on subsequent political events and on the minds of people in my country.

I was in Bangkok, Thailand, on a U.N. assignment when the news of the disaster broke out. While in the Soviet Union an effort was made to minimize it, the Western media dramatized the news and speculated about the possible consequences of the accident. I well remembered the Three Mile Island accident in the United States in March 1979. I had lived in New York in the 1970s so I naturally compared both events and their coverage. At first I thought the effects of the Chernobyl accident might be contained, but I soon understood, even before returning to Moscow, that a real tragedy that would have far-reaching consequences had occurred.

I knew a little about the effects of nuclear radiation, and when data became available I understood that although it was bad it was not the end of the world. But Moscow was close to panic. The city was rife with rumors, and few people believed the official version of the events. Glasnost was then not even a word widely used, much less an accepted concept. Government-run media were minimizing the disaster, both out of habit and for fear of causing even greater panic. But the mood in Moscow was of gloom and often anger. It was a mood of distrust of the authorities. In retrospect, I think it caused a rift between the people and the government that never quite closed. It was perhaps the beginning of a powerful wave of rejection of authority and the loss of legitimacy of the country's leadership in the eyes of the people.

Gorbachev was struggling with a difficult situation. I watched his addresses on television and saw him in person one or two times during those days. I interpreted at his meeting with Dr. Robert Gale, an American physician and specialist in radiation biology, and American industrialist Armand Hammer, who were actively helping to deal with the medical consequences of the disaster. Gorbachev chose his words carefully, and it was clear that he understood how much hinged on every word he said. I am not sure he was fully aware of the enormity of what had happened, for even the data he was given might have been doctored. He later recalled how Yefim Slavsky, minister of "medium machine building" (code name for the atomic weapons industry), had assured him that the dangers were being exaggerated and that similar accidents had happened before without any terrible consequences.

Gorbachev could not afford either to downplay the disaster, which would have made him look callous, or to react in a way that would be too emotional by the standards of that time, which might have caused even greater panic and possibly catastrophic consequences. So he had to engage in a kind of balancing act. It was not the first time in his career, and not the last. Unfortunately, he had to do it again and again, and he sometimes continued to balance even when it was time, as they say, to fish or cut bait.

Shevardnadze in London

In the summer of 1986 Shevardnadze went on a visit to London. It was one year after his surprise appointment as foreign minister, and he was not yet the globally known and popular figure he would become. But working with him during the London visit, I was impressed by him. It had taken him exactly one year to gain full command of the issues and the confidence of a real professional. He had his priorities on arms control and regional issues, and a realistic ability to see what was possible and what was not. He did not need as much expert help and advice as before, even when answering questions on rather technical matters, such as the Stockholm talks and chemical weapons negotiations.

It was not an easy visit. In addition to problems at the talks, during which there was much repetition of the sides' standard positions, which were still widely different on many issues, the atmosphere of the visit was poisoned by some hostile demonstrations, particularly those associated with Chernobyl and Afghanistan. The demonstrators were noisy and harsh. Shevardnadze handled it with outward calm, but I think he felt that we were not being treated fairly. He was particularly upset when a demonstration was allowed right near Covent Garden, to which he had been invited by Sir Geoffrey Howe for a night at the opera. But he did not say so to the British minister.

The atmosphere at the talks was good. While keeping close to the Western position on practically all issues, the British were willing to listen to the Soviet position being presented in a new and more flexible way, and hinted that flexibility was possible on their part too, at least on lesser issues. The reception by the British was warm; they made a real effort to make the Soviet minister feel at home. Although I was not present at Shevardnadze's meeting with Prime Minister Margaret Thatcher, I understood from his remarks later that he was pleased.

Shevardnadze's Trip to the United States

The next event of 1986 was the annual visit of the foreign minister to New York to attend the session of the United Nations General Assembly. Once again the speech in the general debate, and meetings with Reagan and Shultz, were to be the high points of the visit. Shevardnadze was carrying to

Washington a letter to Reagan from Gorbachev with a proposal to hold a meeting "in London or Reykjavik"—not quite a summit (it was again believed in Moscow that a full-scale summit should not be held without the prospect of a major arms control agreement) but a get-together to discuss an open agenda quietly and informally. None of us was at all certain that would be acceptable to the Americans, who were insisting on a full-scale summit "without preconditions." But it seemed worth a try.

I was going to New York a married man again. Lena and I had hesitated during the summer before taking the plunge. Our wedding ceremony was held on September 12 in a civil registration office one subway stop from her home, and we then had a small party with a few friends at the Restaurant Prague. Lena has been a friend and great support to me in good times and bad. Our daughter Liza was born the next year. I hope she is growing to see a better world.

On the eve of Shevardnadze's departure for New York a bombshell threatened to undermine all our efforts. A Soviet official from the United Nations Secretariat, Nikolay Zakharov, was arrested in New York on charges of spying. It was not done quietly, in a way that would have made it possible just to expel the man and avoid complications. The case was covered in the U.S. media in a big way, which was bound to arouse anger and suspicion in Moscow. The KGB countered by arresting Nicholas Daniloff, the well-known *U.S. News & World Report* Moscow correspondent, who was, in the view of his colleagues, "clean."

As we were leaving for New York there was every indication that the incident might develop into a full-scale scandal that could embitter the U.S.-Soviet relationship for a long time to come. The mood among people on Shevardnadze's plane was quite pessimistic. Some openly doubted the wisdom of Daniloff's arrest. Everybody believed that it could doom the effort to arrange a Reagan-Gorbachev meeting. Teimuraz Stepanov, one of the foreign minister's closest assistants, was in one of his dark moods, and I halfheartedly tried to comfort him by saying there were ways to patch things up. He was not convinced. I think he felt that the incident could undermine Shevardnadze.

The reporters' first question to Shevardnadze as he left his plane in New York was about the Daniloff-Zakharov affair. I remembered a similar incident in 1977, when two Soviet U.N. staff members in New York and an American businessman in Moscow were arrested. It took months for the two countries to disentangle themselves, and it was messy. This time, I thought, much more was at stake, and it was not at all clear that a compromise was possible, given the various agency interests and the pride and prejudice that were involved.

Shevardnadze's Meetings with Shultz and Reagan

Soon after arriving in New York, Shevardnadze went to Washington for his second White House meeting with President Reagan. He had talked with Shultz in New York and given him a preview of Gorbachev's letter to the president. The talk with Shultz went better than some of us had expected; the two men had already established a rapport that allowed them to discuss quietly and without rancor even the matters that obviously upset both of them. But the underlying tension was unmistakable. Shultz cautiously indicated that the proposal for a "nonsummit" might get favorable consideration—but, he strongly hinted, only if the Daniloff matter were cleared up first. And there was no doubt about the U.S. position on that, which was that there had been no justification for the arrest and that Daniloff had to be released unconditionally.

As we were riding in the Soviet ambassador's car to the White House, Shevardnadze was silent. I have seen many of his silences, which can mean different things to a careful observer. This silence did not seem to bode well.

The meeting with Reagan was a real one-on-one, with only the interpreters present. As we were driving back to the embassy about an hour later, the minister's silence was the same as before. He went right to the second floor of the embassy building, where the ambassador's office was located. Ambassador Yury Dubinin, Deputy Foreign Minister Alexander Bessmertnykh, Sergey Tarasenko, and Teimuraz Stepanov were waiting there. Shevardnadze indicated that I should enter too.

For a couple of minutes everyone sat in silence waiting for someone to utter the first word. Then Dubinin said, "Eduard Amvrosiyevich, how does it look?"

"How does it look? Not very good," Shevardnadze answered. He then looked at me and said softly, "What would you say?"

I was surprised that he had asked my opinion. It was unusual. So, maybe out of surprise, I stood up and was silent for a moment. The natural and expected thing would be to echo the minister's words. But I heard myself saying, "Well, Eduard Amvrosiyevich, it did not look that bad to me. Of course, Reagan repeated the American position on the espionage matter, and that's quite natural. But he did not put it very harshly. And his other remarks seemed more constructive than I had expected. And he did not reject the idea of a meeting with Gorbachev."

The foreign minister listened and did not object, although my assessment probably seemed too rosy to him. After this episode, he began to ask my opinion again from time to time, particularly after one-on-one discussions. I always tried to "tell it like it was," though the temptation to echo the prevailing mood and to say the expected things was always strong.

Shevardnadze then began to discuss with his aides the strategy for talks with George Shultz. It was clear that a way to strike a compromise had to be found.

As always, a complete record of the conversation with President Reagan was sent to Moscow. Shevardnadze had to weigh his every word carefully because he had to look firm in both capitals—for different reasons, of course. Shultz was in a similar predicament. Both men had a limited range of options, and both wanted to find a way out. This is the stuff diplomacy is made of. It deals mostly with unpleasant situations. A lot of effort is expended on untying knots tied stupidly by others—and when the dust settles it all looks simple.

It did not look simple during the dozens of hours that Shevardnadze and Shultz spent together, alternating their meetings between the Soviet and U.S. missions in New York. Discussion of the Daniloff-Zakharov affair paralleled talks on arms control and regional issues. And the "nonsummit" was always in the background, waiting for the vexing espionage issue to be resolved. Some of the meetings were held unannounced, and once we had to arrive at the U.S. mission by the garage entrance. But as we were leaving in the same way, a few reporters stood watch near the garage door.

Alexander Bessmertnykh and Roz Ridgway, Shultz's deputy for European and Soviet affairs, were always present during the discussions of the "espionage affair." Negotiators with many years of experience, they were tough bargainers and skillful diplomatic technicians. In a way, it was a pity that their skills had to be used on such a thing. But all of us were working for an important reward—not a personal reward, but a reward for both our countries.

At some point in the conversation the name of Yury Orlov was mentioned. A physicist and a friend of Andrey Sakharov, Orlov had been jailed and sent to internal exile under Brezhnev. Although, as later became clear, the question of releasing almost all remaining political prisoners and exiles was then being considered by the Soviet leadership, Shultz's suggestion to include Orlov in a kind of swap was not a readily acceptable option.

For the Americans too it was important to make sure that the release of Nicholas Daniloff from a Moscow prison not appear to be a formal part of a spy swap. And although I think Shultz understood early in the whole game that Zakharov, whose arrest had started the incident, would have to be released, he insisted that his release would have to be arranged differently from Daniloff's. It was to be made clear, he hinted, which man was "the real spy." In this diplomatic minuet everyone had to save face.

In the end, a compromise was struck. Zakharov would be let go after a court hearing in New York at which the judge would say that he believed the man was guilty but was dismissing the case for political reasons at the request of the administration. Daniloff was to be released at about the same time, and Orlov a few days later. Shevardnadze and Shultz worked on the final details of the scenario for hours, and several times the outcome appeared doubtful. Shevardnadze later said to Shultz that he too was not sure Moscow would approve the deal. But it did, and after a few tense moments of waiting for a call from the court building with the news that Zakharov was free, the nerve-racking episode was over.

I did not have much sleep those days. The record of every conversation had to be made immediately, to be cabled to Moscow. A two- or three-hour talk sometimes takes twice as much time to record and check. On some days I came back to my hotel in the small hours of the morning and slept for a few hours before rushing back to the Soviet U.N. mission. I rarely had time for walks in my favorite areas of Manhattan: the East Sixties and Central Park. Shevardnadze seemed to work around the clock, and though I would have liked to show New York to him, I understood that he did not have the time and was in no mood for that. In his five and a half years as foreign minister he did not do much sightseeing.

The Gorbachev-Reagan Reykjavik Summit

We were returning to Moscow with a date set for the Reykjavik meeting between Gorbachev and Reagan. I did not know what kind of meeting Gorbachev had in mind, but the agenda seemed certain to focus on arms control. The talks in Geneva had stalled once again, as they would so many times afterward. The ability of the U.S. and Soviet bureaucracies to entangle any negotiation in a web of abstruse technical details was amazing, and I often saw how impatient Gorbachev was with that, although he appeared to have no difficulty grasping the technical issues. But he must have felt how much better it would be to strike a grand bargain that would cut through the mass of details and make the negotiations proceed at a different pace toward a clear outcome. Such a change would also strengthen his position at home, leaving him with more time for dealing with the difficult domestic issues.

Reykjavik does not look very hospitable in mid-October. It is cold, and the little snow on the ground does not make it feel warmer, as the big banks of snow do during Russian winters. The motorcade with Gorbachev and the accompanying officials was long; it is never possible to organize "a really small, informal get-together with as few people present as possible," as Gorbachev had suggested in his letter to Reagan. As the cars sped to the city, I was wondering whether in their second meeting Reagan and Gorbachev would get along.

They started off one-on-one the next day, with my colleague Nikolay Uspensky interpreting for Gorbachev. I stayed with Shevardnadze and Shultz, who started a conversation on the overall U.S.-Soviet relationship and the accumulated range of issues. In about half an hour, however, word came from the room where the two leaders were talking that the foreign minister and the secretary of state were being invited to join them. The talks then went on in the two-on-two format until their dramatic finale.

Gorbachev had started by proposing to Reagan a simple deal on strategic arms: 50 percent reduction in all categories. He wanted to simplify the Geneva negotiations and put them on a fast track to an agreement. He also proposed that the two sides limit their strategic defense programs to research conducted "in laboratories."

When Shevardnadze and Shultz joined their leaders in the small room at Hofdi House, where the talks were held, Reagan seemed to be somewhat confused. He was not used to discussion of arms control matters in any detail, and even Gorbachev's simple proposal was not something he was ready to discuss alone. The four men then started a review of the overall arms control situation, dealing with its three main areas: strategic offensive arms, defense and space, and the INF missiles.

Space defense—"Star Wars"—was the most sensitive issue, a "neuralgic point" for the Soviet Union. Many on the Soviet side thought that the U.S. SDI (Strategic Defense Initiative) program could not be stopped, but they hoped to restrain it at least enough to prevent a full-scale arms race in space. There was also what turned out to be ill-informed concern that space arms—for example, laser weapons—could be used to strike targets on earth. (In Reykjavik I heard Soviet nuclear physicist Yevgeny Velikhov, who accompanied Gorbachev there, say that this was technically extremely difficult, and impossible from the cost-benefit standpoint.) Reagan was prepared with an elaborate explanation of his concept of SDI and of why it should not be regarded by the Soviet Union as a threat.

Reagan's arguments for SDI have become well-known since then—often repeated and, with a new world and new issues emerging, regarded by many as "overtaken by events." He said that the goal of SDI was to make nuclear weapons "impotent and obsolete." He emphasized that relying on nuclear weapons for global security was immoral. Gorbachev countered that the answer to this was to destroy nuclear weapons and recalled his program for nuclear disarmament by the year 2000.

Then Reagan produced a relatively new line, that SDI was needed as a kind of "gas mask," the ultimate protection against nuclear weapons even if the superpowers decided to destroy them. Imagine, he said, a madman like Gaddhafi having nuclear weapons and threatening to use them. With space defenses, we would be protected against this eventuality, he said. He even suggested that he would be ready to share the Star Wars technology with the Soviet Union, to ensure that both countries were safe.

In hindsight some of Reagan's arguments may not sound so bad, but in the circumstances of 1986 they appeared quite implausible. Gorbachev was particularly skeptical about the offer of SDI technology to the Soviet Union. "I may believe you, Mr. President," he said, "but would your successors repeat the offer?" Even many American officials were incredulous that their president would suggest something like that.

By the end of the day, Reagan and Gorbachev had decided to ask their experts to consider the issues in light of their discussions. Gorbachev went back to the Soviet ship *Georg Ots*, where he and his team stayed. He met with his delegation, including Marshal Sergey Akhromeyev and such advisers as Georgy Arbatov, Yevgeny Primakov, and Valentin Falin, and foreign ministry officials, including Shevardnadze's deputies Bessmertnykh and veteran arms control negotiator Victor Karpov.

Gorbachev asked me to read through my notes of his discussion with Reagan. I did so while everyone listened, and he commented from time to time on certain points. He then appointed Akhromeyev to head the Soviet group of experts that was to discuss the issues with the U.S. group, led by Paul Nitze, overnight.

The next morning the experts reported that they had agreed on the general scheme of a fifty percent strategic arms reduction, which was more complicated than what Gorbachev had proposed but still fairly simple and nontechnical. Then Gorbachev proposed to Reagan a deal on INF: zero missiles in Europe and one hundred warheads elsewhere. Reagan immediately accepted. But they stumbled again on the SDI. Reagan said he could not accept confining SDI research and testing to the laboratory, and Gorbachev asked why he did not want to consider it in combination with the elimination of all nuclear weapons, say, within ten years. To my surprise, Reagan answered that he would not be against the destruction of all nuclear weapons, including tactical and battlefield ones.

I frequently wondered afterward why Shultz did not try then to restrain Reagan, who was suddenly saying something quite contrary to the U.S. strategic doctrine. I think that as an expert Shultz understood very well that what Reagan was saying was heresy, but he did not interfere.

Was it because the rationale of Star Wars, upon scrutiny, was equally inconsistent with the dogmas of nuclear deterrence? Or did Shultz want to see how far his boss would go to probe what could be achieved in serious negotiations? I don't know. But I remember that years later, when George Shultz, retired and teaching quietly at Stanford, met with Shevardnadze in New York, he said something like this: "When our leaders, each in his own way, began to speak of a world without nuclear weapons, the experts thought that they were wrong and that this was a goal that could never be achieved. But the experts did not understand that Reagan and Gorbachev were on to something: they felt what people wanted in a profound way." Shevardnadze agreed. I hope they were right.

In the end, of course, there was no agreement in Reykjavik. Reagan continued to insist on the need for SDI as protection against a madman and therefore refused to accept limits on it. Gorbachev said that without an agreement on defense there could be no agreement on offensive weapons—the two things were linked. What is more, he included the INF missiles in that link.

As Reagan and Gorbachev left Hofdi House, the reporters did not know what had happened, but Reagan's dejected face told the story. Their final exchange was picked up by reporters and was in most newspapers the next day, as well as the photo of Gorbachev and Reagan saying goodbye to each other in front of Hofdi House, with me standing between them.

Shultz gave a gloomy press conference right afterward, saying that promising agreements had been discussed, but fell through because Gorbachev insisted on limiting SDI. As Gorbachev entered the crowded auditorium where his press conference was to be held thirty minutes later, everyone was expecting a similar assessment. But as I interpreted his words, I sensed that Gorbachev took a completely different line.

The talks in Reykjavik, Gorbachev said, had not produced a deal, but they were not a failure. In fact, they were a breakthrough, because for the first time the leaders of the United States and the Soviet Union were discussing the possibility of destroying all their nuclear weapons. Was he putting a good face on a bad situation? Or was he looking beyond the details of the day to the deeper meaning of what had occurred? I wanted to believe that the latter was true.

The next day, I drove to the airport with Shevardnadze. The foreign minister was pensive. I try never to ask too many questions, and so did not ask him what he thought. I remember one remark he made: "Well, now it is all tied together again." As a diplomat whose mind focused on the practical tasks, he understood that it made reaching specific agreements more difficult. While the link between strategic offensive arms and strategic defense was quite natural and inevitable, throwing in INF was more difficult to justify and complicated the efforts to reach agreement on the one area that looked more promising—intermediate-range missiles. So both the overall arms control situation and the prospects for some agreement that would justify holding a full-scale U.S.-Soviet summit seemed uncertain once again.

Once the U.S. experts and bureaucrats had a chance to analyze what had happened in Reykjavik, they immediately began to backtrack from Reagan's incautious remarks about destroying nuclear weapons. The argument that Star Wars would make nuclear weapons obsolete was one thing, but discussing the abolition of nuclear weapons in the context of specific arms control negotiations was quite another. The European leaders too were concerned, for they still regarded nuclear weapons as the ultimate guarantee of their security and the only weapons that were genuinely reliable.

A round of megaphone diplomacy began, with the Americans trying to alter what had actually transpired at Reykjavik, and the Soviets countering with quotes from my transcripts of the talks. I found the exchange quite distressing. It was quickly degenerating into a transatlantic shouting match and did not bring agreement on any issue closer. I thought it played into the hands of those who did not want any agreement. And the longer we would insist on lumping all issues together in one package, the less likely an agreement could be reached. In the endless discussions with my colleagues in Moscow, that was, for me, the bottom line.

The Gorbachevs Go to Delhi

A month later Gorbachev went to Delhi on a short official visit. We left on a cold wintry day, but when we landed it was, by Moscow standards, summer.

The atmosphere was also warm. Crowds waited at the airport and in the streets, and enormous flower arrangements decorated the welcoming signs.

Gorbachev found it much easier to talk with Gandhi than with Reagan or some other leaders. Their rapport was total, and their discussions were genuinely frank. I noticed a special warmth between Raisa Gorbachev and Sonya Gandhi too. Mrs. Gandhi was quite reserved and sometimes seemed uncomfortable in the role of "first lady," but she and Raisa Gorbachev had much in common—above all, I felt, concern and alarm for their husbands.

Then and later I frequently thought about why Raisa Gorbachev was not popular in her country. Like others, I sometimes tended to attribute that to her somewhat didactic manner of talking or to the way her personality was projected on television. I now believe that the reasons went much deeper. After years and decades of almost inhuman facelessness at the top of Soviet society, she now had a special role to play. Gorbachev was the first Soviet leader with a wife who could be observed, judged, and commented on. And the judgments of many people reflected not so much her real pluses and minuses but rather their own long-suppressed emotions and inferiority complexes. I later came to know Raisa Gorbachev quite well, particularly in 1991, and came to genuinely respect her.

Gorbachev's talks with Rajiv Gandhi were long and for the most part very private. The trust between them continued to grow. Some of Gandhi's proposals, if fully accepted, would have meant a tilt in policy, so Gorbachev had to react cautiously. Gandhi seemed to understand that Gorbachev could not be forthcoming on some matters, and it did not hinder their developing relationship, which, I thought then and later, could become an important moral factor in the world for years to come. The Delhi Declaration on the nuclear-weapon-free and nonviolent world, which the two leaders signed at the end of the visit, was often criticized as being just a rhetorical statement without much real meaning. It was indeed put together hastily, but it was much better written and had more substance than the usual statements of this kind. The Indians seemed to be pleased that the Soviets did not try to foist on them what they had perhaps expected—a long tract with a lot of "anti-imperialism" phraseology. The emphasis on universal human values made the Delhi Declaration one of the first documents of the "new thinking," and its value will probably be lasting.

Gorbachev was accompanied on the Delhi visit by a large group of official and academic experts, including Roald Sagdeyev, Yevgeny Primakov, and Georgy Arbatov. I was present during some of his conversations with them, and, frankly, I did not find their contributions particularly edifying. Their main effort seemed to be to speak in tune with the boss, even when, as was clear then or later, they had a different view of some question. At the end of his final talk with the entire Soviet contingent, Gorbachev suggested that they might want to send to him ideas and suggestions in preparation for the party plenum "on personnel matters," which was to be held shortly.

The visit to India was a difficult one for me. I interpreted so much in a little more than two days that at the end of the visit I lost my voice. When Shevardnadze asked me something on the plane home, I said I would write him a note—and I did, setting forth some of my impressions. I wrote that some of our people in Delhi seemed rather arrogant toward the Indians and regarded their work there as a kind of exile. I did not know what could be done about that, but I felt I had to share that impression. Shevardnadze showed the note to Gorbachev, who said it was food for thought. Generally, the mood on the plane was cheerful, and I wondered whether it was fully in tune with the situation in the country and in the world.

Shevardnadze and Shultz Continue Arms Debate

The international debate about what had happened in Reykjavik and what must follow was continuing unabated, and I wondered whether anything constructive could come out of that debate. When Shevardnadze met with Shultz in Vienna in early December on the margins of a meeting of the CSCE (Conference on Security and Cooperation in Europe), they had perhaps the most difficult talk of all the years in which they worked together. Shevardnadze later recalled that talk as the least fruitful. I think it was because there was enormous confusion then in the capitals, with the bureaucracies fighting it out and trying to understand, correct, or preempt their leaders.

Shevardnadze and Shultz were clearly on different wavelengths. Shevardnadze wanted Shultz to confirm the goal of nuclear disarmament as a part of the agenda discussed in Reykjavik, and insisted that the Soviet Union and the United States should not retreat from the goals set by their leaders. Shultz objected in a tepid way, saying among other things that there was an uproar in Europe, where leaders wanted to hear nothing about nuclear disarmament, and he proposed that the Soviet Union and the United States should focus on agreements that were feasible in the immediate future. He wanted the START, space defense, and INF issues to be treated separately. There was a feeling of impasse in the room.

Later I often discussed with Shevardnadze and Tarasenko this frustrating conversation. Both ministers obviously had no room to maneuver, and in the confusing overall situation the most they could do was maintain civility and keep the channels of communication open. In the past a similar lack of understanding at the very top could have resulted in months, if not years, of mutual recriminations and propaganda bickering. This time, fortunately, a civil tone was preserved, and things were back on track within a few weeks.

As 1987 approached, it was clear that important decisions would have to be made soon. I did not yet have a clear idea how urgent some of the domestic problems were, but, being better informed on international issues, I felt that we had come to a watershed on things like Afghanistan and INF—decisions could not be postponed for long. And the issue of human rights was a problem that focused both domestic and foreign policies around one simple question: Do we want to behave in a civilized way accepted in the international community, which means that people can think and say what they like without fear of being thrown out of work, jailed, or kicked out of their country? I was not sure that the Politburo of the time would be ready to give a clear answer to that question, but the return of Andrey Sakharov from his exile in Gorky to Moscow at the end of 1986 seemed a good sign.

Four
ON THE ROAD TO THE WASHINGTON SUMMIT
1987

Glasnost and Gorbachev's New Vision

The Central Committee plenum that Gorbachev mentioned in Delhi was held, after some delay, in January 1987. Gorbachev's report at the plenum was a revelation to those who had continued to be skeptical about his intentions. It was that report, I think, that convinced many people at the time that the general secretary's intention was not to repaint the facade of the existing system and strengthen the party's power, but to find a way to make the country a modern and civilized society with a way of life that would be perceived as more normal—a society kinder to the people.

In envisioning such a goal, Gorbachev was ahead not only of the party but also of many of the people. His report to the plenum was so different from what people used to hear from the party that some were not ready to take it seriously. Until January 1987 many ordinary people and people in the party, the military, and even in the foreign ministry—the older generation—thought that perestroika must mean a tightening of the screws: greater order and discipline, a crackdown on corruption, and a return to Andropov's ideology and vision of a rather regimented society. Therefore Gorbachev's emphasis on glasnost—more openness and a freer press—was a surprise to many. As a linguist, I felt perhaps more than others that there was a new vocabulary and a new way of talking to the people.

But I was disappointed that there was little new on the economy, and I was not enthusiastic about the few economic ideas in Gorbachev's report. I remember discussing them with Roald Sagdeyev, whom I had known since 1985. We both wondered what good could come out of things like having factory managers elected by the employees. The words "market economy" did not appear in the report, and it was not clear whether investment would be redistributed toward the consumer sector.

Nevertheless, there was much enthusiasm about Gorbachev's speech. The limits of glasnost still had to be tested, and no one knew yet how far freedom of thought and expression would be allowed to go. But most people felt that something new was beginning, and among my friends in the Moscow intelligentsia there was a lot of willingness to support the new leader and help him in some way. For the first time in many years, party reports and decisions were discussed as though they really mattered, not in a detached, uninterested, or sarcastic way.

It was then that I began to think seriously of leaving the foreign ministry's translation department to try something new. Over the years, I had received offers to join one of the ministry's departments dealing with substantive issues—arms control or U.S. affairs. It was tempting, but somehow I never got around to accepting those offers. Something had prevented me from making that decision. I did not want to become totally involved, or maybe did not want to forgo the relative freedom that went with the position of interpreter, somehow regarded as not quite a government official but more one's own person.

Shevardnadze's Trip to the Asia-Pacific Region

In late February, Eduard Shevardnadze went on an extended trip to the Asia-Pacific region, including Australia, Thailand, Vietnam, Laos, and Cambodia. The goal was to explore the prospects of Soviet relations with countries in the region and to see what could be done to bring to an end the conflict in Cambodia. That conflict was another regional sore point, which, although it was not as much of a drain on our resources as the war in Afghanistan, poisoned relations with a number of countries. I was told that the foreign minister had included me on his team for the entire trip, not just Australia.

There had been a lot of discussion in the foreign ministry about separating INF from other arms control areas, and everyone seemed to agree that was desirable. (Even Andrey Gromyko, in a talk with his former counterpart Cyrus Vance, had said that the three arms control areas had to be considered "in context" rather than "as a package.") Nevertheless, no one expected it would happen soon.

When Shevardnadze announced in a speech in Australia the decision to untie the package so far as the INF missiles were concerned, it was a surprise to me. I still find it interesting that this announcement was hidden deep in a routine speech at a lunch given by the Australian government. Apparently the shift in position had to be performed inconspicuously, as if it were nothing important. But I had no doubt that it was a crucial turning point. The most difficult thing in politics, I still feel, is not the enunciation of grand political concepts but specific decisions, particularly those that correct recent errors.

As we went on to visit the countries of Indochina, I was wondering whether something dramatic could be done to end the conflict there. Of course, regional problems, which involve the interests and ambitions of many countries and their leaders, are more difficult to resolve than any others. Too many factors have to be considered, and the solutions finally arrived at look easy only afterward.

I had more time for myself in those countries than in Great Britain or Australia, and as I discussed the problems and the progress of Shevardnadze's talks with his assistants and foreign ministry experts, it sometimes looked hopeless to me. But I was encouraged to hear Igor Rogachev, Shevardnadze's deputy for Asian affairs, who was always restrained in his assessments, say of his boss, "He will find a solution. He can talk to all of them."

There was also something else that really struck me on that trip. I compared the bustling capital of Thailand, with its vibrant economy and its people, who looked busy and dynamic, with the economic decline and people's apathy that was so obvious in the countries of Indochina, particularly in Vietnam. The contrast was dramatic. It could no longer be explained by the ravages of war, and the officials of our embassy in Hanoi were candid in their criticism of the huge and inefficient "economic cooperation" projects on which we were wasting enormous resources and efforts. Even Laos, where a little private initiative had been allowed, seemed different from Vietnam. I could not understand why our well-paid academic economists were not shouting about it, for the conclusions to be drawn seemed starkly clear.

When we returned to Moscow, I finally decided that the time for a change in my career had come. I talked to Sergey Tarasenko, and he suggested that the best place for me would be in the arms control section of the USA and Canada department, where I could focus on an area I knew well and also get a closer view of all the other issues that the "U.S. desk" was keeping track of. Alexander Bessmertnykh welcomed the idea and took me on immediately. So on an April day I became one of those officials who are the workhorses of any foreign affairs bureaucracy. Their work can be boring or fascinating, unrewarding or exciting, dull or intellectually challenging, and it was all of that for me during the four years that followed.

Difficult Talks with Shultz in Moscow

Shevardnadze agreed to my reassignment on the condition that I continue as his interpreter, which was also my intention. So when Secretary of State Shultz came to Moscow that April, I was already on my dual job. I was looking forward to that visit for a number of reasons, and there was a general feeling in Moscow that it would be extremely important in setting the tone and the pace of the U.S.-Soviet relationship.

Shultz came to Moscow to discuss the entire range of issues and to see when a full-scale U.S.-Soviet summit could be held. Gorbachev had an invitation to come to Washington, and it was clear that the summit was necessary—a "new chapter" is never open without it. But maneuvering on the substance of the summit continued both in Moscow and in Washington. Shevardnadze had made the summit his highest personal priority, and he was not quite happy, as he clearly indicated to me on the first day of Shultz's visit, with the way things were going. Indeed, separating INF missiles from the arms control package, and agreeing on broad outlines of the deal, was not enough to bring the talks into the home stretch.

The question of shorter-range missiles emerged almost immediately to cast doubt on the prospects of an agreement. I believed that the question could be dealt with as such, but some people on both sides were sticking to their guns and making things difficult precisely because they were not happy about any agreement. The feeling was reinforced by the emergence of another espionage problem on the eve of Shultz's arrival. It soon developed into a real and long-playing scandal over the bugging of the new U.S. embassy building in Moscow.

Both countries had by then almost completed their new buildings, and the Soviets were ready to move into their new "Brezhnev style" embassy. Everyone probably assumed that both countries' intelligence services had made some efforts to penetrate the other's building electronically. This, after all, is what had been going on for years. Our people had found some bugs in the Washington building and were apparently not surprised. But the Americans took a dramatic stand. Shultz said the new U.S. building was "honeycombed" with listening devices but refused to produce any of them.

Shevardnadze was extremely unhappy about the whole affair. He was sure that some people on the U.S. side were just trying to scuttle the summit. But I believe he also felt that the Soviet KGB was not being quite up-front with him and with Gorbachev, and, as he indicated much later, this made him think there was something like a second government in the country. Interpreting the discussion of the embassy problem was one of the most disheartening experiences of my entire career.

Overall, the talks were quite difficult. Not only INF, START, and ABM, but also nuclear testing and chemical weapons, gave rise to endless tugs-of-war between experts on the two sides. Regional issues were not much easier. And not everyone on the Soviet side was pleased with the new way in which human rights were being discussed—without rancor and recriminations, and with Shevardnadze ready to talk about the specific cases the Americans raised. "Why do we allow ourselves to be held answerable by them, responding to their complaints and forgetting about our pride and dignity?" was the question I heard more than once, and sometimes from people I would not have expected to hear it from.

To me too, the U.S. position on many issues seemed to amount to a continuing escalation of demands, many of them not unreasonable, but with little understanding that Gorbachev's and Shevardnadze's freedom to maneuver was limited and that opening them to criticism by conservatives at home was a dangerous tactic. I still wonder how much George Shultz understood it. But he did make a visible effort to preserve and strengthen a warm personal relationship with Gorbachev and Shevardnadze.

Shultz's talk in the Kremlin with Gorbachev was long and often difficult, but in the end they seemed to clear some obstacles, particularly the shorter-range-missiles problem, and their parting handshake was a cordial one. The arms control delegations in Geneva received firm instructions to work toward an agreement that could be signed during a summit in Washington before the end of the year. Yuly Vorontsov, Shevardnadze's first deputy, who had been named our chief delegate in Geneva, looked upbeat and optimistic.

Summer Geneva Arms Talks

But the arms control talks are never over before they are over. As the summer round went on in Geneva, and as I followed the proceedings by reading the cables in Moscow, the horizon for the summit seemed to become increasingly clouded. Problem after problem seemed to emerge, mostly concerning verification — that was still the minefield for disarmament.

The pattern was always the same: the Americans would raise some technical difficulty, the Soviets would object, almost automatically, that there was no need for overly intrusive verification, and the issue would soon assume political significance and thus become more difficult to resolve. With Shevardnadze's quiet prodding, our delegation was changing its approach. It often agreed to look at a U.S. proposal and then tried to hold the Americans to their own stringent standards. The approach seemed to work on some technical issues, such as the monitoring of production facilities. Nevertheless, the mass of verification details and the danger that our military would revert to the old approach made it doubtful that the INF train would arrive in Washington on time.

What made the verification negotiations particularly difficult was the problem of the final one hundred warheads that were to be left outside Europe. The need for them was not clear to me. In fact, they were already complicating our relations with Asian countries. And the problem of monitoring their production and deployment created endless difficulties in Geneva. So the best thing seemed to be to drop that "final hundred," perhaps as a goodwill gesture to the Asians. That is what was finally done, but I can imagine how hard it was to push that decision through the bureaucracy and the Politburo. To many, it must have looked like just another unwarranted and unrewarded concession.

On some other issues too, the attitude of the U.S. administration, while justifiable in absolute terms, so to speak, seemed to take too little account of the internal Soviet factor. They sometimes seemed to deal with Gorbachev as if he were just another Soviet leader in the Brezhnev-Chernenko mold. I even wondered why the Americans seemed more willing to compromise with the old Soviet leaders than with the new ones. My doubts grew as I watched the Americans take what seemed to be a particularly tough and uncompromising position on the problem of Pershing-1A missiles belonging to Germany.

The problem was more political than military or technical. Formally, the Americans were right to insist that the treaty was between the Soviet Union and the United States and that the "German" missiles had no place there. But missiles of the same type were to be taken out of Europe and destroyed, and so politically the Soviet demand for the removal and destruction of U.S. warheads for German P-1As was logical, especially given the still-sensitive nature of anything associated with Germany. But in Geneva the United States stood firm. It was a great relief when, in August, Chancellor Helmut Kohl announced that the Federal Republic of Germany would destroy its missiles within three years. At the time, it was a courageous step. When I got the news of that decision I felt that prospects for the treaty had finally brightened.

The SDI-START Impasse

As Shevardnadze was preparing for his regular trip to New York and Washington in September, the prospects finally looked good. We had achieved what had seemed impossible: a dual zero on both INF and shorter-range missiles. True, a less tortuous way to this goal could have been found and things could have been handled more elegantly, but things are rarely very elegant in real life. There were still some doubts that the Soviet leadership and bureaucracy would agree that the INF treaty alone justified a full-scale summit with Reagan (there was even talk about signing the treaty on "neutral ground"). It was becoming increasingly clear that some people were unhappy about the "dual zero," and even more unhappy because there seemed to be no give on the U.S. side on the painful issue of SDI.

I felt the growing tension between Shevardnadze and most foreign ministry officials, on the one hand, and the military, on the other. Although Gorbachev and Shevardnadze were making every effort to make the military-industrial community a part of the arms control process so that they could feel comfortable with the decisions made there, they had only limited success. It was clear — one sometimes saw it in their eyes — that although people like Marshal Akhromeyev eventually agreed to the solutions worked out in the talks, in which the military were well represented, they hated the outcome that was emerging. I often asked myself why. Then and later, I read some analytical papers prepared by various American institutions that sought to explain our military's position by citing profound strategic or military-technical considerations. But I believe it was something much simpler: the inertia of the old approach and the habit of countering any apparent military problem by building more and bigger weapons.

In the summer of 1987 the foreign ministry was doing a good deal of thinking about what could be done to find a way out of the SDI–START impasse. Without something on the SDI–ABM treaty problem, many of us felt the summit could fall through. If the link between ABM and START could be dropped, that might speed progress toward the START treaty, but that was by no means certain. And although some people, such as Andrey Sakharov, had begun to call for it openly, dropping the link was taboo for our military and looked difficult to others on the Soviet side too. The interrelationship between offense and defense did exist, and the Americans admitted it. So unlinking them openly was politically impossible for us at the time.

But it was clear that a fresh look at the entire space defense problem was needed. To many people, our objection to any ABM defense appeared increasingly difficult to justify and ripe for reassessment. I remember Lev Mendelevich, a veteran diplomat whom Shevardnadze profoundly respected, arguing at a closed meeting in the ministry that we should look at the problem from the long-term perspective of the country's security and think seriously about limited defenses. But that suggestion looked too bold to most other officials.

The big question was what kind of compromise could be struck on SDI and linkage. One idea that came to mind was to include a provision recognizing the relationship between strategic offensive and defensive arms in the text of the START treaty and in Geneva begin discussing the limits of testing activity permitted under the ABM treaty, with a pledge that both sides would make a good-faith effort to resolve the issue. (Two years later something like this was agreed on in the ministerial talks in Wyoming.) We discussed the idea informally with two U.S. embassy officials in Moscow, and it seemed interesting. They said they would talk to the ambassador and get back to me. I promised that I would discuss it with Victor Karpov, and I did. But my colleagues from the U.S. embassy never mentioned the idea again.

Facing Domestic Economic Problems

Overall, there was a sense of direction and purpose in the country's foreign policy, but not in the domestic economy. Although economic growth, which had stalled during Brezhnev's last years, had resumed, the structural problems, primarily those of investment and prices, were getting worse. The distorted, militarized economy demanded huge investments in the nonconsumer sector, and no one seemed able to break that inertia, and the artificially set prices were distorting the economy in yet another way. The government prepared proposals to adjust the price system, which meant, of course, raising the prices of food and most consumer goods. Gorbachev seemed ready to take that risky step and began to mention in his speeches and interviews that a new price system was needed. But this news was not well received, and no decision was made.

I remember how Shevardnadze explained that in one of his private talks. Raising prices is necessary, he said, but if we were to do it after just two years of perestroika people would say that is all perestroika meant—solving the problems at the expense of the people. This, he said, would undermine popular support for perestroika and could mean its end.

I wondered then and I wonder now what would have happened if the Politburo had had enough courage to raise prices. Would it have created a healthier economy and thus saved the entire system? Would it have provided the conditions for a gradual movement toward economic reforms on the basis of a model similar to Hungary's development in the 1970s? I don't know. Another scenario was also possible. Because, as we saw later, the country was not quite ready to accept the price hikes in 1989 and even 1990, it might have exploded in strikes and protests if prices had been raised in 1987—and that might well have meant the end for Mikhail Gorbachev. He would have been appointed, say, ambassador to Burma, and things would gradually have returned to the old ways "under new management."

The Difficult Road to the December Washington Summit

While the country's economic problems seemed intractable, we believed that as much as possible had to be done to change things for the better in foreign affairs. Almost all the time there was some big or small crisis to be dealt with, but we had already learned to handle such situations. Before Shevardnadze's Fall 1987 trip to the United States, for example, another espionage crisis between the Soviet Union and the United States broke out. The United States demanded a substantial cutback in the number of Soviets stationed at our New York mission, on the grounds that many of them were engaged in espionage.

Shevardnadze believed this was a dangerous diversion from the important work of preparing for the Washington summit and said so to Shultz. Such things, if they were to be done, could at least be arranged quietly and without media hoopla. But he also sought to defuse the situation by asking Shultz to postpone some of the expulsions and by postponing the Soviet countermeasures, which in the end turned out to be hard-hitting. He wanted to focus on INF, START, and the regional issues and bilateral agreements that would form the substance of the summit, but there always seemed to be something that could scuttle it.

I had no doubt that the INF treaty would be completed and ready for signing at the summit in Washington. The two sides had invested too much in it to just abandon the effort. But I did not know how hard the remaining part of the road would be and how many agonizing hours in Moscow, Washington, and Geneva would be required before the happy ending. Everything seemed to be on track after Shevardnadze's talks in September in Washington and New York, and both he and Shultz were saying that only a few technical problems remained to be cleared up by delegations. Prudently, they admitted that another ministerial meeting might still be necessary to wrap things up. I remember that meeting quite well.

The problems that were still open when Shevardnadze, Akhromeyev, and a group of arms control experts went to Geneva in November had to do almost entirely with verification. I was present at the delegation's briefing for the visitors from Moscow, which began right after their arrival at about 8:00 P.M. and lasted for more than four hours. The problems seemed as much on the U.S. side as on ours.

The Americans now did not want to go too far on verification. In bargaining over the issue of monitoring the INF production facilities, they sought to protect some of their plants and insisted on selecting other sites for monitoring. This issue took the longest to settle. Colin Powell, then White House National Security Adviser, and George Shultz, both of whom understood the problem well, were visibly just as nervous as we were and frequently consulted with Washington. We expected that the issue would be settled at a final meeting in the Soviet mission, but Shultz asked for another meeting at the U.S. mission. We waited nervously. Things were hanging in the balance.

When we returned to the U.S. mission late that evening, Shultz offered tea and cookies and took some time before announcing the U.S. decision. "Reluctantly," he finally said, "we agree to Magna." This was the site of the U.S. production plant we had insisted must be monitored. The two ministers then went outside to the press and announced that they were both confident that all the problems had been resolved and that the only task that remained was to record their decisions in treaty language.

This was true, but it did not mean there would be no hitches and critical moments in the days that remained. Problems continued to crop up as the INF delegations were toiling in Geneva. In the final days before the summit, they had to work almost around the clock.

I remember reading a cable in early December, a few days before Gorbachev departed for the summit, starting with the words "It is 4 A.M. and the meeting of the treaty text working group continues, discussing a package on the remaining issues. The following set of decisions, if approved, would provide a solution." It was a nervous time for all of us, and I was not surprised when I learned that the head of the U.S. group, Ambassador Maynard Glitman, whom I remembered well from the INF talks of 1981–83, fell ill and could not take part in the final bargaining. Another man I knew, James Woodworth, completed the work on the U.S. side.

But it was an episode at the end of October 1987 that made us doubt that the summit would take place at all and that the treaty would be signed. It happened during Secretary Shultz's visit to Moscow, which initially appeared to go very well. There may be different interpretations of what happened and why, so I want to record it the way I saw it, and also what I thought at the time and afterward.

Shultz came prepared to discuss the entire U.S.-Soviet agenda and the summit format. The talks between him and Shevardnadze on INF resulted in seemingly full agreement on the substantive issues. They did less well on START and ABM, but because everyone seemed to agree that it would be an "INF summit," the other issues could be set aside for the moment, we all thought. We went to the Kremlin meeting between Gorbachev and Shultz in a confident mood. Gorbachev began with a wide-ranging discussion of the situation in the country and his vision of the U.S.-Soviet relationship. By that time I had interpreted such talks by Gorbachev quite often, and would do so many times afterward. His speech might seem rambling at times, and his expressions awkward. He seemed to be thinking aloud, never content with ready-made formulas and prepared lines. And though listening to him and interpreting his words I sometimes thought his meaning was not too clear, later when I recorded his conversations I almost invariably found that he had provided a fresh angle on the issues of the day and clarified at least his own view of the situation, if not the situation itself.

Shultz was a good listener. As Secretary James Baker did after him, he always took notes on what Gorbachev was saying, though there usually were some aides present who were also making notes. I think everyone expected this meeting basically to ratify the understandings on INF and maybe to explore some of the other issues for further discussion at the summit. But SDI still had enormous "irritant potential" for both sides.

At one point, when Gorbachev asked what progress could be made at the summit on the ABM issue, Shultz answered with a listing of the usual U.S. arguments, and the discussion began to go off the rails. Gorbachev suddenly seemed flustered, and I felt on both sides of the table a mounting irritation at having fallen into some kind of trap. It was one of those moments when the interpreter almost wants to shout, "Stop! There's got to be a better way to do it. Why not take a break, come back in an hour, and see if there's a chance to come to terms."

Finally, Gorbachev said that it appeared no agreement on ABM was possible. He then suggested that he was not sure the INF treaty alone would be enough to hold a productive, full-scale summit in Washington. Shultz then indicated that the United States would not change its position on ABM for the sake of holding the summit. It looked like a total impasse. At the last moment, Gorbachev said, "I'll write the president a letter."

The meeting ended without harsh words, but we all knew what had happened. As the Soviet side, which included Shevardnadze, Dobrynin, Akhromeyev, Bessmertnykh, Vorontsov, and Chernyaev, went to a waiting room nearby to sit down and have tea with Gorbachev, there was a heavy silence. No one spoke for at least a couple of minutes, and when Gorbachev finally did, it was a summary of the talk that had just ended. Again, silence followed.

It was Anatoly Chernyaev, Gorbachev's assistant, who broke the silence. "So did we try in vain? Did we bend over backward on INF and come so close to the treaty just to see the whole thing ruined now?" he asked.

His courage was a total surprise for me, for I did not know him well then. He certainly said what at least some people in the room might have been thinking but were not saying.

Gorbachev responded, "Don't boil over, Anatoly. We'll have to think over what happened, and I said I would write the president a letter. I'll do it soon."

Bessmertnykh gave me a lift to the foreign ministry. He did not seem perplexed. "This is a new ball game," he said. "It's tougher, but I like it."

But Shevardnadze did not. The talks in Moscow were over, and one of his deputies normally went to the airport to say goodbye to Shultz. But this time he quickly decided that he had to do it himself to help George Shultz cool down. It was a thoughtful gesture. Perhaps, as a result, nothing was said at high levels in Washington or in Moscow that would finalize the apparent sudden breakdown in the relationship.

I often wondered why it had occurred in the first place. There may have been multiple reasons, but one, I think, is being overlooked. The Shultz visit took place just a couple of days after the party plenum at which Boris Yeltsin announced his decision to resign from the Politburo. Of course, at the time no one knew what ramifications this would have for Gorbachev and for the country, but it could not but affect the atmosphere and Gorbachev's state of mind. First, such an event was then highly unusual. Second, it had to make Gorbachev wonder what the trouble was and where the main danger to his course was coming from. I think he felt, rightly, that the main danger was from the conservatives, who could use any concession to the Americans as a pretext to attack his foreign policy as too soft.

The next day my friends at the foreign ministry suggested, rather cautiously, that Shevardnadze believed the episode had to be put aside quickly. At the U.S. desk, work started on a draft of the letter that Gorbachev had promised to write to Reagan. We understood that the purpose of the letter was to put the preparation for the summit back on track. I think both sides quickly saw what they could lose if that was not done. But it was obvious that it would take some diplomatic footwork to get out of the impasse.

About a week later Shevardnadze went to Washington with Gorbachev's letter. On his plane was an unusually small group of officials, including Tarasenko, Bessmertnykh, and Karpov. The letter was conciliatory. As for the Moscow episode, I thought both sides could just let it be, and it would in time be forgotten. But in the plane Bessmertnykh and Karpov gave Shevardnadze a draft for a ministerial joint communiqué that contained, in veiled form, the same old position on ABM that caused the rupture in Moscow. Perhaps they thought it was right to propose the text as a tactical "demand position" that would be bargained off in Washington. But there was no longer any time for tactical ploys.

Sergey Tarasenko was particularly angry when he saw the proposed text. "They will refuse to discuss anything like this seriously," he said, "and we'll return empty-handed."

On a pad of notepaper he wrote, and I quickly translated, a much shorter draft, basically a joint announcement that the two sides would hold a full-scale summit in Washington to sign INF and discuss other issues, including ABM and START. The draft was carefully worded, and I felt that its language on ABM could satisfy both sides. In the end, that is what actually happened, and the text issued as a result of the Washington talks was very similar to what Tarasenko wrote down in the plane.

The talks in Washington began in a rather nervous mood, and I was not at all sure that we would clear both the substantive and psychological barrier. But it quickly became apparent that Shultz really wanted to help find the way out. It took less time than we had thought, and because we returned to Moscow earlier than expected, it even turned out that we had been overpaid our per diem allowance by one day.

But most of the speculation, among both the Americans and the Soviets in the embassy, was about the Yeltsin resignation. By that time word had filtered out, and both the *Washington Post* and the *New York Times* ran stories that gave an accurate account of what had transpired in Moscow. I did not know much more than what was in the papers, but I was asked many times by friends from the embassy what I thought about it. They regarded it as something quite extraordinary. Any friction in the Soviet leadership was then supposed to be either nonexistent or out of bounds for any serious discussion. I was at a loss what to say.

Finally I said to an old friend with whom I had worked a decade before in New York: "Listen, in normal countries political debate and disagreement in government are nothing extraordinary, so we'll probably have to get used to it in our country too." The problem, of course, was that no one knew what exactly had happened and whether it was a real political disagreement, a clash of personalities, or just a fluke.

It was perhaps all of that. As we were returning to Moscow, Tarasenko told me how things had gone at the plenum. He said that Yeltsin's statement was rambling and thin on substance but reflective of the widespread feeling of unease that things were not going well inside the country. Yeltsin did not use words like "reform," "democracy," "market economy," or anything similar. His speech did not contain specific proposals. It was a statement of a frustrated party official who did not know how to get things moving. Gorbachev, I was told, was displeased, but he tried to postpone any decision until after the November 7 ceremonies commemorating the 70th anniversary of the October Revolution, among other things because he did not like the speeches by members of the old guard, which followed Yeltsin's. They clearly wanted a party vendetta. (Unfortunately, there was a vendetta later, orchestrated by Yegor Ligachev, in Gorbachev's presence at the Moscow party organization plenum in mid-November.)

Knowing everything in minute detail, Shevardnadze had a difficult time in Washington. Shultz did not ask him about Yeltsin—domestic politics was not yet considered appropriate for U.S.-Soviet diplomatic discussions—but the press did at every opportunity. He could only reply that he thought the situation in the country was evolving ("Normalno," he said, which can be rendered as "normally" or "fairly well") and that profound processes of change were under way. Under the circumstances, and given all the conventions in our domestic politics of the time, it was not a bad answer, but we felt that Shevardnadze was not happy with it.

We still had a long way to go to wrap things up for the December summit. A lot of things happened in November, some of which I have already described, and they pushed the Yeltsin problem into the background. But during a pre-summit interview that Gorbachev gave to American newsman Tom Brokaw, he was asked about Yeltsin. He answered, I thought, cautiously and without taking it out on Yeltsin. Look, he said, such things happen in politics—people disagree and fall out sometimes, so let's not overdramatize it. This remark may sound ironic today. The drama had begun, and what a continuation it was to have!

The Reagan-Gorbachev Summit

The December 1987 U.S.-Soviet summit in Washington was an event I will always remember, for many reasons. Many people thought something would happen to scuttle it, and it was indeed a nerve-racking experience until the very end. As we were working in Moscow on the final preparations, the organizational details and the speeches, the tension was in the air. I came back home after 10:00 P.M., and sometimes had to answer telephone calls after that.

I wrote drafts of some of Gorbachev's speeches and saw the final texts, reworked by Gorbachev, Yakovlev, and Chernyaev, when they were returned for translation. (It was occasionally a funny experience to struggle over the translation of a line I had written myself.) That was in addition to all the other work that Victor Sukhodrev, then acting chief of the foreign ministry's USA department, and I had to do. The cables from Geneva and from the advance team in Washington, headed by Bessmertnykh and Vladimir Kryuchkov, then first deputy chairman of the KGB, indicated that there were still many snags and hitches.

As Gorbachev landed in Washington with his delegation and was met cordially by Shultz at the airport, there were still problems. Bessmertnykh reported that Shultz was asking for a meeting with Shevardnadze on that very day, when no official events had been scheduled, and it was obvious the meeting was not just for coffee or tea. Bessmertnykh whispered to Shevardnadze in the car on the way to the embassy, "Shultz will probably be asking you for a photo of a naked missile." Indeed, it was this request—possibly the last problem on the way to the INF treaty—that made Shultz ask for an urgent meeting.

The two sides had agreed, for verification purposes, to exchange photos of the missiles that were to be destroyed under the treaty. The exchange revealed that while the U.S. Pershing-2 missile was photographed "naked" (it had no launch canister), the SS-20 was in a canister, for that was the way it left the production plant and that was how it would be destroyed—that is, blown up together with the canister. So the Soviet delegation's answer to the American request for a picture of the missile "in the nude" was that it was not necessary for verifying its destruction. Shultz argued to Shevardnadze that the treaty called for other verification procedures too, and a photo of the missile would facilitate them. "After all," he said, "both missiles should be treated equally, and we have given you the picture of ours."

Regardless of the merit of Shultz's argument, it was obvious that something had to be done. Akhromeyev talked to his people in Moscow, and they faxed something that the Americans accepted, on the understanding that they would get a real photograph as soon as technically possible. (Nothing is ever smooth and easy about these things, and when our military were reminded of the arrangement later in Moscow, they stalled, I have to admit. Finally, after persistent reminders and telephone calls, Victor Sukhodrev and I handed the photo to a U.S. embassy counselor in January 1988.)

The summit, when it finally started, was not just "signing and dining." As Shevardnadze and Shultz had agreed in late October, there would be an extensive joint statement that should include agreements and understandings on the entire U.S.-Soviet four-part agenda (arms control, regional issues, human rights, and bilateral relations). The section on START was to include a kind of outline for the future treaty. The delegations were bargaining over every word, and some issues, such as the number of warheads to be attributed to each type of missile, proved to be extremely difficult. Gorbachev seemed to spend more time huddling with his people at the Soviet embassy than in talks with Reagan. A few things had to be cleared through the interagency process in Moscow, but eventually the START details were hammered out.

The SDI–ABM matter, however, turned out to be a cliff-hanger again. Everyone agreed it should not be allowed to spoil the summit, but something on ABM had to be included in the joint statement, so the question of the ABM treaty interpretation inevitably emerged. The United States was then insisting on the so-called broad interpretation of the treaty, which would make it possible to deploy almost any kind of defense system in space. We felt that it would make the treaty meaningless and that it could not have been the intent of the treaty's authors. On that we had the support of almost all Americans who had participated in working out the ABM treaty in the 1970s, but Reagan was not about to agree with this.

The Americans proposed that the question of the treaty's interpretation should be left out of the joint statement. Gorbachev insisted that the statement include a reaffirmation of the ABM treaty "as signed and ratified in 1972." As the final events of the summit approached, the two sides were deadlocked on that and some smaller START issues. Gorbachev was consulting with his people and with Moscow when Vice-President George Bush came to the embassy to have a formal talk with him and to accompany him to the White House for the signing ceremony.

After the talk, which was warm though not very substantive, Bush was told that the Soviets would need some time before going to the White House. He said he would wait, and insisted on that even when it became clear that the wait could be quite long. As he was sitting in a small room downstairs at the embassy I conveyed to him Gorbachev's apology and asked what his decision was. "Oh, I'll wait as long as it takes," he said casually, and smiled.

Bush probably did not regret that decision. Almost an hour later they went together in Gorbachev's car to the White House, smiling to each other and chattering as the car turned onto Connecticut Avenue. A small crowd of people there were waiting to catch a glimpse of the Gorbachev motorcade. Gorbachev suggested getting out of the car and talking to the people, and he asked what Bush thought of the idea. Bush did not mind and the motorcade stopped. It was obviously a nightmare for both U.S. and Soviet security people, but it was one of the summit's high points.

Gorbachev worked the crowd in an expert way. He was telling them what they obviously wanted to hear—that our countries had been adversaries for too long but that it had to stop and that we would go from confrontation to cooperation. He said the people already understood that our countries should be friends and now the politicians seemed to understand that too. We need your continued support, he said, and when I shouted the translation of that very American phrase to the crowd, it roared back its approval. As Gorbachev was shaking hands with the onlookers, who had been joined by dozen of people from nearby offices and restaurants, Bush had part of the limelight, and I don't think it did him any harm in the election year that followed.

As Bush and Gorbachev returned to the car, they both looked pleased and excited. They had had a good time. I will speak of their relationship later; they do have a lot in common. And one thing was obvious then: they both liked the people, the crowds, the faces, and the handshaking. It was genuine and not contrived.

Gorbachev and Reagan had a talk in the White House while the final touches were being put on their joint statement. The summit was a little behind schedule, but the large group of officials and guests invited to hear the final speeches at the White House lawn were waiting patiently, despite a light rain that had begun. It will take a little more time, Gorbachev and Reagan were told when they asked whether the statement was ready, but everyone was somehow sure that nothing would interfere with the outcome. When they approved the final compromises and went outside, where the rain was getting worse, there was almost a sense of anticlimax. I was exhausted.

In the car on the way back to the embassy, Gorbachev was at first silent. He too seemed tired. He then said to me, "Well, Pavel, it's a great day. Those two countries were enemies for too long. And many bad things happened because of it." After a pause he added, "We too have messed things up [*nalomali drov*, a Russian expression he uses a lot] quite a bit."

I thought I knew what he meant. After some hesitation, I said as half-question and half-statement, "Afghanistan."

He answered, "It's time to decide."

At Ease with George Bush

Vice-President Bush accompanied Gorbachev to the airport—about a thirty-minute ride there from midtown Washington. The motorcade was moving rather slowly, and the two men talked frankly and warmly, I thought. Bush was enthusiastic about the results of the summit and about the prospects for U.S.-Soviet cooperation. He told Gorbachev that he would run for president and expected to win, although it would not be easy. There are certain things about U.S. election campaigns that Gorbachev should know, Bush said, and candidly described how messy and unpleasant they can be. "Things are sometimes said that we all regret afterward, and they should be disregarded."

But he assured Gorbachev that there should be no doubt about his commitment to cooperation with the Soviet Union.

They discussed a few other things in the car, and Gorbachev has now let the details of that remarkable conversation be known in his published memoirs. In this book I try to indicate only the general sense of the talks that I interpreted, and my impression of them. I felt that an important relationship was beginning. And in the plane Gorbachev said to me, "Pavel, I know that you could not take notes, but try to write a record of that conversation with Bush in the car. It was not a routine talk." Indeed, it was not.

Later Gorbachev often recalled that talk. Bush too remembered it well. They sometimes reminded each other of it, and at various points in the ensuing years the "conversation in the car" was mentioned as a kind of password. It stood for a personal mutual commitment to work together in spite of possible complications and obstacles. I too recall that talk often. I had a good time interpreting it. The two men seemed to be at ease with each other. Their pledge was, I felt, sincere. Did they keep it? Were they always faithful to that commitment? It is for them and for the historians to answer these questions, but my answer would be yes.

Reflections on Foreign Policy Breakthroughs

This time, as we were returning to Moscow, I fully shared the festive mood on the plane. What had seemed impossible had happened on that day in December 1987: a major arms control treaty was signed between the Reagan administration and the Soviet Union. Just a few months before, Alexander Bovin, a respected foreign affairs observer for the newspaper *Izvestiya*, wrote that we would probably have to wait for a new administration to achieve anything significant. Many people agreed. Having spent months and even years working in the frustrating field of U.S.-Soviet disarmament, particularly INF, I knew that reaching agreement on the basis of the zero option, initially proposed by the United States, would require a supreme effort of will on the part of the Soviet leaders. How did it finally become possible? I frequently wondered, both then and afterward.

Why, in the end, was it possible to break through the logjam of old positions that had seemed unshakable and ideological dogma, and conclude agreements on INF and then on Afghanistan and other regional conflicts — agreements that were a decisive break with the past and that cleared the way for new relations? Why was such a breakthrough possible in foreign affairs and not possible in domestic affairs, specifically in the economy? There has to be more than one reason for this paradox, which became so dramatic in subsequent years and eventually resulted in Gorbachev's domestic troubles and his resignation.

First, the foreign policy conducted by Gorbachev and Shevardnadze was based on a sound philosophical foundation, much of which had evolved gradually in the years before Gorbachev and was given a stamp of approval and authority by him. The basic principles of what was later called "the new thinking"—the indivisibility of the world and its interdependence, mutual security, and defense sufficiency—were spelled out in 1986, but they were not inconsistent with our previous rhetoric on international affairs. The West did not immediately believe us, but of greater importance was the fact that those principles did not arouse too much suspicion among our conservatives. So Gorbachev and Shevardnadze could begin to put these principles into action, which was more difficult than just proclaiming them.

They were not professional diplomats, but particularly in the initial stages they had full support from the foreign policy bureaucracy and academic experts. Most of that bureaucracy was competent and knowledgeable. Later many had doubts, but they continued to show loyalty, perhaps partly out of inertia. And they could always be relied on at least for giving expert advice and carrying out their instructions faithfully and professionally, if not for political vision and courage. For years they had had to deal with the real world in normal diplomatic ways and were thus much better prepared to work under new leadership, committed to reforms, than our economists and ideologues, who lived in an abnormal world of essentially Stalinist dogma.

Finally, when the time came to make difficult decisions and painful choices, Gorbachev was often able to take advantage of the old command system's methods, of the residual authority of the party and its general secretary, and of the fact that the conservatives did not immediately catch on to the consequences of the changes they were witnessing and taking part in. I am not saying that the changes were crudely imposed, but they would have been much more difficult to push through had a full-scale nationwide debate been initiated about foreign policy. In such a debate, conservatives could have taken advantage of the people's patriotic feelings and pride, or the fear of "looking weak," which is ingrained in many Russians. Later the conservatives did launch a debate on foreign policy, and in 1990 Shevardnadze was attacked increasingly openly. Gorbachev's turn came later, in 1991. But by that time most of the changes in the country and in the world had become irreversible.

I never discussed this paradox with Gorbachev—a fully democratic debate about foreign policy would have made changing it in a democratic way more difficult. But I talked about it with Shevardnadze. He agreed that there was nothing preordained about the shift that Gorbachev brought about. Each decision took a lot of time and effort to push through, and our Western partners did not make it much easier. Too often they claimed victory when the Soviet Union took the steps prompted by common sense. In an environment of complete freedom of expression—which was not yet the case in the Soviet Union in 1986–87—that would have opened Gorbachev and Shevardnadze to fierce criticism for being "soft." Actually, that kind of criticism was heard even then, but it was still subdued.

And as 1987 was closing on a note of optimism following the signing of the INF treaty, only a part of the priority foreign policy agenda had been dealt with successfully. Regional conflicts still inflicted on us a high cost in lives and resources, and there were the problems of conventional forces and other issues of disarmament that proved less tractable than INF. Generally, relations with the West were still not free of suspicion and mutual mistrust. No one yet knew that history would soon gain unprecedented momentum and that in a few years the reasons for such suspicions would be, as the phrase goes, overtaken by events.

A SHIFT OF FOCUS

Five

1988

Preparing for Another
Reagan-Gorbachev Summit

We still had one year to go with the Reagan administration, and the question on everybody's mind was what we could expect to achieve in that year. By that time our understanding of Ronald Reagan had evolved. He was respected, grudgingly by some and more enthusiastically by others, as a man who gave expression to something that his country felt and wanted strongly. He had been able to turn the mood of the nation around, and that was no small achievement. He delegated a great deal to George Shultz, who was respected as a reliable and honest man. Gorbachev, so far as I know, was never tempted to stand back and wait for a new U.S. president.

That was a temptation I know some people felt when the Iran-contra scandal broke out in 1986. I had arguments with some of my colleagues about the scandal and what it could mean. I felt strongly that it should be disregarded in our handling of U.S.-Soviet relations. No matter how it would turn out, I felt that we should just go on working with the administration. I argued that the Americans, all of them—the politicians, Democrats and Republicans, the man in the street, even the media—did not want another Watergate. The nation could simply not afford another ordeal like that, and therefore it would not happen. Some of my colleagues, and experts at the famous Institute of USA and Canada Studies, felt differently. Our political leaders were wise enough to disregard their advice.

So we were dealing with Ronald Reagan, no doubt about that. How much could be achieved during his last year in office was a different question. Would we conclude a START treaty? Would there be a solution to the Afghan problem? Would we achieve what Gorbachev called the dynamization of U.S.-Soviet relations? Most of us were not very optimistic about all that.

Concerning START, we felt soon after the Washington summit that the talks had again gone into one of their interminable phases, with the experts bogged down in the details that fewer and fewer people understood. (I, as an interpreter, had to try to follow them and their increasingly esoteric language.) The U.S. administration seemed to lack the political will to work through those details and meet us halfway. But there had to be a summit before the end of the Reagan administration—we knew that "Ronnie" wanted to come to Moscow—and neither side made a START treaty a condition for that. So we began thinking what agreements could be prepared for signing at the summit. The idea of the two leaders meeting on a regular basis without some "crowning achievement" was not yet generally accepted.

There had to be, of course, the exchange of the ratification documents of the INF treaty. I had no doubt that the treaty would be ratified, though I expected problems to emerge in the process. We wondered about some other arms control accomplishment. Could the talks on banning and destroying chemical weapons be speeded up? Possibly, but not enough to have a convention ready for signing soon. Besides, the talks were multilateral, not just U.S.-Soviet talks. Could anything be achieved on nuclear testing? That was an issue with a long and tortuous history, and I was working on it at the time in the USA and Canada department of the foreign ministry.

The On-Site Verification Issue

Before Ronald Reagan, the goal of a complete test ban was accepted by both the Soviet Union and the United States. Both countries also thought that the ban could be verified by seismic instruments, without on-site verification. All that changed under Reagan. The administration declared that nuclear testing would have to continue as long as nuclear weapons existed. It disregarded

Gorbachev's moratorium on nuclear tests in 1985–86, leaving him vulnerable to criticism from the military-scientific community. It also said that, to verify the previously negotiated limits on the yield of nuclear explosions, seismic methods were not enough, and it proposed CORRTEX—a complicated and costly method of on-site verification. It was transparent that the administration's goal was to have a free hand to continue testing for creating a new generation of nuclear weapons and for SDI experiments.

The usual impulse of our foreign policy establishment in such situations was to fight it out in the propaganda arena. The temptation was strong this time, because many respectable U.S. experts were critical of the administration's position and of CORRTEX in particular. As I found out later, even many government experts believed CORRTEX was a needless and even bizarre venture. So another campaign to "unmask what is really behind the U.S. position" could easily have been mounted, but of course that would have been a mistake. Even if we won the propaganda contest, there would be no political gain. In fact, such a victory would have created problems in our relations with George Shultz, who had to defend the U.S. position.

But there was also something else. I talked with an arms control expert from the foreign ministry, whom I heard say for the first time, "Our military don't want a test ban. They need testing, or at least they think so." So accepting CORRTEX in some form was a good idea from many standpoints, and Shevardnadze was persuaded that we should move in that direction. It was proposed that the two countries hold a joint experiment at their test sites in Semipalatinsk and Nevada, detonating nuclear devices and verifying their yield both with the seismic method and with CORRTEX. The experiment was preceded by visits of teams of experts to the two test sites. I was included in the Soviet team.

We came to Semipalatinsk on a day in January 1988 that would be regarded as cold in Moscow but was mild by the standards of Northern Kazakhstan. The Americans had brought an enormous amount of warm clothing and footwear, some of which looked quite exotic to me. But it became even warmer the next day—something like minus 20 or 25 degrees Celsius—and the trips to the "ground zero" sites in the steppe turned out to be quite easy. The U.S. and Soviet teams, packed with weapons-testing experts and intelligence officials, soon established a chatting and joking relationship. They were much more candid in their conversations than I had expected.

The cordiality that emerged in Semipalatinsk grew when the teams moved on to Nevada. The facilities at the U.S. test site were, of course, much more comfortable—our people marveled at the cafeteria and its menu—but a lot of other things seemed similar. The experts understood each other easily, and the preparation for the joint experiment went quite well. Some of the Americans frankly admitted that CORRTEX was dispensable.

From my conversations with the nuclear scientists on the American team, I got the impression that they were driven most of all by scientific curiosity and professional perfectionism rather than by any idea of national security. But they were also sure they would not be left unemployed if the testing program were suspended or reduced. It would be nuclear waste storage or something else, they said to me, but the Nevada site would still be used for some purpose. The Americans, I thought, are always practical, while we tend to look for grand ideas and all-embracing explanations. And the results are as different as the two test sites in Nevada and Semipalatinsk.

On my return from Nevada I had a talk with Alexander Bessmertnykh. We both knew that on this question too we could be criticized for playing by U.S. rules. But what was the alternative? At least some kind of process that could end the fruitless propaganda bickering on the issue of nuclear testing had begun. What worried me was the larger U.S.-Soviet relationship. A drift seemed almost inevitable for the duration of the year. Bessmertnykh too seemed to accept that the Moscow summit would be largely "atmospheric"— with ratification of the various arms control treaties as its centerpiece, plus a warm farewell to Ronald Reagan.

Soon afterward, however, George Shultz sent a message indicating that he regarded the goal of signing the START treaty at the 1988 summit in Moscow as feasible. Frankly, I was surprised. Was this Shultz's own idea, his personal initiative? Did he do it for Ronald Reagan, thinking that the INF treaty would not be enough of a pedestal for his boss's place in history? Or did Reagan himself think so? We all wondered about that. Whatever it was, I felt, as I interpreted Shultz's talk with Shevardnadze, that both men believed the START treaty was a practical possibility.

START Treaty Issues for the Summit

Like SALT before it, START was so often declared "98 percent ready" that we grew cynical about such statements. Ironically, they were not untrue. The remaining 2 percent of the treaty issues were normally resolved after inter-agency squabbles and more and more nearly incomprehensible articles were added to the text. But in the meantime, other problems emerged from the depths of both countries' bureaucracies, and those technical molehills quickly became political mountains. The experts often did not make their discussion any easier. I often saw how frustrated Shevardnadze was by the entire process. Karpov alone seemed capable of explaining the issues in clear terms to him. Once an issue had been taken care of, it looked easy. But the tug-of-war between the Moscow and Washington bureaucracies never ended.

Shultz proposed that Shevardnadze and he should meet often, maybe once every six or eight weeks, to discuss the issues and settle them. He seemed to think that setting deadlines would push the bureaucrats and subordinate them to the political needs of the two countries' leaders. Both he and Shevardnadze were genuinely committed to the goal of an early START treaty, and after their first meeting it began to seem to me that it was not impossible. I was to be disappointed. The agencies in Washington and Moscow were ingeniously inventing ever new "important issues" on which the hopes for an early treaty finally foundered.

INF Treaty Ratification Problems

In the meantime, problems with INF treaty ratification inevitably arose. Most of them were totally spurious. We understood that the U.S. Senate had to make some kind of splash, even though the treaty was so obviously in the country's interest. From the very beginning it was clear that the Americans had nothing to lose from eliminating an entire class of nuclear missiles. They had, of course, persuaded many Europeans—and perhaps even themselves— that the Pershings were needed for the strategic "coupling" of the United States and Europe. So when it became clear that "Zero" would be real and not just for propaganda, it took the West some time to adjust. But by 1988 the adjustment had been completed, and it was impossible to imagine that the U.S. Senate would refuse to ratify a good treaty signed by a popular president. And yet Moscow had to watch with some frustration the emergence of ratification issues, such as the "exotic INF warheads." What if, the senators asked, the missiles were to be equipped not with nuclear warheads but with something like a laser weapon? Would the treaty, as negotiated, be applicable then? The answer was certainly yes, but it did not satisfy some senators.

So Shultz and Shevardnadze had to spend an inordinate amount of time discussing how to put that issue to rest. The Geneva negotiators had to work out elaborate language, which finally satisfied everyone. But I was disappointed that time was being wasted on such pseudo-issues.

U.S.-Soviet Discussions on the Problem of Afghanistan

Still, we were not worried about INF ratification. I was saying to everyone that the treaty would be ratified. What worried me much more was how the Afghan problem would turn out. Was there real and definitive commitment on the Soviet side to end our presence in Afghanistan? And would the Americans help us do it instead of making the decision itself and carrying it out even more difficult? In January 1988 I did not know the answers to those two questions. But soon afterward I got a clear answer to the first one.

By that time Shevardnadze had made several trips to Afghanistan, some of them unannounced. I did not go with him, but his assistants kept me posted on the main developments. He also discussed with Shultz drafts of U.N.-sponsored agreements that were to facilitate our withdrawal and establish a basis for peace and reconciliation in Afghanistan. Both negotiations were extremely difficult. It thus took great courage to decide that our troops would just have to leave that country to itself and its fate. Again, the decision seems inevitable, and even easy today, but persuading the Politburo at the time must have been quite a challenge.

The question everyone asked was: What would happen to our friends once we have left? Would there be a bloodbath? For Gorbachev and Shevardnadze, those were not easy questions. They had to move forward while carrying the dead weight of an outdated and bankrupt ideology, of commitments assumed by their predecessors, and of people whom they had to treat as friends. The legacy of the past was nowhere as apparent and as ugly as in that set of people—men like North Korea's Kim Il Sung, East Germany's Honnecker, or Romania's Nicolae Ceausescu, whom I felt they privately despised. But there were others, more difficult to characterize. They did not despise Fidel Castro or Afghanistan's President Najibullah.

In a frank talk Shevardnadze once spoke of Castro as, in a way, a tragic figure who wanted to do something good for his people but missed the moment when it was necessary to change. Of their relations with Najibullah, neither Shevardnadze nor Gorbachev ever spoke in my presence, but they seemed to respect him for being serious about achieving national reconciliation in Afghanistan. Shevardnadze said many times to Shultz and to Baker that it was a genuine effort rather than a tactical ploy.

The problem for both Gorbachev and Shevardnadze was that they could not just abandon the commitments and the people that, as they understood at about this time, 1988 and afterward, already belonged to the past. They were looking for a more or less smooth way to dismantle those commitments. And as for the people, I heard Shevardnadze say on a number of occasions, "If they stand for something and have any real support among their people, they must cope themselves." In Afghanistan that meant that our troops had to leave.

Shevardnadze tried to work out with Shultz a formula that would stop the flow of arms into Afghanistan. But "the negative symmetry" could not be just U.S.-Soviet. The resistance received much of its weapons from Pakistan, Saudi Arabia, and other countries. The Americans refused to discuss how that flow could be halted. They also did not want to discuss any link between an end to arms shipments and a cease-fire in Afghanistan. Therefore, U.S.-Soviet "negative symmetry" would have meant ending the supplies to Kabul but not to the resistance, and certain defeat for the Kabul government. The Soviet Union could not accept signing such a death sentence.

Shultz and Shevardnadze spent hours on diplomatic language that would make the two countries guarantors of the Geneva agreements on Afghanistan. The agreements were to allow us to save face while withdrawing the troops. On a brief visit to Washington in early 1988, Shevardnadze finally proposed that the Soviet Union and the United States could assume the role of guarantors while leaving the question of arms supplies open—in fact, allowing them to continue to ship weapons into Afghanistan, what the Americans later called "positive symmetry." Shultz did not reject the formula, and he asked Shevardnadze to wait in a State Department conference room while he consulted with his experts and the White House.

It is incredible how nerve-racking such waits can be. Shevardnadze, Tarasenko, one or two other persons, and I sat near a fireplace—Shultz liked to keep the fire well stoked during the discussion. We almost did not talk; it is difficult to find topics for discussion while you wait for something crucial to happen. The twenty or so minutes seemed interminable. I thought Shultz would accept, but I said, "He'll probably ask for more time."

Shultz came back saying the answer was no. He had the tired, sullen look he often had. Sometimes it was a mask, but this time we felt a genuine sense of defeat—a defeat for all of us.

On the plane to Moscow I cautiously asked Shevardnadze whether we were not exaggerating the importance of what had happened. We could just leave Afghanistan without an agreement with the Americans, right?

There was silence. The others probably thought, "Yes, without even a fig leaf to cover up the defeat."

After a pause Shevardnadze said, as I recall, that it would be more difficult.

A day or two later U.S. Ambassador Jack Matlock asked for an urgent meeting with Shevardnadze. He had a letter from Shultz. At such meetings I would normally quickly translate the letter for Shevardnadze. A very good listener, he captured the meaning of the letter immediately, as I did. Shultz was accepting what he had rejected a few days before in Washington. I even hesitated on that line and reread it quickly.

There was no mistake. A few weeks afterward the agreements on Afghanistan were signed in Geneva. They did not make Shevardnadze very happy, because he continued to feel something like a human obligation to Najibullah and a few others in the Afghanistan government. He had also met some people on the other side. From several of his remarks, I gathered that he liked some of them too. Shevardnadze had a sharp sense of human tragedy.

The Conservatives' First Attack

Our trip to Geneva to sign the agreements on Afghanistan coincided with the flap in Moscow over an article by Nina Andreyeva in the newspaper *Sovetskaya Rossia*. The article complained about "ideological permissiveness" that resulted from glasnost. It was a purely Stalinist piece, badly written and crude, and I thought it meant nothing at all. So I was surprised when Teimuraz Stepanov, who was quite knowledgeable about the intricacies of Moscow ideological struggles (he had worked for several years at the newspaper *Komsomolskaya Pravda*), said to me in his usual metaphoric manner as we were boarding the plane, "Pasha, Nina Andreyeva's article means the end of perestroika. It's 'About-face—and march!' " He was worried that the clock was being turned back.

I attributed that remark to his tendency to overreact to newspaper articles and noted that Shevardnadze did not seem disturbed. But, looking back, I understand that I just did not know what my friends knew well. Andreyeva's article had become the battle cry for the hard-liners in the party apparat. Considered to reflect the new line coming from the very top in Moscow, it was "recommended material" in the provinces for ideological studies. The worst was that no attempt was made to challenge the article or to show in any way that it was not the new line. Even the boldest newspapers were silent about it. It was like a pall that fell on almost everyone among the Moscow liberals—a pall of fear and of silence. It was then that people understood that glasnost could just be taken away from them.

But that did not happen. After two or three weeks of scary silence an article calling the Nina Andreyeva piece "the manifesto of antiperestroika forces" and refuting it point by point appeared in *Pravda*, approved, it was rumored, by Gorbachev himself. Moscow's intelligentsia breathed a sigh of relief. Many of us thought that, now that a return to the past had been rejected, perestroika would gain a second wind. Others were more skeptical. But I don't believe those who now say they predicted big trouble was ahead. They certainly did not predict the kind of trouble that awaited us. Perhaps they foresaw some continuation of the conservatives-versus-liberals fight. But just as the generals do, they were fighting the last war. History is unpredictable, and it was already preparing its surprises—in Vilnius and Baku, Tbilisi and Kiev, Moscow and Sverdlovsk.

Meanwhile, we were still preparing for the Moscow U.S.-Soviet summit. It was almost routine, and no one was looking forward to anything special. We thought it would be "mostly style, not much substance," and that is how it turned out. Ronald Reagan came to Moscow with a fresh set of Russian proverbs and a smile for everyone. The U.S. Senate delayed the ratification of the INF treaty until the last moment, but no one doubted that they would ratify it.

The Reagans in Moscow

The main fact was that Ronald Reagan was in Moscow as a president who had succeeded in much that he sought to accomplish. He did not gloat and he praised Gorbachev. He said he no longer considered the Soviet Union an "evil empire." He had a nice walk through the Kremlin and Red Square with Gorbachev, and he obviously enjoyed the majestic hall of the Kremlin, the churches, and the beautiful dignity of Red Square. I think he had been "prepared" by George Shultz, who once said to Shevardnadze, "I don't know anything that looks more majestic than Red Square, particularly in the evening." His words reminded me of a poem by Osip Mandelstam: "The Earth is roundest in Red Square."

Reagan saw Red Square in broad daylight and was impressed. He enjoyed the visit, as he enjoyed life. He was eager to please and to be pleased, and he was a simple man in what I think is the good sense of the word.

The joint statement to be signed by the two leaders had been prepared in advance and, like many other such documents, was rather thin on substance. At a meeting with Reagan in the Kremlin, Gorbachev suggested adding a paragraph saying that both countries supported the principle of freedom of choice for all nations. Reagan said he liked the idea, but members of his delegation frowned. He asked for a break and huddled with Shultz, Powell, and others for maybe ten minutes. Following the break, he went back on his agreement, and Shultz offered explanations, which seemed rather lame to me.

Why did they reject the inclusion of those few words, which seem difficult to dispute and which Gorbachev later proved—in Eastern Europe and elsewhere—that he regarded as more than just rhetoric? We can only guess. The answer may be quite simple, that they did not believe Gorbachev meant it and that they thought in the usual geopolitical terms and could not imagine we would ever abandon Stalin's "conquests" in Europe. And they were not alone in having these doubts.

"Freedom of choice" was a phrase that had already appeared in statements by Gorbachev and Shevardnadze. And the Soviet Union was already in the process of dismantling some of its costly foreign obligations—in Afghanistan, for example—thus honoring that principle. But it was a slow process that ran into obvious resistance at home and among our "friends" abroad. What is more, the main question was not yet answered: Was this principle absolute? Would it apply to, say, Poland or Hungary or Czechoslovakia?

Many in the Soviet Union thought that it should not. Many others thought it should, but that Gorbachev, in a crisis, would not be able to choose freedom rather than "geopolitical security." In my discussions in the foreign ministry and elsewhere, no one expected the events in Eastern Europe to unfold as rapidly as they soon did, but few doubted that those countries would eventually go their own way—go West. Similar discussions went on in the higher echelons. I don't know whether they were always frank, but their hidden meaning must have been clear to all.

The Reagan visit was moving toward its conclusion when an incident that could have marred it occurred. Gorbachev and Reagan were to go to the Bolshoi Theater on the last full day of the visit. After a ballet a very private supper was to be held at Gorbachev's dacha for the two couples only. But the start of the show at the Bolshoi had to be delayed because Reagan's people insisted on some additional security precautions. It was reported to Gorbachev that they wanted to check all spectators themselves.

This was one of the few occasions that I ever saw Mikhail Gorbachev really angry—in a rather quiet way though. Waiting at the Kremlin with Mrs. Gorbachev for word from the Bolshoi that everything was ready and they could go there, he wondered aloud: "Well, if they don't trust us . . . I don't know—should we have that supper over there? Maybe a snack at the Bolshoi would be enough?"

Raisa Gorbachev was silent for a moment and then said, "And they must be tired too."

Vladimir Medvedev, the Gorbachevs' chief security guard, chimed in, "Let's cancel that supper if they don't trust us. We have tried to make it such a good visit but they . . ."

Gorbachev looked at me.

"What do you think?" Raisa asked.

"Frankly," I responded, "I think that if you can avoid canceling the supper it should not be canceled. It would leave a bad taste at the end of a good visit."

A few minutes later we went to the Bolshoi. The Reagans came beaming, obviously looking forward to the ballet. Gorbachev said to Reagan, "Mr. President, I understand there has been a security scare. Have your people found anything? Maybe a bomb?"

Reagan said he was not aware of anything like that.

"We were all so concerned," Gorbachev continued. "But now that it's over, let's enjoy the performance and then we'll go to our dacha for a nice little supper."

I was relieved to hear those words.

The next day the visit was over. All's well that ends well, and this visit succeeded on its own terms. But I had a feeling we were losing valuable time, that relations were not as dynamic and trust not as deep as I would have liked them to be. We had wanted so much to wrap up START and put the whole tedious and unproductive process behind us, but now that would have to wait for at least a year. And START had symbolic meaning—it was an indicator of the status of U.S.-Soviet relations, a signal to the various government bureaucracies. And because they did not have that signal, a go-slow attitude seemed to reemerge on many other matters. That was disappointing.

As I learned later, I was not the only one who was disappointed. Until rather late in the game, George Shultz had been hopeful that the treaty could be signed in Moscow. He told us later, in 1993 at a conference in Princeton, that he believed failure to sign the treaty was due mainly to the differences within the U.S. government and that this was one of his biggest disappointments in as secretary of state. In that role, Shultz had always been careful to present the U.S. position as a "united front." But more than four years afterward he was under no obligation to hide his bitterness about the hardliners in the U.S. government, who had been able to do a lot of harm.

Gorbachev and Shevardnadze Seek New Approaches to Foreign Policy

The apparent lull in the everyday business of foreign affairs, which always occurs in U.S. presidential election years, gave us time to think about more fundamental aspects of the country's foreign policy. Both Gorbachev and Shevardnadze had already seen how flawed the old foreign policy was: how it involved us in an endless cycle of "steps" and "countersteps" that always resulted in confrontation and an arms race; how it lacked clear goals; how it was often based on sheer inertia and propaganda stereotypes. They wanted to return to normalcy, to an understanding of the country's national interests based on common sense rather than ideology. But, as Shevardnadze often complained, in making specific decisions they had to rely on intuition and instincts rather than on carefully thought-out concepts. Shevardnadze frequently told us he was worried about that. He was looking for a more sound basis for foreign policy decisions. More and more often we heard from him calls for "a genuinely scientific approach to foreign policy."

Both Gorbachev and Shevardnadze liked the company of academic experts, who often had their own views of things and knew how to express them clearly and attractively. Shevardnadze, who knew that much in his own actions was based on intuition and improvisation, had set up in 1987 a research coordination center within the ministry, as its link to the academic community. He was looking for two things: alternative approaches and workable concepts for the development of foreign policy. I was interested, and became actively involved in the efforts of people like Vladimir Shustov, who helped Shevardnadze build bridges with the academic world.

I was not disappointed, but neither was I fully satisfied. I did not share the antiacademic sentiment—indeed, anti-intellectualism—which was then typical of quite a few of my foreign ministry colleagues, not only members of the "old guard." As I met more frequently with people from the various academic institutes and research centers, I found many among them who were interesting and thoughtful. Some were really capable of providing a totally new perspective on the issues. But there were also quite a few others who were not particularly knowledgeable and very shallow in their judgments. And yet they were self-confident to the point of arrogance, which made it difficult to talk to them. Certainly my patience with some of them was far less than that of Shevardnadze, who always listened to them carefully and never shrugged off anyone.

Scholars and academic foreign policy experts are an interesting bunch. They have a lot in common as a class, but certain groups also share some fascinating peculiarities that may well reflect larger political and psychological aspects. I noticed quite early, for example, that there was a big difference between our "Americanists" and "Germanists," both inside and outside the government. Whereas most experts on the United States, regardless of differences of view on particular issues, seemed genuinely to like America and the Americans, our Germanists often did not even bother to hide their dislike and resentment of the Germans. Again, this was regardless of their different viewpoints or intellectual caliber.

Even the best of them seemed to assume that, given the history of Nazi aggression against the Soviet Union, it was right and also "politically corrrect" for them to be wary and suspicious of Germany decades after the end of the war. I believe that in this they were out of tune with the people, who had gone beyond such simplistic thinking and, perhaps instinctively, felt that Germany—and, in the minds of most people, the Federal Republic was the "real Germany," richer, more successful, and more attractive than the German Democratic Republic—had changed and should not be feared.

Partly as a result of their anti-German bias, I believe, our experts did not serve the country well at a crucial turning point in 1989–90, when it was necessary to take a clear and unbiased view of the rapidly unfolding events and advise political leaders. Most of our experts were as taken aback by the developments as the leaders, and unable to suggest anything that would be really helpful in policymaking.

The U.S. Sovietologists were in a somewhat similar situation in 1991. As a group, their attitude toward the Soviet Union and the Russian people was not uniform, but most of them tended to be instinctively anti-Soviet, and some even anti-Russian. Many had been trained by Russian émigré scholars, and it showed; others overemphasized the importance of Communist ideology in Soviet policies. The views of almost all of them were affected by the Cold War and U.S.-Soviet rivalry in it. Few academic experts were ready to give an open-minded analysis of the country and its people.

When the changes in the Soviet Union began, most Sovietologists were not ready for them. First they underestimated their extent and genuineness, then they oversimplified the situation and, like our radicals, often ignored the country's complexity and the resilience of the old ways. It will take time for a new, well-educated, and broad-minded generation of experts to emerge in both our countries.

In the summer of 1988 Shevardnadze presided at a conference of diplomats and academic experts on the future of Soviet foreign policy. He delivered the keynote speech, which struck me and my colleagues as unusually frank, intelligent, and often courageous. His assistants told me that Shevardnadze wanted his report to record his definitive views: that international relations must not focus on "the struggle of the two social systems"; that peaceful coexistence was not a form of class struggle; and that national security does not have to depend on equality in every category of weapons.

Shevardnadze had come to the conclusion that the country had drawn the wrong lessons from the Second World War. He came very close to admitting that creating a "security belt" in Eastern Europe had been a mistake. But he could not yet say it openly—we had "friends" there. Talks with those "friends" had by that time become an ordeal for both Gorbachev and Shevardnadze, and I sometimes heard them vent their feelings, but not in public.

In the United States that fall, Shultz told Shevardnadze he had read his speech at the academic conference and found much to admire in it. It was recommended reading at the State Department, he said. I think the speech made him really appreciate Shevardnadze as a policymaker and as a man. But I also heard from some of my American friends that Reagan and Shultz were already being criticized as two sentimental old men who were too soft on the Soviets. I thought that was the most unfair criticism I had ever heard. On practically all substantive issues those two old men were tough as nails.

The year 1988 was not yet the year when open criticism of the foreign policy of Gorbachev and Shevardnadze was heard in the Soviet Union. Even in June 1989, Shevardnadze was reappointed as foreign minister by the new and more democratic Supreme Soviet almost unanimously. The main issues for the country, everyone agreed, were in domestic policy, and they were to be argued at the Party Conference in the summer.

Gorbachev Calls for Democratic Elections, More Glasnost, and Rule of Law

The 19th Party Conference was eagerly awaited in Moscow and in a few other centers of intellectual ferment. The rest of the country was still quiet, and many of the delegates elected to the conference were conservative. But they did not determine the shape of things at the conference. The agenda was set by Gorbachev's report, which called for democratic elections, more glasnost, and rule of law. It was a powerful speech, but either as a consolation prize to the conservatives or out of his own party-bred illusions, Gorbachev included in it one proposal that irritated most Moscow intellectuals. He said that the post of the chairman of soviets should at all levels be filled by the secretary of the party committee at that level—provided, of course, that he is elected by a popular vote.

This could be interpreted as a kind of screening, so that unpopular bosses could be fired after they failed to win the election. That was how Gorbachev explained the proposal. He may have been right on substance. Even today, if one looks at who is president in many of the republics (amazingly, even in the Baltic states), it is mostly the former party bosses. Most men capable of governing were then in the party, but people still did not like Gorbachev's proposal; they saw it as an attempt to railroad party officials into the new democratic positions.

I soon saw that it was futile to try to explain to my friends what I thought Gorbachev's idea was. They still chided him for proposing it, even though they agreed with the main thrust of his speech. But the more I thought about it and about the decisions adopted at the 19th Party Conference, the more it seemed to me that something was missing from them. All right, we shall have free elections as a guarantee against a return to the Stalinist past. I agreed wholeheartedly. But what will the candidates propose? Will they have substantially different programs? I thought they should.

The conference avoided discussion of a multiparty system, and I, like many people, thought it might be too early to contemplate that. But who will develop alternative policies? Why not allow different factions within the party so they could do it? After all, it was clear even then that the party was not a monolith, that, say, Alexander Yakovlev, Boris Yeltsin, and Yegor Ligachev represented quite different tendencies. To me, Yakovlev stood for Western-style reforms, Yeltsin for populist radicalism ("Just do something, and kick the old bastards out"), and Ligachev for conservatism pure and simple, but without "the excesses" of Stalinism.

I suggested something like this at a party meeting in the ministry and no one supported me. Indeed, they did not pay much attention. But the record of that meeting must be somewhere in the party archives. Others spoke of the economy. Gorbachev's report contained little on it, and Leonid Abalkin, the economist who later became a member of the cabinet responsible for economic reform, openly wondered, "Well, you are going to have free elections, but what well these new democratic bodies do with the economy?" Gorbachev was not yet persuaded that the only solution to the country's problems was to move toward a market economy. Neither, of course, was Yeltsin, who squabbled with Ligachev at one of the meetings which caught everyone's attention, even though it seemed to me it was over totally irrelevant matters. The incident revealed only two things: that the maverick Yeltsin was popular and that the conservative Ligachev was almost hated by the increasingly politicized populace.

I tended to be much more tolerant of Ligachev than most of my friends were. Why should I hate him if he stands for a group in the party, and a set of views, that does exist? But I disagreed with those views. I remember his famous statement at a meeting following the conference: "Comrades, some people call for political pluralism, but if we allow that, plus a so-called market economy, not much will remain of socialism."

Well, I asked, what do we need more—his kind of socialism or a decent standard of living for the people? But Ligachev was enthusiastically applauded by a group of Party functionaries and automobile factory workers.

Ethnic Conflicts Begin

The prospects for the economy worried me. But we were all even more worried by the ethnic conflicts that were beginning to shatter the foundations of peace and tranquillity among the country's dozens of nationalities. We had grown so used to interethnic peace that the first clashes came as a terrible shock, a tragedy of an extraordinary kind.

It all began in Nagorno-Karabakh, a small Armenian enclave in Azerbaijani territory. Its people wanted to reintegrate with Armenia, and they thought perestroika gave them what might be their last chance to right a historical wrong. But the Azerbaijanis regarded the territory as theirs, and the Soviet Union's constitution—and international law—prohibited any change in the frontiers without the consent of the republic concerned. So Gorbachev was faced with another quandary, another problem that had no solution, at least not under the old system. I believed that the only answer to problems like that was to have legitimately elected authorities whom people trust to sort out all problems through negotiations. I still think so. But as far as the Karabakh problem is concerned, it was already too late. Too much hatred and mistrust had accumulated between the two peoples, who were, on top of it all, "heated up" by some of their favorite writers and artists. The democratic process came too late to change that. In the meantime, almost all my friends among the Moscow intelligentsia took the side of the Armenians. Andrey Sakharov and his wife, Yelena Bonner, took the lead. But how could Gorbachev and the Moscow authorities favor one side?

When Eduard Shevardnadze came to the United States in September for his annual U.N. speech and meetings with U.S. officials, he was met with demonstrations by local Armenians. Such shows of hostility had not happened for some time. Shevardnadze was not surprised, but I saw sadness in his eyes. More than any one of us, he knew how many latent ethnic problems existed in the Soviet Union, particularly in the south, and I think he knew better than we did that most of those problems had no easy solutions and might take years to sort out. For the Soviet mind this was difficult to accept. We had been taught about "the friendship of the peoples," and parting with that myth was difficult.

For the first time in my travels with him, Shevardnadze did not come out to talk to the demonstrators, who shouted, "Reunite Karabakh! Karabakh is Armenian!" Shevardnadze did not want to take sides, but he did meet at the embassy with a group delegated by the demonstrators. Most of them were nice, soft-spoken people who had lived for a long time in the United States. The group also included Paruir Airikian, an Armenian dissident recently expelled by the government. Shevardnadze always disagreed with expulsions as a method of solving problems. He was willing to listen to Airikian and to try to help him.

Airikian began aggressively and stridently. It seemed he would never stop. Only some of those who were with him understood Russian, but they certainly caught on to his tone and spoke apologetically to Shevardnadze, asking him to understand Airikian's plight. Airikian was later allowed to return to Armenia and was even a candidate in the presidential election, coming in a distant third.

Shevardnadze Meets Bush and Dukakis

Shevardnadze's visit and his intensive consultations at the United Nations continued against the background of the U.S. presidential election campaign. He followed it with real interest. The night of the first Bush-Dukakis televised debate, he invited me to his suite at the Soviet mission and asked me to interpret the substance of the debate. It was not an easy task, and I had to explain a few things along the way. But the thrust of the debate was clear.

The campaign had started to go Bush's way by that time, and I thought the debate strengthened that trend. Shevardnadze was careful to express no preference for either candidate, which was a change from our past practice. The previous Soviet leaders and our propaganda usually had a clear preference and had often expressed it crudely and aggressively. I was told that the first question Andrey Gromyko asked Ambassador Dobrynin when he came to the United States in an election year was "Whom should we support?" The story may be apocryphal, but it reflects a certain way of thinking that existed even among diplomats.

Shevardnadze met with both Bush and Dukakis. They did not go into any details. I remember Shevardnadze emphasizing to both men how important it was to put an end to the arms race and cut military spending. He said that the Soviet Union ought to have stopped some of its military programs, such as the production of chemical weapons, years before. And he said that the American people's needs, mentioned in the debate by both Bush and Dukakis, cannot be met, *and* the budget deficit cut, without a major reduction in defense spending.

Many in the United States and abroad criticized the election campaign as very thin on substance and sometimes dirty. I too saw much that could be criticized. But as we discussed the campaign I tried to emphasize its positive side. I felt that things like contested elections and debates on the issues should be transplanted to our soil.

"It can't happen in our country," said Shevardnadze's doctor, objecting to a remark I made, "because all the candidates in our system must be approved [by the party], and so what difference can there be between them?" Later I thought many times that in a way he was right: "our system" was incompatible with real elections. But, of the two, Gorbachev chose the elections.

Compromises in a Politburo Power Struggle

Shevardnadze had to return to Moscow hastily, several days earlier than planned. A cable from Moscow informed him that a Central Committee plenum was to be held shortly. There were signs of a power struggle in the Polituro, and there was concern in the United States about its outcome. Shevardnadze was questioned by anxious reporters about the reasons for his quick departure. He said the plenum had been planned for about this time but that the date had not been finalized; now that it had, he was returning to

Moscow. There was probably more to it than that—another occasion when I felt I was translating the truth but not the whole truth.

On the day of our departure I was having lunch in the mission's dining room with Andrey Kozyrev, recently appointed head of the foreign ministry's International Organizations Department. He asked me what I thought might happen in Moscow, and I replied that I did not expect any earthshaking events, that Gorbachev's positions were still quite strong, including in the party. "You never know," he responded. "Anything can happen in our country."

The mood on the plane that carried us to Moscow was not very cheerful. We felt that something was afoot, but I at least did not venture to start talking to the foreign minister about it. He was not forthcoming either, although I think he may have talked much more frankly with Tarasenko and Stepanov— his assistants, confidants and friends.

I learned in Moscow that, before the plenum, hard-liners in the Central Committee and the provinces mounted a fierce assault against Alexander Yakovlev. They accused him of "ruining the ideology" by permitting the papers and literary magazines to "publish anything." Glasnost had not yet become irreversible, and the term "freedom of the press" was still taboo in most places. The long-delayed publication of Boris Pasternak's novel *Doctor Zhivago* and some other previously banned books, and the intelligentsia's demands for the return of Solzhenitsyn's novels to the Russian reader, were regarded as dangerous by most of the party apparat. They demanded the removal of Yakovlev from the Politburo.

At the plenum, Gorbachev dealt with the problem by means of what I regarded as a bureaucratic maneuver. He proposed that Yakovlev be given the post of a Central Committee secretary responsible for international affairs and that the ideological post would go to Vadim Medvedev, another Central Committee secretary. At the same time Ligachev, who had become the leader of the Politburo's conservative faction and attacked Yakovlev in an increasingly open way, was transferred from his number two position in the Central Committee Secretariat to become the "supervisor" of agriculture. It was obviously a compromise and, like all difficult compromises, a somewhat ugly one.

Compromises on Election Procedures

This was the autumn of compromises. A few weeks later the draft law on the election to the Supreme Soviet was published. It was a huge step forward, compared with the old system of uncontested elections. The procedures it would establish were much more democratic. The important thing, I felt, was the acceptance of the principle that the candidate whom the authorities preferred could be challenged through a democratic electoral process—and be defeated.

But signs of compromise were everywhere in the draft law. The authorities did not believe that people would always make the right choice, so instead of a clear procedure they invented something much more complicated: a two-step election process through a Congress of People's Deputies, of which one-third was to be elected not by a popular vote but by various groups such as official organizations and government-approved trade unions. There were also some other "filters."

Later, after adoption of the law and the elections based on it, all these flaws and less-than-democratic provisions were pointed out by many increasingly bold critics. But no one objected openly at the time. What is more, many democratically minded people even took advantage of those provisions to become people's deputies. Andrey Sakharov, for example, chose to be elected not in some Moscow constituency but in one of the official organizations. I saw an irony there, and a recognition of the fact that not only the authorities but also the country as a whole was still rather conservative. But as the democratic process began to heat up, that changed very quickly.

While there was no real debate on the draft election law in the media, we discussed it frankly and critically. I thought the pluses far outweighed the minuses. Establishing the democratic principle of contested elections was more important than the flaws and the filters built into the law, which most people felt was only a beginning.

Ethnic Conflict in Azerbaijan Continues

But the country was not waiting for the democratic process to unfold and to ease the conflicts that were bursting into the open every day. The Karabakh problem had already become the fuse that ignited the fire of hatred and increasingly frequent bloody clashes between the Armenians and the Azerbaijanis. Reports of those clashes were difficult to take—one's instinctive reaction was disbelief or rejection. We had been brought up to believe that the "nationalities problem had been solved in the Soviet Union." When I was growing up, a person's ethnic origin was rarely if ever mentioned. I still believe that nationalism is irrational and more often destructive than constructive. I could not understand why perestroika had to open that Pandora's box.

Among my colleagues at the U.S. desk of the foreign ministry were people of various nationalities, including an Armenian and an Azerbaijani. They were both good people, and though they were different we never regarded those differences as ethnically based. I saw that the Karabakh conflict saddened both of them. Sometimes, after particularly upsetting news from the region, all of us were too depressed to look them in the eye. But "the show must go on." We went on working, preparing for Mikhail Gorbachev's trip to New York in December for his first address to the U.N. General Assembly.

Drafting Gorbachev's U.N. Speech

The speech was being drafted by a group of people working under the close supervision of Gorbachev himself. The idea was to summarize the "new thinking" and its practical consequences for us and for the world in such areas as human rights and disarmament. By that time human rights had been accepted as one of the pillars of the new thinking, and the last vestiges of the Stalin-Brezhnev constraints on them were being removed. Almost all the political prisoners had been released, and more and more refuseniks were allowed to emigrate, despite sometimes fierce objections from the military-industrial complex. Gorbachev could go to New York with a clear conscience so far as this area was concerned.

As for disarmament, the need for unilateral steps was finally accepted by the Politburo, and there were calls for a dramatic reduction in the size of the Soviet Army and in the numbers of weapons, particularly for forces deployed in Eastern Europe. In the foreign ministry, rumors circulated that the army could be reduced by a million men. It was risky territory, we all agreed. After all, Khrushchev's impulsive, drastic, and perhaps not very careful reduction of the armed forces was the reason he was disliked not only by the top brass but also by many officers. It was one of the reasons for his downfall. The army had to be reduced; Gorbachev understood that its size was way beyond any imaginable security requirements. But he had to move carefully to obtain the consent of the General Staff to the specific reduction figures. The result was less than revolutionary but still impressive: the U.N. speech included the announcement that the Soviet armed forces would be reduced by 500,000 men and that large amounts of weapons would be withdrawn from Eastern Europe.

But the speech was important not only for its disarmament initiatives. As I was reading the final text delivered by messenger from Gorbachev's office, I felt that I would be translating a truly historic statement. In thinly veiled form, it was a rejection of many dogmas of Marxism-Leninism and also of the post-Stalinist ideology that was behind the foreign policy of Gorbachev's predecessors.

Gorbachev was thinking in terms of a single global civilization, of one world whose problems could not be solved on the basis of our outdated "theology." I thought this was a speech by an intensely moral man who meant what he was saying, a man who really wanted to bring together morality and policy. I felt that it was a truly novel speech, which would be read long after Gorbachev's U.N. appearance. But I also thought about how much would have to change both in the country's foreign policy and in its domestic affairs to meet the high standards set by the speech.

Gorbachev in New York

As we were preparing to board the plane for New York, more news came about the ethnic clashes between the Armenians and the Azerbaijanis. Men, women, and children had been killed on both sides, and thousands of refugees had to flee from their homes. This was a real shock; we had not had refugees in our country for decades. Some of us hoped that a way could still be found to ease the crisis and make people return to common sense, but many had a premonition of even worse things to come.

Gorbachev was taken to New York from J. F. Kennedy Airport by the longest motorcade I ever saw. Traffic in many parts of Manhattan was blocked by the police, and there was gridlock in much of the city. Television and radio had warned motorists not to come to Manhattan during the two days Gorbachev was to be there. It seemed to be a lot of inconvenience because of one man, and I was worried it might make many people angry. Georgy Arbatov, who was hovering near Gorbachev, even suggested that the whole thing might have been arranged in order to set New Yorkers against Gorbachev. But judging by the interviews shown on local television, people were quite willing to put up with the inconvenience. Gorbachev was a popular man in New York.

The day of the speech I came to the Soviet U.N. mission early to check the final arrangements and look at the morning papers. As I was leaving the ambassador's office to wait for Gorbachev downstairs, an item about an earthquake in Armenia on a television news program caught my attention. There was no word about the death toll, and though it was clear that the earthquake was quite powerful, there was no information about whether large population centers had been affected.

A few minutes later I was entering, with Mikhail Gorbachev, the U.N. building in which I spent five years of my life in the 1970s. So much had changed since then! As Gorbachev spoke, there was extraordinary, almost tangible, silence in the General Assembly hall. The applause after the speech was loud and long, and it was clear that the politicians and diplomats in the audience were genuinely impressed. From the General Assembly building, Gorbachev immediately went to Governors Island, where a meeting was scheduled with Ronald Reagan, the outgoing president, and President-Elect George Bush.

On the way to the island, Gorbachev admired the bridges—the Brooklyn Bridge, which I pointed out to him, in particular. I told him briefly the story of the bridge and of its architect, John Augustus Roebling: how an accident killed Roebling at the outset of construction and how his son took over but was later crippled by caisson disease. He continued to direct construction from his apartment in Brooklyn, watching the process with field glasses and sending messages to the site by his wife. Gorbachev was impressed by the story. "To build things like this, one has to reach beyond the possible," he said.

The motorcade came to the place from which the cars were to be taken by ferry to Governors Island. As the cars stopped, Yury Plekhanov, chief of the KGB government security department, who accompanied Gorbachev on all his foreign trips, came up and asked Gorbachev to go to the communications car. There was a call from Moscow, he said.

Gorbachev returned a few minutes later, sat in the car for a moment in silence, then spoke: "Ryzhkov was calling. The earthquake in Armenia is really bad. They don't know yet how many people have been killed, but it is bad. Enormous destruction. They have started to mount the rescue operation. I have asked Yazov and everyone else to get involved. I'll have to get in touch with them again right after this meeting. It's bad."

Bush and Gorbachev Set the Tone

The meeting with Reagan and Bush was a complicated mix of themes and emotions. It was a farewell to Reagan and a starting point with Bush. It was stock-taking and an attempt to look into the future. There was hope and, at the same time, concern. Gorbachev told them about the news he had just heard from Premier Ryzhkov, and help was immediately offered. He spoke mostly about his vision of his country's future and about how difficult it would be to get there.

"We have made our choice," Gorbachev said. "We will be moving toward a society that is consistent with the general trends of global civilization. We know full well how much we will have to change. And we want you to understand that the road will be difficult for us. It cannot always be a straight line. There will be some zigzags and maybe even backsliding from time to time, but the overall direction has been chosen—democracy, freedom, and genuine cooperation with the outside world—and we will not swerve from it."

When the lunch talk was over, Bush took Gorbachev aside for a brief private chat. They understood each other well. There would be many private talks between them in the subsequent three years, and the tone they struck from the outset never changed. They were similar men in many respects. They were both the product of their country's systems, but both seemed to have an understanding of the complexity of real life. I think both of them understood the limitations of any system and felt that the politicians have basically one task: to establish certain values and goals and then do their best—and stick to the universal principles of morality in the process. They may not have put it in those terms, but this is what I felt was the gist of their approach to policymaking.

Bush and Gorbachev also seemed similar in the way they verbalized their political approach. Both were not very keen on ready-made formulas and the rhetorical flourishes that speechwriters and journalists like so much. They did not like to repeat the positions on the issues, which they expected their counterpart to know. Rather, they preferred to think aloud—not only in their one-on-one talks but even at the press conferences and interviews. That made their syntax contorted and their speech sometimes rambling and groping, but the attempt to go beyond the formula language and the automatic repetition of positions was genuine.

Their talks were not easy to interpret, but I found working with both Bush and Gorbachev professionally rewarding and fascinating. Here were two men caught in a tremendous historic whirlwind and trying to deal with it using the instruments of political management that were available to them. No one had invented other, better instruments, and often they were not much help. History was moving on implacably, and it fell to Mikhail Gorbachev and

George Bush to be in the midst of it. Perhaps all that could be asked of them in this situation was that they acquit themselves honorably.

The White House public relations people had arranged a photo opportunity against the backdrop of New York Harbor and the Statue of Liberty. A podium was installed for Gorbachev, Reagan, and Bush, on which they had to stand, chatting or whatever, with no one in the vicinity. "It's the three of them only," the White House people insisted. "They'll find a way to communicate. An interpreter would ruin the picture." It was decided that I and my U.S. colleague would stand near the podium, which was at least a couple of feet high, and shout up the translation of whatever the three men said. As could be expected, the arrangement did not quite work, and after a few awkward moments Gorbachev and the others waved me up to join them.

Gorbachev had several events scheduled for the remainder of the day, but he said he would rush to the mission to get an update on the earthquake and to decide with the rest of the delegation what to do. He was already inclined to cut the visit short, and of course to cancel the visits to Cuba and Britain, which were to follow, and return to Moscow. On the way to Sixty-seventh Street he made just one stop, at the World Trade Center. We climbed to the 100th floor for the view of Manhattan and the harbor. A small ceremony was also scheduled, which he asked the organizers to make as brief as possible.

I watched as Gorbachev walked along the perimeter of the observation platform looking down intently and listening to the explanations. He was fascinated and awed by the view of New York. Unlike many other leaders, he had the natural ability to admire people and places, to enjoy and to be fascinated by things. The skyscrapers of Manhattan, built on solid rock, impressed him the most. During the brief ceremony that followed the tour, Gorbachev mentioned the Brooklyn Bridge story. "I've been told how immensely difficult it was to build. And I think that this story is a kind of symbol of how this nation was developing—this vast and great land, America. We are trying to rebuild another vast country, to make it a modern and civilized country, open to cooperation with everyone."

Huge crowds had gathered on Third Avenue in Manhattan near the Soviet mission. Gorbachev asked me where we might stop the car to go out and say a few words to the crowd. It was always a nightmare for his security people, but he insisted on doing it. I said we might stop after we pass the Queensboro Bridge intersection. The unscheduled stop was hasty and disorganized, and at some point I feared that the crowd might just swamp Gorbachev. He pressed the flesh and said the simple things that politicians always say. He was tired and prepared for the bad news at the mission, but the few minutes with the crowd seemed to recharge him with fresh energy.

In contrast, Raisa Gorbachev's mood was somber. She seemed unable to keep her mind off the news of the earthquake and the interethnic strife in the area. "If this tragedy does not make them forget their quarrels," she said, "then I don't know whether anything will." She spoke in a low voice, sounding uncharacteristically perplexed and concerned.

Armenian Earthquake Aid Tensions Arise

The cables from Moscow waiting for us at the mission outlined the extent of the damage from the earthquake. It was even worse than Ryzhkov's information a few hours before suggested. There was no doubt that the trip would have to be cut short. Gorbachev asked Shevardnadze to hold a brief press conference to announce his decision. The next morning we were all on the plane flying to Moscow. At some point Gorbachev joined the "lesser" members of his delegation—aides, secretaries, communications and security people—in the compartment of the plane where we were all crammed in. He thanked everyone for their help during the U.N. visit and told us in some detail about the earthquake.

"I will be going to Armenia shortly," Gorbachev added. "Probably the day after we return to Moscow." This was a natural thing for him to do. He went there to be with the people who were suffering and to help in organizing the rescue and rebuilding operations. He also expected that the tragedy would bring people together, making them forget the ethnic problems at least for a time and concentrate on the task of rebuilding.

But that did not happen. People did not forget, and the pain from the various tragedies that the Armenians had gone through was only amplified by the earthquake. When people assaulted him in Yerevan with questions and demands about Karabakh, Gorbachev exploded. He could not understand, having seen the devastation and the sufferings, how anyone could talk about things that seemed far less important. Many armchair critics in Moscow who watched his outburst on television judged it severely. Well, Gorbachev was not a clockwork politician, capable of calculating his every step and weighing every word. He was a human being with emotions that he could not always control. If that reaction was a mistake, I thought I would have made the same one.

When Gorbachev left Armenia, Ryzhkov stayed behind to coordinate the rescue operations and the foreign aid that began to flow into the country immediately. He held daily televised sessions of the coordinating committee to discuss the work under way. I did not think the process was particularly effective, but apparently it raised Premier Ryzhkov's rating. People saw a hardworking official who cared and was trying to do something to whip the bureaucracy into action. At least, that was the impression the television people sought to create.

Shevardnadze sent Ernest Obminsky, the foreign ministry's top expert on economic affairs, to help coordinate foreign relief and to sit on Ryzhkov's committee. One day in December television news showed Ryzhkov questioning Obminsky about the confusion that was the inevitable result of both the quake and the sheer amount of aid received. Obminsky tried to answer the best he could, given that the foreign ministry had no management responsibility in this whole effort. At one point, unhappy about Obminsky's answers, Ryzhkov exploded, "This is no answer at all. You should tell them that we are not satisfied with the way the foreign ministry is working here."

It was obviously unfair. Ryzhkov had a difficult and frustrating time. He reportedly slept just four or five hours a day, so perhaps the outburst was understandable under the circumstances. But it was shown on prime-time television, and Shevardnadze was always concerned about the foreign ministry's public image. Shevardnadze, his aides told me, was furious.

The day after the Yerevan incident was televised, Shevardnadze was leaving on a trip to Japan, the Philippines, and North Korea. As always, most of his team had boarded the plane before he even arrived at the Vnukovo airport. As we were waiting for him, it became obvious that he would be late. For the first time in years, I had a feeling something was wrong on the first day of the trip.

Shevardnadze finally came, gloomy and distracted. I did not see anyone from the Politburo see him off at the airport, which was still a firm rule then. This time he just didn't want it. He had protested against the attack on his ministry. I heard he had told Ryzhkov he was prepared to go to Yerevan himself instead of Tokyo. He was, of course, persuaded to do nothing of the kind. I do not know what his relations with Ryzhkov were before the Yerevan episode, but afterward I began to detect signs that they were quite cool, and getting cooler as the economic reform efforts stalled more and more obviously.

Shevardnadze Travels to Japan, the Philippines, and North Korea

Shevardnadze's visit to Japan was part of a long saga to which both countries were, I thought, doomed by fate. It focused on the problem of four South Kuril islands. The Japanese claim to them had some merit, certainly so far as the two southernmost islands were concerned. Khrushchev had promised to return those and to discuss the two others, but later the promise was rescinded and the two countries were locked into two mutually exclusive positions: the Soviet Union said there was no territorial problem, and Japan was claiming the islands, all four of them. The problem was an obstacle to increased economic cooperation and to genuinely normal relations between the two countries. I heard Shevardnadze speak of that problem many times, both in private and in public. He felt the problem could have been avoided in the first place, but now that we had it on our hands, there was no easy or obvious solution.

In rough outline, the approach that Gorbachev and Shevardnadze favored, and which Gorbachev later proposed to the Japanese, looked something like this: recognize the existence of the territorial dispute; create a mechanism for discussion of all aspects; seek an overall improvement in relations and wait for an opportune time—perhaps not very soon—when the problem could be resolved to the mutual satisfaction of the two countries.

Nothing that happened since 1988 has changed my mind about the sensibility of this approach. If the problem is not politicized in either country, sooner or later it will work. Gorbachev and Shevardnadze were able to take the first two steps—recognizing the problem and creating a negotiating mechanism— and were not rewarded much for it. An immediate reward was not what they were looking for. Still, I felt that their efforts ought to have received greater recognition.

Shevardnadze's visit to the Philippines had no drama of a big issue behind it. It was a get-acquainted call. Both Philippines President Corazon Aquino and Foreign Minister Raul Manglapus turned out to be interesting interlocutors. Aquino made a great speech at lunch for Shevardnadze. Like him, she was concerned with the problem of morality and politics—could the two be combined? Her answer was yes, but she spoke frankly to Shevardnadze about how difficult it was to stick to certain principles, to be in touch with the people, and to govern effectively. She also agreed with Shevardnadze that too much ideology was harmful in both foreign and domestic politics. Shevardnadze recalled a phrase he had heard a few months before from Argentina's foreign minister, Dante Caputo, and liked very much, about the danger of political and ideological fundamentalism.

In North Korea, Shevardnadze had the unpleasant task of informing his host that the Soviet Union would be moving toward normalizing relations with South Korea. I was not at the talks and could only guess what an ordeal he had to go through. Pyongyang was a depressing sight: it was cold, there was no snow, and the wind was raising little storms of dust in the gray streets of the city. People went about with lowered eyes, unsmiling. The statue of Kim Il Sung towered above the city. He seemed ever present, and I almost felt his shadow in the government residence where we were lodged and in the huge "guest house" to which we were taken for the official dinner.

As Tarasenko and Stepanov were working on the draft of the minister's answers to the questions of the government newspaper, they were struggling to describe his meeting with Kim Il Sung. They could not bring themselves to include any of the expected formulas of admiration, but the foreign minister had to be diplomatic. They finally came up with a formula: "The meeting with Comrade Kim Il Sung, as always, produced a very powerful impression." From the discussions on the plane to Moscow, I understood that things did not seem too bad. The North Koreans were obviously displeased with Moscow's intentions, but there were no tantrums.

Six

A MATTER OF PACE
1 9 8 9

U.S.-Soviet Relations on Hold

The plane brought us back to Moscow, to the country's numerous problems, and to the inevitability of a slowdown in international developments as a result of the decision by newly elected U.S. President George Bush to reassess the administration's foreign policy, and relations with the Soviet Union in particular. In a way, it seemed to be a sensible decision, and in endless discussions with my colleagues at the foreign ministry and elsewhere I defended it.

Bush was by nature a cautious man, I argued, so taking his time to look around and get his bearings following his election was a natural thing for him to do. Even if the results of the reassessment were not much different from the starting point, it had to be done. He could not afford to be seen as just "a follower" of what Reagan and Shultz had established. Spending eight years in the shadows was difficult enough for him, I said. Give him time to pause and then come out with some big speech. We would then move forward fast with his team, for it seemed to consist of eminently competent and reasonable men. I expressed that view in a commentary I wrote for the government news agency TASS under a pen name.

Based on what I heard him say in private as well as publicly, Gorbachev was more or less of that view. Bush was sending him various signals of his goodwill and of his intention not to drag out the review unduly. The Western press was full of all kinds of commentaries and conjectures; some doubted that Bush would continue to seek a close relationship with the Soviet Union. Some of the cables from the embassies were not very optimistic either, nor were quite a few people in the corridors of the foreign ministry. But the view that we should take an understanding attitude and not criticize Bush for "wasting time" prevailed easily. Anyway, we did not have much choice. Starting out with a new administration on a critical note would be counterproductive.

Afterward when events in Eastern Europe and then the Soviet Union began to develop at a pace that no one had foreseen and few were comfortable with, I often asked myself whether that mutually accepted pause, even if inevitable, was a good thing after all. It did not produce any significant change in U.S. policy toward the Soviet Union, or in any other aspect of American foreign policy. Bush came back with a number of speeches that sounded right, including one in which he declared his intention to seek "new closeness" with the Soviet Union.

If there had to be a pause, could it result in something more substantial? A proposal, perhaps, that would cut through the accumulated clutter of the START issues and open the way to a quick signing of the treaty? Or a similar proposal in the conventional arms negotiations? Something like this could create a situation, or at least an impression, of controlled development, of managed evolutionary change.

Instead, when things that changed the geopolitics of Europe and the world began to occur, they were moving much faster than anything the Soviet Union and the United States were doing. I continue to believe that the overall effect of those changes will be positive, but there is still this question: Could a more manageable process have been created? And could it be that the Soviet Union and the West lost valuable historical time in 1989 instead of beginning to shape such a process?

Perhaps there are no answers at all to these questions. The ability of policymakers to affect historic changes of such magnitude is not great. Or perhaps the final answers will be negative. But these questions must be asked when thinking about the revolution that followed in the subsequent months.

Gorbachev and Shevardnadze understood that relations with the United States were decisive, and those relations now had to wait. They were also preoccupied with domestic developments, but they believed the country needed to continue to be active in the foreign policy arena. They also felt that the time had come to put forward a constructive regional agenda, since the most difficult problem, that of withdrawal from Afghanistan, would soon be behind us. Two things had to be done without delay: definitively normalizing our relations with China and developing a new and realistic policy in the Middle East. Much had already been done to lay the groundwork for both developments, and in the first months of 1989 major steps were to be taken to push them forward.

Shevardnadze Talks with Deng in China

In early February 1989 Shevardnadze went to China to prepare for Gorbachev's visit there later in the year. Many saw it as part of a continuing geopolitical game in the U.S.–U.S.S.R.–China triangle. But the lines in that triangle had already blurred. It was no longer clear who was doing what to whom, and for what purpose. Most of all, the three countries wanted a normal relationship with one another. True, all had their own commitments and agendas, but those seemed to belong more to the past. I felt that Gorbachev, Deng, and Bush wanted to look to the future.

A number of irritants in Soviet-Chinese relations still remained, dating back to the time when Asia, and the whole world, seemed to be up for grabs in the ideological and political struggle between the two superpowers. Cambodia was the stickiest problem. During Shevardnadze's visit to Peking it became apparent to me from talks with our experts that both the Soviet Union and China were increasingly displeased with the behavior of some of their friends and clients in that country. But neither was willing to say so openly. The talks consisted of hints, suggestions, hidden meanings, and gestures.

Shevardnadze went to Shanghai to meet with Deng when the discussions with the Chinese foreign minister and among experts on Cambodia seemed to be deadlocked. At that moment he seemed not at all sure that the main goal of his visit—setting the date for Gorbachev's trip to China that would seal Soviet-Chinese normalization—would be achieved. But he came back in high spirits.

As Shevardnadze told us on the plane, the talk with Deng had gone well. They recalled the years of closeness between the two countries, both to recapture the human warmth of those years and to agree that there would be no return to that relationship of virtual alliance. Although the Chinese had said that the Cambodian issue would have to be resolved before final normalization, Deng agreed to set the date for Gorbachev's visit without insisting on that condition. Shevardnadze, of course, did not claim victory. In the game of hints, gestures, and implied promises, this is never done. The implied promise was that the Soviet Union would do its best to persuade Vietnam to withdraw its troops from Cambodia, and the promise was kept.

Afghanistan and a Meeting with Pakistan's Bhutto

Another troop withdrawal—one that was much more important for us and far-reaching in its implications—was being completed during those days. As we were flying from China to Pakistan, the last units of the Soviet army were leaving Afghanistan. Although I had never been to Kabul with Shevardnadze, I knew what it had cost him to make that happen. The question that was then being debated everywhere, by experts and nonexperts alike, was whether the government of Najibullah would survive the withdrawal.

The international press was full of predictions of the impending final assault of the mujaheddin on Kabul, the fall of the regime, and a subsequent bloodbath. This was also the conventional wisdom in the Soviet foreign ministry, particularly in departments not directly concerned with Afghanistan. The experts on the Afghanistan desk were more prudent. Some went openly against the current and predicted that Najibullah's regime would survive, but they were a minority.

Shevardnadze did not make any predictions in my presence, but I felt he did not share the most pessimistic assessments. I once talked to him about the phrase "self-fulfilling prophecy," which is difficult to translate into Russian and had to be explained. That was something that could happen in Afghanistan, I said. He answered to the effect that the strength of the Najibullah regime should not be underestimated.

This, I thought, was the message he was taking to Islamabad, but the Pakistanis were not receptive to it. From the outset of Shevardnadze's talks in the foreign ministry, they were taking for granted the early defeat of Najibullah. They said they were looking forward to a rapid improvement in relations with the Soviet Union, now that the Afghan problem was almost behind us. Once the current regime was gone, they suggested, a political solution would be easy to achieve, and they were ready to cooperate. Shevardnadze's attempt to persuade Foreign Minister Yakub Khan that Najibullah was an indigenous and viable force that at least had to be reckoned with in a political solution was ignored. He just couldn't get through.

A meeting was scheduled with Prime Minister Benazir Bhutto, and Shevardnadze believed it was his last chance to explore possible political approaches seriously. He had some messages from Kabul to pass on to her. Part of the meeting he expected to be one-on-one, as is usual during such visits, but when we came to the parliament building, where the prime minister had her office, the events proceeded according to a different scenario.

We were kept waiting for about ten minutes in one of the many halls of the building. As we waited, through an open door I saw Bhutto talking with someone. I could not hear what she was saying, but she seemed concerned. She was dressed in a red native outfit, her head covered with a shawl, and Shevardnadze, who did not recognize her, later said she might be taken for a young secretary. Finally, we were invited to join Bhutto and led into her office.

But Bhutto's private talk with Shevardnadze turned out to be short. A few minutes later the door of the office opened, armchairs were brought in, and we were joined by Yakub Khan and two or three other officials. Bhutto smiled apologetically. She seemed to be encircled by people who, though not openly hostile, owed her no allegiance. The discussion did not add anything to what we had gone through before, and the overall feeling was eerie and frustrating.

We made one final attempt to get through to Bhutto. At Shevardnadze's request, I talked with her personal assistant for foreign affairs, a man I remembered from my years at the United Nations, but he too seemed isolated and not quite free in what he was saying. The next day, when Yakub Khan came to the airport to say goodbye to Shevardnadze, he indicated he was aware of what I had privately conveyed to Bhutto. He and the military were clearly in charge, and they wanted to win big in Afghanistan.

The withdrawal of Soviet troops was completed a few days afterward. There was some panic in Kabul and other cities; many were waiting for a coup against Najibullah, but it did not materialize. Dozens of Western reporters were in the city, ready to chronicle the finale of the Afghan drama. But nothing happened. After a few days of waiting they began to trickle out of Kabul. The city was, after all, not a spa.

In a meeting with India's defense minister, Gorbachev said that predictions of Najibullah's imminent rout had been proven wrong but that it only underscored the need for a political solution. The Indians were pleased that the rout had not occurred, for it would have meant a great victory for Pakistan. As for the political solution, no one had any workable ideas about how to achieve it. The problem was that the Pakistanis and the mujaheddin were still hoping for a clear victory and wanted to divide the spoils among themselves only.

It was then, perhaps, that a formula, a phrase, which he later suggested to U.S. Secretary of State James Baker, began to gel in Gorbachev's mind. It was not some new concept of a settlement, but rather an approach to settlement that reflected both the intractability of the Afghan problem and the two powers' diminished interest in Afghanistan's affairs. During his first talk with Baker, Gorbachev remarked that the Afghan equation was extremely confusing. "So maybe we should let them stew in their own juices," he added almost in passing. Baker's reaction was noncommittal, but he often quoted those words later. They became a kind of code for what I called a policy of diminished interest.

Was it the right policy, and was it policy at all? Both Gorbachev and Bush often said to each other that a victory for Islamic fundamentalism in Afghanistan was not in the interests of either the United States or the Soviet Union. I believed that was reason enough to try to develop something like a common policy aimed at preventing that outcome and achieving stability in Afghanistan. With some effort, a coalition that would be acceptable to almost everyone — and "almost" would be enough in that case — could perhaps be put together in Afghanistan. But apparently the Soviet Union and the United States were not equally interested in such an outcome.

Letting them "stew in their own juices" seemed to be the most realistic option, but it also indicated how difficult it was to develop cooperative U.S.-Soviet policies now that the Cold War was on the way out and the old assumptions were no longer valid. This, in my view, is a difficulty the Gorbachev-Bush partnership never really overcame. It haunted their relationship on many issues — there were some shared goals and a large measure of mutual understanding, but often no clear common policy.

The Middle East Equation Shifts

With the Afghan issue defused if not resolved by the Soviet withdrawal, a subtle shift was also occurring in the Middle East equation. Our military involvement in Afghanistan had marred the Soviet Union's relations with moderate Arab regimes and oil-rich Gulf countries. Relations with Israel were also difficult, for diplomatic ties had been broken during the six-day war in 1967 and never resumed, despite the efforts of people like the longtime Soviet

Ambassador Anatoly Dobrynin, who once told me that during one such attempt in the 1970s he thought he had persuaded most members of the Politburo but could not "get past" Mikhail Suslov. That left us with a small and unpleasant bunch of partners in the Middle East, including mostly Syria, Iraq, and the Palestine Liberation Organization (PLO).

Gorbachev and Shevardnadze wanted to change that. They were attracted to a more equidistant policy in all regions, and they were aware of the advantages of closer relations with the Gulf regimes. Ideological inertia did not mean much to them, at least so far as the Middle East was concerned.

I remember Gorbachev's meeting with King Hussein of Jordan a year or so earlier. The king insisted on speaking English. He impressed Gorbachev as a good and pragmatic man—in contrast, Gorbachev told me after the talk, to some of his other Middle East partners (he named one or two). At about that time we began to get closer to the Saudis—talking to them through our embassy in Washington, mostly about Afghanistan—and other Gulf Arabs. Gorbachev often said that we had to find a new role for our country in the Middle East, in order to become an honest broker for peace based on a balance of interests.

Shevardnadze often said that we should talk to everyone. He wanted to find a way to reestablish diplomatic relations with Israel, and he used every session of the U.N. General Assembly to have a talk with the Israeli foreign minister. He had thus talked with Shimon Perez, Itzhak Shamir, and Moshe Arens. Superficially, those talks did not seem very productive, but gradually they led to reopening ties in various areas. Economic and cultural relations were being rebuilt quite rapidly. The ice was melting; diplomatic relations were just a question of time. The Arabs understood this too, and that created a new underlying dynamic in the Middle East. The time was ripe for the Soviet foreign minister to visit the region. It was a long and exhausting trip, with stops in Syria, Jordan, Iraq, Egypt, and Iran on the way back.

As we were flying from Moscow, frozen in February, to Damascus, someone noted how close the Middle East was to our country. With less than four hours flight time, it was indeed quite obvious. The Middle East is "Near East" in Russian, and Shevardnadze referred to that on several occasions. The visit's keynote was Shevardnadze's speech in Cairo, offering a new Soviet approach to the Middle East, which was different from the old one in both rhetoric and substance. No more talk about the "national liberation struggle," no more cheap criticism of U.S. policy. No longer was the Soviet Union allowing its allies to shape its policy in the Middle East. In that, I felt, it was paradoxically showing a kind of example to the United States. Later, the U.S. policy on the Middle East became more independent as well.

Selling the New Policy in Amman, Cairo, Baghdad, and Teheran

Shevardnadze had to sell the new policy to our friends in the Middle East. Some were more receptive to it than others, but he seemed to have infinite patience, sitting down for hours and hours with the presidents and foreign ministers, trying to break through the confrontational mind-set many of them had. He seemed more relaxed and at ease in Amman and Cairo, where he met the Israeli foreign minister Moshe Arens and PLO Chairman Yasir Arafat, as well as Egyptian officials. His visit to Iraq seemed almost an appendage to the Middle East tour.

The Iran-Iraq war, which had ended recently and inconclusively, was a "thing in itself," and our Middle East experts thought we should explore the kind of factor Iraq was going to be in the region now that the war was over. Shevardnadze and Tariq Aziz, the Iraqi foreign minister, seemed to have a good rapport; they talked as two professionals. Shevardnadze also expected to have a meeting with Iraqi President Saddam Hussein. On the day we arrived in Baghdad he was told that Saddam was in Basra and it was unclear whether he would return to Baghdad before our departure. A few hours later the Iraqis told us the president was ready to have a meeting in Basra. Shevardnadze flew there and had a long talk with Saddam. Most of the delegation stayed behind in Baghdad.

I did some sightseeing. The city did not bear any scars from the long war with Iran. The gold-domed mosque of Kazimayn was spectacular. Women in black garb and those wearing modern clothes coexisted without apparent conflict. I asked the embassy's minister-counselor to summarize the country for me. "It's a cruel regime by any standards," he said, "and they are broke after the war with Iran." I recalled those words eighteen months later, in the Siberian city of Irkutsk.

The last stop on our route was Teheran. There was more than a little nervousness among our team as the plane was approaching that city. Although we all expected the withdrawal from Afghanistan to improve Shevardnadze's chances for some success, certain things worried us. For Shevardnadze, as a Georgian, it was not an easy excursion. Historically Georgia suffered from Persia's aggression, and unlike other Soviet leaders Shevardnadze was not a man without ethnic memory, though he approached the visit in a cool and professional manner. There was also the fact that the visit coincided with the stormy debate over Salman Rushdie's book *The Satanic Verses* and Ayatollah Khomeini's *fatwah* against the author. There was some question whether it was prudent to go to Teheran at the height of the scandal. Shevardnadze decided that he must go.

I was the only one in our group to have read the book. I liked it, and did not think it could be offensive to all Muslims. But it certainly complicated the picture, particularly because the British had asked Shevardnadze to intervene on the author's behalf. Frankly, I could not imagine how that could be done in any effective way.

At the Teheran airport Shevardnadze was literally assaulted by a group of journalists and cameramen—so much so that his security guards had to make a special effort to keep him safe. We went to the embassy, which features a statue of Alexander Griboyedov, the Russian poet and diplomat who was killed in Teheran in 1828 by a fanatical mob that attacked the Russian embassy. I had the whole next day free. The Western-style hotel where we stayed was clean and well run. There were dozens of security guards everywhere—the Iranians were taking no chances. Contrary to expectations, they were cheerful and smiling. Also somewhat unexpectedly, most embassy officials praised the Iranians and said that on both the human and the diplomatic level they were good to deal with.

The visit to Iran went well. Shevardnadze had already built a professional relationship with Foreign Minister Ali Akbar Velayati, and this time both sides agreed to forget some episodes from the past and start more or less afresh. Shevardnadze had a talk with the Ayatollah, who was already quite frail (he would die within a few months).

The officials who were present at that talk were at first a little enigmatic about what had transpired, but a few hours later the Iranians published almost the entire minutes of that talk. Shevardnadze gave the Ayatollah a letter from Gorbachev, to which he responded that the Soviet president should think more about life and death—in a word, a useful talk to conclude a long and fruitful visit. We landed at Vnukovo airport bumpily amid a moderately severe snowstorm.

Election Campaign in the Soviet Union

The talk of Moscow was the election campaign. Whatever our criticism of the election law, most of us agreed that this was the closest thing to real elections the country ever had, including during prerevolutionary times. The debates between the candidates were shown openly and uncensored on television. Issues were discussed, and people had a real choice.

Boris Yeltsin was among the candidates running in Moscow, and he was enormously popular. People sympathized with him as a maverick, already an outsider, and a man who was giving utterance to their discontent. He was not calling for a rapid transition to a market economy, for allowing private property, or for a more democratic legal and political regime. He had other issues to which the crowds responded. He called for ending the privileges of the party apparatchiks and attacked unpopular members of the Politburo, such as Yegor Ligachev. When the party press ran an article criticizing Yeltsin, his rating soared even higher.

I discussed the election campaign with friends, colleagues, and my family. Almost everyone intended to vote. But almost everyone was not quite pleased with the way things were evolving. I too had my doubts. The fact that we had a choice was obviously welcome, but I felt that real issues were not being debated. And how could they be debated when we still had a single party, which had an election platform but paradoxically did not run an official slate of candidates? And in the party itself there were people of all views and persuasions, not structured into any organized factions or groups.

In the end, 85 percent of those elected to the Congress of People's Deputies turned out to be Communist Party members, but it was no victory for the party, and certainly not for its apparat. At the time, I did not talk about that with Gorbachev—we were not that close then—but I discussed it with Shevardnadze. He too felt uneasy about the demagogues and populists who had won in many places, and he said the party should have organized the campaign differently. But was he receptive to the idea of factions within the party, and eventually a two-party or multiparty system? I did not try that idea on him. Perhaps he would have just smiled, or looked at me pensively. Anyway, he said to us and to his foreign guests many times that he thought the pluses in the elections far outweighed the minuses. And on that I fully agreed with him.

Gorbachev and Castro on Different Wavelengths

The Congress of People's Deputies, which was to elect the new Supreme Soviet, the country's legislature, was due to start in mid-May. In the meantime, Gorbachev scheduled one foreign trip. There were debts to pay to Fidel Castro and Margaret Thatcher; his visits to Cuba and Great Britain had been canceled in December 1988 because of the Armenian earthquake. They were now rescheduled for April 1989.

Latin America and Cuba were not my area, but I knew enough from cables and my contacts in the foreign ministry to understand that our relations with Cuba were going downhill. The Cubans were not happy about Gorbachev's policy of disengagement from regional commitments. Castro, even more than the Communist leaders in Eastern Europe, saw the world in ideological terms. In 1987 he said to Shevardnadze that the rehabilitation of such Soviet leaders of the 1920s and 1930s as Nikolay Bukharin would be difficult for Cuban Communists to accept. He found it even more difficult to accept internal democratization in the Soviet Union and Gorbachev's emphasis on improving relations with the United States. Castro's comments about perestroika—first private and then, in veiled form, public—were becoming increasingly harsh. It was obvious that ideologically he and Gorbachev were parting company.

Gorbachev was receiving advice that he should take a tougher line on Cuba, using as leverage—and also as a positive signal to the United States—Soviet supplies of weapons to Cuba, but he was reluctant to do that. In addition to his inborn caution, I believed that another factor contributed to his reluctance. Castro was probably a hero to Gorbachev in the 1960s. I know he was a hero to many Soviets who were much less ideologically minded than Gorbachev, a regional Komsomol leader, must have been in those years. And Gorbachev was not a man who abandoned past attachments easily. So he made what I thought was a final attempt to talk it out with Fidel—to explain himself and maybe to persuade Castro to try some reforms.

It was clear even during that visit that he could not succeed. Gorbachev and Castro were obviously on different wavelengths. I saw only glimpses of that visit, for most of the time I was working with Chernyaev on the texts of Gorbachev's London speeches. But the atmosphere of the visit was clearly cheerless and pessimistic. Gorbachev was greeted warmly everywhere he went, and the crowds that lined the streets on the days of his arrival and departure were numerous and enthusiastic; they probably wanted to see him as a messenger of hope for change. But the slogans painted on the walls of increasingly dilapidated buildings of Havana were "Socialism or Death"—the alternative Gorbachev clearly rejected. On the fight from Havana to London, I, for one, felt relief that it was over.

Gorbachev's London Visit

The London visit was the first time I had a chance to get a close look at Margaret Thatcher. I had specialized in the United States and worked with British officials only rarely, but I had certainly observed her with great interest. My countrymen were enormously fascinated with the British prime minister. Everyone remembered how in 1985 she literally demolished a group of Soviet journalists interviewing her, who had tried to mumble some ideological bromides that other Westerners used to leave unchallenged. Shown in full on television, the interview was one of the first signs of glasnost.

I did not fully share people's enthusiasm about the episode, for I did not believe it should be a politician's goal to savage a reporter. But I respected Thatcher for her passionate commitment to Western values and for her clarity and consistency. During Gorbachev's visit to London, I admired something else in her: a total lack of condescension and a seriousness in the discussion of issues. She did not believe that some things are better left unsaid; she had a passion for issues, ideas, and opinions.

Thatcher came to Heathrow Airport to welcome Gorbachev, and when we were getting into Gorbachev's car I bumped my head against the door and bruised it rather badly. It was dark, and no one noticed there was blood on my forehead; I was holding a handkerchief to it all the way to the Soviet embassy. Thatcher and Gorbachev spent the time during the ride talking about the issues. As I now recall, they discussed trouble in Namibia on the eve of the elections there and some other regional matters. They never had time or enough interest to talk about the weather or protocol niceties.

Prospects for the Soviet Union's relations with the new U.S. administration were implicit in everything that was discussed during the visit. Thatcher was enthusiastic about the new administration and said Bush would be good to deal with and would take the issues head-on. The Bush administration was then completing its foreign policy review, and Thatcher sought to assure Gorbachev that as a result of that review relations would be put on a fast track rather than slowed down. This was what Gorbachev wanted to hear; he was eager to start out with Bush.

Another discussion topic was democratization in the Soviet Union. Both Gorbachev and Thatcher took an optimistic view: the country was ripe for democracy, and democracy was the only answer to its many problems. Later, when developments took a dramatic turn, Gorbachev was often accused of starting the process of reform with an overly optimistic view of things. But pessimists never start any reform. Realists sometimes do, but they tend to stop or scale them down once real trouble begins. I believe that by that time Gorbachev had decided he was prepared to accept all the consequences of the democratic reforms that were beginning to shake up the country. Of all Western leaders, it seemed then that only Margaret Thatcher fully believed him.

On the last day of the visit, Gorbachev was invited by the Queen to

Windsor Castle, the royal residence outside London. Our protocol officials suggested that I go in Shevardnadze's car, which would put me close enough to the Gorbachevs once they left their car and the welcoming ceremony began. During the half-hour drive, we talked about some aspects of the visit and about the British character—national character is one theme that fascinated Shevardnadze. But most of the time he was silent, brooding over something I could only guess at.

Bloodshed in Tbilisi, Georgia

The news about street demonstrations in Tbilisi was probably being relayed by cable to London. I don't know how troubling it was to Gorbachev and Shevardnadze at the time. There had been similar demonstrations six months before, but they ended peacefully after Gorbachev's appeal for calm was read to the crowd. And though Georgia was a web of problems, there seemed to be no reason for an explosion similar to the one in neighboring Armenia and Azerbaijan.

The explosion came a day or two after our return to Moscow. As we were waiting for our luggage at the airport I saw Gorbachev talking to a large group of Politburo members who had come to meet him. He said later that he then asked Shevardnadze to go to Tbilisi the next day. I am sure that Shevardnadze would have helped to sort things out there. But on April 8 Dzhumber Patiashvili, the Georgian leader, sent a cable to Moscow indicating that the situation was returning to normal and that Shevardnadze could stay in Moscow. Indeed, the crowd near the government building had thinned, and the demonstrators showed no signs of being in a violent mood. But on the night of April 9 troops were used to push the crowd out of the square where they were demonstrating, and eighteen people died.

I heard the news on the radio on Sunday, April 9. They said only that there had been casualties, without giving the number, but I understood immediately that even one person killed was a catastrophe. Those deaths detonated a chain of events leading to upheaval, independence, and, eventually, war in Georgia, which everyone knows about today. Georgia soon became the place where the price of change was perhaps the highest in terms of death, destruction, and human drama. It was so bad that I often thought that some or even much of it could probably not have been avoided. Still, I was troubled by this question: If Gorbachev and Shevardnadze had disregarded Patiashvili's cable, if Shevardnadze had gone to Tbilisi on April 8, could the worst have been avoided?

It had always been a matter of conjecture and debate in the foreign ministry how much Shevardnadze was interested and involved in what was happening in Georgia, his native land. So far as I knew from Stepanov and other people close to him, so far as I could guess from some of Shevardnadze's own remarks, he was avidly following the events there, but he made a point of not interfering and not posing as a kind Moscow-based overseer. Patiashvili would certainly have benefited from his advice, and perhaps Shevardnadze would have been ready to give it in a discreet way. But to my knowledge Patiashvili did not seek advice. He was a confident man, and he only visited Shevardnadze in the foreign ministry once or twice, when things were already turning badly. Even then, it looked more like a courtesy call. As Shevardnadze's people were telling me, those two were very different men.

Shevardnadze went to Georgia after the news of the killings reached Moscow, canceling his scheduled trip to Berlin. Stepanov and Tarasenko went with him. From what was shown of that trip on television, I could guess what kind of experience it was for them — and above all for Shevardnadze. He later sometimes mentioned those days in Tbilisi to us, and even to some of his foreign counterparts. He discussed it in some detail with Shultz, who came to see him in New York in late September. It was still an open wound then.

Shevardnadze was bitter about Patiashvili, whom he initially tended to believe — or so it seemed to me — and particularly about the military and the interior ministry troops. The people who commanded the troops had lied to him about many things, admitting the truth only under the pressure of incontrovertible evidence, and one thing Shevardnadze absolutely detested was lies.

This was the beginning of our sleepless nights. It was disturbing to think of all those problems springing up everywhere, and of the system's inability to handle them in a civil way. Even if it was necessary sometimes to disperse an unruly crowd, why must it end in bloodshed and carnage? I wondered about that. The instincts of the people in charge of defense and law enforcement seemed to be to crush them and let them know who's boss. Formally, Gorbachev was the leader of that regime and that system, and Shevardnadze was their representative on the international scene. But their instincts were quite different. It was, at that time, a clash of instincts.

Doubts, Vacillation, and Too Much Debate

Gorbachev was starting a journey toward democratic government and the rule of law, and he wanted the whole country to be with him on that journey, including the party, the military-industrial complex, and the KGB. The open question was whether those institutions were capable of changing, adapting themselves to democracy and to the instincts of leaders like Gorbachev, or whether they would try to bend the democratic process and Gorbachev to their own instincts and needs. We were discussing those questions endlessly. We used words like "the system," "the invisible government," and "the state security," but most often we just said "they" or "those people."

The Americans were engaged in a similar debate then. Perhaps they put the question more starkly: Was Gorbachev for real, or was he one of "them"? My impression was that many in the U.S. government, and quite a few academic experts and influential journalists, did not trust Gorbachev and doubted his commitment to democratic change, in a way that was less than fair to him.

Some of the American debate about Gorbachev was open and some was hidden. The fact that the administration took so long to reassess its Soviet policy created an opening for the conservatives and "the agencies" in Moscow. They had their own interpretation of the pause and the debate, which they were putting into cables and memorandums sent to Gorbachev. Their "incisive analysis of the correlation of forces in the Bush administration" boiled down to a simple message: "Mikhail Sergeyevich, they don't like you, they don't trust you, and they want you out."

The Americans themselves did not always help those in the Soviet Union who counseled patience and a continued emphasis on relations with the United States. So on both sides, instead of developing a clear policy of cooperation for the coming years, there were doubts, vacillation, and too much enervating and futile debate. Nevertheless, I went out of my way whenever I could to defend "the pause" and insist on the need to give the new administration time to sort things out. That was also the view of most people in the foreign ministry, including even cautious and relatively conservative people such as Alexey Obukhov, a knowledgeable and respected diplomat and arms control expert who was appointed to head the USA and Canada department of the foreign ministry following Alexander Bessmertnykh's promotion to the post of first deputy foreign minister.

Kissinger and Gorbachev in Mutual Doubt

Former U.S. Secretary of State Henry Kissinger came to Moscow in late January 1989 with a good but rather brief and carefully written letter to

Gorbachev from George Bush. Right after his inauguration the new president had telephoned Gorbachev, and their conversation was warm and friendly. Bush obviously wanted to reassure Gorbachev about his intentions. Kissinger's visit was awaited for possible additional clues.

Kissinger came as a member of a Trilateral Commission delegation, which also included former French President Valery Giscard d'Estaing and former Japanese Prime Minister Yasuhiro Nakasone. Gorbachev brought to his meeting with them members of what was then his foreign policy brain trust — Alexander Yakovlev, Vadim Medvedev, Falin, Arbatov, and Primakov. The questions Kissinger asked, some of them quite specific, concerned Gorbachev's intentions with regard to the economy and to Eastern Europe. He also made suggestions that were later interpreted by the press as a proposal for a second Yalta — some kind of grand bargain on Eastern Europe. Later, in 1992, Kissinger confirmed to Gorbachev that indeed that was his intention, though my impression at the time was that it was something less than that.

Kissinger did not seem to trust Gorbachev fully. Whether he mistrusted his intentions or his ability, I did not know, but there definitely was a layer of mutual doubt under the surface of the meeting's cordiality. This was obvious after the meeting, when Gorbachev discussed the talk with his advisers. I did not find their remarks particularly helpful to Gorbachev. Maybe they too had not yet decided how serious Gorbachev was about change and about "freedom of choice" — the words that he kept repeating — for Eastern Europe.

"There will be a crisis in Eastern Europe," Medvedev said.

"Whatever it is, they will have to decide themselves how they will live," Gorbachev replied.

I believed he meant it, but I don't know whether everyone on Gorbachev's side of the table, in the Central Committee and elsewhere, thought so.

Baker and Shevardnadze in Vienna

Arms control continued to be the main indicator of the status of U.S.-Soviet relations. Gorbachev wanted the bureaucracy to come up with our own proposals on START and conventional forces in Europe (CFE) so that whenever the Bush administration was ready we could hit the ground running. On CFE some important issues requiring a political decision awaited resolution; on START it was already more a matter of arcane technical details that were fully understood by only a few people on both sides. But work on the new proposals was proceeding rapidly, and I believe that most of them were ready in March and April. Gorbachev and Shevardnadze were set to go as soon as Bush and Secretary of State James Baker let them know they were ready. Shevardnadze and Baker met in Vienna at a Conference on Security and Cooperation in Europe (CSCE) meeting in March. It was not bad for a first meeting, but I could not help thinking that Vienna was somehow not a lucky city for U.S.-Soviet ministerials. The one between Shultz and Shevardnadze in 1986 was certainly quite discouraging.

This time both sides were careful to lower expectations. It was billed as just a get-acquainted meeting. Baker was not yet ready to deal on most issues, and Shevardnadze was willing to give him time. Their meeting was carefully orchestrated and warm, with both of them obviously determined to avoid any faux pas. But it worried me that the tone of their CSCE speeches was somewhat different.

Shevardnadze outlined a broad and long-term vision of the European process, leaving certain aspects vague. Baker's speech seemed more like a set of demands for very specific steps on the part of the Soviet Union and its allies—with a clearly stated goal, a kind of central and all-embracing demand: an end to the division of Europe, a Europe whole and free, as Baker put it. I was sure by that time that Gorbachev and Shevardnadze accepted that goal; certainly it was more than consistent with Gorbachev's call in his U.N. speech for an "integrated global civilization." But it is always more difficult to accept explicitly what sounds like an imperious demand. The way it was phrased, I don't think Baker's speech in Vienna helped Gorbachev and Shevardnadze in the internal Soviet debate.

Working with the Baker and Shultz Teams

As I watched Baker in Vienna and later in Moscow, I was inevitably drawn to assess him as a person and as Shevardnadze's counterpart, and to compare him with George Shultz. The press too was full of assessments and comparisons, but I honestly thought I had a better view.

Temperamentally, Baker was obviously tough, unsentimental, and vigorous. He was smart, attentive, and had a good reaction. Where Shultz sometimes seemed to be content to work on the broad framework and let some things stand and work themselves out later, Baker wanted to grasp every detail and go at it, if he could, immediately. Baker was also more inclined to rely on prepared formulas and to use his briefs almost verbatim. In Vienna and afterward, he seemed to be more dependent than Shultz on his close circle of advisers. He also trusted them more, and they seemed attached to him in a very personal way.

I later developed a good relationship with Dennis Ross and Margaret Tutwiler. Those two and Bob Zoellick were ready to go to bat for Baker any time; they played an important part in his subsequent success. Ross and Tarasenko soon became friends, and that too helped at some difficult moments. Neither they nor their bosses ever said anything to each other that they knew to be untrue.

Among the people who accompanied Baker to his first meeting with Shevardnadze and Gorbachev, there were few holdovers from the old Shultz team. One was Roz Ridgway, a tough but fair negotiator. Baker called on her a couple of times to explain the intricacies of the U.S. position on short-range missiles planned for deployment in Europe. It was a nasty issue, potentially extremely harmful to Gorbachev, and Ridgway seemed uncomfortable reciting the U.S. line, either because she had doubts about it or because of the tensions that were brewing between members of the outgoing State Department team and the incoming people.

New Proposals on START and CFE

When the Bush administration finally announced the end of the pause we felt great relief. As expected, the reassessment did not produce any revelations. It was said that one result was Bush's decision to emphasize CFE at the expense of START. Some in the Soviet Union attached great importance to that and even saw something sinister behind it, whether or not there really was a change of emphasis. I took a different view. I believed that for all intents and purposes the START treaty was already working. The ceilings and sublimits agreed to in Reykjavik in 1986 and fleshed out in Washington in 1987 were there, and they were tacitly observed by both sides. The numerous details regarding verification and some less central weapons systems could be worked out in four months, or four years, but did not seem to be of much strategic importance.

My remark that the treaty was already working struck some as going too far, but my opponents found it difficult to refute that or to prove the strategic importance of the remaining issues. In fact, many were openly beginning to doubt the importance of START and arms control as a whole. Against the background of our deteriorating economy and ideological confusion, extreme views were expressed openly on the question of whether we needed significant strategic nuclear forces. An article in the leading liberal newspaper, *Moscow News*, by an academic expert and a former KGB official, called for cutting Soviet strategic nuclear forces to 5 percent of their current level.

That kind of talk was meaningless and dangerous, I thought. It was "the red cloth"—a needless irritant to our military and also a cavalier approach to what had been built at tremendous cost to the country and its people. This kind of investment should not be written off lightly. When the dust settled, it could be of strategic value not only to the Soviet Union but also to the world, I said to an American friend of mine around that time. I still hold that view. I also believed then and believe now that our strategic forces should be reduced as rapidly as technically possible to a level of reasonable sufficiency—perhaps 20 or 30 percent of the current level. With the changes that have now taken place, we could move toward this goal quite rapidly.

The new proposals on START and CFE were approved by the interagency "group of five"—including Shevardnadze, Vladimir Kryuchkov, Dmitry Yazov, Oleg Baklanov (the Central Committee secretary in charge of the defense industry), and Yury Maslyukov (deputy prime minister in charge of defense industry)—in time for Baker's visit. Later, when the military and their advocates in the Soviet media screamed about the arms control treaties, calling them unequal and accusing Shevardnadze of betrayal, he countered with the argument that all Soviet positions in the talks had gone through the "group of five" process, in which the military played an active and often decisive part.

As I followed that process from the vantage point of the foreign ministry, I noticed that the defense ministry was often more accommodating than the representatives of the defense industry—the Council of Ministers military-industrial commission. In the end, the necessary decisions were as a rule made by Yury Maslyukov, the commission's chairman and a man whose outlook was broader than that of many of his colleagues. In 1988 he was appointed chairman of Gosplan, the State Planning Committee, and Baklanov began to play a more important role in the interagency process. He too normally agreed with the decisions hammered out by the experts, but afterward often complained privately that we had caved in.

Baker and Shevardnadze Talk in Moscow

The Soviet proposals prepared for Secretary of State Baker's first Moscow visit, May 1989, were perhaps not revolutionary but certainly far-reaching enough to push the negotiating process forward. Shevardnadze looked quite confident and relaxed as his talks with Baker began. Baker suggested that the four-part U.S.-Soviet agenda, including arms control, regional issues, human rights, and bilateral relations, be broadened to include discussion of "transnational problems," such as the environment, global warming, and drug trafficking. After several months of foreign policy reassessment, such a proposal did not sound like much, but it did no harm.

Shevardnadze had his own proposal: to discuss, at the foreign minister level, internal developments in both countries. In effect that signaled a readiness to be even more open and frank than before about our domestic affairs, which he knew would become more and more difficult. He also indicated that the Soviet Union was ready to move faster on the remaining regional issues now that the withdrawal from Afghanistan had been completed. Baker, like Bush a few months before in New York, emphasized Central America. The U.S. mistrust of Soviet intentions in various regions was still strong, and Central America was a case in point. But some other irritants were disappearing, and the general tenor of the talks was good.

A "Bumpy" Meeting on Arms Control and Domestic Issues

Gorbachev's meeting with Baker in the Kremlin was bumpy. Who knows what cable or "analytical paper" had landed on his desk before that talk? It was probably something about the debate in the U.S. administration on policy toward the Soviet Union. National Security Adviser Brent Scowcroft, Defense Secretary Richard Cheney, and Robert Gates were portrayed in the press and in most of the cables and papers as the ones who most distrusted Gorbachev. Gates was on Baker's team in Moscow. Whatever Baker's intention was in bringing him to the Kremlin to sit in on the meeting with Gorbachev, the effect was not good.

Gorbachev began to comment at length on some Central Intelligence Agency report about the Soviet Union that questioned his intentions. He challenged Gates to deny that the administration wanted to take advantage of problems inside the Soviet Union to improve its global position at Soviet expense. Gates's cold and unsympathetic manner, not so much his actual answers, obviously irritated Gorbachev. For a while I thought we were in for a replay of the October 1987 incident, when a meeting between Shultz and the general secretary ended on a sour note, but fortunately that did not happen. Gorbachev regained his composure and went on to explain to Baker and his team the new Soviet arms control proposals, which seemed to impress the Americans.

One matter was quite vexing to the Soviet leaders: the issue of U.S. "modernization" of short-range tactical missiles to be deployed in Europe. Although their range was a little below the 500 kilometers that would have made them illegal under the INF treaty, the Soviet Union had just destroyed missiles of a similar range, and deployment of such missiles by the United States would have been a huge embarrassment to Gorbachev.

The Soviet Union proposed negotiations on tactical nuclear weapons, during which the United States would have suspended the modernization. Baker called the proposal attractive politically but said the United States had to go ahead with the new missiles because the Soviet Union had overall superiority in tactical nuclear weapons. He cited SS-21 missiles and modernized nuclear artillery and said the U.S. needed a minimum number of nuclear weapons in Europe for its "flexible response" strategy.

The elimination of INF missiles had clearly undermined the credibility of that strategy and made the talk of "coupling," "graduated response," and so on less convincing than before. Did Baker understand that Gorbachev's credibility with the military was at stake? Did he know that discontent with Gorbachev's policies was already brewing? Did he want to show a tougher line, in contrast to that of Reagan's final year, after the "strategic review"? Whatever it was, the unwillingness or inability of our U.S. partners to fully understand all the implications of the issue for Gorbachev and Shevardnadze was deeply troubling to me. It was only a year later, when German unification created much more severe problems for Gorbachev, that the West abandoned the modernization plan.

In the discussion of Soviet domestic developments, Baker sounded quite encouraging, calling the changes in the country dramatic and revolutionary. "We very much want your plans to succeed," he said, "and there is no one in the administration who would want you to fail. The success of perestroika would make the Soviet Union a stronger, more stable, open, and secure country," Baker added, clearly implying that he saw nothing wrong with that.

It is up to the Soviet Union—the Soviet leaders and the Soviet people—to make perestroika succeed, Baker said, not the West, whatever the West does or does not do. He was, however, ready to give advice. He said that it is better to make tough economic decisions, such as changing the price system, sooner rather than later. It is better to do it when people tend to blame the previous administration for whatever hardship they have to go through, he added, looking at Gorbachev.

Gorbachev remarked, "We are already twenty years late so far as price reform is concerned, so another couple of years do not make much difference." He was soon proven wrong, of course. Baker did not belabor the point. As someone who was U.S. treasury secretary for more than three years and dealt with the International Monetary Fund, he said, he knew that the political leaders of a country know better what they can afford politically. Baker also had a private talk with Gorbachev, with only Shevardnadze, Chernyaev, and Dennis Ross present, and it was a good talk—not warm yet, but friendly and cordial.

Baker and Shevardnadze Begin a Friendship

On the last evening of Baker's stay in Moscow, Shevardnadze invited him to his apartment at Plotnikov Pereulok, right behind the foreign ministry building. He had already come down to welcome Baker when the U.S. embassy called to say, with apologies, that the secretary would be perhaps ten or fifteen minutes late. It was a nice—warm and clear—evening in mid-May, probably the best time to be in Moscow. Shevardnadze and I walked in the backyard of his apartment building for about half an hour (the Americans called again to apologize for another delay). We talked about the visit, about Gorbachev's upcoming trip to China, and about the elections of the people's deputies.

Shevardnadze was quite well informed about domestic developments and was worried about the situation in the republics. He knew some of the leaders of the Baltic republics from his Komsomol years. They were reasonable people, he said, and if handled reasonably the situation there would calm down. The Baltics were not the place where nationalism would turn violent, he was certain, but he was worried about nationalism—which he believed could be particularly dangerous if the Russians were to support extreme nationalists, such as the group "Pamyat." I said I did not think Pamyat would get much support. Even a milder nationalist candidate did badly in a constituency near Moscow where my mother voted, I told him.

The only way to address all the problems is to go ahead with the democratic process, Shevardnadze said, and I felt that those words came earnestly and sincerely. After this episode my talks with Shevardnadze about all kinds of things became more frequent and frank. I soon noticed that, even though he was much older than I, he was sometimes more realistic, imaginative, and bold in his remarks. His thinking was evolving rapidly in those months.

Baker finally arrived, the two men went to dinner, and that was the beginning of a personal relationship that soon became a real bond of friendship. They talked about some aspects of U.S.-Soviet relations in light of what had been agreed during the visit, but mostly about other things that do not normally come up for discussion between diplomats.

Shevardnadze told Baker about his Middle East trip and his talk with the Ayatollah. He talked about his youth in Georgia in the World War II years. He spoke about the country's postwar development and the drama of those years. "The country was lying in ruins," he said. "We had to rebuild it, and at the same time we were developing the nuclear bomb and ballistic missiles. Undertaking such tremendous industrial and scientific projects in a wartorn country meant that all the country's resources had to be concentrated on them. People were left with very little, and a more democratic economic and political system was probably impossible then. But soon afterward the country was ready for democratic reforms, and we should have begun them years and even decades ago. Well, we are beginning now, and it won't be easy."

I saw that Shevardnadze's remarks impressed Baker, who talked about his years in business and in the Reagan government, and then told Shevardnadze about his youth and about a Russian-born teacher of history who had influenced him greatly as a student. Like most Americans, he seemed fascinated with the Russian soul, and he was fascinated with Shevardnadze. Baker was a cool and sober-minded politician and negotiator, but he was not a cold man, and later I saw many times that he had genuine personal sympathy for Gorbachev and Shevardnadze, two men with whom he spent more time than any other American. They went through a lot together.

Gorbachev's Trip to China

Gorbachev's last remaining foreign commitment before the first session of the newly elected Congress of People's Deputies was his trip to China. In a way, he was rounding off his foreign policy agenda before concentrating on internal affairs, which everyone was saying he should have done earlier. They were right, but only up to a point, I felt. What would an emphasis on internal affairs have meant for a country that had no democratic institutions in place yet? Probably another campaign like the one against drinking, another round of exhortations for greater order and discipline, another attempt to get a little more mileage out of the old economic system. But that was a dead end. And could Gorbachev or anyone else accomplish something domestically if things continued as before internationally? With relations with the U.S. frozen or deteriorating, the military-industrial complex would probably have foisted on the country more costly arms programs, and without glasnost and a new international atmosphere, there would be no way to challenge that.

By mid-1989 Gorbachev's international achievements, completed by his trip to China, were impressive by any standards. A country that four years earlier was at loggerheads with just about everyone, including the entire "big league," was now genuinely at peace, with no Soviet soldiers fighting abroad. Its relations with almost all countries were good and getting better.

It was spring in China when Gorbachev arrived, the Peking spring that had begun a few weeks before with student demonstrations for democracy and human rights. The demonstrations were now in full swing, and they created all kinds of problems for Gorbachev's visit—logistical but, above all, political problems. The students were demanding greater freedom and democracy, and Gorbachev was of course sympathetic to their demands. They asked for a meeting with him and showed their admiration, but Gorbachev was well aware that the demonstrators were straining the patience of his Chinese hosts. Some of the students were carrying signs with slogans against Deng Xiao-ping, which was their biggest mistake. Once again Gorbachev had to tread a fine line.

I worked on the translations of his public speeches, which were published as press releases, but that was about all the workload for me on that visit—much lighter than during Gorbachev's trips to English-speaking countries. That left me with enough time to watch the developments and talk about them with embassy staff, among whom I had several friends. They all welcomed normalizing relations with China, but had different views about future prospects for our relations with China and about the current developments in that country.

The dividing line among the diplomats seemed quite clear, and it was generational. The younger ones were more or less sympathetic to the students, while senior officials, with the exception of the ever-prudent Ambassador Oleg Troyanovsky, expressed their disapproval of them. All agreed that the students' specific demands were vague and that the time for full democracy had probably not yet come. And no one ventured to predict how the crisis would end. The demonstrations were expanding even as Gorbachev's visit continued. As his motorcade went from the government residence to various appointments, the route often had to be changed. The pivotal meeting with Deng in the Great Hall of the People coincided with a huge rally in the adjoining Tiananmen Square; the noise and the chanting were heard in the spacious rooms where we waited for the meeting to end. It sealed Soviet-Chinese normalization after decades of estrangement. But with all the turmoil around, the appropriate sense of triumph was somehow lacking.

The students continued to demand a meeting with Gorbachev. The Chinese officials indicated that the choice was up to the Soviet leader, but their attitude was clear—they did not like the idea. Gorbachev finally decided to invite some student representatives to attend his address to a large group of Chinese intellectuals. He navigated through his visit in his usual style, while the reporters were trying to draw him out and get him to talk more candidly. They accompanied him on an excursion to the Great Wall of China, rushing after him with their cameras, tape recorders, and other equipment. They asked the questions that might be expected, hinting at the parallel between the Great Wall and the Wall in Berlin. "Do you think the Berlin Wall will one day disappear?" an American reporter asked.

Even such a liberal as foreign ministry spokesman Gennady Gerasimov was surprised at Gorbachev's answer, which went something like this: "We must work to improve the international atmosphere, and I hope that would create conditions when all unneeded walls would disappear." The implication was unmistakable, and it was quite different from what the East German leaders were saying—that the Wall would continue to stand for a hundred years.

Gorbachev's final press conference was to be held in the Great Hall of the People. Gerasimov, I, and our Chinese-language interpreter left the residence well in advance of the motorcade to come to the Hall before it and check the arrangements and the equipment. As we came closer to the center of the town the sea of demonstrators seemed to be engulfing every street. "Look," our interpreter said, "there is a sign indicating that this group of demonstrators is from the government information agency and the Central Committee's propaganda department." It really was amazing.

We were starting to worry whether we would reach our destination. One street after another appeared to be impassable, and our driver, though calm, was clearly at a loss. For the first time I saw the imperturable Gerasimov losing his cool. "Well, do something, say something to the driver," he shouted at the interpreter. "We can't be late for this." We even considered walking the remaining distance, but our driver, who did not say much in response, ended up by finding a way.

When we came to the Great Hall, however, Gerasimov was told that for security reasons the press conference was to be held at Gorbachev's residence, "shortly." Apparently, the decision had been made moments before, and they were informing the press of it. We were not sure we would make it, but we rushed to our car to get back. The rescheduled press conference started an hour later, and after a bumpy and noisy ride we were there on time.

Of the questions Gorbachev had to answer at that press conference, I remember one vividly. He was asked whether in times of change violence and the use of force, as had happened in Tbilisi and might happen in Peking, was inevitable. He answered that his policy was aimed at avoiding the use of force, and that he hoped the Chinese leaders wanted to resolve problems peacefully. It was probably the best answer under the circumstances. But as we were leaving Peking, the demonstrations were growing and getting more chaotic. I was going to the airport in the same car with Deputy Foreign Minister Igor Rogachev, an old acquaintance. The sirens of ambulances filled the air; the crowds seemed to be all around us, and groups of people were running in an unknown direction. There was a sense not only of alarm but also of doomed fearlessness. Rogachev noted the increasing number of anti-Deng slogans.

In Moscow, colleagues asked my impressions of the visit and of the situation in Peking. I remember a long conversation with a colleague on the U.S. desk who sometimes shared with me interpretation duties during Gorbachev's visits abroad. I told him that I thought the students were pushing it too far without quite knowing what they really wanted, but that Deng probably would like to avoid the use of force. Still, I said, I worried that it could all end very badly quite soon.

We both remembered that talk when a few days later we were watching CNN news reports of tanks and carnage in the streets of Peking. An American reporter I knew, who had just returned from Peking, said to me, "I think there can be no peaceful democratic reform in socialist countries. It just had to end this way." She hinted that her conclusion applied to the Soviet Union too.

Andrey Sakharov denounced the Peking killings immediately and vehemently. And who would have disagreed that they were abhorrent? But Gorbachev was in an awkward position. Issuing a public condemnation right after the long-awaited normalization of relations with China might have undermined one of his most important achievements. Both for him and for Shevardnadze it was a real quandary.

Even later, Shevardnadze, whose abhorrence of the use of force was then nearly absolute, refused to be drawn into denunciations of the Chinese government when some of his colleagues asked him leading questions about the Tiananmen Square massacre. "It is a terrible tragedy, and everything possible should have been done to avoid it," he said to one of his African counterparts several months later, "but I know that the Chinese government could not afford chaos and destabilization in their vast country."

Reluctantly, I had to agree with that. I also believed that things were never as simple as Sakharov sometimes seemed to believe. The dilemma of choosing between instability and chaos, on the one hand, and continuing change and reforms, on the other, would haunt Gorbachev, as it will probably haunt the new generations of reformers in my country.

Seven
STORMY WEATHER
1 9 8 9

The First Congress and the Transition to Democracy

On the eve of the first Congress of People's Deputies of the Soviet Union, no one knew whether it would really mark the beginning of a transition to democracy. Many were doubtful, saying that the old system would reassert itself behind the facade of a parliament elected in a less than perfectly democratic manner. I think that concern was behind the behavior of the more-radical deputies, who used the Congress to begin an aggressive push for change without much regard for the need to maintain at least some stability in the vast country.

On May 25 we were glued to our television sets watching the live broadcast of the first Congress. The carefully prepared script of the proceedings went wrong in the very first minutes, when a delegate from Riga called for a minute of silence in memory of those killed in Tbilisi, and for an investigation and punishment of those responsible. When the speeches began, only a few were in the old mold; some others were cautious; still others were openly defiant of the system. A few, like the speech of former weightlifter turned democratic political activist Yury Vlasov, were in my view extremely unfair to Gorbachev personally. The great "national disobedience day" was beginning.

A country starved for freedom of expression was finally beginning to understand that it need not fear: you could speak critically and irreverently, you could even offend the country's leader. Many really enjoyed it. There were not too many speeches that discussed the real problems of the country's sputtering economy and the need for a radical market-oriented economic reform. Premier Nikolay Ryzhkov stated in his report that the government did not agree with the economists who believed that taking dramatic steps toward a free market was the answer to the country's problems. Instead, he favored a slower transition. To my regret, this did not become the subject of a great debate at the Congress. The big and noisy arguments were about other things that, I thought, were less relevant.

In June, a few days before the Congress was due to end, there was a terrible railway accident in Bashkiria. A cloud of natural gas from a ruptured pipeline caused a powerful explosion when two passenger trains were passing at the same time near the pipeline. Hundreds of people were killed in what was the deadliest such accident in the Soviet Union's history. In the overall atmosphere of excitement and unease caused by the Congress, this tragedy traumatized the nation. The Congress was interrupted, and Gorbachev went to the scene. Many people thought he should also cancel a trip to West Germany scheduled a few days after the Congress. Some saw the disaster as a bad omen, a premonition of things to come.

The Heated Phase Begins

Overall, it was clear that the first democratically elected Congress had not cooled the passions or put developments on a smooth track. The heated phase was far from over; it was only beginning. The republics were demanding greater sovereignty, but it was not yet the war cry it became a year later. Everyone still seemed to regard the problem as one of "interethnic relations," which was indeed how it had started. But now a new specter was looming. It was becoming increasingly clear that political activists and increasing numbers of local people in the Baltic republics, particularly in Lithuania, wanted not just real sovereignty within the Soviet Union but independence, a secession from it. To many, it was a shock. It had to be a shock to the Party Politburo, and the process of accepting or rejecting that reality was painful and full of conflicts. I think few in Russia were then ready to take a stand one way or another; the conflict was often in the individual's mind. At least that's how I felt.

In July, a few weeks after the Congress, the coal miners' strikes were shaking the country, which also came as a tremendous shock to the Soviet Union's leaders, who had hoped the working class would continue to show patience. That was not to be. The Congress had heated up the mood of the workers too. Doubts whether the whole experiment with glasnost and democracy was worth it were being expressed openly. Some, and not just the conservatives, were saying that it had been a mistake to convene the Congress. An article by leading political scientists Igor Klyamkin and Andranik Migranyan made quite a splash. They argued that a direct transition from totalitarianism to democracy was impossible and that there should be an authoritarian phase in between. It sounded like a suggestion for Gorbachev, but they did not make any specific recommendations.

As the strikes were expanding and beginning to look more threatening, Gorbachev's old friend Rajiv Gandhi came to Moscow on a short and apparently routine visit. Gorbachev had talks and a long private lunch with him. Much of what he was saying looked like an answer to those who were calling for a more authoritarian approach. It might look plausible and even attractive on the surface, he argued, but in Russia democracy had never really been tried, and if it was not tried now, when? It was easy to call vaguely for stronger rule, but what specifically did the word "authoritarian" mean? In Russia it always meant suppressing democracy and denying people freedom of expression. Once you started doing that, Gorbachev said, where do you stop? He defended this line of reasoning passionately, as if debating with someone.

A few days later Shevardnadze was talking to James Baker in Paris, where they both were to attend the opening of the conference on Cambodian settlement. He said that although things were difficult the democratic process was under way. It was bringing to the fore new people who were honest and had pure intentions—for instance, in the new Supreme Soviet and among the striking miners. He hoped the democratic process would channel their energies in the right direction.

Debate over Party Unity and Alternative Platforms

I agreed, but I had my doubts. At a party meeting in the foreign ministry, I said that a democratic political process required clearly formulated, differing positions on various issues, and that this could be done only by political groups or movements. I suggested once again that the party should allow factions to form within itself to generate alternative platforms and positions on the issues. Otherwise, I said, it would be disorganized and everyone for himself: miners would demand more money, the intelligentsia would demand more freedom, the man-in-the-street would demand "order," and the party apparat would say that things should have been left the way they used to be. I didn't say so, but I thought that developing an alternative platform within the party would lead to the emergence of a new, perhaps social-democratic political party, and subsequently to a two-party system in the Soviet Union.

Much later, Anatoly Chernyaev told me that at about the same time Alexander Yakovlev had suggested to Gorbachev a similar approach. He thought that 15 percent of the party's members would go with him and in effect create an alternative democratic movement. Gorbachev discouraged Yakovlev from doing so. He had a different idea: he wanted the whole party to evolve in the reformist direction. This may have been one of his biggest mistakes in the years of perestroika, but the tactic did not seem implausible then. What's more, he did not want to take responsibility for "breaking up the Party."

Reluctantly, I would instead have to fault Yakovlev in that episode. He was a good man, and his ideas and suggestions were always fresh and interesting. Of all the leaders of the party, he was the most ready to break with the dogmas of Stalinism. But he was not a man of action. He could have insisted, he could have just gone ahead and done what Gorbachev did not want him to do. Instead, he continued, as late as 1990, to defend in press interviews the dogma of party unity, which I think misled many people. The alternative platforms inevitably began to emerge at about that time, but they were supported by well-intentioned political lightweights who could not assume leadership of the entire democratic movement, which left it rudderless and often misguided.

The democrats at that time were a curious and very mixed bunch of people. What united them was their discontent with the way things were. Most of them were populists who tended to expect an easy solution to every problem. They liked to demand "radical steps" and "specific measures." Frankly, I doubted the commitment of many of them to democracy. The frail Dr. Sakharov was of course beyond suspicion in that regard, but why should I believe the democratic credentials of government prosecutors, former KGB generals, nationalistic orators, old and new party apparatchiks, professors of Marxism-Leninism, and "doctors of agricultural sciences"? Their chorus sounded bizarre—a song of protest at best, often cacophony without much meaning.

But like most people of my generation and background, I wanted the democratic process to continue despite its deficiencies. There were a few conservatives among my colleagues at the U.S. desk, even among the younger ones. As for the older generations, some were going through painful soul-searching, others were cynically ready to serve any policy, and still others were waiting for a change in direction, thinking that Gorbachev would not last long.

Positive Signals from the Americans

The Americans too were watching our developments. Baker's meeting with Shevardnadze seemed to point to the possibility of more rapid movement on arms control and bilateral relations, but the debate in the administration was clearly not yet over. The signals from President George Bush were positive, though, and Gorbachev decided it was time to have a very private and in-depth discussion with him.

I was on annual leave in late July, spending it with my family at my mother's place near Moscow, when I got a call from the office of then Deputy Foreign Minister Alexander Bessmertnykh. He was sending a car to take me to the foreign ministry to help him with something urgent and sensitive, his assistant told me. I was intrigued, but not too much. I had been in this business long enough to guess that it was either a letter from Bush to Gorbachev, or one from Gorbachev to Bush. Another possibility was an urgent phone call. What I wondered about was the substance. Nothing particularly special seemed to be happening. It was a lull—a lull before the storm, as it turned out soon afterward.

Bessmertnykh told me he was going to Washington on a sensitive mission of which few people were aware. Gorbachev and Bush were exchanging messages of a very positive nature. He gave me for translation Gorbachev's letter to President Bush about a "nonsummit" in some secluded place— without protocol formalities, a large retinue of aides, or a fixed agenda.

The idea, initially suggested by Bush, struck me as a good one, but unfortunately, as I saw later, it is almost impossible to implement. No protocol formalities? The meeting at Malta, which resulted from this idea, was indeed relatively free of formalities, but even during the state visits nonsubstantive events had already been cut down to a minimum. A secluded place? There can be no such place when heads of state meet. Few aides? This also turned out to be a very elastic formula.

As for "no fixed agenda," that part worked well. The discussions in Malta were free-flowing, mostly philosophical, and helpful in building trust on the eve of—indeed, in the midst of—revolutionary changes in the world. But in that sense too they did not fully meet my expectations. That, though, was several months later.

The East Europeans Go Their Own Way

In the meantime I was ending my vacation near Moscow. August is not a month when there is much news of any kind. One thing was happening, however, that was the beginning and a sign of something much bigger. Thousands of East Germans were crossing the newly opened border between Hungary and Austria to go on to West Germany. The Honnecker government was furious, and helpless.

One of the Soviet ambassadors cabled to Moscow his view that the Hungarians had presented Helmut Kohl with "a royal gift." He stated that the Berlin Wall was the only way to maintain stability in the GDR for the foreseeable future. The East German leaders wanted an outer wall too. They asked Gorbachev to intervene with the Hungarians to get them to stop the flow somehow. He declined. This was the second important specific decision he made regarding freedom of choice for Eastern Europe. A few months before, he had indicated to Polish Prime Minister Mieczyslaw Rakowski that the Polish government should seek agreement with Solidarity rather than try to end the strikes by using force, as some were prepared to do. When I learned of that, I truly appreciated Gorbachev's political courage.

Letting the East Europeans go was perhaps the most difficult decision in the years of perestroika. Of course I fully supported it. But I belonged to a younger generation. I had friends in Eastern Europe, and I knew that culturally and psychologically they did not belong in the quasi-Soviet system. But even many people my age were doubtful that Eastern Europe could just be allowed to go its own way. What about our security? And, some said, we won the war and there were millions of our soldiers buried in the soil of Eastern Europe. Had that been in vain?

The fear was deep and in many ways irrational, but it was there. It became stronger when German unification began to unfold at a pace more rapid than anyone could have expected. This is what the Soviet leaders faced as they made their momentous decisions regarding Eastern Europe. But there was more. Their own Communist past, and present. They had been reared within the system and by the system. I don't think that in 1989 they had already severed the ideological umbilical cord of adherence to the system. It was, at the very least, a part of their lives that they never fully negated. And like most of us, they could not just close their eyes to the security aspect of the problem. It had to be troubling.

Finally, they could not but feel that their decision would carry a domestic political risk: the military would find it difficult to accept its consequences and larger implications, and the psychological trauma for the older generations of Soviets could not be ignored. Yet the decision to "release" Eastern Europe was made, and they did not go back on it when the full implications became clear.

Was that a victory for the West? Perhaps. But even more, it was a victory of Gorbachev and his supporters over themselves, over the past in themselves—the most difficult victory anyone can achieve. I do not believe that the coming generation of leaders will ever have to make decisions of such magnitude or such agonizing difficulty.

Baker and Shevardnadze Talk at Jackson Hole

In September Shevardnadze was preparing to go to the United States for an unusual trip. Secretary of State James Baker had invited him to hold their full-scale ministerial meeting in Wyoming at the mountain resort of Jackson Hole. They had already decided to meet sometimes outside the capitals, starting a tradition that was repeated only once, in Irkutsk and at Lake Baikal. But before Wyoming, Shevardnadze went to Washington to discuss with President Bush the idea for an informal summit. By that time Shevardnadze had become a hit in America. People recognized him and waved to him in the streets. But his smile was often interrupted by an expression of concern and even alarm. Things were beginning to move fast, and that had to be unsettling.

At their White House meeting Bush was very friendly. He seemed to understand the problems the Soviet leaders were facing in adjusting to the developments. He said he liked the idea of a "nonsummit," which resulted in the meeting at Malta, and asked whether the Soviet side would find it awkward if it were held on a Navy ship or ships. Shevardnadze could not give a final answer, but he said that he personally saw no difficulty with that. They agreed to work on the idea and on the date of the meeting quietly. In the meantime, there was much work to be done on the substantive issues.

Meanwhile, Baker's invitation to Wyoming took us to a mountain hotel right in the Grand Teton National Park. It was the end of the tourist season, and the large group of U.S. and Soviet diplomats and experts descended on an almost deserted hotel surrounded by the eternally silent lakes and mountains. The view from my cottage was breathtaking. The Tetons illuminated by the colors of a fall sunrise are a sight I shall never forget. The moose and Rocky Mountain elk completed the picture, and the coyote calls were sometimes heard. Everyone was saying that they would like one day to return to Jackson Hole for a vacation. Meanwhile, it was back to arms control and other issues.

Shevardnadze brought to Jackson Hole a new Soviet position on START and ABM. It was a position I had been waiting and working for. It had been quite clear for some time that our insistence on the formal linkage between the two arms control areas—offensive and defensive strategic arms—had become counterproductive. The position calling for "nonwithdrawal" from the ABM treaty for a specific period of time was even more so. In fact, the hardliners on the U.S. side, who were looking for a way to kill the ABM treaty and develop space-based SDI without any restrictions, were exploiting that position to achieve a result quite opposite to our intentions: the end of the nonwithdrawal period, they suggested, would mean that both sides were henceforth free from their obligations under the treaty. In memos to Shevardnadze and Bessmertnykh, and in conversations with Karpov, Tarasenko, and others, I had argued that both positions should be dropped. They all seemed sympathetic to my view, but it was difficult to change an established, Politburo-approved position.

At last, in September 1989, we had a new position, similar to what we and the U.S. embassy officials had discussed informally in Moscow two years before. Now that the Americans had agreed that START-1 would not require the destruction of Soviet heavy missiles, which our military valued as a possible counterweight to SDI, the unlinking of START and ABM made even more sense for us. True, Shevardnadze added that we would consider violation of the ABM treaty sufficient ground to withdraw from START, but that would be formalized in a unilateral statement rather than an article of the treaty itself.

The Americans seemed surprised at the change in our position. "Are you delinking ABM and START?" Richard Burt, the chief U.S. negotiator in the Geneva talks, asked as the two delegations sat facing each other in a small conference room at the Jackson Hotel. Baker repeated the question. The answer was yes. Should it have been done earlier? And would it have meant that the START treaty might have been signed in 1988, before the change of administration in Washington? It is one of those questions for which I have no answer.

Baker and Shevardnadze Discuss a Free Market Economy

The talks on other issues went reasonably well. Eastern Europe was not discussed at any length; the two ministers were obviously leaving that hot potato to their presidents. But on the plane to Wyoming there was an interesting discussion of economic reforms in the Soviet Union. Baker and Shevardnadze had agreed they would talk about internal developments, and they did.

To help him talk on the Soviet economy, Shevardnadze brought with him Nikolay Shmelyov, an academic free-market economist who became popular in the Soviet Union following several smart articles and televised speeches on the need to radically change our economic system. We all remembered Shmelyov's words at the Congress of People's Deputies: "This country has tried everything to make the economy work, including concentration camps, but it has never tried a free market, which is how the entire civilized world lives. So we shall inevitably have a free market one day. The question is how to get there."

That was precisely the question. And I was not sure Shmelyov had the answer. Like other academic experts, he did not know the existing system of production too well, and therefore tended to propose remedies that looked good only at first sight. And no one seemed to have an answer to the question of how much the real market reforms would hurt an ordinary citizen and how much pain would he or she be ready to accept. But so far as the concept of the reform was concerned, Shmelyov and Baker understood each other well.

Baker recommended steps to soak up excess money in order to stabilize the consumer market, rapid introduction of a price system based on supply and demand, and privatization, among other measures, to end the monopoly of the state in the economy. Compared with what some of our increasingly radical economists were saying just a few months later, this was a moderate program. Of course, Baker did not say he knew the answers to various specific questions, or that he knew how to push the changes through the entrenched system. "It is up to you to make the specific decisions," he kept saying. "We can only suggest."

Talks with Baker on Interethnic Relations, the Republics, and the Baltics

Another theme Baker and Shevardnadze discussed on the plane and later was interethnic relations in the Soviet Union, relations between the center and the republics, and the Baltic issue. Those were sensitive issues, but Shevardnadze was well qualified to discuss them. It seemed to me that Baker's main interest was clarifying the Soviet leaders' intentions on the Baltic issue. He also wanted Shevardnadze to understand the U.S. position, arguing that it was not aimed at undermining Gorbachev. By September 1989 Baker had come to trust Shevardnadze enough to believe the main point the foreign minister was making: that the leaders of the Soviet Union wanted to preserve the unity of the country but would seek to do it by political methods in a democratic way.

Shevardnadze explained the idea of adopting a law on withdrawal of republics from the Union, which would create a mechanism for orderly secession—if a republic's intention to secede has been firmly established through a referendum. The idea was that this should be a lengthy process, which would give the republics time to create a viable economy that could survive separately from the Soviet Union or, alternatively, to change their mind and stay in the Union in some form, perhaps a loose association. The center's hope was that the second option would prevail in the end, but Gorbachev and Shevardnadze would be ready to accept the first choice too, provided the change was not too abrupt.

Two other options were being discussed by the leadership at that time, but the overall picture of that debate began to emerge only later. One was the possibility of opening up the entire problem of relations between the center and the republics by launching a process of negotiating a new Union treaty. This was first discussed seriously in 1988 but, Shevardnadze told us later, the idea was shot down by the conservatives in the Politburo supported particularly by regional party leaders in the Russian Federation. They argued that the process would not only be used by the Baltic republics to leave the Union, but also put the idea of secession into the heads of others and launch a similar process of disintegration in Russia. Subsequently, of course, the Union treaty process had to be initiated as the last hope for saving the Union—or for making its dissolution orderly. But it was too late.

The other possibility, which Anatoly Chernyaev later told me he favored, was letting the Baltic republics leave the Union quickly as soon as it became clear that their peoples insisted on seceding—and he said it became clear to him in August 1989, when there were massive popular demonstrations there denouncing the Molotov-Ribbentrop pact. That was certainly tempting, and it left the hope that the process would stop there, for the economic disadvantages of secession would probably become evident soon. It would also earn the goodwill of the West. But the domestic political consequences of such a strategy were difficult to predict, and they could well deal a deadly blow to Gorbachev. Also, no one could vouch that a chain reaction of secessions would not follow immediately. So, in retrospect, the Union treaty approach would probably have been preferable, though the process would have been extremely painful anyway, and its results unpredictable.

Baker Explains the U.S. Position on the Baltic Issue

Anyway, Baker listened quite receptively, it seemed to me, to the strategy outlined by Shevardnadze: giving the republics greater sovereignty and at the same time adopting legislation providing for orderly withdrawal. But there was also something that Shevardnadze wanted to find out from Baker. He asked questions about the intentions of the U.S. government. The U.S. position of refusing to recognize the incorporation of the Baltic states into the Soviet Union had survived the Second World War, the Cold War, détente, and perestroika. It was obviously something that could not be changed. But was it just an opening to help initiate the breakup of the Soviet Union? Many in the Soviet Union—certainly all conservatives and many foreign ministry officials—were extremely suspicious of U.S. intentions in that regard.

The Soviet Union, not only the conservatives but popular mentality as well, had not yet adjusted psychologically to the idea of Baltic secession, and many believed it should be prevented at any cost. Traditionally, the U.S. position had been described as interference, unacceptable nonsense, and worse. Explaining it to most members of the Politburo then as anything other than that was an exercise in futility. It later seemed to me from some of their remarks that Bush and Baker regarded that position as something of a burden, to the extent that they feared the Baltic problem might trigger events leading to Gorbachev's ouster and a return to the past. Subsequent events showed that such a fear was not unfounded.

In Wyoming, Baker was careful to explain that the administration regarded the Baltic republics as a special case. It did not recognize their incorporation, and had always said so, but it was aware of the problems that this position — and the Baltic issue more generally — created for Gorbachev. It did not want to aggravate those problems, Baker assured Shevardnadze. It would like to see some kind of mechanism that would make it possible for the Baltics to leave the Union in an orderly way and to preserve economic ties with the Soviet Union.

Three more countries like Finland as neighbors to the Soviet Union would be much better for everyone, including the Soviet Union, than keeping those republics attached despite their will, Baker said. He added that the administration would understand if the Soviet government continued to express its preference for a different outcome, but it ought not to be imposed by force. That, Bush indicated, would destroy much of the new U.S.-Soviet relationship. In the meantime, the administration would try to steer a prudent course and would not push the process with any special eagerness. Baker did not say that in so many words, but he left me with the clear impression that that was what he meant.

Shevardnadze seemed to believe Baker. He was aware of differing views on the Baltic issue within the U.S. government, but he trusted Baker's good intentions. The two men were in agreement about the basic course of the relationship: from confrontation, which had already become a thing of the past, to mutual understanding and cooperation, and eventually to partnership. And between the two of them it looked increasingly like friendship.

On the last day of the Wyoming ministerial meeting, Baker and Shevardnadze fished in Snake River. The fish in the river was cutthroat trout, and catching it required some mastery of the reel rod. Baker was an expert with many years of practice; Shevardnadze and I were novices. The park warden tried to teach us the ABCs of reel fishing but was not too successful; we had fun but no catch. Baker did much better, and the media emphasized it the next day.

History Just Beginning:
Germany and Eastern Europe

Shevardnadze returned to New York for his annual speech at the United Nations, the usual meetings with foreign ministers, and a speech and question-and-answer session at the Council on Foreign Relations, a prestigious New York group. East Germany was in turmoil, with the outflow of people continuing and getting worse. Probably the last remaining resort of the Honnecker government was to play on our security concerns, and they were doing it in a desperate way. In his talk with Shevardnadze the East German foreign minister raised the specter of "revanche," always a raw nerve with Soviet leaders and Soviet society. "What is happening negates the results of the war," the East German government was saying to us at every level.

Shevardnadze eventually included a warning against "revanchism" in his speech, but defending the East German regime in any way clearly made him uncomfortable. We all understood that their days were numbered. Finally, our "German experts" were saying that too—the same experts who had been confident of the regime's stability just a few months before.

On the eve of his departure Shevardnadze appeared at the Council on Foreign Relations and fielded questions expertly, like an old and cool pro. One question he promised to answer later was about Francis Fukuyama's article on "the end of history," which he had not yet read. We discussed the article on the plane that was taking us back to Moscow. Essentially, Fukuyama argued that history had centered on a conflict between liberal capitalism and revolutionary Marxism; now that revolutionary Marxism had lost any appeal globally, history as we knew it was ending and something different was beginning—something less cataclysmic, less interesting, and generally rather boring.

It was typical of Shevardnadze's open mind that he did not reject out of hand either the author's premise or his line of reasoning, even though he disagreed with the conclusion and said it could be that history was just beginning. I called Fukuyama's piece "a dream article"—an academic scholar could only dream of writing something that would not join the dusty rows of books and journals in the libraries but instead focus the debate and concentrate people's minds on a real problem. Shevardnadze agreed, and I heard him saying something similar to our scholars and scientists, with whom he continued to meet quite often.

In the final months of 1989 there was history galore, if by history one understands events that change people's lives in a fundamental way and for a long time to come. Honnecker invited Gorbachev to Berlin to attend the ceremonies marking the GDR's 40th anniversary. I was not there, but from what I saw and heard I could guess what kind of an experience it must have been for him. The agony of the East German regime was not a pretty sight. A torchlight parade of young people was organized, to show there was some loyalism left, but the youths shouted "Gorby! Gorby!"—which, translated from the East European of 1989, meant "freedom."

The crumbling of the "socialist camp" was quick and almost simultaneous in the GDR, Czechoslovakia, and Bulgaria. Hungary was moving toward a new system in a much smoother way. Romania was the only holdout, but that, I thought, could not last long. CNN was showing scenes of the "velvet revolution" in Prague, the end of the Berlin Wall, and the fall of Todor Zhivkov in Sofia. Soviet television was showing those scenes too. An era was ending. It was epitomized in vivid and effective television images, and this made the historic change more joyful for those who welcomed or accepted it, and more painful for those who rejected it.

Turmoil and Conflict

In the Soviet Union many people were confused and some were indifferent. The still powerful party apparat was scared; some quickly understood that it was their death knell too, others demanded that the collapse be stopped, and still others simply panicked and reacted with a kind of rhetorical flailing about. Amid all this, we were preparing for the Bush-Gorbachev meeting at Malta in December.

As Gorbachev was going to Malta to meet with Bush, the situation in the country was again heating up. On the anniversary of the Bolshevik Revolution, November 7, 1989, thousands of Muscovites demonstrated with slogans condemning the revolution and the Communist Party. The rift between Gorbachev and Yeltsin was growing, and with the economy deteriorating rapidly the people's sympathies were increasingly shifting toward Yeltsin and against Gorbachev. The coal miners were still unhappy: a long strike was under way in the northern coal-mining region of Vorkuta. And the Karabakh problem had expanded into an all-out conflict between Armenia and Azerbaijan.

Gorbachev believed all those problems could be dealt with through a democratic process, but that implied a willingness to compromise on both sides of any issue. That is precisely what was lacking in the country's political culture. In a fight, everyone wanted a total victory. I recalled the words of an American friend of mine who commented on our political rallies, Supreme Soviet sessions, and even arguments among friends: "In other countries, people argue in order to find the truth. In this country you argue in order to prove that you are one hundred percent right and to destroy your opponent."

A few months later a Soviet newspaper published a letter from a former prime minister of Czechoslovakia, Tadeus Masarik, to Stalin written in the late 1940s, before Masarik's suicide. In a democracy, Masarik wrote, no political force or party can gain a total victory. The original goals erode or change, and a compromise is achieved. "But your country has a different tradition." That was true. Gorbachev often made a similar point to his foreign counterparts and in speeches and private discussions.

Gorbachev's Official Visit to Italy

Gorbachev was going to Malta by way of Italy. His official visit to that country was marked by a special warmth. The crowds in Rome and Milan were more enthusiastic than anywhere I had ever seen. I could not attribute that to the southern temperament alone. I believed that, with the developments in Eastern Europe made possible by Gorbachev's commitment to the freedom of choice, Europeans had become convinced beyond any doubt that the division of their continent was over. The fear generated by that division, the fear that had pervaded their lives, was over too. The Italians saluted the man who had the courage to rid them of that fear.

Gorbachev was clearly impressed by that enthusiasm. In Rome I was present when he talked to a large group of intellectuals who accompanied him on the trip. The group included some of the leading lights of the democratic movement: economist Stanislav Shatalin, political scientist Yevgeny Ambart-sumov, *Moscow News* editor-in-chief Yegor Yakovlev, and Sergey Alexeyev, a Supreme Soviet member and professor of law. Gorbachev said that the common European house was becoming a reality and we had to move forward more rapidly to be a part of it.

The discussion turned naturally to developments within the Soviet Union. What struck me was that the intellectuals seemed worried and concerned, but they did not propose any particularly novel or radical solutions. Indeed, what they said seemed quite timid. Alexeyev suggested that a movement be launched to support leasehold as a way of phasing out state property. But no one mentioned private property as such. Those two words were no longer taboo, but many were still uncomfortable using them.

Shatalin, who soon afterward became one of the most radical Soviet economists, seemed particularly cautious then. When Gorbachev said, "Any radical change is always accompanied by chaos," Shatalin remarked: "Perhaps, Mikhail Sergeyevich, but don't say that publicly. They simply won't understand."

Shatalin was a difficult man who later worked closely with Gorbachev and then turned against him, criticizing him vehemently. And yet I never heard Gorbachev attacking him or others who zigzagged in a similar manner. Gorbachev was not easily offended; he was always ready to resume cooperation.

Bush and Gorbachev at the Malta "Nonsummit"

I don't know what the weather system developing in the Mediterranean during those days is called, but it was foggy in Milan as we were boarding the plane, and windy in Malta when we landed there. Gorbachev had a short talk with the prime minister of Malta and then went to the cruise ship *Maxim Gorky*, where he was to stay. The meetings with Bush were to be held alternately on board a Soviet naval ship and a U.S. naval ship, which had arrived a few days before. "An informal meeting at a secluded location" had turned into a huge media event. Malta was full of U.S. and Soviet government officials, diplomats, and reporters from around the world.

The first thing I heard the next day was that holding the meeting on board the naval ships was very much in doubt. The winds had become stormy overnight, and it would probably be impossible to get the heads of state onto the ships safely. A protocol official told me that two other possibilities were being considered: holding the meeting ashore or inviting Bush to come to the *Maxim Gorky*. Furthermore, it was rumored soon afterward that Bush, who was staying on a U.S. ship anchored in the storm-swept harbor, was seasick.

Everyone seemed more nervous than I remembered them at other summits. It was said that Bessmertnykh was pressuring Admiral Vladimir Chernavin, commander of the Soviet Navy, to find a way to get the two leaders on the ship despite the weather. Chernavin was firm: it was too risky and he would not agree to it. It was finally decided to invite Bush to the *Maxim Gorky*. I remember Chernavin saying to Gorbachev: "Mikhail Sergeyevich, I talked to the officers and sailors, and they would very much like to welcome you and the president to the ship. They would be proud to, and they are sorry that it is impossible. But your safety is paramount." Chernavin had the aristocratic bearing and the clear manner of speaking that naval officers in all countries seem to share.

The arrangements at the *Maxim Gorky* had to be made hastily, but it is a big ship and there was no problem finding a suitable room. Finding a table long enough for the two delegations was more difficult, so two tables of somewhat unequal height had to be put together and covered with a green tablecloth. Bush arrived with no sign of seasickness—he had an ability to recuperate quickly—and the Malta summit began almost on schedule. The storm continued and soon got worse, so the *Maxim Gorky* became its venue for the duration.

Bush's New and More Flexible Positions

As Bush said from the start, suggesting a meeting with Gorbachev at this stage was a departure from his initial position that a summit should take place only when arms control agreements were ready. He must have realized that this display of "post-review" toughness could only damage Gorbachev at a time when he was beginning to need all the help he could get. And Bush came to Malta well-prepared with new and more flexible positions on arms control and other issues. His two main arms control proposals were to abandon the binary chemical weapons program, subject to a bilateral agreement on major cutbacks in chemical weapons arsenals, and to give up U.S. insistence on prohibition of mobile intercontinental ballistic missiles (ICBMs), thus removing a major irritant to the Soviet Union, which was planning to make such missiles the mainstay of its land-based strategic forces.

Bush announced some long-overdue shifts in U.S. position on economic relations with the Soviet Union. He promised to take steps toward suspending the Jackson-Vanick amendment, thus opening the way to grant the Soviet Union most-favored-nation status in trade, and the Stevenson and Byrd amendments, which limited loans to the Soviet Union. He made a point—a politically sensitive one at the time—that the United States was making its proposals on economic issues in the spirit of cooperation and trade rather than aid. He added that the United States would no longer object to Soviet membership in GATT (the General Agreement on Trade and Tariffs), a global free-trade organization.

Bush's remarks and suggestions, which he made during the very first hour of formal talks, clearly impressed Gorbachev. "It is the best proof," Gorbachev commented, "that President Bush's administration has made a policy decision on its relations with the Soviet Union." He said he had gone to Malta in a rather critical mood, believing that U.S. expressions of support for perestroika were not supported by deeds, but that what Bush had just told him changed that impression. Clearly, the meeting started on a very good note.

Also on the first day of the Malta "nonsummit" there were some frank discussions—both private, one-on-one, and delegation-level—about Eastern Europe, German unity, and domestic developments in the Soviet Union. Bush emphasized that, despite some advice to the contrary, he was taking a moderate line, seeking above all not to create problems for the Soviet Union. "Some people were suggesting that I should jump on the Berlin Wall," he admitted, adding that, although the U.S. administration could not be expected to disapprove of German unification, he would continue to act with restraint.

Gorbachev appreciated this stance. No one could then predict that events would soon begin to develop in a vertiginous way. The general promise of restraint, coupled with the good understanding of Soviet domestic developments that Bush showed in his private talks with Gorbachev and sensible U.S. positions on arms control and trade, created a new atmosphere.

Focus on Western Values and Intentions

The next day, December 3, Gorbachev came back with a major political statement. He told Bush the Soviet Union was ready not to regard the United States as its enemy. Both Gorbachev and Shevardnadze later often recalled that moment. It certainly was a watershed. Saying something like that in 1989 required courage. I do not know at what level the statement had been "cleared" with our military, but it certainly had to be cleared. Gorbachev would not make such a momentous statement offhand. But it had to make quite a few people in the Soviet Union uncomfortable. The military, almost by definition, need an enemy, and the "image of the enemy" had helped the totalitarian state and the militarized economy to survive for decades.

Was Gorbachev's statement ahead of its time? Perhaps. Certainly Bush was in no hurry to respond immediately. (He did so in April 1990, saying in a talk with Shevardnadze: "The enemy is not the other side, but instability and unpredictability.") But being ahead is what a statesman's courage is all about, and in my heart I applauded Gorbachev. I was, of course, wondering whether the U.S. administration would respond in kind with a clear policy of support for Gorbachev and his team of reformers.

The Malta summit was one of those rare meetings where the discussion of philosophy and generalities took a great deal of time. There was an interesting exchange, involving Gorbachev, Bush, Baker, and Alexander Yakovlev, about "Western values" and whether reforms in the Soviet Union should be based on them. Gorbachev was piqued by remarks often made by Western politicians that the reforms should amount to our acceptance of Western ways. He disagreed with such remarks in substance, but he also hinted that such "propaganda" was hurting him politically.

Democracy, glasnost, and a free market are not just Western values, Yakovlev chimed in. They are universal, added Gorbachev, for whom the idea of universal human values was a favorite subject. Baker suggested, "as a compromise," that both Americans and Soviets could say that the positive changes in the Soviet Union and Eastern Europe were based on democratic values, but I thought that Bush understood better what Gorbachev had in mind. "Let us avoid incautious words and speak more about substance," the U.S. president said. "We welcome these changes wholeheartedly."

The important thing was to be clear about each other's intentions. Americans probably still wondered whether the Soviet Union would try to stem the revolutionary tide in Eastern Europe. And how would it react to similar developments that had already started in its own territory? Would the United States exploit the turmoil to weaken the security and the position of the Soviet Union in the world?, Gorbachev was asking Bush straightforwardly. Did the United States understand the consequences that such a policy would have within the Soviet Union, and its global implications?

Bush seemed quite alert and sensitive to what Gorbachev was saying, reacting to his suggestions and hidden meanings with a great deal of understanding. He was not, I thought as I listened to him, the kind of politician who would crudely take advantage of someone else's plight. He believed Gorbachev, and he wanted him to succeed with his plans of reforming the Soviet economy and society. He understood how daunting the task was and how powerful the traditions, institutions, and people that Gorbachev had to contend with were. He did not appear to regard Gorbachev as just "one of them," a tactician whose goal was to save the Communist system. He seemed to trust Gorbachev to be a democrat in his heart. But as I saw it, he doubted whether it was right for him to try to help Gorbachev, and he did not know how it could be done even if he wanted to.

Bush clearly disagreed with those in the United States who said "The worse it is for Gorbachev the better for us." He could not support this, if only because he was a prudent man and knew what the alternative to Gorbachev was at the time. But I believe that his policy then and for too long afterward was to do nothing that would undermine Gorbachev. Both then and for some time afterward, I believed that was a good policy, but for various reasons it turned out to be not enough. As the changes in Eastern Europe were reaching a high point and having a radicalizing impact on Soviet society, particularly on the Moscow intelligentsia and the Baltic republics, Gorbachev was still faced both with the old system and with the flaws of the new and more democratic bodies.

The Congress of People's Deputies, conceived at a time when Gorbachev's aura of power and authority made it easier for him to influence people, was no longer capable of having a stabilizing effect on developments. This became obvious at its second session, held in December. The Congress started amid calls for strikes, supported by influential deputies, and an increasingly unstable situation in many republics. The nationalist leaders and the radical intelligentsia were coming to the view that Gorbachev's goal was to preserve the old system more or less intact. Andrey Sakharov was planning to openly oppose Gorbachev. An opposition without a party or a political movement to rely on did not seem to me to be a good idea, but a few days later Sakharov was no longer there to debate that point. He died on December 16.

German Unification Issues to the Forefront

On the day of Sakharov's funeral Shevardnadze left for Brussels, where he had an intense program of activities: a major speech on European developments, including the issue of German unification, and visits to the Europarliament, NATO headquarters, and the European Community (EC) Commission. On the plane all talk was about German unification. Few people in the Soviet Union then were ready to accept rapid unification, and even fewer would have predicted that it was only a matter of months.

Many Europeans were worried about the developments. Giulio Andreotti said, only half-jokingly, "We love the Germans so much that the more

Germanies there are the better. Let there be at least two." Diplomats at the French embassy in Moscow were telling me about concern in Paris. Those who believe that unification would come rapidly, they told me, are depressed, and their number is growing; no one is happy.

No one was happy in Moscow either. Men as different as Shevardnadze and Ligachev said the same thing at the Central Committee plenum in January 1990: the pace of Germany's unification was alarming, and its membership in NATO would be dangerous. But even in December 1989, on the plane to Brussels, one thing clearly emerged from our heated discussion: we were dealing with a national issue and a national drive; unification was inevitable; we could perhaps slow it down but we could not stop it.

The big question was how this would be received in the Soviet Union. Could it become the straw that would break the back of Gorbachev's perestroika? Could the people, with their "genetic memory" of two devastating wars started by Germany in the twentieth century, regard its unification as a trauma and react in an explosive way? Those questions were real, and in December 1989 we did not know the answers.

Shevardnadze was perhaps better prepared than many for what was happening. He was extremely sensitive to ethnic and national feelings and issues, which he believed had been badly neglected by the Soviet government. He told me he had asked Yuly Kvitsinsky in 1986, when the latter was appointed Soviet ambassador to the Federal Republic of Germany, whether he believed the "national factor" in Germany would become important and the question of unification would arise. Kvitsinsky had answered that he did not think so, that too much had changed in the forty years of separation, and that the Germans in the East and in the West had in effect become two different peoples. Those who wanted to believe that regarded East Germany's membership in the Warsaw Pact and the presence of our troops there as the only real guarantee of our security. It was a mistake to stick to this view. Paying for old mistakes—the mistakes of our fathers—and for our own unwillingness to challenge them was what we were doing in 1990.

As I was translating Shevardnadze's Brussels speech I could not take a purely professional attitude. Unlike many of my older countrymen, I had no anti-German feelings, but at some profound level I was worried by the questions Shevardnadze raised in the speech. Were there any guarantees that German unity would not threaten our security? Would the united Germany be a neutral country? Would it have the strongest military forces in Europe? Would it be a member of NATO, which we still traditionally regarded as our adversary? I was prepared to look at such questions in a more-or-less matter-of-fact way and hope that they would become irrelevant with time, but I knew how many people back home had grave doubts.

Shevardnadze on Building a New Europe

Shevardnadze's speech also called for speeding up the process of building a new Europe, of developing new CSCE institutions with real authority in dealing with political and security questions. The speech was well received, but I was not sure many believed the European process could be synchronized with the increasing pace of German unification, as Shevardnadze suggested. CSCE institutions were only being conceived and were of questionable value to the Europeans, while NATO and the EC were real and had been proven useful. But those were West European institutions. Shevardnadze visited both of them in Brussels.

The visit to NATO headquarters was a real breakthrough. Here was the Soviet foreign minister in the building where the targeting of Soviet territory with nuclear missiles was discussed. He was welcomed in the lobby by a crowd of officials, clerks, and secretaries; the scene was floodlit by television news crews. The crowd applauded, and the young and middle-aged secretaries were reaching out to shake hands with Shevardnadze, who was smiling broadly in his unique and somewhat bemused way.

Talks with NATO Secretary-General Manfred Worner were followed by a cocktail with NATO ambassadors, and then we rushed to the European parliament. In the rush Shevardnadze forgot the folder with the text of the Europarliament speech and the notes for talks with Worner. Neither I nor his security guards were vigilant enough to notice. As soon as we became aware of the problem I called Worner's office from the Europarliament and the folder was promptly delivered, "probably photocopied," Shevardnadze said half-jokingly, "many times over."

In the Europarliament, Shevardnadze had to answer questions about the events in Romania, the only place in Eastern Europe where the regime did not want to leave quietly. There were as yet unconfirmed reports of police shooting at crowds in a town near the Hungarian border, and numerous casualties. Romania was still regarded as our ally, and Shevardnadze was constrained by the dogma of "friendship." So his answer was pioneering, by the standards of Soviet policy of the time. He dissociated himself from the use of force against demonstrators—if, he added, the reports of the killings were true. It soon turned out that they were, and President Ceausescu had to leave the scene in a violent way that was unique in the East European revolutions of 1989: he and his wife were summarily executed after a short trial. But Romania had always been a special case in the region, and both the East and the West bore part of the blame for the tragedy of that country. The Soviet Union had imposed an alien system on it, and the West had tended to forgive Ceausescu a great deal for his "independent attitudes."

Shevardnadze and Thatcher Talk on East Germany

From Brussels, Shevardnadze went to London for a brief stop and a frank talk with Prime Minister Thatcher. He spent only a few hours there, but that was enough to get the sense that Thatcher was alarmed by the events in East Germany. For the first time I saw her worried and even confused. She did not have her usual ready formulas to react to the developments. When during the talk with Shevardnadze an aide brought her a piece of paper with a wire service report of the East Germans' intention to open additional passage points on the border, she read the news aloud and looked at Shevardnadze questioningly. Shevardnadze was silent. Thatcher's remarks were alarmist, but she made no suggestion about what might be done under the circumstances. In effect she was fueling our own worries. I thought this was unnecessary and could be dangerous.

As usual, the four hours in the plane back to Moscow were full of arguments and frank talk. We had long ago become a close and mutually trusting team. To Tarasenko, Stepanov, and Vitaly Churkin, the minister's press secretary, I could say what I really thought. I could also talk candidly with Shevardnadze himself. For about thirty minutes we talked privately. I told him my impression of his conversation with Margaret Thatcher. The Europeans, I said, were clearly worried about German unification, but they did not know how to stop it or slow it down. So they were stoking our fears, which they knew must be nagging us, at least at the subconscious level, I said. Maybe I put it too bluntly, but Shevardnadze did not disagree. He commented that the Europeans were probing to find out how concerned we really were and what we might be ready to do.

"Should we be worried?" I asked.

"If you look at the big picture, we shouldn't," Shevardnadze answered. "If we succeed in changing our country, then we really would have nothing to fear in Europe or in the world. It's a big 'if,' of course, but the Europeans— they have to worry about the balance in Western Europe, in NATO, and in the European Community."

I often recalled that conversation. Perhaps our position on German unification ought to have taken that analysis more into account. But it turned out differently. Throughout the entire process in the ensuing months, we appeared to be the country that had the most to fear from the unification and that raised the most objections.

Gorbachev's Dilemma

Before the end of the year something happened that I learned, indirectly, only a few weeks later. It was Shevardnadze's first attempt to resign. The facts, as I know them, are still sketchy, but both in 1990 and later I thought a great deal about the episode, and my view of it changed. I now believe that almost everyone underestimated that event at the time and failed to see its potential implications. The reason for Shevardnadze's step was, as he described later, Gorbachev's agreement to let the office of the chief military prosecutor present to the Congress of People's Deputies its findings about the events in Tbilisi in April. Technically, the Congress did not have to listen to the prosecutor's report, for it had set up its own investigative commission, headed by Anatoly Sobchak, which submitted a report placing on the Georgian officials and the military and KGB commanders full responsibility for the bloodshed. Gorbachev felt, however, that the investigation conducted by an official government body could not be ignored. He was under tremendous pressure from the military, who wanted to whitewash its commanders.

This was a classic example of the duality of Gorbachev's position. He was the initiator and leader of reforms in the Soviet Union, but he was also a head of state—a state that still had the institutions, traditions, and personnel inherited from the past. Declaring war on those institutions and individuals, or even openly ignoring them, would have been suicidal for Gorbachev. He felt he had to maneuver to make time for the new democratic institutions to take root while "reeducating" the old ones. Like the symbol of the old Russia, the two-headed eagle, he had to be ambivalent, at least in some situations.

The problem was that the old institutions did not want to be reeducated—

they were allergic to change. The report of the military prosecutors, setting out to prove that the military commanders should not be held accountable, in effect suggested that the demonstrators themselves were to blame for the deaths. At best, it was a case of extraordinary moral deafness, even though the Georgians themselves later confirmed some of the facts contained in the report, particularly concerning the provocateur role of Zviad Gamsakhurdia, later elected president of Georgia. Clearly, the prosecutors' report should not have been allowed to appear at the Congress, on both formal and ethical grounds, but the fateful decision to consider the report was made, with no objection from Gorbachev, and even though it was presented in closed session, the Georgian delegation was furious. They literally accosted Gorbachev, and he had trouble calming them down. The harm had been done.

Shevardnadze Tries to Resign

Shevardnadze disagreed vehemently with what had happened. I think that the ordeal that he went through in April 1989, when he was sent to Tbilisi after the killings and was faced with the anger of his own people, came back to him. His gesture of protest was to resign. I do not think there was anything more than that behind his decision. He talked with Stepanov and Tarasenko, his confidants, and they supported the decision to submit the resignation. He then told Gorbachev about it and left for his dacha.

As I was told later, Gorbachev, Yakovlev, and Kryuchkov called Shevardnadze in his car and tried to persuade him to call off the resignation. I don't know how long it took, but they finally succeeded. As Tarasenko told me, one of the principal reasons Shevardnadze allowed himself to be persuaded was his expectation that 1990 would be a crucial year in foreign affairs; he had in mind specifically the completion of the START and CFE treaties. So he changed his mind and for a few weeks did not tell anyone.

When sometime in February 1990 I understood what had happened, my first reaction was close to fright. Gorbachev and Shevardnadze had seemed an unbreakable team, and a rift between them on any issue seemed next to impossible. I wondered why the foreign minister's two closest aides did not try to discourage him from even mentioning resignation. My reasoning was that Shevardnadze and Gorbachev should be together, for the hard-liners were becoming too strong for them to afford any disagreement. I was glad the resignation had been called off, and I hoped that, whatever had happened, my two bosses would patch things up. Besides everything else, I liked both of them.

The Mirror Is Cracked

Today, in light of much that happened afterward, and having given a lot of thought to that crucial episode, I think I was naive. We were all still quite naive at the time. Things are never the same after such incidents. The mirror had cracked, and the crack ran through the entire picture. Once Shevardnadze decided to resign, he should have made the resignation stick, even though, as I came to believe later, he resigned for the wrong reason.

Let me explain. The months that I am describing were the last chance for the launching of a responsible democratic movement. The conservative opposition to the reforms was becoming increasingly visible, aggressive, and well-organized. Its base was among the high-ranking members of the KGB and the military, and in the Central Committee and regional organizations of the party.

Gorbachev, as I have said, could not ignore those institutions. He had to maneuver, to try to contain or to neutralize them, but in order to do so he had to be, at least to some extent, "one of them." He could not dissociate himself from them. But the politically active segments on whom Gorbachev had relied greatly in the first years of perestroika, particularly the intelligentsia in the big cities, were increasingly impatient to break with the dogmas, traditions, and institutions of the past.

They needed a leader or leaders who would provide them with a sense of balance, make them move a little more prudently and talk a little less stridently; a leader who would help make a movement out of a crowd; a leader who would be a real democrat rather than a populist or an opportunist. They needed a Shevardnadze or a Yakovlev—or, better yet, both of them. Eventually this would have led to the development of a two- or three-party system, with Gorbachev at the center, where he belonged both by temperament and by political logic.

Attacks on the New Thinking and Foreign Policy

But that was not to be, and partly as a result of it the tenor of politics in what turned out to be the Soviet Union's two final years was aggressive, strident, radical, and extremely intolerant on both sides. There is no doubt that, initially at least, the conservatives bore a much greater part of the blame for it. In the last days of 1989 they launched an extremely malicious and vehement propaganda attack against the "new political thinking" and our new foreign policy.

In a particularly vicious article in the weekly *Literaturnaya Rossia*, the writer, Alexander Prokhanov, who later openly supported the August coup, argued that the new political thinking had "led to the collapse of the entire geopolitical architecture of postwar Europe," which underpinned the country's security. He wrote of the millions of Soviet soldiers who died in Eastern Europe in the Second World War and of the generations that sacrificed everything to achieve military parity after that. They have been betrayed, Prokhanov said.

Prokhanov's rhetoric appealed to the war veterans, to the military, and to the patriotic feelings that are traditionally strong in Russia. Amid the squalor and poverty of everyday life, many had found refuge and relief in the fact that they were citizens of a superpower that was respected and even feared by the rest of the world. Now, Prokhanov wrote, that superpower was being kicked unceremoniously out of Europe. He was touching a raw nerve, stoking the military's anger, which focused on Shevardnadze. Gorbachev was not yet targeted for public attacks, but in private he too was criticized for being too soft.

Some experts in the foreign ministry and the academic community were also critical of our Western partners, saying they were not doing enough to make things easier for Soviet reformers. If the West wants to help us, they argued, why would it not curb the East Europeans' demands for immediate withdrawal of Soviet troops, demands that were creating enormous economic and logistical problems for the Soviet Union? Was there not a way to make the inevitable process of Soviet withdrawal and the dismantling of its imperial commitments look less humiliating, they asked? Maybe they had a point there, but I did not think such complaints made much practical sense in the world of "realpolitik." Still, the fact that people with democratic and even pro-Western leanings said this was indicative and alarming.

Indeed, some things the Americans did at the time were not helpful. The invasion of Panama in December was one of them. It was not, by objective standards, a big event, and it was not unprecedented; there had been the Dominican Republic in 1963 and Grenada in 1984. But against the background of the Soviet Union's concessions and "good behavior," it looked like an affront, a slap in the face, and more and more people said so.

I was appalled to hear such an interpretation from a foreign ministry official, a man I respected for his expertise and reasonable attitude on most issues.

"See," he said, "we are out of steam, we're down. But we try to look good. We behave ourselves. What are they doing? They are showing who's boss, and they are sticking it in our faces."

We were sitting in the eleventh-floor cafeteria drinking tea. I was in no mood to argue. I thought what the Americans had done in Panama was wrong, but I said, "Look, we don't even have diplomatic relations with Panama. And you can't be a fan of Noriega. So do you want to make a big thing out of it?"

"It's not that," he replied, "it's that they fight for what they think is theirs. And we—well, we're just down, for all to see."

I did not want to argue further. At some point in any argument, if the assumptions are different you just can't go on.

I later had a few similar episodes in the same cafeteria on other occasions with people whose assumptions were, I thought, still imperial.

The Americans made an effort to explain themselves to us. Ambassador Jack Matlock asked for a meeting with Shevardnadze and read out carefully written "talking points." He appeared somewhat embarrassed. His argument was that the invasion of Panama and the overthrow and capture of Noriega were "a special case," even a unique case. He reaffirmed the administration's willingness to cooperate with the Soviet Union on the entire agenda of relations and suggested that the Panama episode be forgotten as soon as possible.

Shevardnadze replied without anger or high emotion. "The Soviet Union does not want to exacerbate the situation," he said. "We disagree with what you have done, but we would like to go on with our relationship. But how do we explain the situation to those who say that we are being taken advantage of, to some of the people's deputies who are already collecting signatures under the demand that we make a strong representation to the United States?"

Matlock replied defensively and with an awkward smile, basically repeating the "talking points."

After Matlock left, Shevardnadze and I talked briefly about a few things. He believed he and Gorbachev would be able to contain the outcry against the Panama invasion. But, he said, once a crisis developed in one of our republics, "they would say immediately, why don't we use force to restore order—see what the Americans did in Panama? And that's a foreign country!"

Clearly, Panama was not Shevardnadze's biggest worry at the time. Things were happening both in the country and abroad at such a dizzying pace that it had to make one's head swim. Shevardnadze was obviously concerned.

Eight

THE ART OF LETTING GO

1 9 9 0

The Problem of Lithuania

In the first weeks of 1990 the Soviet leaders had several irons in the fire, and they were all red-hot. The Lithuanian Communist Party wanted to break away from the Communist Party of the Soviet Union, and that, everyone understood, was only part of a broader trend toward the independence of Lithuania and the other Baltic republics. In Moscow and Leningrad, people were demanding a formal end to the Communist Party's monopoly on power: cancellation of Article 6 of the Soviet constitution. The ethnic conflict between the Armenians and the Azerbaijanis had reached the point of massive pogroms and daily casualties in Baku and elsewhere. Eastern Europe was making a final rush to freedom and its future. And, most threatening to many Soviet citizens, the East German regime was crumbling and on the verge of being absorbed by West Germany. Daily, people heard on radio and television the news that many found unsettling. Today, when almost everyone has come to terms with those changes, it is too easy to forget the troubled confusion of early 1990.

The problem of Lithuania seemed by far the biggest challenge to Gorbachev. Two years later I talked to Justas Paleckis, a former Soviet diplomat with whom we worked together on the INF delegation in 1982. In 1990 he was a secretary of the Lithuanian Communist Party's Central Committee and directly involved in the maneuverings on the issue of the party's separation. "We nearly toppled Gorbachev in 1990 by our initiative," he admitted. "Eventually, we did appreciate his role."

I found Paleckis's admission interesting, for that is precisely what I was saying in 1990 to a longtime friend of mine, a Russian from Riga, Latvia, who was active in the Popular Front—the umbrella organization pushing for Latvia's independence from the Soviet Union. "I can understand your goal of independence," I said, "but the way you are going about it you will just help to topple Gorbachev, and then you can say farewell to independence, and the whole country will have to forget about freedom for another decade."

My argument did not impress him. A people fired up by national emotions, led by an intelligentsia that wants to go all the way, naturally abhors compromise.

My friend was an engineer at VEF, a large producer of electronic and communications equipment. He was a nice, unaggressive man just a few years younger than I. Compromise and conformism had been the substance of his life before "the second Russian revolution" started. But like many of his countrymen he did not want to miss the opportunity to break with the system.

Conservatives and New Radicals Press Gorbachev

So the Lithuanians, Latvians, and Estonians, and the intellectuals in Moscow and Leningrad, were pushing ahead, multiplying their demands and rejecting Gorbachev's counsel of patience and gradualism. As a result Gorbachev was left almost alone, with only a few loyalists around him, facing the conservatives in the Central Committee of the party. On the eve of Secretary of State Baker's arrival in Moscow for a full-scale U.S.-Soviet ministerial meeting, two debates were coming to a head in Moscow—on rescinding Article 6 of the constitution, about "the leading role of the Communist Party in Soviet society," and on the Lithuanian Communist Party's bid for separation. I remember talking with Shevardnadze in January about Article 6.

"It will be impossible to hold on to it," the minister said.

"I don't think we should try," I replied.

Shevardnadze did not object. He came to terms with the idea of a multiparty system rather quickly, I felt, and it was easier for him than for Gorbachev.

But then, Shevardnadze was not the general secretary of the Communist Party of the Soviet Union. Gorbachev was.

Gorbachev faced the daily onslaught of the party conservatives — the appa- ratchiks in the Central Committee, regional party secretaries, the party bosses from the republics supported by Russian-speaking workers who were worried by the rise of local nationalists, and the hierarchy of the army and the KGB. All were vehemently opposed to the cancellation of Article 6. In January Gorbachev did not take a clear stand at first, he appeared to be hesitating, which embittered both sides. They decided to put up a real fight.

On February 4 the democrats held a huge rally in Moscow. Tens of thousands of people chanted "Down with Article 6!" on Manezhnaya Square, right near the Kremlin. The march of a quiet but determined crowd down the Sadovoye Koltso to the city's center, which I watched from my office on the thirteenth floor of the foreign ministry building, was impressive. From the seventh floor Shevardnadze was watching the procession too. On or before that day, Gorbachev understood that Article 6 had to go. He also decided that the country needed stronger executive authority and therefore a president as head of state, rather than a chairman of the parliament.

By the time Baker came to Moscow, the debate on Article 6 at the Central Committee plenum had ended. The conservatives had vented their anger, but they deferred to Gorbachev. They did that at every plenum, but each time more and more reluctantly, and those political fights were increasingly painful and debilitating for Gorbachev. The February plenum was perhaps the first one at which he had to listen to massive and bitter attacks against his policies of new thinking and democratization.

Gorbachev was between the rock and the hard place. While the new radicals were increasingly in disagreement with Gorbachev on the question of the pace of reform, the party, in which he grew as a politician and with which he could not break until the end, rejected his vision of a decent society in the Soviet Union.

Shevardnadze was a member of the Central Committee, and I could imagine how he must have felt listening to the ravings of the hard-liners. On the Lithuanian Communist Party issue Gorbachev had to project firmness. Even Shevardnadze and Alexander Yakovlev sought, perhaps half-heartedly, to persuade the Lithuanians to change their mind. Their speeches were mild in tone and language, but they were clearly a minority at the plenum. Shevard- nadze's own deputy in the foreign ministry, Valentin Nikiforov, also a member of the Central Committee, called for expulsion of Lithuanian leaders from the party. His speech was one of the toughest.

Shevardnadze did not stay until the end of the plenum; the beginning of the talks with Baker could no longer be postponed. We were waiting for him in the foreign ministry's Osobnyak, a grand prerevolutionary mansion of eclectic architecture and style used for meetings with visiting delegations.

When Shevardnadze finally arrived, he was not in a good mood. "It's madness," he said. "They insist on a resolution condemning the Lithuanians. It's that silly rhetoric once again." He still took those things quite emotionally. A few months later he gave up on the party's ability to adjust to change and did not even comment on similar incidents.

Baker and Shevardnadze Discuss Arms Control and Regional Problems

I felt that discussions with Baker were emotionally anticlimactic for Shevardnadze, but there was much to discuss. In Vienna and particularly in Geneva the arms control talks dragged on without apparent prospects for a breakthrough. Shevardnadze often wondered why the START talks were so prone to turn into an endless tug-of-war. Was it because the negotiators were too used to the routine of discussing the technicalities and just forgot about the larger issue involved? Was it a kind of a conspiracy of the military-industrial complexes on both sides? My own view was that our U.S. partners were generally pleased with the parameters of the treaty but put off the signing until they could use it as a political plus for Bush and perhaps a "reward" for Gorbachev. That view was probably an oversimplification, but I still believe it was generally plausible.

In the meantime new esoteric issues were being raised by both sides, cruise missiles with poetic names like "Tacit Rainbow" were getting in the policymakers' way, and the circle of experts on both sides who supposedly understood all the technicalities was getting increasingly smaller. Later, at the Moscow summit in 1991, Bush said to Gorbachev, quite seriously I believe, that he felt even "the experts" did not really understand some of those bizarre issues.

Baker and Shevardnadze always gave the negotiations something of a push at their meetings. After tough discussions in expert working groups, which never amounted to much, there was a lot of cable traffic between Moscow and Washington, and eventually some memorandum of understanding, letter of intent, or agreement in principle emerged, which the negotiators were supposed to translate quickly into treaty language. But I, for one, was no longer fooled. I knew something even more esoteric would come up a few days later, a seemingly innocuous little problem would balloon into a big one and then become a political issue, a real conundrum for the nontechnical minds of the leaders who had many other things to worry about. They were often unable to break out of that vicious circle; details triumphed over policy, which means the policy lacked strength.

Baker also brought with him a group of experts on regional problems. While the Afghans were "stewing in their own juices," it became quite clear that no side could win a definitive victory, and a search for a real disengagement—a "negative symmetry" on arms supplies—seemed about to begin. Soviet POWs held by the mujaheddin were becoming an increasingly emotional issue in the country, and Shevardnadze hoped Baker could do something to help get our soldiers back. He and Gorbachev were under mounting pressure on this issue, and even a little progress would help them greatly.

Baker's regional agenda focused on Central America. I am not sure whether he knew how much pressure the Soviet Union was putting on the Sandinista government in Nicaragua to hold a really free and clean election and to accept its outcome. Baker indicated that he doubted they would. He hinted that Central America was becoming a real test case for judging the behavior of the Soviet Union and its friends. There was still much mistrust then between the Soviet Union and the United States, despite the warm personal rapport between their leaders.

Gorbachev Is Reconciled to German Unification

But it was Germany that was most on the minds of the Soviet and U.S. leaders those days. Just then the East Germans were ransacking the headquarters of STASI, the secret police, and calling for rapid introduction of the West German deutschemark in the GDR. The bandwagon was rolling, and it soon became clear to me that Gorbachev had reconciled himself with the idea of German unity. That was not easy. He was bombarded with papers and memorandums containing warnings about the consequences of unification, some of them coming from the foreign ministry, where the "Germanists" continued to be hostile to a process they could not stop.

I believe that what finally persuaded Gorbachev and his associates that German unification had to be accepted was not only their awareness that it would be enormously risky to try to stop it by political or military intimidation, but also their sense of fairness. Someone once said that in any situation the most important thing was to see the moral issue involved. And the moral issue was simple: Should a nation be kept from uniting? Should this be a goal of our policy? Should we base our security on the division of Germany?

But for a very long time the Soviet Union's perception of security had been based on the division of Germany and of Europe. It was therefore reasonable to hope that the transition to a new situation would not be abrupt, that it would be a process leaving us some time to adjust and to change. In his lengthy talk with Baker on February 9, Gorbachev called for a process of reasonable duration, and one that would take the security interests of the Soviet Union into account. He could not help recalling the war and its consequences for the Soviet people. He mentioned the fact that many German intellectuals were uncomfortable with the breakneck pace of unification and preferred a confederation of two German states. He took a firm position on German membership in NATO: it would radically change the strategic balance in Europe and in the world and was therefore unacceptable.

Baker sought to assure Gorbachev that the West would not use German unification to undermine the Soviet Union's security or to weaken Gorbachev's domestic position, but that was about all he could say at the time. The United States, I felt, did not have a policy that would help the Soviet Union and its leader absorb the shock of German unification. Some people believed it was something of a shock even for the United States. Canada's Prime Minister Brian Mulroney later told Gorbachev that he had talked to Bush in December 1989 or January 1990 and found him perplexed and confused about the enormous long-term strategic consequences of the unification.

When Baker called Shevardnadze on the eve of his visit to Berlin in January, he too sounded less than enthusiastic about the pace of developments. He tried to explain to Shevardnadze that his appearance near the crumbling Berlin Wall should not be regarded as a provocation or an ideological gesture. Baker had come a long way since his ideologically loaded speech in Vienna less than a year earlier. Of course, the psychological atmosphere on the U.S. and Soviet sides was not comparable. While some Americans may have felt a little uncomfortable that the stable old world in which they were so used to operate was giving way to something fluid and unknown, for the Soviets it was the collapse of a universe, of the assumptions that had underpinned our security in Europe, and not merely of ideology or customary practices. Almost daily, painful adjustments had to be made, and agonizing choices could not be avoided.

A few days after Baker's visit to Moscow, Shevardnadze went to Ottawa for the "Open Skies" conference. What would have been a routine diplomatic event stemming from a recently revived U.S. initiative was now transformed into something of a turning point. The presence of almost all major players in European politics, including the United States, provided an opportunity for discussion of the German issue, which was getting hotter every day.

Shevardnadze's team included experts on German affairs; an acquaintance of mine was with us as a German-language interpreter. He was younger than I, but far more conservative on almost every issue. A graduate of the Moscow Institute of International Relations, he had been taught to think in a certain way. It was not just the German issue, which he interpreted in the stark terms of alliance politics, "territorial security," and unconcealed suspicion of the Germans' intentions. He did not believe in the democratic experiment in the Soviet Union, he mistrusted the new politicians, the "so-called democrats" as he put it, and he spoke tolerantly of extreme Russian nationalist organizations like Pamyat.

That a young man with a good education held such views struck me as a bad sign. In some form, disenchantment with the democratic process was being expressed by many members of the Soviet foreign service. Many had been lukewarm about democracy from the start; others were beginning to lose faith as they saw conditions in the country deteriorate and its superpower status being eroded.

Another friend of mine, a classmate at the U.N. language training course years before, was then working at the Soviet embassy in Ottawa. He was a typical liberal intellectual with prodemocratic and even prodissident leanings. He was eager to hear news about the developments and mood in Moscow, and he was obviously concerned. On the day of our arrival, news came of riots in Dushanbe, the capital of Tajikistan, a Soviet republic in Central Asia. At the time, such news still seemed shocking, and mass riots anywhere in the Soviet Union, although increasingly frequent, still seemed a kind of cataclysm to those of us who were used to the idea of stability as an inherent and necessary part of the system. Even though disliked, the system was still "ours"—it was our country, and we could not watch its troubles with quiet detachment.

"What is happening, Pavel?" my friend asked me. "We no longer seem to be a stable country worthy of respect. China, despite last year's killings, is more respected internationally than we are." He had majored in Chinese in college and was prone to make comparisons with that country.

I did not know any easy answer to his concerns, but I disagreed with him. Essentially, I answered that democracy in Russia was bound to be a difficult experiment but that I did not see any other way for it to become a normal country. The same, I felt, would one day happen in China too.

Hammering Out the "2 plus 4" Arrangement on Germany

Unification of Germany would have been difficult for the Soviet Union to accept anyway, but it created particularly difficult political and psychological problems for the leaders of perestroika. Nevertheless, the German people were eager to reunite, and Chancellor Kohl was determined not to miss the opportunity to go down in history as the chancellor who "made it happen." Whatever doubts the Americans may have had initially had been overcome.

Bush and Baker decided they would not try to slow the unification train. They now wanted to help it to arrive at its destination carrying goods for the United States too. But they also wanted to reassure the Soviet Union. They obviously were worried that problems at home and abroad, particularly the changes in Eastern Europe and Germany, could cause Gorbachev's downfall. To some of our people, high-ranking U.S. State Department officials said frankly that Gorbachev was in trouble and that they regarded the threat of his ouster by the military and the conservatives as quite real.

Shevardnadze's talks with West German Foreign Minister Hans-Dietrich Genscher and Baker in Ottawa were unusually long by any standards. They were also difficult, particularly those with Genscher. I thought Shevardnadze expected from him a little more understanding of our predicament. Baker, though quite firmly sticking to the West's general line, including insistence on NATO membership for the united Germany, seemed more forthcoming and willing to look for face-saving formulas. I don't know whose idea it was initially to create what was later called the "2 plus 4" arrangement, including West Germany and East Germany, the United States, the Soviet Union, Great Britain, and France, but hammering out its format in Ottawa was a tough exercise.

The West's initial position was that the negotiators' task and objective was to agree on termination of the four-power rights in Germany, which the United States, the Soviet Union, Great Britain, and France had as a result of victory in the Second World War. Shevardnadze could not agree on an explicit formula of this kind, for it would appear that we were unceremoniously being kicked out. The Germans, on the other hand, insisted that the unification was their business and that the four powers were not to be involved in the discussion of unification as such.

I was waiting for Shevardnadze in the lobby of Ottawa's convention center, a remodeled former railway station, while he was having a long and, as it turned out, crucial meeting with Genscher. The schedule of Open Skies conference meetings had been skewed and almost forgotten. No one seemed to care about Open Skies as the foreign ministers of the six countries and Poland were meeting again and again in various combinations. Some inexperienced East Europeans were even irritated.

At one point, while the ministers continued to work out language for the "2 plus 4" statement, and the others were reduced to the role of spectators at a dark stadium, I heard Jiri Dienstbier of Czechoslovakia say, "Why do they take so long arguing about words?"

Polish Foreign Minister Konrad Skubiszewski quickly retorted, "Words are the instruments of diplomacy."

I often remembered those words later, and mentioned the episode to Skubiszewski months later in September 1991, in Moscow. He remembered it too.

When Shevardnadze finally left the room in which he had been talking with Genscher, he seemed a little more at ease. He went on to talk with Baker. The crucial phrase he worked out with Genscher was that the "2 plus 4" mechanism was intended "for the discussion of the external aspects of building German unity." That seemed to be satisfactory to all, and, as always in such cases, the formula acceptable to all sides was linguistically rather awkward.

What was in it for us? It was vague, but it seemed to point to a process ("building Germany unity") in which we would be involved for perhaps an extended period of time. After his talk with Baker, who found the formula acceptable, Shevardnadze asked me to go to the embassy and draft a cable to Gorbachev about the emerging agreement, asking for his consent. While the foreign minister stayed in the convention center for some further discussion, I rushed to the embassy to write out the draft and talk to Tarasenko, who for some reason had not been present during the decisive talks with Genscher and Baker. Tarasenko liked the language of the "2 plus 4" statement. The hard-liners in Moscow, he pointed out, would of course say that the West's only purpose in this exercise was to make us rubber-stamp German unification. But would we be better off if we refused to participate in the process? The answer was obviously no.

We decided to draft a cable that would strongly recommend endorsement of the "2 plus 4" formula, as agreed in Ottawa. Withholding our agreement to something hammered out with so much effort, including Shevardnadze's arduous talks with Genscher, would look bad. We would have to agree eventually anyway. So a quick answer from Moscow was necessary. We knew we had an important, hardworking ally in Moscow, a man with a quick reaction and the right instincts: Anatoly Chernyaev. He would not put the cable on the back burner, but would make sure it was shown to Gorbachev immediately. And that is what actually happened. The positive answer from Moscow came quickly, to the relief of Shevardnadze and every one of us.

After the exhausting Ottawa marathon, which also included a speech in the Canadian parliament and talks with Prime Minister Mulroney and Foreign Secretary Joe Clark, Shevardnadze gave an extensive interview to Hella Pick, diplomatic correspondent of the *Guardian*, who had been asking for a meeting with him for a long time. She was for some reason in disfavor with the Soviet embassy in London, disliked and distrusted by Ambassador Leonid Zamyatin personally and some members of his staff. But Shevardnadze respected Pick for her professionalism and her balanced view of the issues. He talked to her frankly, without trying to hide that it was not an easy time for him.

On the German issue, Shevardnadze had to tread a cautious line, but whereas just a couple of weeks before, at the party plenum in Moscow, he spoke of the potential dangers inherent in unification, he was now saying that no artificial obstacles should be put in the way of the German people's unity. Still, he insisted on what he called "a smooth process" that would make the transition less painful politically for us and economically and socially for the Germans themselves.

"Do you think this process should take some time?" Hella Pick asked.

"Yes," Shevardnadze responded.

"How long?" asked Pick.

"Well, maybe a few years," came the reply.

I believe that at the time he really thought it should be a process extended to several years and that everyone would be better off for it.

The Contagion of Impatience: German Unity and Lithuanian Independence

In principle that may have been a reasonable assumption. Who knows, perhaps even the Germans would have preferred to avoid the social costs of rapid unification, such as the huge rise in unemployment in the East, and of course a longer and smoother process would have been preferable for us. But in the end the people of Germany thought otherwise. As became very clear just a few weeks later, they wanted to go toward unity on a fast track.

It was not only the national yearning for being one country that played a role in this, I believe. There was also the strong desire to make a complete break with the totalitarian past, a factor we later saw working powerfully in Eastern Europe and then in the Soviet Union. In a situation of "a final reckoning," appeals to reason don't work. Calls to consider all consequences and to take a cautious and prudent approach to change are not heeded; they seem to be intended merely to protect the vestiges of the old system. I think this psychological phenomenon accounts for why the pattern of developments in East Germany, Eastern Europe, and the Soviet Union was so similar. And though the countries involved are so different in many respects, it all happened almost simultaneously because the media, particularly television, spread the contagion of impatience in vivid images that are now engraved in the minds of millions.

In February and March 1990 the Lithuanians were more impatient than anyone else in the Soviet Union. They wanted their independence now, and for them that meant immediate secession from the Soviet Union. They believed there was an easy way to do it: rescind their parliament's decision of 1940 to join the Soviet Union as having been made "under duress" and therefore illegal, and obtain diplomatic recognition immediately. That expectation was based on the fact that the West, more specifically the United States, never recognized the incorporation of the Baltic states into the Soviet Union.

Many people in the Soviet foreign ministry thought they knew precisely what was going to happen. A friend of mine, with whom we shared an office and who had been a high-ranking Komsomol official in Lithuania in the early 1970s, predicted confidently: "They will secede." When I asked him what that meant, he described a scenario that was close to what actually happened in March.

But I disagreed with him on Western recognition. The whole issue of independence, I said, amounts basically to whether the seceding country is recognized by the "metropolitan power" and by the international community. The West, in my view, despite its position of principle on the illegality of the Baltics' incorporation, would not rush to recognize Lithuanian independence for fear that it would cause Gorbachev's ouster by the hard-liners. That would give us time to institute a process eventually leading to a solution, and possibly to independence. But the issue had to be put in blunt terms. Independence had to be real, including trade on the basis of world prices for oil and other commodities that the Lithuanians were buying cheaply for rubles. Such a strategy seemed plausible to me; it could result in an amicable settlement acceptable to all.

Even the Lithuanians could have agreed to some form of confederation in order to preserve the economic benefits of cheap oil. But the strategy could work under one condition only: it had to be clearly stated in the first place and accepted by the principal powers. That was what I later called a more Kissinger-like approach—a real policy that anticipated a certain result and worked toward it by using pressures and inducements.

Unfortunately, no one on either side could propose such a policy. Gorbachev's actions and thinking were constrained by hard-liners and the military, whom he no longer could ignore, Shevardnadze felt increasingly threatened from the same quarters and therefore was in no position to put forward a major initiative of this kind, and Bush and Baker were operating in a reasonable but mostly reactive mode, constrained by anti-Soviet conservatives and the powerful ethnic lobbies. Theirs was a policy of reassuring Gorbachev that they meant no harm and wished him good luck. It was not a policy of prudently guiding history. Overall, I think there was a failure of political imagination on both sides. I hasten to add, however, that at the time I regarded the U.S. approach to the issue as right and reasonable, and said so in frank discussions with friends and colleagues.

Gorbachev Faces Calls for Lithuanian Independence

The opening of the third Congress of People's Deputies, which was to elect Gorbachev the first president of the Soviet Union, was preceded by the election of the chairman of Lithuanian Supreme Soviet. The man the Lithuanians chose was Vitautas Landsbergis, the most aggressive and confrontational of the Lithuanian politicians pushed forward by perestroika. He insisted on adopting the Declaration of Independence the next day, or rather the next night, to preempt Gorbachev's election as president and face him with a fait accompli.

Initially Gorbachev tried to play down the event, saying that he and the deputies would have to look into the situation and assess it legally and from the standpoint of the constitution. I thought that approach was exactly right. But he could not hold on to it. The conservatives accused him of making one concession after another and called for drastic measures to reverse the Lithuanian decision.

Once again I saw how many conservative-minded people we had in the foreign ministry. They were in every department, but perhaps most of all in Personnel, stuffed with KGB officials, former party functionaries, and old-school diplomats not wanted in the substantive departments of the ministry. During one of the first days of the Congress, I went to one of the offices in that department for some formalities and heard a personnel official almost shouting, "He is trying to play it down, but they are not playing his game. They have said they are independent, and that's his reward for being soft." Everywhere the hard-liners were beginning to speak out increasingly openly and harshly against Gorbachev's policies.

But Gorbachev was not getting help from the democrats and the new nationalist forces in the republics either. Their support was grudging and reluctant at best. So when he decided to be elected president indirectly at the Congress rather than by a popular vote, his election was by a comfortable margin but not a landslide. Perhaps he thought he might not win if he chose a popular vote, or that parliaments in some republics would refuse to hold the elections. But I thought then and still think today that "going to the country" would have been the right choice. He could win, and then his position would be much stronger in dealing both with the republics and with the economy.

U.S. Concerns About Lithuania

The Americans seemed quite concerned about the situation caused by the Lithuanian parliament's decision. The State Department made a statement that was, in my view, quite mild. It reiterated the standard U.S. position of not recognizing the incorporation of the Baltic states into the Soviet Union and called for their self-determination, but stopped short of recognizing Lithuania as an independent nation. This gave us some time to try to sort things out. But the Americans knew that radical secessionists in Lithuania and hard-liners in Moscow, for different reasons, did not want a process that would lead to independence gradually. What most worried the United States was the prospect that the deterioration of the crisis might force "the center" to crack down.

Numerous delegations, including American politicians, senators, and experts, were arriving in Moscow and the Baltic republics to assess the situation. Directly or indirectly, they asked whether force would be used against Lithuania. I recall a meeting Shevardnadze had with a delegation of U.S. senators that included Ted Kennedy. Tensions were running high outside the Smolenskaya Square building on that gloomy afternoon of early March. Shevardnadze was obviously worried both by the confrontational attitude of the Lithuanians and by the calls at the Congress for "restoring order." When asked what he thought might happen he said that a reasonable process might be put on track if the Lithuanian leader attended a scheduled meeting of the Soviet Union's Council of the Federation. "This is the test," he said. "Do they want confrontation or talks?"

The Americans seemed receptive to Shevardnadze's argument. They warned against the use of force, but both the U.S. president and the U.S. Senate seemed to be willing to give Moscow time to sort things out. This was our chance, a chance that was reopened subsequently even after such mistakes and disastrous moves as the oil blockade in the spring and the use of force in January, a chance that the Soviet Union missed many times and lost definitively in August 1991. The same people who blocked every opportunity of reaching a settlement with the Baltics caused the collapse of the Soviet Union with their coup in August. The events of 1990–91 were full of what Marx called the ironies of history, and I believe we have not seen the end of such ironies.

Shevardnadze Faces Opposition

Long before, Shevardnadze had scheduled a trip to Africa for late March, and although he hesitated about whether to go, because the situation was so tense in the Soviet Union, he felt he could not cancel the visits. He was going on a grueling trip to one region he had not yet visited. Did he regard it as paying his last debt before leaving the foreign ministry? Some of his remarks and those of people closest to him made me think he did, but he alone could answer the question.

He worked on that trip with his usual quiet and balanced vigor and attention to diplomatic details. The trip was filmed by a crew from the television program "Vzglyad," an opposition-oriented group of young men who obviously liked Shevardnadze and his team. They had asked to accompany him to Ottawa, but their own bosses at government television did not allow them to go. The fact that Shevardnadze allowed them to film the trip, and even to accompany him on his own plane, was a novelty in the Soviet Union, and I knew that some people in the Central Committee and on Gorbachev's staff resented it. They might have accepted a more official television project, but they vehemently disliked "those democrat brats."

Unlike them, Shevardnadze believed in working with such people. He was quite ready to talk with those who flaunted their independence and opposition leanings. He said he could talk with anyone—a liberal or a conservative, a Communist or a Christian Democrat. But he was increasingly irritated by many members of the old Soviet establishment, whose mindless conservatism and orthodoxy he often called "reactionary." That was a new word in his vocabulary, which he did not use lightly. But the campaign of slander and harassment against him was indeed being orchestrated by those people in an increasingly open and vicious way. So, more and more often, his irritation reached the point of anger.

In frank interviews with the "Vzglyad" team, most of which were taped on the plane, Shevardnadze disclosed for the first time that he had tried to resign in December. But he praised Gorbachev's foreign and domestic policies, and also said he believed the country could succeed in democratic reform if it moved ahead radically and decisively. But his concern about mounting instability in the Soviet Union was obvious.

German Unification and the NATO Line

During the African trip we learned the results of the parliamentary elections in East Germany. It had been predicted that the social democrats, who favored a relatively smooth and longer transition to German unification, would win or at least do very well. This is what the polls suggested almost until election day. But the results of the elections belied the polls and the predictions. The Christian Democrats, who made no secret of their intention to dismantle the GDR as fast as they could, won overwhelmingly and could form the government even without the social democrats. They eventually accepted a coalition with them, but it was clear that henceforth they, or rather Chancellor Helmut Kohl of West Germany, controlled the game. The upshot clearly was that we had little time to find a formula that would make the impending unification palatable to the Soviet people, and particularly to the conservatives in the Soviet leadership.

Many find it surprising that the people did not seem terribly worried. Our "German experts" lived in the past and were hopelessly out of tune with the people, particularly with the thinking and clearheaded among them, when they said that on this gut issue the Russians would always be adamantly anti-German. Perhaps the preoccupation with domestic developments and the hardship of daily life made people indifferent to any foreign policy problems, or maybe the relatively quiet postwar decades had had their effect and the wounds had healed, but the anti-German feelings were not widespread, and there was no large-scale outcry against German unification.

The foreign ministry had quietly conducted polls in Moscow and other cities, and the results were surprising. Even among the military, only a minority then objected to unification or even to full NATO membership for Germany. I felt that, based on those findings, we could take a much more confident attitude on the issue of German unity. The problem, of course, was that among the high-ranking members of the still powerful Soviet institutions—the army, the KGB, the party apparat—the prevailing opinion was quite different. Their vehement opposition to unification and to German membership in NATO probably influenced Gorbachev's position even though he accepted the idea of unification. Gorbachev and Shevardnadze needed political help from the West.

The West could, at that time, set aside a full-scale discussion of the issue of Germany's membership in NATO, quietly asking the Soviet Union to do the same. Somewhat later this idea was mentioned to me by a French diplomat in Moscow. Eventually, he said, Germany will be in NATO, and you'll have to accept it. But let us leave that question for later. In the meantime, constraints on the united Germany's armed forces, territory, and behavior would be negotiated, and NATO would try to take steps that would make it look less hostile in Soviet eyes.

I found the idea attractive. I believed that the constraints on Germany would in effect amount to giving it special status within NATO, which could be presented as an outcome palatable even to our hard-liners. But I could not sell this strategy even to Tarasenko, to say nothing of our "Germanists." I still believe it should have been tried. Would the West have accepted it if it had been suggested quietly to Bush and Baker? That is anyone's guess. On the one hand, they probably would have preferred to find a way to include Germany in NATO without humiliating Gorbachev. On the other hand, many in the West would have said that the Soviet Union's policy might soon change for the worse and that the window of opportunity should therefore be taken advantage of quickly. This seemed to be the prevailing view in the United States and in Germany in spring 1990.

Gorbachev's Economic Proposals Meet Opposition from Left and Right

As Shevardnadze was going to Washington in April 1990 to discuss issues and to prepare for Gorbachev's trip to the United States scheduled for late May, my friends and I were not in high spirits. Teimuraz Stepanov said to me, "Pasha, you were always the most optimistic among us, but now even you look and sound pessimistic. You can't hide it."

All of us were worried about developments in the country. Gorbachev had recently been elected president and he immediately appointed Shevardnadze a member of his Presidential Council, kind of a new inner circle. At the Congress that elected him, Gorbachev spoke about the need to speed up and radicalize the economic reform, to move rapidly toward a market economy. That was indeed the only way to go.

The moderate approach to economic change advocated by Ryzhkov and the Council of Ministers was not working, or at least it was not producing any visible benefits for the people. With the standards of living visibly deteriorating, the social fabric was beginning to unravel. The party elite and the conservatives blamed Gorbachev for letting things get out of hand. That should have led to a closer alliance between him and the democratic forces, radicals, and nationalist leaders, but that was not the way it was working.

There was not enough trust between Gorbachev and the new political forces that owed their existence to his reforms. The radical intelligentsia were deserting Gorbachev at precisely the time when he needed their support. They were switching allegiance to Boris Yeltsin, who had been elected overwhelmingly to the Russian parliament. It was clear that Yeltsin had a good chance to become chairman of Russia's Supreme Soviet.

The continued rift between Gorbachev and Yeltsin in 1990 was a prescription for political instability and for the failure of any reform, but many political activists seemed just to be enjoying a good fight and eager to take sides. And they took Yeltsin's side—willingly or unwillingly they were beginning to push Gorbachev to the right.

The hard-liners, the Stalinist institutions, and their leaders were ready to welcome Gorbachev back as a prodigal son who had sown his wild oats and was now returning to the fold, but many of them already distrusted him too much. At the March 1991 Congress of People's Deputies a high-ranking general, Albert Makashov, said Gorbachev should be sent to a course at the Academy of the General Staff to learn what military and political strategy was all about. It seemed increasingly clear that the left and the right despised Gorbachev equally, and there was no center—certainly no organized center.

U.S.-Soviet Talks and German Unity

Germany, talks on conventional forces in Europe, and Lithuania took up most of the time in Shevardnadze's talks with Bush and Baker in Washington in April 1990. There was no longer any expectation that a START treaty would be ready in time for Gorbachev's visit to the United States in May. Shevardnadze appeared reconciled to that; Baker seemed to have other things on his mind. I was deeply disappointed. Of course, the two countries could well live without a formal treaty, because most of its provisions were being quietly observed anyway, but its signing could make a big political splash, favorable to Gorbachev and therefore good for political stability in the Soviet Union. It would demonstrate that the United States was definitely cooperating with Gorbachev, and that it expected others in the Soviet Union to do so too. But George Bush, who at the same time was sympathetic to Gorbachev and cautious and mindful of conservatives in and out of his own administration, was not ready to make such a commitment.

Baker's greatest concern was Lithuania. He and Bush did not hide their dislike of Landsbergis, the Lithuanian leader who was frantically forcing the pace of movement toward independence. They saw how that was endangering Gorbachev's position. But they were also afraid Gorbachev would be tempted or forced to invoke his new powers and introduce presidential rule in Lithuania. That would not only cut the democratic process short in that republic but also result in an explosion of tensions or even violence. This, in broad outline, is what Baker said to Shevardnadze at a private meeting at his home in Washington.

Sipping wine in Baker's basement den, which was decorated with hunting trophies, the two men forgot about their public faces. They seemed no longer to be foreign ministers, but rather two well-informed individuals worried about the developments and sharing their concerns earnestly and directly.

No less than Baker, Shevardnadze was alarmed by the new boldness of the hard-liners and some high-ranking members of the military. He had seemed to be used to their intrigues and remarks against him behind his back. But statements like the one made by General Makashov at the March Congress, he said, were a different matter altogether. He believed the general's statement was seditious, and he told Baker he could not sleep the night after that meeting of the Congress.

I thought the concern was somewhat exaggerated. It still seems to me that at the time the military could be controlled politically, on one condition: that there was a degree of political stabilization in the country. To achieve that, a clear policy was required, particularly toward Lithuania, which was the sore point and the focus of tensions at the time.

I knew Shevardnadze was skeptical, to say the least, about the policy of pressuring Lithuania economically and politically, which most members of the Politburo insisted on, and that he was looking for a different strategy. The oil embargo, decreed by Gorbachev apparently at the insistence of Premier Ryzhkov and others, was definitely a mistake, even if it eventually pushed the Lithuanian leaders to negotiate with the center.

"You need to institute a negotiating mechanism with the Lithuanians," Baker kept saying to Shevardnadze. We knew that he and Bush had encouraged Kohl and Mitterrand to suggest to Landsbergis that he should start negotiations with Moscow without prior recognition of Lithuania's independence by the world community or by the Soviet Union. That was a golden opportunity for everyone, and if history were a reasonable and logical process it would have been seized gratefully. But in real history, only the end result is logical and sometimes even reasonable; the path to it is almost always messy, like Russian roads in late March.

The tone of the discussion about Germany in Washington was good, but in substance it was clear that the "2 plus 4" talks, which would have a first session in early May in Bonn, would be rough going. It seemed that the West had basically agreed on the central argument that appeared unbeatable and therefore had to be accepted by everyone: that the united Germany would be a sovereign country and that its sovereignty must be full and unabridged, and that it therefore had a right to decide for itself which alliances or groups it wanted or did not want to join. The obvious implication was that the question of NATO membership for Germany was predetermined by that and by German leaders' declared position in favor of full NATO membership. Baker outlined that position to Shevardnadze quite forcefully.

Frankly, I did not think that argument amounted to much. It should have been accepted immediately. Yes, the united Germany would be a fully sovereign country. That, however, did not mean it could not decide—in a fully sovereign way—to modify its status in NATO or to accept some constraints on its armed forces, use of territory, and political and military behavior. A special status within NATO was not something unheard of at the time. France had it. Norway did. I believed that constraints, as well as questions such as the definitive nature of Germany's eastern borders and of the unification itself (no more territories to be "reunited" in the future)— questions on which we could not lose—had to be discussed quietly.

Unfortunately, instead of that, a different approach was chosen. Shevardnadze spoke at length about the need to institutionalize the CSCE process and to create structures with expanded responsibilities for all-European security, conflict prevention and resolution, and so on. Those were worthy goals, but, as we saw later, they were difficult to achieve and could promise no immediate benefit. They did not help to achieve a transition to German unity that would cost us less politically. And even when rudimentary European security structures were set up, they did not help to solve or even alleviate the crisis in Yugoslavia.

In the final rush to German unity, the focus of political, diplomatic, and media attention was on the question of NATO membership. Once again I believed it was a failure of imagination on the part of policymakers in both the East and the West to allow this issue to dominate the entire process.

Baker and Shevardnadze also had to spend a lot of time on the questions of conventional forces in Europe. The talks were extremely technical, and without the help of my former boss, Oleg Grinevsky, who was now the Soviet Union's chief delegate at the CFE talks in Vienna, and his U.S. counterpart, James Woolsey, the two ministers would have been lost. But Woolsey and Grinevsky worked well together. They had a good grasp of technical detail and good instincts. They both knew when it was time to call for high-level political help to rescue the negotiations from a technical quagmire. But even Grinevsky, despite his enormous self-confidence, was often perplexed by the problems created by both countries' allies.

Baker, too, often complained to Shevardnadze that an issue that seemed feasible to him bogged down because of the adamant attitude of one or another U.S. ally. But when he said he would try to persuade, say, Turkey or Norway, we knew he would get his way. Eventually he always did. But it took time, and it was becoming increasingly clear that, with the growing demands in Eastern Europe and East Germany for the quick withdrawal of Soviet troops, the CFE treaty was in danger of becoming irrelevant even before it was signed. Soon Baker was saying that openly to Shevardnadze, who couldn't agree more.

When the foreign ministers of the Soviet Union, the United States, Great Britain, France, and East and West Germany met in Bonn on May 5 for the first "2 plus 4" meeting, I had the same feeling of going through the motions in an exercise that was in real danger of becoming irrelevant. On most issues, it seemed to be a "1 versus 5" balance. British Foreign Minister Douglas Hurd and French Foreign Minister Roland Dumas tried to soften the impression, but the East Germans were not playing along, to the dismay even of some members of the U.S. delegation. One of them, generally a most disciplined soldier, said to me, and I agreed, that the East German minister's behavior was awful. Very simply, the man was not a professional.

The German desk of the Soviet foreign ministry, led by Yuly Kvitsinsky, who had just become Shevardnadze's deputy, put together the policy position he outlined to his counterparts. Its essence was that achieving German unity and settling the external aspects of unification should not necessarily coincide, that there could be two different time frames. This approach did not work.

The initial Western reaction was not one of total rejection, but as soon as we returned to Moscow cables from Bonn indicated that the Germans were opposed to the idea and were mounting a media campaign against it. As Gorbachev saluted the military parade in Red Square to celebrate the anniversary of victory in the Second World War, hard-liners everywhere, and some of my colleagues in the foreign ministry, were saying that the Soviet Union was capitulating to Germany forty-five years after the end of the war.

This impression, and the dangers that stemmed from it, was just one of Gorbachev's problems as he traveled to Washington on his third trip to the United States. Lithuania was another one. A few weeks before, it seemed that things were moving toward the end of the oil blockade and the start of negotiations with no prior conditions between Moscow and Vilnius. But something had happened to make Landsbergis change his mind. Apparently he thought that agreement to begin negotiations would hand Gorbachev a propaganda victory on the eve of his U.S. trip. Still, Gorbachev said he was confident that talks would start fairly soon, and he turned out to be right about that.

Gorbachev's Plans for Economic Change Meet Criticism

But even the Lithuanian problem, difficult as it was, paled in comparison with two other problems that almost exploded in the days leading up to Gorbachev's visit. Those problems were the economy and the first session of the newly elected Russian Supreme Soviet.

In the first months of 1990 Gorbachev had made up his mind that a much more rapid transition toward a market economy was required and instructed the Council of Ministers to prepare a plan to be presented first to his Presidential Council and then to the Supreme Soviet. The initial plan, which had been discussed by the Presidential Council in the spring, was criticized both by some academic economists for not being radical enough and by the conservative leaders of some of the republics for being too radical. Following a revision in the Council of Ministers, it became more cautious and less liberal, but that was not the main problem. Any transition plan would have to require a substantial increase in prices of food and consumer goods, which had long before ceased to reflect the costs. But the country, and particularly the workers, who had been brought up to believe in stable, relatively low prices, were simply not ready for that.

People had to be persuaded that changing the price system was the only way, and that task fell to Gorbachev and Prime Minister Ryzhkov. The new democratically elected politicians preferred to have nothing to do with it and continued to insist on "social protection." When Ryzhkov announced to the Supreme Soviet the final blueprint for the reform, including the projected price rises, which were relatively modest, panic buying began almost immediately. People began to hoard in anticipation of the new prices. For the first time in many years there were huge lines in Moscow stores to buy spaghetti, rice, sugar, and similar products, which had never been in short supply. Yeltsin called the proposed prices "plunder of the people," and reformist economists called them "shock without therapy."

Yeltsin's Election Presents Challenge to Gorbachev

On the eve of his departure for Canada and the United States, Gorbachev made a televised address about the proposed reform. He said all the right things about the need to cut subsidies and move toward a more efficient economy, but his speech had little effect. It was characteristically unfocused and lacked punch lines that would make it memorable. But even if it had been better written it would not have been more successful. The people were not yet ready for real, painful reform, and they now had their "champions" in Yeltsin and men like the newly elected Mayor of Moscow, Gavriil Popov, who combined liberal economic pronouncements with populist politics.

Also on the eve of Gorbachev's visit Yeltsin was fiercely battling Ivan Polozkov, a conservative regional party boss from Krasnodar, for the post of Chairman of Russia's Supreme Soviet. Gorbachev was officially neutral, but he did nothing to dispel the impression that he was against Yeltsin. By that time, mutual resentment between them may have reached a point of no return. Yeltsin's election by the first Congress of People's Deputies of Russia was not assured, but it should not have been resisted. When Gorbachev was boarding the plane for North America, several rounds of voting had taken place at the Congress, with inconclusive results. But Yeltsin was inching closer to the required majority.

On the eve of the visit, there was talk that Gorbachev might shorten it because of the tense situation in the country. The atmosphere of tension was felt on the plane too. There was a lot of talk about the economy, Yeltsin's likely election, and the trouble in Armenia, where armed local militants had begun to attack Soviet army garrisons.

Midway to Canada the news came that Yeltsin had been elected. It was not unexpected but people in the section where I was seated naturally began to discuss the possible reaction to the event. Valentin Falin, a Central Committee secretary, and Alexander Dzasokhov, chairman of the Supreme Soviet's foreign relations committee, suggested that Gorbachev send a telegram to congratulate Yeltsin and even drafted something not at all in the Gorbachev style. From that draft I particularly remember one phrase: "You have shown yourself to be a real fighter." The result was a curious mixture: it was both patronizing and somewhat obsequious. Chernyaev reluctantly agreed to show the draft to Gorbachev, who dismissed it with a smile and a comment that he did not need this kind of advice.

Gorbachev Talks with Canada's Mulroney

When the plane landed in Ottawa the question about Yeltsin was one of the first Gorbachev was asked. He said, essentially, that he respected the democratic choice of the deputies and hoped that he and Yeltsin would cooperate. He emphasized that during the campaign, and also in his speeches at the Congress, Yeltsin had spoken in favor of Russia remaining within the Soviet Union. Actually, there were some doubts about Yeltsin's position on that score. Clearly his main commitment was not to the Soviet Union. I think that Gorbachev, a realistic politician, understood the need to work with Yeltsin.

Canadian Prime Minister Brian Mulroney was eager to hear what Gorbachev had to say about domestic developments in the Soviet Union. He and Gorbachev had talked about the prospects of the Soviet federation six months before, during Mulroney's visit to Moscow, and Mulroney understood Gorbachev's problem better than some other visitors. "I will be very happy to see you succeed in reforming your federation," he said. "That would probably be helpful in addressing our own problems in Canada."

Now, only a few months later, the challenges of reforming the Union and the economy seemed even more daunting. Mulroney also asked whether Gorbachev had confidence in his economic team. I know that at the time some people close to Gorbachev were suggesting he should dispense with the increasingly unpopular Ryzhkov; the new democrats were doing so quite openly. During the visit the Canadians and the Americans sometimes appeared to be hinting that that would be a wise thing to do, but Gorbachev did not react to such hints, for obvious reasons and also because he was generally reluctant to part with his associates. Politically, his character was a mixture of that of a boss, who likes to have the final word on everything, and a conciliator, who seeks compromise among all members of his team. Gorbachev rarely fired people and never enjoyed doing it.

Mulroney also wanted to reassure Gorbachev about the West's intentions concerning Germany. In essence, he was saying that the process of unification was not some kind of Western conspiracy and that the West too had some difficulty adjusting to the stunning pace of unification. He did not have to belabor that point. Gorbachev was never keen on conspiracy theories, and by that time any residual illusions he might have had about the Stalinist "socialist camp" were gone. What he really was concerned about was the problem of security, particularly its perception in the Soviet Union. To that problem neither Mulroney nor President Bush in Washington seemed to have an answer.

The Bush-Gorbachev Summit

At their Washington summit Bush and Gorbachev struck me as two men who were concerned about one problem: stability and the fate of democracy in the Soviet Union. Bush knew that a few weeks later Gorbachev was to appear before a very conservative Congress of the Communist Party in Moscow with a record that had to seem appalling not just to the hard-liners but to many of the party regulars as well. A possible break between Gorbachev and the still powerful party seemed a real prospect, and a reversal of the democratic gains of the preceding months was a clear possibility. Therefore, unlike many senators, who at a meeting with Gorbachev sounded more like interrogators, Bush sought to understand, to explain, and to suggest.

Unlike many other visits, this one was mostly about symbols. Lithuania was one of them. From what Bush and Baker were saying, it was increasingly obvious to me that they regarded the Baltics more as an inherited irritant than as a moral or geopolitical issue on which they sought a quick and clear victory. Gorbachev, for his part, had come to understand the need to seek a compromise with the Lithuanians, relying on the more moderate reformers who still had some influence in that republic in 1990.

I recall an episode during the U.S. visit when Gorbachev spoke privately at some length about Lithuania. Waiting in a suite in a San Francisco hotel for his first meeting with the president of South Korea, Gorbachev suddenly switched to internal developments, which were never far from his mind. He said he was sure that talks with the Lithuanians would start soon. They would be difficult, he said, but he was not pessimistic. He expected that Landsbergis's strategy would be to do everything to exacerbate problems. But Gorbachev spoke with respect of people like Lithuanian Premier Kazimiera Prunskene, Lithuanian Communist Party leader Algis Brazauskas, and other moderates, whose names he recalled without apparent effort. Those were reasonable people, Gorbachev said, with whom an agreement on some form of association was possible. I was glad to hear that. Even Landsbergis was saying then that one thing Lithuania really wanted was "to become again a sovereign entity under international law"—the rest would be up for discussion.

Negotiating some kind of association would have been much better than what actually happened afterward. But that would have required a clear negotiating strategy aimed at reaching agreement rapidly. The rather conservative Ryzhkov, who headed the Soviet government's delegation to the talks, was in no mood to support such an approach. The negotiations soon degenerated into a purely formal exercise. Shevardnadze, after his resignation, said often that he could not forgive himself for being so passive in that matter. He had known that the negotiations were being mishandled but had not done enough to try to change that.

The trade treaty between the United States and the Soviet Union and the most-favored-nation trade regime for the Soviet Union were other symbolic issues at the Washington summit. No one expected a big upsurge in trade as a result of the most-favored-nation status, but the issue had acquired great political significance and was therefore important. Years before it had been tied by Senator Henry A. Jackson and Congressman Charles A. Vanick to the problem of free emigration from the Soviet Union. Now all the barriers to emigration had been removed, but the administration was still hesitant and Shevardnadze and Baker had to spend an inordinate amount of time working out a formula on that symbolic issue.

In contrast, arms control issues, which used to take up so much time and energy at previous summits, were almost pushed to the background. Both sides had come to accept the delay in reaching final agreement on START, which meant that some issues of importance to each of them remained unresolved.

The Americans made another effort to persuade Gorbachev to agree to limits on the flight testing of the SS-18 heavy missiles. From some private remarks of Yury Maslyukov I understood that he would have been willing to consider compromises, but not in a situation when the signing of the treaty was being delayed yet again. It was clear, however, that the administration would sign START only after an agreement on conventional forces in Europe had been concluded. Eventually, the administration signed the START treaty, which included no constraints on the flight testing of SS-18s.

Mutual Trust, Closeness, and Warmth

The visit's final symbol was Bush's invitation to Gorbachev to spend a day of relaxing and informal talks at Camp David. It was a symbol of trust, greater closeness, and warmth between them. And it was not a show, but real. As I worked with both of them and watched them at Camp David I thought how paradoxical things were. They were definitely more at ease with each other than with many politicians in their own country. The more complicated and perplexing the situation was becoming, the more they wanted to rely on each other. Each knew that the other man would not intentionally do any harm to him despite the pressures. But I still don't know whether they fully understood the complexity and intensity of those pressures. Maybe they thought mutual trust made all the difference—and it did make a lot of difference, up to a point.

The talks at Camp David were relaxed and businesslike. Gorbachev said to Shevardnadze that when he was talking with Bush and Baker about the various regional issues, he felt as if he were "at some seminar in Moscow." This time the third person on the Soviet side was not Anatoly Chernyaev but Marshal Sergey Akhromeyev, who told me Gorbachev had asked him to take notes. Indeed, arrangements had been made for simultaneous interpretation during which the interpreter is normally unable to write down anything. Still, I decided to take some notes just in case, and I turned out to be right.

When Akhromeyev gave me his notebook—to decipher, as he put it—I found his handwriting barely legible and the notes very incomplete, so that without my own scribblings I would have been unable to make a decent memorandum of conversation. During lunch break I talked to Gorbachev, and he agreed that a colleague of mine should attend the afternoon session to record the talks.

Of course, the initial idea for Akhromeyev's presence was not that he should be a note-taker. I never talked with Gorbachev about it subsequently, but I believe he wanted him to be present as someone who was trusted by the military and the conservatives and could confirm that nothing "improper" happened during those private discussions—no capitulation, no sellout.

Before the talks resumed in the afternoon, Bush showed Gorbachev the grounds at Camp David, including the place where he liked to play horseshoes. We all threw one or two horseshoes, and Gorbachev hit a ringer on his first or second try—a fact of which Bush made much when he talked to the press at the end of the day. Bush was somewhat less successful in his first throw; when he turned away to talk to Brent Scowcroft I came up to the pin and placed a horseshoe right on target. When Bush turned back I laughed and said, "This one is yours, Mr. President!" "You joker," he said, laughing too, and made a mock threatening gesture with his finger. Gorbachev too had a good laugh and said he was overruling the throw.

The Germany and NATO Question

But the serious business was never far from everyone's mind. Decision time on the issue of united Germany's membership in NATO was quickly approaching, and Gorbachev agreed to the inevitable: in a talk with Bush he said that Germany itself would have to decide the matter. This still left open the possibility of some face-saving "special status" formula later. But Gorbachev's advisers on Germany, including Valentin Falin, who was in the Soviet delegation at the summit, seemed unable to suggest anything creative. Nevertheless, it was Falin who later accused Gorbachev of caving in and who said that "dramatic steps" should have been taken to slow down the process of unification and prevent Germany from becoming a member of NATO.

What is most unfair about this criticism is that there was nothing behind Falin's self-important airs. He did not suggest an alternative strategy either then or later. According to a Russian journalist, who heard Falin speak in Berlin in 1991, he said the process should have been stopped "with a million soldiers if necessary." It is always sad to see how a person with a good mind loses touch with reality. In Falin's case, his arrogance often outweighed his intelligence and perhaps clouded his vision. Our American partners did not help matters when in 1992 they began to claim victory on the German issue. The issue was decided by the German people. Whatever political leaders on both sides did concerned only one question: whether the unification would take place in a peaceful and relatively painless manner, or whether it would cause major trouble, perhaps even a conflict, in East-West relations.

Bush's associates later told me he had prohibited them from speaking about Germany, Eastern Europe, or the events in the Soviet Union in terms of U.S. victory. This is consistent with Bush's cautious behavior in 1990. He certainly did his best during the Washington summit to treat Gorbachev as an equal partner, not an enemy on the run.

Whatever the rumors preceding the visit, Gorbachev did not want to cut it short. He went ahead with the whole program, going to Minnesota and to California for brief stops. The news from home was that the situation had quieted down somewhat; in the United States the media coverage of the visit was extensive and generally quite sympathetic. The crowds in Minnesota and in San Francisco were enthusiastic. There were some flags of the Baltic states here and there, but they did not anger Gorbachev, particularly since most people carrying them seemed good-natured and there were almost no hostile calls or chanting of slogans. He mingled with the crowds; there is little that Gorbachev enjoyed more than that.

The Reagans Visit with the Gorbachevs

In San Francisco Gorbachev had a few events on his schedule: an address to the leading members of the business community, a visit to Stanford University, and a talk with the president of South Korea. He also had a reunion with Ronald Reagan, which I thought went well. The former U.S. president and Nancy Reagan came to see the Gorbachevs, who were staying at the residence of the Soviet consul-general, a spacious building with a breathtaking view of the city and San Francisco Bay. Reagan looked older than when we last saw him in Moscow—two years had passed since that visit—but he still had enough power to walk a few sprightly steps from his car to the house, to wave and smile to the reporters and the crowd, and to keep up a lively conversation with Gorbachev during the photo opportunity and half-hour talk that followed. He really was amazing. Eight years of the presidency, the bout with cancer, and the recent riding accident had aged him, but he still behaved and spoke as if he regarded himself as a young man with many years of active life ahead.

Reagan and Gorbachev spoke about the visit, about the old times, and about current events. Reagan was not uninformed. At one point he mentioned Lithuania and said, "Is it not true, Mikhail, that when Lithuania was incorporated into the Soviet Union before World War II the other alternative was that it would be occupied by Germany?"

Gorbachev agreed.

"Well," Reagan said, "that does not come out at all from what is being written about it now."

In the meantime Nancy Reagan and Raisa Gorbachev were having their little talk in the same room, with no sign of tension or any residual resentment. They were both lively and really chattered away. I still think that talk of friction between them was exaggerated. Raisa has her explanation for it: small misunderstandings amplified by protocol mishaps. I have a simpler explanation: the media has to play something up, and the real work of summits is boring.

Right after the get-together with Reagan, Gorbachev went to Stanford—something he was looking forward to. Forty years earlier he had been a provincial lad studying at Moscow University, and since then he had valued the process of learning as such and the academic milieu. Unlike most of his party colleagues and, paradoxically, many members of the intelligentsia, who were often content with the scrapings of education they had picked up at college and afterward, he had a healthy respect for knowledge.

I went with the Gorbachevs in their car. As it sped on the expressway to Stanford we talked about all kinds of things: the impressions of the visit, news from home, recent newspaper articles, and Gorbachev's plans for organizing his presidential staff. Now that he had been elected president, he said, this was a priority task. "But it's tricky. There are many pitfalls. Boldin will be Chief of Staff. But I want Yakovlev and Primakov to supervise the process."

Gorbachev asked me whether I would like to be a member of his staff. "There will probably be a small foreign policy development unit," he said. "And I've been using you a lot for quick reference, so to speak."

The offer was a complete surprise to me, and I think it was an improvisation on Gorbachev's part. I said I needed time to think it over. Frankly, I enjoyed working in Shevardnadze's foreign ministry. The U.S. desk was a good, hardworking team, and I had many friends there.

"It's not urgent," Gorbachev said, and indeed for several months nothing was done to set up the foreign policy unit, and the whole business of putting together the staff dragged on extremely slowly. Without a staff and a vertical system of executive command and control, Gorbachev was often president in name only—his own troubleshooter, negotiator, and fence-mender. The transitional system was, perhaps inevitably, an eclectic mixture of the old regime and new, more democratic elements. Trial and error was the name of the game.

On the way to Stanford, Gorbachev also mentioned something he had read recently in the radical magazine *Ogonyok*: an interview with a former colleague of mine, now a U.N. official in New York. Gorbachev was critical of the interview. He said that attacking Brezhnev now for rudeness and incompetence was like beating a dead horse (he actually used a stronger Russian expression). Whether Brezhnev was a bad man was irrelevant, Gorbachev said; actually he was not that bad. The important thing was that in his time our country became increasingly marginal economically, technologically, and even culturally. But there had to be some dignity in speaking about the country's former leaders, he concluded. Raisa Gorbachev said we had a long way to go before leaders, past or present, would be treated "normally," as she put it.

At Stanford, Gorbachev was greeted by two student representatives, whom he asked—at my instigation, prompted by Condoleezza Rice, a National Security Council staff member and former and future Stanford professor—whether they will "beat Cal" that year.

"We will," the boy said confidently.

Gorbachev wished him good luck. After his address to the students and faculty he walked to a nearby building, where he was to meet with George Shultz and a group of Stanford professors. There were thousands of young people on the streets of the campus, and everyone wanted to shake his hand.

Gorbachev seemed to draw strength from the crowd—their smiles, handshakes, and words of encouragement—or perhaps it was those young men and women who could draw strength from being close to him. They would need a lot of strength and courage in their lives, which were just beginning. Who could say what proportion of happiness and adversity, how many victories and how many defeats, were in store for them? That is what I thought as I watched Gorbachev at Stanford—a small triumph, to be followed by the continued ordeal of a reformer in a tough country.

Shultz introduced to Gorbachev a group of colleagues from the Stanford faculty—professors of history, economics, microbiology, genetics, and I don't remember what else. Each had something to say about the present and the future and the global problems, which, as Gorbachev often said, no country could handle alone.

Gorbachev kept up the conversation, which sometimes became quite specialized, rather well, but he responded with particular approval to economist Milton Friedman, who recalled that prospects for economic reform in Japan after the war were regarded as quite poor; it was said that the Japanese were different from Westerners and that their traditional ways made adapting to a Western-style economic system difficult. "And see what Japan has become now, Mr. President," Friedman concluded. "So you should not be bothered by similar arguments as regards your country."

Gorbachev often recalled Friedman's words later, and never quarreled with their ideological message. He said often that the labels "capitalism" and "socialism" were outdated, and certainly no good for the twenty-first century. And yet Gorbachev was the leader of the Communist Party. He had to deal with its apparat and its rank-and-file members, and he believed that abandoning his position as general secretary would result in a vendetta not only against him but also against perestroika and the beginnings of democracy. So he wanted to reform the party, to help it transform itself into something similar to a social-democratic party of a Western type. This was the party's only chance to survive, as it turned out later, but its leaders preferred suicide. As shaped and structured by Stalin, the party could not be reformed.

Continued Challenges to Gorbachev at Home

Several weeks after the August coup Chernyaev told me that every attempt to reform the party by promoting younger people had made things even worse. The old guard at least was automatically loyal to the chief, but many of the younger bosses were totally cynical, angry, and ready to do anything to turn back the clock. And such people were at every level of administration in the party, the KGB, the army, and various government ministries. They were a majority at the 28th Party Congress, at which Gorbachev had to preside a few weeks after his trip to America.

The hard-liners in the Central Committee, and particularly the regional party secretaries, regarded the Congress as perhaps their last stand—or a golden opportunity to topple Gorbachev. There were many issues they could exploit, and the German problem was one of them. It was clear that no amount of political posturing or diplomatic maneuvering could stop or even slow down the unification bandwagon. It was going to happen, it was going to happen soon, and it was going to happen "according to Kohl."

Whatever misgivings some Westerners, particularly the French, had on that score, they decided to go ahead and ratify the unification and worry about the consequences later, hoping that the European Community would somehow "subsume" German unity. But Gorbachev and his supporters had to worry about how it was going to play at the Party Congress.

Following Gorbachev's visit to the United States, Shevardnadze went to Berlin with a draft document entitled "Main Principles of the Final International Legal Settlement with Germany." A look at the paper, born in the third European department of the foreign ministry, and perhaps "improved" in the Central Committee before being approved by the Politburo, was enough to reveal that it would cause nothing but irritation in Bonn and probably in Washington.

Everything had been thrown in—things that had already been accepted by all, such as the final nature of Germany's postunification borders, and things that were bound to be rejected outright. For example, it was proposed that for a transitional period of five years all international treaties concluded by the FRG and the GDR—including even the Warsaw Pact—would remain in effect. This was, of course, an impossible demand. Indeed, I thought that proposing long drafts at a time when events were developing at a mind-boggling speed would invite certain embarrassment. It might have been a purely formal exercise for domestic consumption, but Shevardnadze felt as if he had been set up. He had a difficult talk with Baker.

For the first time in many months I saw that Baker was clearly disappointed. Asked at a photo opportunity his impression of the Soviet draft, he quipped, "I'm underwhelmed." Sitting with Shevardnadze in a gloomy room in the Soviet embassy in Berlin, a pompous huge palace built to last for centuries, he seemed uncomfortable and sometimes at a loss for words, which was rare for him. But his message was clear: this is not the way to do it.

The United States, Baker suggested, understood that rapid German unification created political, military, psychological, and logistical problems for the Soviet Union. It was ready to help alleviate those problems, but both sides had to approach them in a realistic way. "Tell us what you need to make what is happening more acceptable to you," Baker said. "Tell us what you need," he repeated, "and we'll see what we can do."

Shevardnadze too was disappointed. Only our German experts seemed to be unaware that the time for diplomatic games was over. Thirty years ago the Soviet Union had made a strategic mistake by agreeing with the East German leaders that it was in its best interest to have a permanently divided Germany. For thirty years they had been pursuing a policy that was wrong. Some, like my former boss in the Geneva INF delegation Yuly Kvitsinsky, did it with great intellectual agility and diplomatic skill. None of them, even the younger ones, truly accepted the fact that it was now over and done with.

A few days before the Party Congress, at a reception hosted by an American news organization, a friendly reporter asked me what I expected from the Congress. Frankly, I said, I would have preferred to have no Congress at all. I did not think Gorbachev would lose it, but he would have to justify his policies to people who were obviously out of step with the changing times. I had a vague feeling of foreboding before that Congress, and it turned out to have been justified.

In a way, Gorbachev won. He was able to contain the conservative onslaught by, alternately, haranguing the delegates, deflecting their anger, or pacifying them. But the sight of people like Gorbachev, Yakovlev, and Shevardnadze grilled, booed, or heckled by a mob of party and government bureaucrats was extremely disturbing. True, most of the delegates had the common sense not to elect Yegor Ligachev, who had become the hard-liners' flag-bearer, as Gorbachev's deputy. Gorbachev was able to insist on the election of people he trusted to the Central Committee, but it turned out to be a hollow victory.

The embittered hard-liners did not accept their defeat and soon began to regroup and organize in alternative ways. And the democrats, both in and out of the Party, were not satisfied with Gorbachev's tactic of gradually squeezing out the conservatives and reshaping the party. His efforts earned him polite applause at best, followed quickly by a new set of radical demands.

Gorbachev was increasingly regarded by the democrats as "one of them." The instinctive, rather unthinking admiration for him that much of the intelligentsia felt when he came to power had been replaced by a similarly unthinking knee-jerk rejection of almost anything he said or did. In droves, the intelligentsia were defecting to Yeltsin, ready to give him unreserved and unquestioned support.

Yeltsin Leaves the Party

At the end of the Congress, Yeltsin declared that he was resigning from the party. This was no surprise. He was beginning a new odyssey, which turned out to be the shortest route to the pinnacle of power. His vehicle was the Supreme Soviet of the Russian Federation.

Following Yeltsin's election as Chairman of the Russian Supreme Soviet in May 1990, the Supreme Soviet adopted the Declaration of State Sovereignty of Russia, which proclaimed the supremacy of Russia's laws over the laws of the Union. The other republics soon followed suit. That was, of course, legally untenable, and it turned out to be the first step in the dissolution of the Union, but Stalin's constitution, which was not significantly changed under Brezhnev, contained enough loopholes and inherent contradictions to explain away this "interpretation" of sovereignty.

Yeltsin grudgingly accepted that the Union would continue to be responsible for foreign policy and defense, but he wanted full control of the economy. The other republics, particularly the Ukraine, jumped at the opportunity to try to solve their economic problems by introducing more controls and limiting the outflow of goods in order to protect their consumers and counter the shortages. Almost immediately the established production and trade linkages began to rupture, and panic buying and hoarding became rampant. From then on, the situation in the economy began to deteriorate even more rapidly. Gorbachev was again facing the dilemma of how to respond. After all, the decisions destroying the economy were made by democratically elected parliaments and their leaders. And the problem of sovereignty for the republics was particularly difficult.

Gorbachev understood the need to decentralize the economy. In Fall 1990, when Baker wondered in a talk with him how he must have felt when the republics were adopting those sovereignty declarations one after another, Gorbachev said: "It would have been easy to respond to them emotionally, to call them illegal and so on. But one had to see the objective process behind them and try to channel it properly. And the way to do it was by preparing a new Union treaty that would redistribute authority in the country, transferring much of it from the center to the republics."

Political System Askew

In a country with a responsible political elite, that is precisely what would have happened, but in the Soviet Union the political system was going haywire. It consisted of the remnants of the old system, new politicized groups, mostly of a nationalist kind, populist elected leaders—and Gorbachev, who was almost alone in the political center. It was therefore very difficult to organize an orderly process of redistributing authority.

Shevardnadze was already skeptical about the Union treaty process, and said it might be too late to put it on track. I shared his doubts. In retrospect, I believe it could have gone either way, but in essence it depended on the position of one republic—Russia. Had its leader decided firmly that he needed a Union treaty, and made up his mind about the kind of treaty he wanted, it would have been concluded. But Yeltsin had a different agenda then. His principal goal was to diminish the center.

The U.S. Administration Is Bewildered

The U.S. administration was watching the situation with wonder and dismay. From what Baker was saying to Shevardnadze at their meetings during the summer I gathered that the Americans were not yet clear what turn events might take and what kind of dangers they should worry about. Shevardnadze had already mentioned the possibility of reactionary dictatorship should perestroika fail, but he was not specific about the possible scenarios.

Some Americans who talked with me informally wondered whether I thought Shevardnadze had a specific potential dictator in mind. I did not think so, but things were developing so fast, I said, that someone might pop up quite suddenly and catch the people's fancy. Predicting anything with certainty was extremely difficult.

Listening to Baker, I felt that our U.S. partners were literally swamped with information from the Soviet Union that was puzzling and difficult to transform into policy recommendations. It was also clear to me that Bush and

Baker wanted to help Gorbachev, and soon they were saying that openly. But the administration was apparently not unanimous about that goal. It did not have a policy of supporting Gorbachev, and it had no policy on how to affect relations between the center and the republics.

In Paris in mid-July, Bush asked Shevardnadze whether the administration should deal mostly with the center or with the republics on matters of trade and economic assistance. The question was, at best, premature. Despite their declarations of sovereignty, the republics simply did not have the structures or institutions capable of handling international trade or large-scale economic assistance. This was a fact that the U.S. embassy in Moscow, or any knowledgeable expert, could easily confirm for Baker. In that very practical sense the republics barely existed. Shevardnadze, in his mild and nonpolemical way, explained that to Baker, but the administration was obviously anticipating a redistribution of authority.

The meeting between Shevardnadze and Baker in Paris was marked by a unique blend of emotions: relief, bewilderment, and alarm. I thought relief prevailed, because it seemed that the German issue had finally been defused. The problem of the united Germany's membership in NATO, which both sides had made into such a big issue—unwisely, I believed—was at last behind us.

Kohl and Gorbachev Strike a Deal

Helmut Kohl came to Moscow on the eve of the Paris "2 plus 4" meeting in July. He and Gorbachev, accompanied by Genscher and Shevardnadze, then went on to the Stavropol region, Gorbachev's birthplace. They had talks at a mountain retreat in Arkhyz, a place no one seemed to have heard of before. Its name would go down in history, at least in German history, but we did not yet know it when our plane was landing at the Mineralnye Vody airport, where it was to pick up Shevardnadze after the Arkhyz talks and proceed to Paris. The passenger list included most members of Shevardnadze's team, journalists, and a group of the foreign ministry's German experts, led by Alexander Bondarenko, a veteran official whom his subordinates disparagingly called "Shurik" behind his back.

No one knew what was going to happen at Arkhyz, and when the reporters asked me my prediction, I told them I had no answer. To myself I thought that two things had just occurred that could make one hopeful.

First, at the Party Congress, Gorbachev had outmaneuvered the hard-liners and now had his hands free, at least in foreign affairs. Second, the NATO council, meeting in London, had issued a helpful declaration that marked a real change of emphasis in NATO's strategy. NATO stated that it was ready to regard members of the Warsaw Pact no longer as enemies and that it was reviewing its concepts of forward defense and flexible response—the strategies for first use of nuclear weapons.

I felt this was precisely the kind of straw at which we should clutch. Under my old pen name, P. Vorobyev, I wrote an article entitled "Living Without an Enemy" for the mass circulation newspaper *Trud*. NATO, I wrote, should no longer be regarded as a bogeyman; we must learn to live without an enemy.

As our plane was waiting at the Mineralnye Vody airport, time seemed to crawl. It was a tense wait. Some of us stayed inside the plane, others went into the airport building, where the V.I.P. lounge was decorated with a huge portrait of Lenin. We bought some souvenirs, talked with the local people, and watched the highway for signs of the approaching motorcade. Waiting forms a large part of a diplomat's life. It is boring, but the results are sometimes worth the wait. They certainly were this time.

The helicopters and the motorcade with the officials and reporters who had gone to Arkhyz and then to Stavropol, where Gorbachev and Kohl did a little barnstorming, finally arrived, and the usual predeparture commotion began. We were all inside our plane, waiting for Shevardnadze and Kvitsinsky, who accompanied him in Arkhyz.

Kvitsinsky entered our section of the plane with his enigmatic smile that was like a mask he was always wearing on his face. Bondarenko looked at him questioningly, and Kvitsinsky said: "Germany will unite, the four-power rights will be terminated, and Germany will pledge to reduce the size of the Bundeswehr to 370,000."

"And NATO?" Bondarenko asked.

Kvitsinsky replied, "It will be a member of NATO. The territory of East Germany will have special status. Our troops will stay there for a transitional period of four years, and NATO's structures will not extend to it."

As I watched Bondarenko it was clear to me that, despite the sweeteners listed by Kvitsinsky, he was shocked. It was obvious we would have some explaining to do at home, but that was the best deal we could hope for. In fact, it was more than I had expected. For the first time ever, Germany would pledge to limit its troops to a very low level. This alone enhanced our security more than anything weapons experts could invent and our industry could produce.

When he learned of the deal, Baker was perhaps surprised, but he said he was pleased that Gorbachev and Kohl had struck a deal. American reporters in Paris asked me whether I thought it was a kind of snub at the other players in the "2 plus 4" game. I told them frankly, though not for attribution, that the "2 plus 4" and our other attempts to work out a formula on the NATO membership issue with the United States and other Western allies had not been particularly productive, and that therefore striking a deal directly with Kohl was all that remained for us to do. If the United States was not totally comfortable with this fact, it was a small problem compared with those Gorbachev and Shevardnadze had to face.

It seemed to me that Baker would have preferred a U.S. role that was more assertive, a role of greater apparent leadership and resolve. He looked a little different in Paris—more thoughtful, vaguely wary of something he was afraid might happen. At one point he said to Shevardnadze: "Things seem to be going well for us. The economy is good, and President Bush's standing in the opinion polls is high. But in the nature of things it has to end one day, and things may turn difficult fairly soon."

Baker suggested that a combination of problems on the U.S. side, and instability in the Soviet Union, could create a situation that would have to be managed skillfully and might require the two countries to rely on each other much more than ever before. Listening to him, I thought that such talk would have been difficult to imagine even a few months before. And two weeks later his prediction came true, though probably not in the way he had thought of.

I interpreted for Andrey Gromyko only a few times. Here, he is talking to the Ethiopian Ambassador to the U.S.S.R., Nesibu Taye (far left), at the Sheremetyevo airport while waiting for the arrival of the foreign minister of Ethiopia in September 1981. To Gromyko's right is Anatoly Kovalev, his deputy, who continued as deputy to Eduard Shevardnadze. I am second from the left. (Photo by TASS)

My first assignment with Gorbachev (right) in May 1985. He was interviewed in his office at the Central Committee in Moscow by a reporter for the Press Trust of India news agency. I am between the two men. (Photo by TASS)

During Rajiv Gandhi's official visit to Moscow in May 1985, Gorbachev invited
him to take a walk on the grounds of the Kremlin. They are shown here with a
group of Indian officials and Indian and Soviet security guards. I am second from
the right, between Gorbachev and Gandhi. (Photo by TASS)

Shevardnadze's first meeting with President Reagan in September 1985. I had entered the White House only once before, as a tourist in 1976. I am seated at Shevardnadze's left. (Photo by Eduard Pesov)

In November 1985, Gorbachev had his first summit meeting with an American president. This was also my first U.S.-Soviet summit. Here, I am interpreting at a one-on-one meeting between Gorbachev (right) and Reagan (middle) on November 20, 1985, at the Soviet mission in Geneva. (Photo by Yury Abramochkin, Novosti Press Agency)

During a break in the negotiations at the Geneva summit in November 1985, I am standing at the far right with Secretary of State George Shultz and Soviet Foreign Minister Eduard Shevardnadze. Seated are, left to right, Alexander Yakovlev, then Secretary of the Communist Party Central Committee, and Leonid Zamyatin, then head of the Central Committee's International Information Department. (Photo by TASS)

I interpret for Gorbachev (right) when he meets with Senator Edward Kennedy (left) at the Kremlin in February 1986. My "working relationship" with Gorbachev began to be closer from about that time. This was also the first meeting attended by Anatoly Chernyaev as Gorbachev's assistant for international affairs. (Photo by TASS)

On Gorbachev's official visit to the United States in December 1987, talks at the White House with the two delegations present. As can be seen in the picture, simultaneous interpretation, which Reagan liked, is used (I am sitting next to Gorbachev, with the microphone). Members of the Soviet delegation, shown on Reagan's right, are, from left to right, Sergey Tarasenko, my colleague Sergey Berezhkov, former Soviet Ambassador to the United States Anatoly Dobrynin (at the time, head of the Central Committee's International Department), Alexander Yakovlev, and Eduard Shevardnadze. Next to Reagan is Dmitri Zarechnak, State Department interpreter. The Americans present are seated on my left. From left to right they are White House Chief of Staff Howard Baker, National Security Adviser Colin Powell, and Secretary of State George Shultz. (Official White House photograph)

This photograph was taken in President Reagan's study at the White House during the Washington summit in December 1987. The invitation to this private room was Reagan's sign of friendship toward Gorbachev, second from the left. At the far left is William Hopkins, a State Department interpreter. I stand at Reagan's left. (Official White House photograph)

The next summit, Reagan's last, was in Moscow in the summer of 1988. The arrival ceremony was held in the ornate St. George's Hall of the Kremlin, and the President and Mrs. Reagan were clearly impressed by the grandeur of the setting. In this photo, the Gorbachevs and the Reagans talk right after the ceremony. I stand between Gorbachev and Mrs. Reagan, and Raisa Gorbachev stands at President Reagan's left. (Photo by Eduard Pesov)

Following the election of George Bush, Gorbachev had talks at Governors Island in New York with President Reagan and President-elect Bush. Shown in this picture are, from left to right, George Bush, Ronald Reagan, National Security Adviser Colin Powell, Soviet Deputy Foreign Minister Alexander Bessmertnykh, Soviet Ambassador to the United States Yury Dubinin, Shevardnadze, Gorbachev, Gorbachev's assistant Anatoly Chernyaev, and Central Committee Secretary Anatoly Dobrynin. I am standing. (Photo by Yury Abramochkin)

At the end of the talks at Governors Island, Gorbachev, Reagan, and President-elect Bush talk on the porch of the building where the talks had taken place. Others in the picture are myself, far left, and U.S. State Department interpreter Dmitry Zarechnak.

In February 1989, Shevardnadze went to Pakistan to discuss the implications of the withdrawal of Soviet troops from Afghanistan. The talks were difficult, though the atmosphere was quite civil and at times seemed cordial. Shown in this picture are, from left to right, Deputy Foreign Minister Igor Rogachev, Shevardnadze, myself, and Teimuraz Stepanov, Shevardnadze's close assistant. On the Pakistani side of the table are Prime Minister Benazir Bhutto, with her adviser Iqbal Akhund to her left and Foreign Minister Sahabzada Yakub Khan to her right. (Photo by Eduard Pesov)

On Shevardnadze's plane, returning from his trip to Asia in February 1989,
Shevardnadze explains his thinking to, from left to right, me, Deputy Foreign Minister
Igor Rogachev, Shevardnadze's assistant Sergey Tarasenko, Oleg Bostorin, head of a
department at the foreign ministry, and Yury Alexeyev, head of the foreign ministry
department dealing with Afghanistan. (Photo by Eduard Pesov)

Shevardnadze and Baker fishing at Snake River after the U.S.-Soviet ministerial meeting (the first to be held outside of Washington, D.C.) in Jackson Hole, Wyoming. Shown from left to right are Shevardnadze, Baker, a park warden, myself, and Peter Afanasenko, a U.S. State Department interpreter.

Shevardnadze and Yevgeny Primakov, then Chairman of the Supreme Soviet's Council of the Union, with Secretary of State James Baker at the Moscow studio/home of the Georgian painter Zurab Tsereteli in May 1990. There is no sign of the tensions that strained relations between Shevardnadze and Primakov a few months later, during the Gulf crisis. From left to right are myself, Baker, a U.S. State Department interpreter, Tsereteli, Shevardnadze, and Primakov. (Photo by Eduard Pesov)

During the summer of 1990, as the pace of German unification accelerated, Shevardnadze made numerous trips to various European capitals. Shown here on his plane are, from left to right, Deputy Foreign Minister Yuly Kvitsinsky, Sergey Tarasenko, Alexander Romanov, one of Shevardnadze's private secretaries, myself, Shevardnadze, and his assistant Teimuraz Stepanov. (Photo by Eduard Pesov)

Gorbachev's visit to the United States in June 1990 for a summit meeting with George Bush was preceded by a visit to Canada, where he had talks with Brian Mulroney (left). They are in the Prime Minister's Office in the Canadian Parliament building in Ottawa. I am on Mulroney's left, Gorbachev is at the right. (Official Canadian government photo)

At a reception in the Soviet embassy during President Gorbachev's visit to the United States, Mr. and Mrs. Gorbachev (left and second from left) are being greeted by Patricia Montandon, organizer of U.S.-Soviet children's exchange programs. I am between the Gorbachevs. (Photo by TASS)

An informal moment at Camp David during the U.S.-Soviet summit in June 1990. President Bush is with a group of U.S. and Soviet interpreters; from left to right, Dmitry Arensburger, Galina Tunik (both U.S.), Bush, myself, and my Soviet colleague Oleg Krokhalev. (Official White House photograph)

Shevardnadze and Baker are in excellent spirits after a fishing trip at Lake Baikal during their meeting in Irkutsk in August 1990. They are as yet unaware of Iraq's invasion of Kuwait—the news came the next day. From left to right are Baker, Shevardnadze, and myself, making sure Shevardnadze does not misstep on the gangway. (Photo by TASS)

Returning from Irkutsk in August 1990, Shevardnadze is a lot more concerned—I suspect more about the domestic situation than foreign affairs. Here we talk over a cup of tea in his plane. (Photo by Eduard Pesov)

Gorbachev and Bush had a hastily arranged "single issue summit" in September 1990 in Helsinki, Finland, to discuss a common strategy to reverse the Iraqi invasion of Kuwait. Here, before the talks began, Gorbachev gives Bush a cartoon depicting the two of them as boxers knocking out the Cold War and the arms race. I stand at Gorbachev's right. (Photo by Yury Lizunov)

President Bush greets me at the White House before his meeting with Shevardnadze (center) in December 1990. We did not know it then, but this turned out to be Shevardnadze's last visit as foreign minister to the United States. (Official White House photograph)

Gorbachev and Bush have just signed the START treaty. This photograph, taken on July 31, 1991, may be one of the last photos of the two men as presidents together. From left to right: Ambassador Joseph Vernon Reed, U.S. Chief of Protocol, Bush, U.S. official, Gorbachev, and myself. (Photo by Yury Lizunov)

One of the high points in U.S.-Soviet relations was the informal and candid conversation between Gorbachev and Bush at Novo-Ogarevo, near Moscow, during Bush's visit to the Soviet Union in the summer of 1991. The two "principals" and the few others present were in shirtsleeves. From left to right, U.S. interpreter Peter Afanasenko, Gorbachev, myself, Bush, and U.S. National Security Adviser Brent Scowcroft. (Photo by Yury Lizunov)

I remained close to Gorbachev in his "post-presidential" years, working in the Gorbachev Foundation and accompanying him on his trips abroad. This photo was taken during a visit to the United States in October 1993.

Nine

THE GULF WAR TEST

1990–1991

Baker and Shevardnadze Meet in Irkutsk

Shevardnadze and Baker agreed to have another meeting, in Irkutsk, a quiet city on Lake Baikal in Siberia. Baker was on the way to Asia, but Irkutsk was quite a detour. Nevertheless, they believed more talks would be worthwhile. They wanted to compare notes on the entire agenda before going on vacation.

The Angara River and Lake Baikal provided a great setting that early August 1990. Shevardnadze and Baker marveled at the sights—some of the most beautiful I have ever seen and rivaling those of Wyoming—and did some fishing. The Siberian grayling is not unlike the cutthroat trout of Wyoming, but it is bigger; catching it takes patience and skill. The warden who helped the ministers did well, of course, but they were less successful. I would have hated it if Shevardnadze had failed to catch anything again, as had happened in Wyoming. I saw he did not want to fail either. The signs of tension were visible on his face as he held the rod and watched the water intently. Finally the fish bit and he started to wind the reel back quickly. He brought in the fish, to the delight of Baker, Stepanov, and myself.

The discussions in Irkutsk went well, though they were tinged with worry about developments in the Soviet Union. Things were getting increasingly chaotic, and the dangers were obvious; Shevardnadze was saying openly that it worried him more than any international problem. One ray of light was the agreement between Gorbachev and Yeltsin to set up a commission of leading economists to reconsider plans for economic reform, taking into account a crash program of price liberalization and privatization called "500 days." The fact that Gorbachev and Yeltsin were cooperating on the economy seemed promising. Shevardnadze had been telling Baker for some time that almost any program would do, provided the leading political players agreed to work together vigorously to implement it. Ryzhkov and the bureaucracy in the Council of Ministers were known to be against the "500 days" plan, but we hoped they could be persuaded to go along with whatever Gorbachev and Yeltsin agreed on.

"Iraqi Troops Have Crossed the Kuwait Border"

As Baker and Shevardnadze were sitting in the room of the former regional party committee guesthouse, now used by some joint venture hotel, and discussing some CFE issue, U.S. State Department spokeswoman Margaret Tutwiler came in with an apology for interrupting and a note for Baker. He read it and said without visible emotion: "Gentlemen, the State Department operations center has received information that Iraqi troops crossed the border of Kuwait. The Kuwaiti ambassador in Washington does not believe that it is yet a full-scale invasion."

I don't recall any reaction on the part of Shevardnadze to that. Baker said something like "Let's monitor the situation," and they went on discussing CFE. The reporters had not yet heard the news. It came after the brief press conference Shevardnadze and Baker gave from the porch of the guesthouse. No one understood yet that a major crisis had just begun.

We often wondered why the various intelligence services and the embassies had been unable to predict the invasion. It was a political failure. Technically the information about Iraqi troop concentration on the borders of Kuwait was available both to the United States and to the Soviet Union. In the fall I talked to a Soviet intelligence official whom I had known since we worked together at the Geneva talks. He said the troop concentration had been picked up by satellites and reported from various capitals, but no one had predicted that Iraq would occupy Kuwait. The conventional wisdom was that Iraq was pressuring its neighbor in order to get the best possible terms in their disputes about oil and territory.

The Soviet Union was not paying much attention to feuds between the Arabs, and the Americans seemed to have a kind of grudging respect for Saddam Hussein. From a frank conversation I had with Dennis Ross, Baker's senior assistant and Middle East expert, a little later, I understood that he blamed the U.S. ambassador to Kuwait for being gullible and unprofessional in her talks with Saddam Hussein. She had probably fallen victim to the dilemma any ambassador faces in a country ruled by a despot. Do you approach him as above all a son of a bitch or as a rational man with whom you have to deal and who may have a point from time to time? It takes a cool head and a first-rate mind to find the golden mean. I knew quite a few Soviet ambassadors who faced similar if less dramatic situations, and a few did not measure up to them.

Baker went on to visit Mongolia, and Shevardnadze returned to Moscow. Dennis Ross was on our plane; he and Tarasenko decided to spend a day in Moscow to discuss the Middle East. Shevardnadze also let Ralph Begleiter, a CNN reporter who covered all his meetings with Baker, fly with us and tape an extensive talk with him. Begleiter asked searching questions on a wide range of issues, including Soviet internal policy questions. He was very well informed, and Shevardnadze enjoyed talking with people like him. Comparing American reporters with ours, I often despaired. Where our guys asked questions that were verbose, unclear, and often biased, their American colleagues were concise and to the point—they obviously did their homework. It will take years to create a culture of real news reporting in our country, I often thought.

Shevardnadze and Gorbachev on Party Politics

Among the questions Begleiter asked were some about the recent Party Congress. It was obvious how much Communist Party politics depressed Shevardnadze. He had not wanted to stand for election to the Central Committee, and he had been shocked by the numerous votes against him when Gorbachev included him on the list of candidates. When Begleiter asked him whether he thought Gorbachev was right to continue to hold on to the position of the general secretary while being president of the country, Shevardnadze said yes, that was still necessary. "But this is the last time," he added. "It will have to be different in the future."

That was not too logical. After all, in many countries the president or prime minister is also the leader of his party. And Gorbachev often indicated that he stayed in the party in order to contain the party conservatives. More and more often Shevardnadze's remarks reflected his resentment of the party's inability to reform itself and to adapt to change.

Gorbachev, I felt, was still committed to the party. He also had some respect for the conservatives. He was wary of their strength, but it was more than just that. He respected the convictions of people like Akhromeyev and Ligachev. He did not regard all conservatives as incapable of changing; he wanted as many of them as possible to be on board and working together with him rather than in open opposition, fighting against his vision and his reforms.

In the end, this policy did not serve Gorbachev well. He could not imagine that some of those people were not just committed to their own outdated values and ideas but also ruthless, capable of breaking the law and trying to topple him illegally. Gorbachev was seeking compromise on most issues. He was blamed for that, and he was accused of wavering by friends as well as foes. But seeking compromise is a normal way of doing things in most countries. It should become the rule in this country too.

Gorbachev was, of course, deliberately fed a lot of compromising information and even misinformation about the democrats, but he never refused to work with them. He respected them more than they thought. I remember someone talking in his presence about how most of the democrats had just repainted themselves, with former professors of "scientific communism" becoming, chameleon-like, leading radical liberals almost overnight.

"Well," Gorbachev said, "this is true, but you should not take this criticism too far. I don't like the word 'chameleon' and never use it. People were not allowed to express themselves freely. But they thought, and their thinking evolved in a certain way and they reached certain conclusions. So what's wrong with that?"

I mentioned that when Leo Tolstoy was accused of changing his view on some problem he answered: "I am not a sparrow to twitter the same thing all my life."

I wanted to take a day off on August 3, but for some reason changed my mind. Georgy Mamedov, my boss at the U.S. desk, said I did the right thing. "It's moving fast," he said somewhat enigmatically, in his usual way. He added after a pause, "Baker is cutting short his visit to Mongolia and he will probably be stopping over in Moscow." A little later he confirmed that Baker would be stopping over and would meet with Shevardnadze to discuss the Iraqi invasion, which, it was now clear, was full-scale aggression. We went to the airport. I did not know how much had happened in Moscow in the meantime.

Debate over Statement Condemning Iraqi Aggression

As I later pieced it together from conversations with Shevardnadze and Tarasenko, it went something like this. Tarasenko and Dennis Ross were at a foreign ministry guesthouse when the news revealing the scale of the Iraqi invasion started to come in. Ross went to the U.S. embassy and got in touch with Washington and with Baker in Mongolia. Tarasenko alerted Shevardnadze, who called in experts on the Middle East. Ross then telephoned to propose that the Soviet Union and the United States issue a joint statement condemning the Iraqi aggression and calling for its immediate end.

It was not an idea that everyone on our side jumped to accept. Later the foreign minister often criticized our Middle East experts to me for their narrow-minded and one-sided attitudes. "The first thing they mentioned," he said, "was our treaty of friendship with Iraq. So what? If your friend kills, do you still call him a friend? And do you defend him when he is brought to trial?"

The experts also said it was an inter-Arab feud in which we should not become involved, particularly on the side of the Americans and the "Gulf fat-cats, whom the Arab masses hate." Finally, they pointed out that we had thousands of people, including oilmen and technical and military specialists, in Iraq and therefore had to be particularly cautious. Who knows what Saddam might do to them?

This last argument turned out to have some merit, but I don't think it was foremost in the minds of our Arabists. They wanted to go back to the old dance. The day after the U.S.-Soviet statement condemning Iraq's aggression was adopted, I lunched in the foreign ministry cafeteria with one of them, a young man who was a second-generation Middle East expert and, like his father, was well respected by his colleagues for wide-ranging knowledge and astute analysis.

"We could play a good game in this crisis," he said, "if only we did not let ourselves be had by the Americans."

I told him I disagreed with that. "The Americans did not thrust the joint statement on us," I said.

He did not pursue the conversation, and we finished our meat and potatoes in silence.

Shevardnadze came to the airport with a look of unusual concern. I attributed it to the overall uncertainty of the situation, but he had been in such situations before and always handled them with cool assurance. This time there had to be something really disturbing for him to wear his look of concern. I found out later that discussions in the ministry and outside it about our attitude toward the Iraqi aggression had been difficult and sometimes bitter. Shevardnadze was able to insist on a statement that the Soviet Union was stopping arms sales to Iraq, but even that was not easy, despite the fact that during the Iran-Iraq conflict we had a policy of refusing to sell weapons to the belligerents.

Generally, Shevardnadze's uncompromising stand against Iraq was resented by many officials, who reacted to the invasion with instinctive anti-Americanism. In the months that followed, I discussed the situation with some of them and often wondered at how this anti-Americanism made them forget both about the moral issue and about the balance of forces. Iraq was clearly the aggressor and had no chance of winning. Both morally and politically it was right to take a stand against Iraq. But the idea of being on the same side with the United States, instead of being welcome, caused a reaction of acute allergy among many people with influence in the Kremlin.

Shortly before Shevardnadze was to leave for the airport the KGB told him and Gorbachev that reliable sources were predicting a U.S. air strike against Baghdad within hours or days. Gorbachev had what I thought was inordinate respect for KGB intelligence and tended to believe Kryuchkov's stories about its efficiency. Shevardnadze had to ask Baker whether the rumors about the impending U.S. strike were true. Baker denied it strongly. The U.S.-Soviet statement was approved by the two ministers and read by them to the press in the V.I.P. building at Vnukovo airport.

Baker told Shevardnadze that he was not going to cancel his vacation and would go to his retreat in Wyoming, but would be in touch with him, including telephone calls if necessary. Shevardnadze decided to spend a couple of weeks vacationing near Moscow.

The next day, I talked to my boss, Georgy Mamedov, about my own vacation. I needed one, and I wanted to go to Czechoslovakia to visit friends in Zatec, a small town about sixty miles from Prague.

"It's a tough call," Mamedov said. "What if the Americans do strike

Baghdad? There'd be a crisis, and you would be difficult to reach. Do you think they will do it?"

I replied that on the basis of what we had heard from Baker and just my instincts, I did not believe they would.

A few days later, Lena and I were on a train going to Prague. Meeting our friends in a new Czechoslovakia after "the velvet revolution" was an unforgettable experience. We spent most of our vacation in Zatec, but on August 21 we went to Prague. Our friends had not been able to persuade us that on the day of the twenty-second anniversary of the Soviet invasion it was prudent for two Russians to stay out of Prague. We did not regret our decision. We saw a city that was saying farewell to those past years—the years of conformism, quiet suffering, and waiting. There was merry excitement in the eyes of young people, and sadness in the eyes of those who remembered August 1968. Two days later we returned home. The future of our own country was shrouded in mystery.

What Will the Americans Do About Iraq?

Baker had called Shevardnadze several times during his vacation, mostly to ask for Soviet support in the U.N. Security Council. The Americans were applying increasing pressure on Iraq, but they had problems getting support in the Security Council for their draft resolutions, particularly the one concerning the blockade of Iraq.

As I learned later, it seemed to Shevardnadze that Gorbachev accepted his recommendations to support the U.S. proposals each time with some reluctance. Cracks in their once 100 percent solid relationship were not yet visible to many people, but at about that time I was beginning to suspect something was wrong. As the political process became more and more complicated and confusing, it was perhaps inevitable that two individuals with strong but different personalities had to part company one day, but watching the erosion of their friendship was painful. As I said to my wife on the day of Shevardnadze's resignation in December 1990, it was a rift that went through my heart.

I returned to work in the final days of August. The main topic of discussion at the U.S. desk and almost everywhere in the foreign ministry was what the Americans would do and when they would do it. As I followed the news from Czechoslovakia, where I did not have the complete picture, my impression was that the administration might be tempted to undertake a surgical strike against Baghdad.

In Moscow I read Henry Kissinger's article, dated August 17, calling for such a strike. This certainly strengthened the positions of those in Moscow whose argument went something like this: the Americans are trigger-happy; they are spoiling for a fight and will strike soon; the result will be an explosion of Arab anger that will affect us because, after our votes in the Security Council, we are seen to be on the U.S. side. Answering such arguments was not always easy. Neither the moral nor the legal counterarguments carried much weight with those people.

My own argument, set forth in a series of articles in Moscow newspapers during the months of the Gulf crisis, was both moral and pragmatic. Bush was committed to reverse the Iraqi aggression, and he would persist, prudently but resolutely, until he saw it through to the end, I argued. Supporting him is both right and a good bet. Those were what I called the simple truths: keep it simple and even the difficult choices are easier. I think Shevardnadze, though he later made one or two missteps, managed to keep it simple. As for Gorbachev, he was in a much more complex situation.

Gorbachev Gets Conflicting Advice on Gulf Situation

Gorbachev was bombarded with conflicting advice and dire predictions not only from the military and the KGB but also from Yevgeny Primakov, a man he—and Shevardnadze too, just a few weeks before—trusted and respected. All this was happening against the background of increasing attacks against the Gorbachev-Shevardnadze foreign policy and a mounting confrontation between radicals and conservatives on the economy and other domestic issues. Every politically active group was accusing Gorbachev of waffling and hesitating. He saw himself as a conciliator and a seeker of compromises, but his authority was increasingly rejected by both the radical and the conservative camps, which hated each other more and more with every passing day.

We were all relieved when Gorbachev and Bush agreed to meet in Helsinki to discuss the Gulf situation. Both of them needed the meeting: Bush had a difficult problem abroad, and Gorbachev was increasingly in trouble at home. This was a time when they should help each other, and I believed they really wanted to.

My expectation was that they would agree to issue a strong condemnation of the Iraqi aggression and a demand that Iraq leave Kuwait, and Bush would ask Gorbachev not to object to the use of force if other efforts failed. I had no idea how Gorbachev would react. It would confront him with another problem at a time when he had many others on his hands. It was not easy for him and Shevardnadze to talk with the Americans in Helsinki when people in Moscow were queuing for bread; there had been another round of panic-buying, sparked by fresh rumors of an impending price rise and possibly other reasons that will never be fully explained. Shevardnadze believed it might be sabotage by old-line bureaucrats against the newly elected democratic city government of Moscow led by Gavriil Popov, but I doubted that.

U.S.-Soviet Policy on Iraq Debated and Discussed

Gorbachev and Bush talked almost one-on-one, with only Scowcroft and Chernyaev present. They were on the same wavelength emotionally and politically and understood that a joint statement would benefit both of them, but they both also wanted clarity about each other's intentions. I believe that during the talk, Gorbachev became convinced that Bush was not eager to go to war with Iraq, that he would prefer to avoid it if possible but was not sure Iraq could be expelled from Kuwait by peaceful means.

Bush listened to Gorbachev's arguments about the need to use all possible avenues for a peaceful outcome with his usual close attention and respect. He seemed to understand the problems and pressures that Gorbachev was facing and that made him want to avoid certain choices. I think he could not but appreciate that Gorbachev showed more understanding of his position than many Democratic senators in Washington.

Shevardnadze and Baker worked out a joint statement more or less along the lines I had expected. When Bush and Gorbachev discussed the statement in the presence of the two ministers and Primakov, there were a few hitches, but compared with the Baker-Shevardnadze draft not much was changed. The result was a strong statement with little of the usual diplomatic vagueness. It warned Saddam Hussein that other measures would be taken if he did not leave Kuwait peacefully. At one point during the discussion of the statement Primakov demurred, but not very strongly. It was the phrase in which the two presidents were telling Iraq that it was isolated in the international community. "Isolation? Why speak of isolation?" Primakov said. But this time Gorbachev ignored his remark.

During a break before a working lunch with the Americans, the Soviet delegation, including Shevardnadze, Primakov, Akhromeyev, Chernyaev, and Tarasenko, gathered in one of the rooms of the presidential palace where the talks were held. Not much was said. The statement had been agreed on and would soon be scrutinized by the diplomats, experts, and the media. Gorbachev mentioned the press conference he and Bush were to hold after the lunch. There was silence.

I ventured, "I wonder, Mikhail Sergeyevich, what you will answer if they ask you about the deadline. What is the moment when the peaceful efforts would be regarded as exhausted and the use of force as all right?"

Primakov said at once, "Yes, that's a good question."

Gorbachev looked at everyone, as was his habit in such situations, and said, "They will probably ask Bush about that, and if they ask me I will say we hope force will not have to be used." It was something like "we'll cross that bridge when we come to it"—and probably the right answer in those circumstances. The question was raised at the press conference, and it turned out that the Americans too were not yet ready to talk about deadlines.

Baker came to Moscow a few days after the Helsinki summit. Many things were happening at the same time: the Gulf crisis, the quick finale of the German unification story, and, what was probably Gorbachev's top priority, the maneuverings on the issue of radicalizing the economic reform. In a subtle way, all these developments were linked. They brought closer the day when the old issues would disappear and an era would end, leaving us to face a more uncertain yet promising future. But first the various vestiges of the past had to be dealt with, such as Saddam Hussein, the little regional Stalin grudgingly respected by Middle East experts everywhere.

In the case of Yevgeny Primakov, a member of Gorbachev's Presidential Council, I sometimes felt that this respect was more than grudging. Saddam was a dictator, he said, but also a rational human being. If given "an outlet," a chance to save face and perhaps even something as booty, Primakov continued, he might leave Kuwait quietly, which would be an outcome preferable to everyone. Gorbachev was receptive to such arguments and inclined to allow Primakov to try out his theory.

From the start Shevardnadze was quite skeptical of it. His moral outrage against what Saddam Hussein was doing was great and quite genuine, as I saw in private talks with him. He also believed that working together with the

Americans was of paramount importance, given the situation in the country and in the world. (Gorbachev shared that view—and that eventually proved decisive, even after Shevardnadze's resignation.) Finally, Shevardnadze could not like the fact that Primakov was assuming some foreign affairs tasks, which no foreign minister ever wants to share with anyone.

Several times during the unfolding crisis I discussed the situation with Sergey Tarasenko. He never hesitated in his analysis or his predictions, and although his predictions were not always accurate he saw the sense of the developments much clearer than anyone I talked to at the time. We agreed about several things: in a crunch, it's important for the United States and the Soviet Union to stand together; the Bush administration was not too eager to use force but would if it had to; it was our job to make sure that the Americans kept us posted about their intentions so there were no surprises.

Our views differed regarding how soon the administration might use force. Tarasenko felt it could happen within weeks, while I thought that Bush and Baker would seek to demonstrate to the world that they have used every opportunity to achieve their objectives peacefully.

In Moscow the two of us had a frank talk with Dennis Ross, whom Shevardnadze and all of us on his team trusted. That talk was almost accidental. We were waiting for Baker in the lobby of the Osobnyak. Tarasenko and Ross talked about a few things in what I called the warm-up mode. At some point either I or Tarasenko—I don't remember who—said that our situation would be quite difficult domestically if the military option was exercised quickly and without some kind of warning to us.

I was not sure the Americans were fully aware of the mounting criticism of our cooperation with them in the Gulf crisis. They were not taking it for granted, but whether they really understood how much heat Shevardnadze and Gorbachev were taking from the military and the Arabists was not clear to me. From Ross's reaction I saw that he at least was aware of our problem. Ross assured us that there would be no surprises and that the administration felt it could wait about four months and try all possible peaceful ways in the meantime. He did not ask us to be careful with what he said—that went without saying.

We were embarking on a long journey. I was sure that at the end of it Saddam Hussein would be out of Kuwait. The rest—what would happen to Saddam, how much blood would be spilled, and whether U.S.-Soviet cooperation would remain intact under the pressure of events—was by no means clear.

What was already clear at the time is that our cooperation had survived the short but stormy passage to German unification. In Moscow that September the last episodes of the "2 plus 4" drama were being played out, and there were surprises until the end. The Germans wanted an understanding that NATO maneuvers could be held in eastern Germany. Shevardnadze demanded a clear statement to the contrary.

On the morning of September 12, when the final meeting of the "2 plus 4" group was to be held, it was still not clear whether the issue would be resolved. As Shevardnadze, Kvitsinsky, and some others were waiting in the Oktyabrskaya hotel, the site of the final ceremony and of Gorbachev's meeting with the four ministers—for word from Genscher, the air was heavy with tension. Shevardnadze had a worried and not very optimistic look. He called Gorbachev to tell him the final ceremony was still in doubt. Gorbachev said he would come only if the matter were resolved in a satisfactory way. At long last, after Kvitsinsky talked with the Germans, it became clear that we had a deal. Genscher had conceded on the issue of maneuvers.

Gorbachev arrived for the ceremony and then had lunch with the ministers. It was clear from their talk that economic reform was the problem that preoccupied him most. The group he and Yeltsin established had completed a plan that had quite a few similarities with the Polish "shock therapy" and was more radical than anything the Ryzhkov government could accept.

Plans for a Market Economy

As always, Gorbachev tended to accentuate the positive. We all agree, he said, that transition to a market economy is the only way for us, but we would like to ease the shock. Even for East Germany, with all its relative advantages compared with the Soviet Union's situation, revamping the economy would not be easy, he said. (East Germany's Lothar de Maiziere agreed.)

Gorbachev went on to say that a market economy functioned differently in different countries (on this he was supported by Roland Dumas) and, given the peculiarities and complexities of the Soviet Union, its future market economy would have to differ in important ways from that of Western countries. It was difficult to argue with that. But behind Gorbachev's words was the struggle that was then raging in the country, and, I believe, in his own mind about the economic future of the Soviet Union. Gorbachev said he was in favor of moving toward a free market more rapidly and that he found the "500 days" plan, reworked under the direction of economist Stanislav Shatalin, a member of his Presidential Council, attractive. That seemed to seal the fate of Ryzhkov's government, which would not want to implement a plan that was not of its own making.

But the govenment was not willing to go without a fight. It was the government, rather than the Politburo, as many thought at the time, that was the most adamantly opposed to the Shatalin plan. As Chernyaev told me, in September Gorbachev was being bombarded with papers and analyses predicting total economic chaos and disintegration, massive unemployment, and hyperinflation should the more radical plan be adopted.

Paradoxically, many independent economists thought that both the Shatalin and the government plan had much in common and differed only on a few points that could be reconciled. This was the view of Shevardnadze's economic adviser, Alexander Shokhin, who later became deputy prime minister in Yeltsin's government. "I'm being told that the two plans are 90 percent similar," Shevardnadze said to Baker. "The important thing is to choose and go ahead with determination."

This was what Gorbachev seemed unable to do; the pressure from his own government was too great. When he met with Baker and Commerce Secretary Robert A. Mosbacher, who headed a delegation of leading U.S. businessmen, he brought with him both Shatalin, who insisted that his plan had to be accepted intact, and the government's chief economist Leonid Abalkin, who was persuading the Supreme Soviet to stick with the government's plan. It was bizarre to see the two men, gloomy and obviously hostile to each other, on Gorbachev's side of the table while he was making a pitch for U.S. help in the Soviet Union's transition to a market economy.

The help, actually quite modest, was needed to stabilize the consumer market and to create a dollar reserve to facilitate transition to a convertible ruble. In fact, it would be needed regardless of which plan was adopted. But the Americans were not eager to discuss such help. Until the end they doubted Gorbachev's commitment to a free market. It almost seemed that they wanted to see a radical "Thatcherite" facing them in the Kremlin's top seat; more likely they were just waiting for the power struggle to play itself out. No one knew when that might happen. The country was in turmoil with no end in sight.

Shevardnadze Becomes Critical of Gorbachev

On the international scene the pace of events was fast and getting faster. Shevardnadze and his team were caught in that never-ending whirlwind. One member of the team was not with us when we were leaving for New York a few days after Baker's visit to Moscow. Teimuraz Stepanov was in a hospital, hoping to join us a week later in New York. In the plane, Tarasenko was working on what turned out to be the foreign minister's final speech at the U.N. General Assembly.

In two respects Shevardnadze's annual New York visit in late September 1990 differed from the previous ones. Reporters and diplomats noticed that his speech at the United Nations contained hints that this was his last appearance there as foreign minister. Shevardnadze was ambiguous on that point. When reporters asked whether that understanding was true, he denied it, but not very forcefully. The phrase in the speech that was an almost undisguised farewell to his colleagues spoke for itself.

There was also something that astute observers may have noticed but so far as I remember no one mentioned publicly: in interviews and in talks with foreign leaders Shevardnadze sounded notably cooler toward Mikhail Gorbachev than even a few months before. He mentioned him less frequently, and when he did there was no enthusiasm in his voice. He was asked about Gorbachev in an NBC interview and he used the Russian word *yeдinomyшlen-niki*—meaning something like "we share the same philosophy." When he was asked about Yeltsin, he called him a major political factor and said Gorbachev and Yeltsin should work together.

I did not think this new coolness was fatal to the Gorbachev-Shevardnadze relationship, but I was looking for an explanation. It was not that difficult to find. One reason, I thought, was the episode in the summer when thousands of pieces of military equipment, including tanks and artillery, had been shipped, surreptitiously and without Shevardnadze's knowledge, from Eastern Europe and the Western part of the Soviet Union to Siberia, where they would not count against the ceilings under the CFE treaty and therefore would not have to be destroyed as part of the treaty-mandated reductions.

In hindsight I believe Shevardnadze overreacted to that ploy of the Soviet General Staff, undertaken in order to save as many tanks as possible from being scrapped. After all, when the dust settled Baker said to Shevardnadze in December that technically the move had not been a violation of the terms of the CFE treaty. But in September, when the story first broke in the Western press, Shevardnadze was appalled. He was sure that if the military had been honest with him and informed him of their intentions, he might have been able to work out some kind of gentlemen's agreement with Baker and the Europeans. Instead, he was in an embarrassing position because of something he felt was inconsistent with the spirit and possibly even the letter of the treaty.

Shevardnadze wrote a "letter of protest" to Gorbachev, whom he suspected of being well informed about the whole operation and too susceptible to knuckle under pressure from the military. Later, when Marshal Akhromeyev, whom Gorbachev asked to look into the situation, provided an explanation that was sent to the Americans, Shevardnadze and Tarasenko were openly scornful of it. Tarasenko called it a shell game, and Shevardnadze hinted that he found it difficult to defend our position. Of course he was right about the spirit of the treaty, and things emerged later that made it clear that our military had tried to circumvent the letter of the treaty as well. The unenviable task of extricating us from the so-called naval infantry and coastal defense issue fell to Shevardnadze's successor, Alexander Bessmertnykh. That was downright embarrassing and left an extremely bad aftertaste. More about it later.

Another thing that made Shevardnadze's relations with Gorbachev more difficult was the Gulf crisis. I did not know all the details then, nor do I know them now, but differences between them in interpreting both the U.S. intentions and the ways of dealing with Saddam probably arose earlier than became apparent.

Shevardnadze favored maximum forcefulness toward the Iraqis and was ready to define the Soviet position in terms of quasi-alliance with the Americans. In the General Assembly speech, he mentioned the possibility that the Soviet Union might participate in U.N.-authorized action against Iraq. When Teimuraz Stepanov joined us in New York about a week after our arrival there, he said that Shevardnadze's words had created an uproar in the foreign ministry, while the military and the KGB were simply furious. Since the recent Soviet experience with the use of force in Afghanistan was still fresh in people's minds, Shevardnadze's remark was unpopular and therefore unfortunate. Those who criticized the very idea of cooperating with the Americans in the Gulf crisis used it against him.

Shevardnadze felt that Gorbachev was not showing his solidarity with him strongly enough, now that he was increasingly under fire from the conservatives. He believed Gorbachev should take a clear stand in his defense. A few months later, when "Stalinists" in the Central Committee of the Russian Communist Party and in some republics launched a vicious attack against Yakovlev, I learned that Yakovlev was bringing similar complaints to Gorbachev.

I found such complaints difficult to understand. After all, you have to be able to stand the heat. Both the radicals and the conservatives were getting increasingly vicious in their public criticism of each other and of the country's leaders, including Gorbachev. Perhaps the right thing was not to dignify the most rabid attacks with an answer.

Behind Shevardnadze's complaints was, I now think, a more profound feeling of unease. He suspected that Gorbachev was retreating from the new thinking in foreign and particularly domestic policies. He believed that too much time had been lost while Gorbachev was alternately fighting or pacifying the hard-liners in the Communist Party. So while internal reforms were marking time, the impression was that foreign policy was moving too far too fast, and Shevardnadze knew how dangerous that was.

In New York I talked with him privately a couple of times, mostly about the Gulf crisis. I shared his view that a clear and simple position that did not rule out the possibility of using force against Iraq offered the best hope of reversing Saddam's aggression. But, watching the Senate hearings and anti-war demonstrations on television, I saw that things were not so simple even in the United States.

Some Democratic U.S. senators and peace activists were saying things that were closer to the position of conservatives in Moscow than to that of Shevardnadze. And Primakov, who was no conservative, was close to Gorbachev and insisted that war should be avoided at almost any cost and that the Soviet Union would benefit from playing a visible part in preventing it. In hindsight it is clear to me that such a policy did not have any chance to succeed, but at the time it did not look implausible. I think I can understand why Gorbachev allowed Primakov to go on his own "peace mission" to Baghdad. Shevardnadze thought it was wrong and in private made no secret of his view.

The Negotiating Process on CFE and START Continues

An important goal for Shevardnadze on that September visit to New York was to advance the negotiating process on the CFE and START treaties. On both of them, particularly on START, the situation was frustrating. Baker was pointing out that the CFE treaty could soon become irrelevant because the situation in Eastern Europe was changing fast. But both sides, Shevard-nadze and Baker agreed, should not forgo the political benefits of concluding the agreement. So the two tore into the arcane technical details of CFE, seeking to push their bureaucracies and complete the negotiations before it was too late.

Watching them sit down with James Woolsey and Grinevsky and grapple with the ceilings, quotas, and "sufficiency rules," I sometimes pitied those two no-longer-young men who had to bend their minds on questions that even the experts found puzzling. Nevertheless, they persevered, and Grinevsky and Woolsey displayed miracles of technical ingenuity in coming up with solutions to problems that kept cropping up. Shevardnadze spoke highly of the two ambassadors. He once said to Baker that, unlike the START negotiators, they always tried to cut through the mass of details and suggested ways out of the maze. At their last meeting in the Soviet mission, Baker and Shevardnadze were able to sort out the last remaining ceilings and quotas and even announced that, subject to agreement by the allies, which was likely, they had a deal on CFE. We were all smiling that day, unaware of how many agonizing moments we would have to go through in the weeks that followed. Those moments really shook up Shevardnadze.

On START, things were moving much more slowly. Of course, the political pressure for that agreement was not nearly as great as for CFE. Hard-liners on both sides were trying to protect their positions on issues that seemed insignificant to many of us. Shevardnadze believed the chief negotiators were not working hard enough to devise solutions to pending issues. Nevertheless, that September in New York I noticed that the U.S. position was becoming more flexible, perhaps because Baker was giving the talks more of his personal attention. The Americans had conceded some points on which they could have continued to insist. For the first time in a few months I felt there was a chance to wind up the START negotiations quickly.

Gorbachev Faces Open Criticism from Right and Left

October 1990 was not a good month for Mikhail Gorbachev. His decision to try to fashion a compromise between the "500 days" plan and the govern-ment's economic program, made under heavy pressure from Premier Ryzhkov and the conservative majority of the Supreme Soviet, was probably fatal. Afterward, both Yakovlev and Chernyaev told me they regarded that decision as perhaps Gorbachev's worst mistake.

It is true that the "500 days" plan was full of flaws and would probably have resulted in high inflation and economic hardship for most of the people, but politically it had the support of the new leaders in the republics and of the intelligentsia, now fully in the Yeltsin camp. They declared themselves ready to assume responsibility for the problems and hardships caused by radical reform. They did not want to be responsible for a program that in their view kept much of the old system intact. The reaction of Yeltsin and his allies to Gorbachev's decision to compromise was a total and definitive break with Gorbachev. The harshness of their criticism of Gorbachev surprised me.

For the first time in decades the Soviets were allowed to attack their top leader openly, and many were doing so enthusiastically. With the breakup of government authority, crime was rising and the economy was crumbling faster than ever before, and people had much to complain about. Few were ready to defend Gorbachev. The party hard-liners and the conservatives took advantage of the deteriorating situation to put pressure on Gorbachev and call for a crackdown and a "restoration of order."

At a meeting organized by the political administration of the army—the Communist Party's military wing, so to speak—Gorbachev was told bluntly that he was in danger of "losing the army." Similar meetings aimed at putting pressure on Gorbachev were convened by Ryzhkov's government. The managers of big factories and production enterprises, many of them linked with the military, demanded, in essence, a return to the old system.

Ernest Obminsky, Shevardnadze's deputy for international economic relations, drew my attention to a speech by Anatoly Tizyakov, director of a military plant in Sverdlovsk, at one such gathering. It was downright hysterical. Overall, the problem was not so much that Gorbachev was being attacked from both the left and the right, but that there was no political center on which he could rely. This condemned him to choosing between the alternatives, both of which he often disliked, or maneuvering—often awkwardly.

Gorbachev was similarly torn apart on the Gulf crisis. Primakov was telling him that siding with the Americans was making him even more vulnerable to criticism by the conservatives and the military—and also ran the risk of trouble in the Soviet Union's Central Asian republics with a majority Muslim population. As I saw from my discussions with colleagues in the foreign ministry, this view was shared by most of the ministry's officials, and not only in the Middle East department.

The Cold War anti-Americanism became latent when Soviet foreign policy changed course, but it was waiting for a chance to reemerge. I did not find many supporters even for a policy of pragmatic alliance with the Americans in a crisis in which they were determined to prevail. As for the moral argument — that Iraq's gobbling up of an entire country should not be tolerated — that had even fewer takers.

The Break Between Shevardnadze and Primakov

I found relief talking with Tarasenko. We both agreed that Primakov's mission to Baghdad and other capitals stood little chance of success. His cables were not encouraging, despite his efforts to present his talks in the best possible light. It was clear that he did not impress Saddam Hussein. Their long acquaintance probably did not help, and may even have been harmful to Primakov's chances of success — he did not look mysterious or threatening enough to Saddam. Overall, the impression his cables gave was vague. Unlike Shevardnadze, Primakov sent a kind of short summary instead of a full record of his conversations. Shevardnadze believed that what Primakov was doing was wrong, and he said so to Gorbachev.

It was amazing how quickly the personal relationship between Shevardnadze and Primakov had deteriorated. I remembered them a few months before sharing a meal with Baker at the Moscow home of Shevardnadze's friend Zurab Tseretely, the famous Georgian painter. The room was full of Tseretely's enormously colorful paintings and there was a lot of Georgian food and wine on the table. The atmosphere of "southern hospitality" was clearly much to the liking of both men. Primakov too was from the South — he was born in Baku — and he and Shevardnadze had many friends in common. Philosophically they seemed to be on the same wavelength; politically, no major differences divided them. Now, with Primakov apparently infringing on the foreign minister's turf and becoming increasingly close to Gorbachev, they barely talked. Their break was painful to observe.

U.S.-Soviet Discussion of New U.S. Gulf Strategy

In late October, Baker let Shevardnadze know that he would like to come to Moscow for an important discussion. He hinted that because the current policy was apparently having no effect on Saddam Hussein's behavior the Bush administration was thinking about the next phase in ratcheting up the pressure and that Gorbachev and Shevardnadze were the first leaders he wanted to consult about the new strategy. In addition, new problems with CFE had emerged just three weeks before the treaty signing was scheduled in Paris. Given the events of 1991 and later, those problems now seem almost irrelevant, but at the time they threatened to derail the CFE treaty. Gorbachev delegated General Mikhail Moiseyev, chief of the General Staff, to discuss the issues with Baker's team.

Baker's talks in Moscow were scheduled for November 8. He was due to come at the end of the day of November 7, the anniversary of the Bolshevik revolution of 1917. It was clear that the routine celebrations formerly organized by the official authorities would be challenged in Moscow and other cities by counterdemonstrations of radical anticommunists. An air of tense expectation pervaded the city, and Shevardnadze, when asked by Alexey Obukhov, his deputy in charge of relations with the United States, what he thought might happen on November 7, said, "Frankly, I don't know what will happen." We also did not know what new ideas Baker would propose.

Among my colleagues on the foreign ministry's U.S. desk there were all kinds of conjectures, including one that Baker would be asking us to support an imminent U.S. military action against Iraq. I was among the few who thought that the United States was not too eager and certainly not yet ready to undertake a military operation. My own guess was that the administration planned to announce that it was ready to resort to an article in the U.N. Charter allowing the use of force for individual or collective self-defense, and that Baker would be asking us not to object to that. Such an announcement would leave the administration's hands free to act whenever it was ready, but would allow other countries, if they chose, quietly to put some distance between themselves and the U.S. actions.

But that was not what Baker had in mind. He gave the Soviet Union and other members of the U.N. Security Council a more difficult choice. Still, we appreciated the fact that he followed the policy of "no surprises" he and Shevardnadze had agreed on in August. He had set out the U.S. position and plans in clear and straightforward terms.

The United States wanted the U.N. Security Council to adopt a resolution stating that, because Iraq was in violation of the previous Security Council decisions, it was authorizing, as of a certain date, the use of "other appropriate means" to reverse the Iraqi aggression. In other words, the United States wanted U.N. authority for its actions in the Gulf, which would mean the

Soviet Union would at some point have to accept whatever the United States decided to do against Iraq. That was the Americans' approach, put very bluntly, and one's attitude toward it depended on how much one trusted the administration. That trust could not be taken for granted.

Shevardnadze listened with intense attention. "This is a statement that cannot be made lightly," he said. "You have to be sure that if the time comes to act on it you will do it," he added. "Are you sure?"

"We are," Baker replied.

A high-ranking Pentagon official who accompanied Baker gave Shevardnadze a description of the kind of forces and weapons the United States was marshaling in the Gulf and would be ready to use to expel Iraqi forces from Kuwait. The descripton impressed Shevardnadze, who said he would use some of that information in his contacts with the Iraqis. Baker trusted Shevardnadze to talk with them in a way that would not undermine the U.S. approach—unlike some others, whom he did not trust at all. In his talk with Shevardnadze he spoke scornfully of all those "amateur peacemakers, journalists, and retired politicians" who went to Baghdad to talk with Saddam as if anything but a complete Iraqi withdrawal could be discussed. He named Nakasone and Willy Brandt, but he also clearly had Primakov in mind. Shevardnadze listened to Baker with an inscrutable expression, but I could guess what he was thinking.

Baker expected to be able to talk with Gorbachev, and despite the official holiday the meeting took place. Gorbachev received Baker in Novo-Ogarevo near Moscow, which was soon to become famous as the site of talks on the new Union treaty. Shevardnadze went to Novo-Ogarevo in advance of Baker, in order to talk to Gorbachev first, and he invited me to go in his car.

From our talk in the car, I gathered that Shevardnadze was cautious about Baker's idea. He wanted to cooperate with the Americans but he clearly had doubts, which he did not discuss with me, however. He asked what I thought of Baker's proposal. I agreed that it was important to cooperate with the U.S. administration and said that the basic approach, as outlined by Baker, seemed sound. I felt that more time should be given to the Iraqis and that, judging by what Baker had said, the administration was probably willing to do so. Indeed, Baker had said the administration would find it almost impossible to maintain its forces in the Gulf after Spring 1991, which seemed to suggest that February or March was the deadline.

Baker did not rule out that in the meantime Saddam might withdraw from Kuwait peacefully, but he was clearly skeptical. He said so to both Gorbachev and Shevardnadze but pledged that the administration would do its best—

short of bargaining with Saddam over conditions—to persuade the Iraqis to leave and thus avoid war.

After listening to Baker's outline of the new U.S. stratey, Gorbachev reacted cautiously. Essentially, he said he would consider Baker's ideas in the spirit of cooperation with the United States. He also said something that I considered quite important. He welcomed the fact that the administration, rather than going it alone or just with its allies, was acting within the framework of the United Nations. Of course, this was a commitment on the part of the United States, but it was also a commitment on Gorbachev's part. After all, he could have taken a different attitude, which would leave his country on the sidelines but free to pass judgment, approve, or criticize. Gorbachev's quick decision left the opponents of cooperating with the United States little room for maneuvering and, I later thought, largely predetermined the course of subsequent developments.

While Baker was focusing on the Gulf, his deputy Richard Bartholomew was discussing the final details of CFE with General Moiseyev and a group of foreign ministry and defense ministry experts. At one point, Georgy Mamedov told me later, they thought they had nailed down all the issues—and even embraced—a new way of congratulating each other. But it was too soon. Something else was brought up almost immediately, and they had to send word to Shevardnadze and Baker that they were not yet through. Almost an hour passed before they came downstairs with the final package.

The two negotiators were smiling. Did they know there still were issues waiting to explode, such as the resubordination of some Soviet divisions as naval infantry and coastal defense forces, that would soon imperil the treaty? I am sure that at least some people on both sides knew but decided to close their eyes to the problem so as not to fatally postpone the signing, and hoped it could be worked out at the political level later. It was a little U.S.-Soviet "conspiracy of negotiators," perhaps a tacit understanding at the head of delegation or at an even higher level.

Preparing the Soviet Response to the U.S. Gulf Proposal

The day after Baker left, Shevardnadze gathered a small group of officials in his Smolenskaya Square office to discuss Baker's proposal on the Gulf. He was leaving with Gorbachev on a visit to Germany the next day, and he asked Anatoly Kovalev, his loyal first deputy, to coordinate the work on developing the Soviet position. Shevardnadze looked tired and concerned, but I believe his concern was more about what was happening inside the Soviet Union. Most of the talk, though, was about the Gulf crisis.

Shevardnadze asked Kovalev to prepare a memorandum that would outline various options, but it was clear where his sympathies lay. He was bitter about some of the Middle East experts in his own ministry. "I've not invited them today," he said, "because they talk to me and then run around telling stories." He said that the decision would not be easy for us to make and that the Americans should be given to understand that. "And we must talk with them frankly about our own situation," he added. "They have to take a clear stand against separatism here."

I had long thought that we should try to elicit from the administration a stronger statement of support for the Soviet Union's integrity and for Gorbachev's efforts to reform the Union. But even more important would have been some quiet work by the administration with the nationalists in the republics, telling them that there was a point beyond which it did not want them to go. Perhaps November 1990 was too late to initiate such an approach. And in the end it was the actions of the Soviet hard-liners, the August coup-plotters, rather than anything the West did or did not do, that precipitated the collapse of the Soviet Union.

When Shevardnadze left, Kovalev called me into his office to go through the discussions of the day before. I had known him since January 1987, when I accompanied him to Pakistan for talks with Mohammad Zia ul-Haq about Afghanistan on behalf of Gorbachev. It was a sensitive assignment, and even though Kovalev was not an expert on Asia, he handled it in a competent and professional manner.

Kovalev had worked in the foreign ministry so long, outliving so many up-and-coming stars and clashing from time to time with so many people, that he could not be especially popular. He wasn't, but even his critics grudgingly admired his ability to see through complex issues and to end up on the right side almost every time. Another thing about Kovalev deserved recognition: he stood for something. In the 1970s he actively promoted the CSCE process, even earning the wrath of some Central Committee officials, including ideology chief Mikhail Suslov. Kovalev had a heart attack after one particularly bad clash and was said to fall out of favor with Gromyko, but he survived and later became one of the men Gorbachev and Shevardnadze trusted.

Kovalev tried to extract from me every nuance of Baker's conversation with

Gorbachev and Shevardnadze. He could spend hours discussing the fine print of a document or the hidden meaning of some phrase. That is what he was doing now. He seemed to be going in circles around the various aspects of the problem. One thing he emphasized was that there should be a clear pause between the adoption of the resolution allowing the use of "other appropriate means" and the actual moment when force could be used.

Gradually, we were moving toward a concept of what Kovalev called "a pause of goodwill." The resolution, he said, should be strong enough for the Iraqis to understand it as a threat, but it must also leave them an opening and enough time to go if they chose to. Kovalev was clearly pleased that he had hit on good wording, a nice-sounding formula—"pause of goodwill." He believed he had something he could recommend to Shevardnadze, but he decided to wait for an options paper being drafted by Vladimir Petrovsky and Alexander Belonogov, two other deputy foreign ministers.

The senior deputy, Kovalev, was capable of speaking to the others frankly and even bluntly, and that is what he did when he had read their paper. "It is verbose, vague in outlining the options, and does not contain a clear and attractive recommendation," he said to them.

Indeed, even though it recognized the need to cooperate with the Americans within the United Nations, the paper was so vague that it could be interpreted as suggesting a policy of procrastination. Kovalev asked Georgy Mamedov and me to join the two deputy ministers in reworking the paper, which was to go to Shevardnadze and then to Gorbachev.

We got down to work immediately, incorporating the concept of the "pause of goodwill" and certain points on which we thought we should insist in drafting the Security Council resolution. For example, we wanted to make sure that "other appropriate means" would not include the use of nuclear or other weapons of mass destruction, even though none of us suspected the Americans of being willing even to threaten that. But the paper's basic thrust now became quite clear, without any ambiguity. I wanted to include a statement that would, in a way, summarize that. Something like "Baker's basic approach appears reasonable and deserving of support." Eventually that phrase was watered down or excluded, but the overall meaning of the paper remained. Kovalev liked it and, after some tinkering with the language, he agreed to recommend it to Shevardnadze.

On November 17 Gorbachev and Shevardnadze went to Paris to participate in the ceremonies drawing a final line under the Cold War in Europe: the signing of the CFE treaty and the adoption of the Charter of Paris on the New Europe. But as we were going to Paris, there was more talk about the

Gulf crisis than about Europe. Gorbachev and Bush were to meet in the residence of the U.S. ambassador to France to discuss the developments. Bush was expecting an answer to the U.S. proposal on a Security Council resolution.

Baker's frantic trips to the capitals of Security Council members had shown that some of them were reluctant to support the U.S. proposal, so a great deal depended on Gorbachev's position. It was my understanding that he basically agreed with Shevardnadze's arguments, but people who objected to it kept trying to influence him.

Primakov was saying openly he did not like the idea of a Security Council resolution because it left no escape route for Saddam Hussein to save face. In his appeals to Gorbachev, Primakov and experts on Arab affairs emphasized two things: first, that the consequences of a major war in the Gulf would be unpredictable and in particular could cause trouble among the Soviet Union's Muslim population; and second, that the Soviet Union, and Gorbachev personally, would benefit greatly from playing a visible peacemaker role. Those were not arguments that could be easily dismissed. Nevertheless, I hoped that Gorbachev would go along with Bush—subject, of course, to the specific terms of the U.N. resolution.

CFE Treaty Problems

The Paris visit began with a call to Shevardnadze from Baker, who wanted to see him urgently on a CFE-related matter. After his first words at that meeting, it was clear that something was wrong, badly wrong. The data exchange, held on the eve of the signing, revealed significant differences between the counts the two sides had made of Soviet weapons in Europe. Baker suggested that some in the Soviet military were not acting in good faith. Some of the weapons listed as having been withdrawn from Europe before the data exchange were, according to U.S. intelligence data, still there and therefore subject to elimination and destruction.

Our military was obviously trying to keep intact as many pieces of hardware as it could. The generals were unhappy about the treaty and were trying to "correct Gorbachev's mistakes" in their own clumsy way, but they disregarded the political damage to Gorbachev and to the country. Baker also said the United States still had questions about the huge transfer of weapons and equipment from Europe to Siberia the previous summer and wanted additional information about their disposal.

I do not recall whether the problem of "naval infantry and coastal defense divisions"—infantry units resubordinated by the Soviet General Staff in order to avoid inclusion of their weapons in the categories to be reduced—was raised in Paris. If it was, it did not look as bad as the other two problems at the time. Overall, I was disturbed by what Baker had to say. Everything was happening in a rush—the Americans did not even have a written memo to hand to Shevardnadze. Perhaps Baker did not want to do it so the legitimacy of signing the treaty would not be questioned. He did say that the United States intended to sign it, but he emphasized the need to get the issues clarified—the sooner the better.

I wrote out a memo to Gorbachev listing the U.S. complaints and gave it to Chernyaev, who understood immediately how serious they were. Gorbachev was having meetings with various European leaders one after another, and it was difficult even to find a slot to alert him to the problem. Still, Shevardnadze talked with him about it, and Chernyaev showed him the memo. Gorbachev instructed Yazov to check things personally and to give clarifications and explanations to the Americans. We all knew now that the signing would be followed by the difficult process of sorting out the various complaints and misdeeds. Ratification of the CFE treaty was now very much in doubt.

Working Out the Language of the Gulf Resolution and Gathering Support

Still, the Gulf was on everybody's mind, and Gorbachev's talks with foreign leaders either began or ended with that problem. Margaret Thatcher, who obviously did not regard Paris as her last foreign trip as British prime minister, was pushing an especially tough line in her discussion with Gorbachev. Saddam should be given no respite, she said. He must be made to expect a strike any moment, and therefore it was doubtful that a U.N. resolution giving him more time to decide to leave was a good idea. It was also wrong, she said, to hope that an air war alone would do the job against Saddam. She seemed to hint that she would prefer a clear decision to fight a war against Iraq, to destroy its army—and probably to topple Saddam. Brian Mulroney seemed to share that view, and implicitly Thatcher's doubts that George Bush would act decisively enough, given his innate caution and the U.S. domestic political situation.

In the one-on-one talk with Bush, Gorbachev finally gave his answer, prefacing it, in his usual way, with a number of general points that on closer examination were not just rhetorical. The Iraqi aggression, he said, had to be reversed, and the Soviet Union and the United States had to be seen working together to achieve that goal—preferably in a peaceful manner. Gorbachev made another point strongly in Paris, as he had done in Helsinki and in his talks with Baker at Novo-Ogarevo: the Middle East issue had to be moved off the ground. He did not link it with the Gulf crisis directly and he agreed that reversing Iraq's aggression had priority, but I thought Bush got his message, and a rethinking of the U.S. position on the Middle East was partly the result of Gorbachev's insistence that some movement was needed there.

Gorbachev also praised Bush for going the United Nations route in dealing with the Gulf crisis. He emphasized the need to draft the kind of Security Council resolution that would command the support of all its members and pledged our cooperation in working on the resolution. That put the Soviet Union in a strong position to influence the terms of the resolution, which proved important a few days later.

I was at home on a Saturday when the telephone rang in our apartment. It was Shevardnadze, and one of the few times he called me personally. "We are sitting here trying to recall everything that has happened since November 8," he said. "I have asked my assistants to check the memcons, but let me also ask you. Is it your clear recollection that the [U.S.] proposal called for a pause after the adoption of the U.N. resolution?"

I replied that Baker clearly had not suggested force could be used immediately after the adoption of the resolution.

"Okay. Vorontsov has cabled from New York that the U.S. draft calls for something that differs from our understanding. It would just authorize the use of force."

This was puzzling. We were both silent for a moment. I don't always react quickly, but this time I did. "Eduard Amvrosiyevich," I said, "I think this is either a tactical move, an initial position, or a misunderstanding. I am sure we are entitled to insist on our understanding."

"Okay," the foreign minister said, "we'll work from that."

A few days later we were flying to New York for the Security Council meeting that was to adopt the resolution. By that time the Americans had agreed to state specifically in the resolution that Iraq was being given more time to make a decision on withdrawal from Kuwait and actually leave. The time given Saddam was six weeks, which I thought was a decent interval. Shevardnadze's final instruction sent to Vorontsov before we boarded the plane to New York was to insist on inserting the words "a pause of goodwill" to make the resolution sound categorical but more positive and therefore more acceptable to some Security Council members who were still hesitating.

I did not know whether the United States would accept that language, and I was still wondering what was behind the language they had proposed a few days before. Was it really a tactical maneuver—to start out tough and then show flexibility? That would be something George Shultz, for example, would not want to do but Baker might be tempted to try. Still, I did not think it likely. But I recalled what Thatcher had said in Paris, and I thought that her views probably had supporters within the administration. That was a more likely explanation for the initial U.S. draft. It also suggested that Baker's position within the administration might be more difficult than we had thought.

In New York, Vorontsov gave us the latest on the resolution. It seemed to be well on track. China would probably not veto it, and although the votes of Cuba and Yemen, two nonpermanent members, were doubtful, they could not affect the resolution's passage. The Americans had accepted inclusion of "a pause of goodwill." Baker was having a final round of meetings and wanted to talk with Shevardnadze.

When Baker came to the Soviet mission for that talk, he looked quite exhausted. He had logged dozens of hours flying to the various capitals to raise funds for the military operation and secure support for the U.S. strategy. The accumulated exhaustion, nervous strain, and jet lag had clearly taken their toll on him. He was less alert than usual and sometimes seemed ready to doze off. Even Dennis Ross, a much younger man, was less sprightly than usual.

But Baker was pleased with the results of his efforts. He would have preferred, of course, to have China vote for the resolution, and he had made a real effort to persuade the Chinese foreign minister. Shevardnadze too had made a try, going to Urumchi, in Northern China, to talk to his Chinese counterpart. They both succeeded only partially, but it was just as well. An abstention in the Security Council vote meant that the Chinese would not stand in the way of the resolution.

Cuba was a different matter. Baker wanted Cuba to abstain even though its vote did not matter once the necessary nine votes in favor were assured. Shevardnadze felt that Cuba could take a position that would allow it to resume a slow process of accommodation with the United States. He and

Gorbachev made a strong effort to try to persuade the Cubans, who seemed to be hesitating between their usual anti-U.S. line and something more pragmatic. But Baker told Shevardnadze that based on his last-minute talks with the Cuban foreign minister, he thought Cuba would vote against the resolution. This was very disappointing to Shevardnadze. We talked about the Cuban decision after Baker had left. We were both sorry that the Cubans were missing a golden opportunity to take a stand that would benefit them in more than one way.

On the day of the vote I was in the Security Council chamber, a place I knew in intimate detail from my five years at the United Nations in the 1970s. I was then on the other side of the arena. United Nations staff are, in a way, working spectators, and in those years the show was often boring. Confrontation is often predictable and it could make the United Nations irrelevant, a place where everyone was just going through the motions. How different things were now! For the first time in years there was a chance of making the United Nations really an instrument of peace, or at least of reversing aggression.

I watched the Security Council members voting. There were twelve votes in favor. "Who is against?" Shevardnadze, as president of the council, asked. It was Yemen and, not immediately but after assuring himself that he would not be alone in voting against the resolution, the Cuban delegate raised his hand too. China abstained. The resolution was adopted.

A couple of days later I wrote a commentary for *Trud*, under my "P. Vorobyev" byline, which I called "There Is Still a Chance for Peace." I wrote that in real life politicians never have the luxury of choosing between what is good and what is very good, that most often it is a choice between two not very pleasant alternatives, one of which has to be preferred. Unlike many of my colleagues, I felt that Bush and Baker did not relish the prospect of war but that with Saddam Hussein rejecting the option of a peaceful withdrawal they might just have to use force.

A difficult choice had also been made by the Soviet Union, I wrote, knowing what it had taken to make it. The break between Shevardnadze and Primakov was almost out in the open. In New York, Shevardnadze learned that Primakov was going to Baghdad again—he was, as I understood, just faced with that fact. To the reporter who asked about Primakov's mission, Shevardnadze said it was to demand the safe return of numerous Soviet experts and technicians who were still in Iraq and who could become hostages to Saddam Hussein at any moment. But I knew what Shevardnadze thought about the whole thing. As for the Soviet citizens in Iraq, all of us agreed that the demand for their return had to be presented to Saddam in a totally different way: firmly and coolly, without a hint of any quid pro quo, and preferably by the Soviet ambassador. Eventually, this approach was chosen, and it worked.

Shevardnadze and Baker Meet Again on Arms Control, the Gulf, and Other Issues

A few days after the visit to New York, Shevardnadze went to the United States again on what turned out to be his last trip there as the Soviet foreign minister. He and Baker had agreed to meet in Houston to go through the entire U.S.-Soviet agenda, particularly arms control, and to try to achieve closure on START, and to set a date for Bush's visit to the Soviet Union, possibly in February 1991. In mid-December 1990 that still seemed possible.

Shevardnadze went to Houston with a large group of arms control experts. They were expected to do two things: provide a satisfactory explanation for the growing number of questions the Americans and the Europeans had on our compliance with the CFE treaty, and work out with their U.S. colleagues a package of trade-offs on the final technical details of the START treaty. But the first thing Baker and Shevardnadze discussed in the car taking them from the airport to Shevardnadze's hotel in Houston was the Gulf.

Shevardnadze commended Bush and Baker for offering, right after the U.N. resolution was adopted, to meet with the Iraqi leaders in Baghdad and Washington to discuss a peaceful withdrawal. That move, he said, looked good and also gave the Iraqis a real chance. Baker, however, was no more optimistic than he had been during their private discussions in New York, where he said that the Iraqis were rapidly dismantling Kuwait as a viable state and creating a fait accompli that would be difficult to reverse. Now he was worried that the Iraqis were setting conditions for the proposed meetings, clearly trying to make that last attempt to persuade them impossible. And Baker was clearly pessimistic about what the Iraqis would say if the meeting actually took place. Shevardnadze advised patience and perseverance and offered to write to Iraqi Foreign Minister Tariq Aziz, whom he continued to regard as a professional and a not unreasonable man.

The Houston arms control talks turned out to be difficult. Our military officials set out their explanation for the transfer and disposal of CFE-accountable weapons and equipment in greater detail than before. It was basically the same "shell game" explanation that Tarasenko had scorned before and was again critical of now. But this time the Americans seemed more willing to listen to it. Later, on the plane from Houston to Washington, Baker said to Shevardnadze that the U.S. experts had concluded that the transfer was not technically a violation of the treaty. But three other CFE matters seemed intractable, and Baker said they had to be addressed if the CFE treaty were to be ratified and if Bush were to visit the Soviet Union: the data discrepancies, the "naval infantry and coastal defense divisions," and the armored personnel carriers in the security units protecting Soviet strategic missiles and nuclear weapons (the Americans wanted them counted under the overall ground forces ceilings). We still had a long way to go before all CFE issues were resolved.

On START, the U.S. and Soviet arms control experts had a field day. They spent hours working on what seemed to be the final package. Shevardnadze tried to prod them a bit, but the issues were so technical that the experts alone seemed to be able to understand them. The foreign minister was frustrated. "Are you sure these details are worth fighting for and risking the bigger political picture?" he once asked the experts. "Are you thinking primarily about your agency or about your country?" In Washington, when we were in a secure room in the embassy, Shevardnadze used stronger language. "They just don't understand," he said, referring to our military. "We are going through hard times, there is anarchy in the country, and they still want their weapons and hardware. We should have signed the START treaty months ago."

We went to Washington from Houston in Baker's plane. The two men were exhausted, and Shevardnadze fell asleep halfway to the destination. They talked mostly about the Gulf, and their talk was not diplomatic in the usual way. Baker said the U.N. resolution had not had any immediate effect on Iraq's behavior and that war might soon become inevitable. The United States could not afford another period of uncertainty following the end of the pause. "Our military," Baker said, "have detailed plans and a great deal of confidence that they will work. But I know that wars never go according to plan. It's always different." Baker was clearly not as sure about the military option as one might have thought.

When Shevardnadze was asleep, Baker talked with Tarasenko and me about all kinds of things—taxes, the looming recession, and again the Gulf. "One thing we are not sure about is the morale of the Iraqi forces," he said. "Will they fight or will they run?" Sergey and I both thought they would run;

in militarized totalitarian societies the morale of regular armies is rarely high. But that remained to be seen. For the time being there was still hope that Iraq would withdraw.

In Washington, Bush and Shevardnadze made an announcement about the upcoming summit, but it was my feeling that both sides were not really sure about it. The Gulf was the great unknown, but that was the obvious reason for the uncertainty and concern. If there were other reasons, I could only guess what they were. President Bush acted as a hospitable host to us. He and Mrs. Bush gave us a tour of the White House, which was being decorated for Christmas. The White House Christmas tree was a real beauty, and the president invited the foreign minister and all of us to have pictures taken with him near the tree. The White House sent one to me promptly, but I received it after Christmas—and after Shevardnadze's resignation.

On the way to Moscow, Shevardnadze stopped over in Ankara. His visit there was not well organized, and a couple of times I saw him frustrated by the ineptness of some embassy and foreign ministry officials. He had a meeting planned during his stay in Turkey with PLO Chairman Yasir Arafat, but something went wrong and it fell through. It was my impression that neither Shevardnadze nor Arafat, and particularly the Turks, really wanted the meeting to take place, but all tried not to let on. On the plane to Moscow, Tarasenko and Vasily Kolotusha, head of the foreign ministry's Middle East department, worked on Shevardnadze's letter to Tariq Aziz, a strong appeal to cooperate in arranging the meetings proposed by Bush and Baker and to talk peace—that is, unconditional withdrawal from Kuwait.

Ten

RIFTS AND CRACKS
1990–1991

Political Tensions and Human Strains

December in Moscow is a cruel, gloomy, and depressing month. Sunny days are rare, the afternoons are dusky, and the long and dark evenings are not enlivened by the traditions of the Christmas season that make December so festive in Vienna or Paris. December 1990 in Moscow was a month of political tensions and human strain. Tensions had been building up since early fall, and particularly after the stormy debate over the "500 days" program.

The radicals resented Gorbachev's decision to compromise on the economic transition program and were preparing to declare a final break with him. Conservatives felt that their pressure had worked and were now consolidating their gains for what they thought would be a decisive battle with the democratic opposition and the nationalists in the republics. Both sides in that confrontation must have felt that tensions worked in their favor and sought to use the atmosphere of crisis and fear as a political weapon.

The hard-liners issued open letters calling for "firm measures" to restore order and stop the country's disintegration. They did not specify what firm measures they had in mind, but it was clear that it would mean a reversal of the democratic process. The radical opposition, with Yeltsin now installed as its virtual leader, felt that Gorbachev was susceptible to the pressure from the hard-liners and suspected him of siding with them.

In a country with a firm democratic tradition, such a situation would stir up a heated public debate and perhaps a political battle. In the Soviet Union in December 1990 it set the stage for a dramatic social confrontation tinged with rumors of civil war. That was the backdrop for the fourth Congress of People's Deputies, which began with a call for Gorbachev's resignation.

There had been rumors that the hard-liners would attack Gorbachev and demand his replacement. Two journalists I knew well invited me to lunch a couple of days before the Congress and told me about those rumors. Still, the call for Gorbachev's ouster, voiced by the hard-line faction, came as something of a surprise to me. I soon understood that the goal was to blackmail Gorbachev. The hard-liners, the Stalinists in the party, the KGB, and the armed forces were already preparing or hoping for a sharp about-turn, and they wanted Gorbachev either to become its leader or to leave the scene. The resignation call on the first day of the Congress was an ultimatum and a warning to Gorbachev from the hard-liners, who wanted to control him. The Congress, however, refused to include the question of Gorbachev's ouster on its agenda.

Shevardnadze Resigns

Eduard Shevardnadze, Gorbachev's old friend, had a different kind of warning for him: he submitted his own resignation. That event shook the Congress, as it also shook the foreign ministry building at Smolenskaya Square. December 20 will be forever engraved in my memory. It was an agonizing day that ended in a sleepless night.

I was working in my office when a colleague entered, saying "Pasha, how do you explain it? Shevardnadze has resigned." There was a television set in the office next door, and we went there to watch the live broadcast of the Congress. I caught Shevardnadze's final words: "Let this be my protest against what is happening and what is being prepared for our people. I still believe that eventually freedom and democracy will triumph." Shevardnadze then left the hall. Everyone was stunned.

Gorbachev tried to cool things down, saying he would talk with Shevardnadze to make things clearer. Liberal deputies called on Shevardnadze to reconsider his decision. Said Ales Adamovich, a radical author from Byelorussia: "He ought to have known he would have to take a lot of heat from the reactionaries. But why is he quitting under fire from them?" The conservatives demanded an accounting; the democrats, whom Shevardnadze criticized in his speech for being inconsistent and uncooperative, wanted an explanation. Clearly, Shevardnadze had not made his motives or his position clear enough. So the city, the country, and the world were abuzz with rumors, speculation, and predictions. In a way, as a person who was close to both Shevardnadze and Gorbachev, I was in the eye of that storm.

My friends were sensitive enough not to bother me with blunt questions, but I felt the eyes of many people on me as I stood in line in the eighteenth-floor cafeteria. A colleague from the Middle East desk asked me in an indirect way whether I thought Shevardnadze would allow Gorbachev to persuade him to change his mind. "I don't think so," I said. "Not again."

In the office, people were talking about the resignation, going over various hypotheses. Somehow, many were convinced that the main reason was the events in Georgia, Shevardnadze's birthplace, in which he had worked most of his life. Things were really getting out of hand there, with armed Georgian irregulars clashing with army troops and harassing people in South Ossetia, an autonomous region within Georgia. The general breakdown of authority was happening much faster in Georgia than in other Soviet republics, and Shevardnadze certainly had to feel bad about it.

I recalled how two weeks before, when we were flying to Houston, Georgy Mamedov said to Shevardnadze, "They will probably ask you about the developments in Georgia. What do you think will happen there?"

"Anything could happen," Shevardnadze replied in an unusually sharp tone. "Anything. A civil war, and then things will settle down." He fell silent. He definitely did not enjoy thinking about all that.

Nevertheless, Shevardnadze was too big a man and politician to resign just because of troubles in his native republic or because he had plans to return there, as some were saying then. It is true that a large group of Georgian intellectuals had come to talk to him during the previous summer, if I recall correctly, asking him "to come back and save Georgia," but Shevardnadze believed it would be a mistake to do so at the time. He regarded himself as a citizen of the Soviet Union, and even after the dissolution of the Union he said he would probably die as "the last Soviet man." That changed later, under the weight of changing circumstances, but in 1990 his heartache was about the country as a whole.

During those days I was completely frank only with the two persons who were closest to me: my mother and my wife. They were worried. They asked me what I thought was going to happen, and I answered in all honesty that I did not know. They also asked me whether I thought Shevardnadze was right to resign. What could I say? I was ambivalent about his decision. "I think I understand him," I answered, "but I wouldn't do it in his place." I would talk to him soon, I said, and maybe I would find out a little more about what was happening. I also wanted to discuss my own future with him.

Shevardnadze stayed in the foreign ministry for almost one month after his resignation statement. Gorbachev was still trying to persuade him not to leave, and although he was firm in his refusal he agreed to stay until a replacement was chosen. Perhaps Gorbachev thought that he could drag that for some time or even indefinitely, but if so it was wishful thinking. The rift between him and Shevardnadze was becoming more personal every day.

Shevardnadze was particularly angry about hints that his nerves or stamina had failed him, that he had panicked. He said later that conservatives like Supreme Soviet Chairman Anatoly Lukyanov and Vice-President Gennady Yanayev, the plotters of the future August coup, had promoted that theory. That is true, but it is probably not the whole truth. Alexander Yakovlev, Shevardnadze's friend and always a strong advocate of democracy and the new thinking, had similar doubts, and he said so in one of his newspaper interviews at the time, though not in an accusatory manner. In his heart he was no less critical of Gorbachev's tactics in the final months of 1990, but he chose to stay with him. For many people the months that followed in 1991 were a time of choosing, of difficult and sometimes agonizing choices.

I asked Andrey Nesterenko, the foreign minister's secretary, to schedule an appointment for me with Shevardnadze. His days were busy—he continued to have a full schedule of ministerial appointments—but he found an hour for me. We talked in his office. There was an electric heater near his desk; he always needed a little additional warmth and had felt good sitting near the fireplace in the State Department office of Shultz and later Baker. He had numerous papers and documents on his desk, and Gorbachev's photograph was still on the bookshelf to his left. Shevardnadze talked quietly. No one interrupted us for about an hour.

I said to him that, given what was happening, I wanted to consult with him about my future. I told him I had a kind of open invitation from President Gorbachev to join his staff but that there was some confusion about what kind of national security and foreign affairs staff he was going to have. I said that I probably would have decided to remain in the foreign ministry if he had stayed as minister, but that now my options were open. I did not hide from

Shevardnadze that I felt confused and was sorry that he had decided to resign. When he started to answer, I saw he had understood me.

Shevardnadze said that over the years of our work together we had developed a relationship of trust that enabled him to be very frank with me. He had made a difficult decision, and he wanted me to understand him, he said. "This decision is a tragedy," he added. It was not a result of panic or confusion. He had given it a lot of thought and had come to the conclusion that a violent turn of events and a crackdown were probably unavoidable.

"We made many mistakes," Shevardnadze continued. "Sometimes we went too fast, and sometimes we were unforgivably late in making important decisions. As a result, the situation is now out of control." He said "we." He did not try to dissociate himself from the decisions, actions, or inaction of the leadership he was now leaving. "What would a crackdown and the use of force mean in this country?" he wondered aloud. "Who knows? It could be worse than Tiananmen. And I would not be able to represent our country internationally and defend such actions. The quality of relations that we have achieved with civilized countries would be impossible to maintain."

I told Shevardnadze that his resignation had stunned many people but that many of them would like to focus on his final words: that eventually freedom and democracy will triumph. I said I too wanted to view his decision as a protest, a warning—perhaps above all a warning to the president—but not as an admission that the worst was inevitable. I said I was very worried about our democrats. Why do they have to act as mindless radicals or mere nationalists? Later in 1991 Shevardnadze said many times that "the president should rely more on the democratic forces," but this time he agreed with me. "We have to respect democratically elected leaders and parliaments," he added. "But I pin my hopes not so much on them as on the people, on their common sense."

I always doubted whether broad concepts such as "the people" were useful in thinking about something quite specific, and something that might happen very quickly, and I said so to Shevardnadze. My hope, I said to him, was that the politically active groups, all those who support or accept the democratic process, would sober up and seek some common ground. "I may be mistaken," I said, "but I still hope the worst can be avoided." In any event, I added, what has been achieved in our foreign policy will have a long-term impact and cannot be reversed.

After a pause Shevardnadze said, "I am not so sure. If, for example, there is a crackdown in the Baltics—You see, there is increasing pressure on the president to introduce presidential rule. If that is done, if their parliaments are suspended, what happens next? Mass demonstrations, hunger strikes, and so on. What would be the world's reaction?"

I pointed out that some of the achievements could not be reversed anyway. The CFE treaty was a fact, and START was close to completion.

"It's close," Shevardnadze agreed. "The Houston package has now been accepted by the defense ministry, and [Leonid] Zaikov supports it. Only Baklanov is being capricious, but I called him today and hope to bring him around."

"They are criticizing you for CFE, START, and for Germany," I said, "but, given that the unification could not be stopped, how else could we achieve such results: the reduction of the Bundeswehr, restraints on NATO in East German territory, and the goodwill of the Germans for years and decades to come?"

"It was difficult," Shevardnadze said. "You remember how we came to the '2 plus 4' meeting in Berlin with our draft? Baker was perplexed and asked me what had happened. Well, there had been a real battle in the Politburo the day before, literally a shouting match. And it was very difficult to turn it around afterward."

Shevardnadze was well aware of his contribution to the foreign policy of new thinking. He said he wanted to continue to be active in that area. "I thought about what I would do next," he said. "Return to Georgia? Well, a different kind of people are in charge there now, and the attitude toward me has changed. But I cannot retire and do nothing."

He was thinking about setting up a foreign policy association, he continued, which would be a think tank and perhaps a mediator in some domestic situations in which the experience of international conflict resolution could be useful. And he said that Tarasenko would be leaving with him to work in the association and that he wanted me to discuss my prospects with him. "He is a remarkable man," Shevardnadze said. "I owe a lot to him."

I joined the praise of Tarasenko and told Shevardnadze that most people in the foreign ministry, including his deputies, would probably feel just as comfortable with a different foreign policy. But not so Tarasenko, and Shevardnadze agreed. We talked for a few minutes about the old times, about Shultz and Baker, and we said goodbye on a lighter note than when our talk began. But I have always thought about that day with sadness. I have never quite been able to take a clear and unambiguous stand on Shevardnadze's decision. I respected it then and respect it now, but respect does not mean agreement.

Shevardnadze turned out to be correct in his prediction that there would be an attempt to return to the old ways. The August coup was just one scenario, attempted only after the others had failed. He saw that Kryuchkov, Baklanov, and others were pushing Gorbachev to the right, calling for "a return to order" and planning a crackdown. But why then was his warning so vague? Why did he not say to Gorbachev, "Here are the people who are pushing you to do something I cannot and you should not accept—they should go, either they go or I go."

Things are never as clear-cut in real life as they are in hindsight, but it is clear in retrospect that Shevardnadze made a mistake. He left Gorbachev increasingly surrounded by hard-liners, by people like Kryuchkov and Baklanov, who later probably formed the principal axis of the August coup-plotters, or Yazov and Boris Pugo, who probably were incapable of taking a stand and who, therefore, joined the principal conspirators; or bureaucrats like Premier Pavlov, who had replaced Nikolay Ryzhkov after the latter's heart attack in late December (Ryzhkov was due to resign anyway).

The Balance of Power in the Government Shifts

As 1991 was beginning, the media in the Soviet Union and abroad were saying that Gorbachev's perestroika team was no longer with him, that people like Shevardnadze, former Interior Minister Vadim Bakatin, and Alexander Yakovlev had either left or been shunted aside. That was not quite true. Yakovlev was still with Gorbachev, although it was clear that he had less influence than before, and Gorbachev said he would offer an important post to Bakatin, whom Pugo had recently replaced as minister of the interior.

Still, it was true that the balance of forces in the higher echelons of government had changed. The increasing chaos and the opposition's apparent willingness to force the issues may have made the conservatives seem like a more responsible group to Gorbachev, or at least a group he could not ignore. Nevertheless, a few democratically minded people who had begun perestroika with Gorbachev were not leaving.

Alexander Yakovlev and Georgy Shakhnazarov, as well as younger people like Gorbachev's press secretary, Vitaly Ignatenko, and Andrey Grachev, a member of the Central Committee, soldiered on. I was watching those people with sympathy and sometimes admiration. They certainly resented the military and KGB hard-liners and the bureaucrats of the government and party apparat. The resentment was mutual. But many of their own friends among the liberal and radical intelligentsia, whose attitude to Gorbachev had changed, were now much cooler and sometimes even hostile to such people.

I felt some of that resentment myself. My telephone was not ringing as much as in better times, and some people began to avoid me. But most if not all of my friendships survived that test. Among people of my generation, ideological differences do not always result in dramatic personal breakups, but I knew how ideological or philosophical disagreements often made enemies of people older than I, and I knew the kind of verbal abuse to which Gorbachev loyalists were subjected by both the left and the right. The radicals called them the liberal Communist mafia—the softer apparatchiks who are good for nothing, whose time had come and gone.

Today, disparaging these people has become almost a sign of good manners among the new Russian political elite, and of course the vicious and revengeful hard-liners will never forgive them for their role in the dismantling of the totalitarian system. I believe they deserve respect, more respect than they get today. After all, in the Khrushchev and Brezhnev years it was easier to be a self-contented apparatchik, an aloof academic, or even a dissident than a liberal reformer trying to do something within the system.

The post-Stalin Soviet ideology was a complex blend of deadwood ortho-doxy and honest intellectual attempts to create a platform for society's more normal development. There was a rather sharp division within the apparat and the ideological institutions, between the cynics and the basically decent people of a liberal socialist or social democratic persuasion. To them, Gorba-chev's perestroika was more than just an attempt to "put our house in order." Some of them were saying it openly and some were less frank, but essentially they wanted the country to become a Western-style democracy. During Gorbachev's years in power they won some battles and lost some, they had their good days and their bad days. But perhaps not even the days of the August coup were as bad for them—or for me—as January 13, 1991, and a few subsequent days.

Bloodshed in Lithuania Brings the Crisis to a Head

The crisis in Lithuania had been coming to a head for some time. Landsbergis had been behaving as though independence was already an accomplished fact. The hard-liners in the Lithuanian Communist Party, the military, and the KGB were putting pressure on Gorbachev, accusing him of tolerating challenges to Soviet law and violations of the rights of the Russian-speaking minority. Actually, it was true that the Lithuanian authorities were behaving in an undemocratic way, but Gorbachev was clearly unwilling to use force to remove them from power. A few days before the disastrous January 13 he had a telephone talk with George Bush. The "pause of goodwill" was ending, and most of the talk was about the Gulf. But Bush also asked Gorbachev about Lithuania and urged him to do everything he could to avoid the use of force.

It was my impression that Bush would perhaps tolerate the imposition of presidential rule in Lithuania but that he would draw the line at the use of military force and bloodshed. Gorbachev assured him that he had no intention of ordering the use of force, and from his remarks to Ignatenko and me afterward I felt he was sincere.

As Shevardnadze had said to me a few days before, Gorbachev was under heavy pressure to introduce presidential rule, which he could legally do. Perhaps he was considering doing so; even if he did, he certainly would have tried to resume negotiations with the Lithuanian authorities after that. Soon, however, it became a moot point, because the hard-liners forced the situation on the night of January 13, when army tanks and KGB forces stormed the television tower in Vilnius, killing sixteen people. I could not believe that Gorbachev had ordered that.

As Vitaly Ignatenko later told me, the next day he and a few other people urged Gorbachev to go to Vilnius and personally lead the investigation into what had happened. Gorbachev said he was ready to do that, and called Kryuchkov to ask him to make security arrangements. A few hours later Kryuchkov called back saying that Gorbachev's safety could not be guaranteed. The trip to Vilnius had to be canceled. It would have been a golden opportunity to put the situation back on track.

But what happened afterward was even worse. Speaking on January 15 in the Supreme Soviet, Gorbachev failed to condemn the use of force unequivocally, saying that the situation was not clear enough and that an investigation was under way. He seemed confused, not in control, and on the wrong side of the issue. Watching him on television was a painful and frustrating experience for me. The worst part of it was that he had not dissociated himself from the so-called National Salvation Committee, a secret group formed by the Lithuanian hard-liners and the military a few days earlier, which had claimed power in the republic in disregard of the legally elected Supreme Soviet.

Regardless of how wrong or even illegal some of the actions of the Lithuanian Supreme Soviet had been, it was the constitutional authority in the republic, and I was dismayed at the president's failure to see the issue in clear terms. The hard-liners had set him up; his political opponents were using the situation against him, and many unbiased observers were beginning to have doubts about his democratic instincts.

For several days many people were wondering whose side Gorbachev was on. The questions continued even after January 21, when Gorbachev finally came out with a condemnation of the "Salvation Committee" and promised a full investigation leading to punishment of those responsible for the deaths of civilians in Vilnius. But by that time the damage had been done, and although my own faith in Gorbachev was intact, this was not true of almost the entire radical and democratic part of the political spectrum—particularly in Moscow, where the intelligentsia were never very willing to give Mikhail Gorbachev the benefit of the doubt.

Later Gorbachev said he had then been maneuvering, trying to preserve the democratic process despite tremendous pressure he was facing from the hard-liners, who wanted a nationwide crackdown. He saw that the demand for a return to order was coming not only from the conservatives in the party and the army, but also from many ordinary people, whose lives had been deteriorating for months. This, and the intelligentsia's defection from Gorbachev, left him without a clear and broad political base, making maneuvering and a certain swing to the right almost inevitable for him. Whether he was doing it well, whether the democratic process and new relations with the West could still be preserved, was still an open question. I felt that while it was being resolved I had to remain loyal to Gorbachev rather than float away from him.

From Foreign Ministry to President's Office

My days of doubt about and disagreement with Gorbachev had been difficult. I had been having sleepless nights during which all kinds of thoughts entered my head. I thought of asking for an assignment abroad, or of leaving the foreign ministry to join Shevardnadze's Foreign Policy Association. Finally, sometime after January 20, I had a talk with Anatoly Chernyaev, which ended my doubts and prompted my decision to join the foreign affairs unit of the president's staff.

I laid out my situation for Chernyaev and asked for his advice. I could, I said, continue as before, but felt I needed a change. My wife was not pressing me, but I understood that she would prefer assignment to a quieter place abroad to living in our crammed two-room apartment in Moscow and seeing me come home after nine o'clock or later, every night. The new foreign minister, Alexander Bessmertnykh, spoke fluent English and would not need me as much as Shevardnadze had, I said. I also told Chernyaev that Shevardnadze had suggested I consider joining his Foreign Policy Association. Finally, I said, there was Gorbachev's offer to work on his staff, and I was ready to think about that if it was still in effect.

Chernyaev's answer boiled down to this: If I preferred an assignment abroad, he would understand and try to help me; if I wanted to go with Shevardnadze, he wished me good luck; and if I was ready to join the president's staff, he would take me on. The foreign policy unit of the staff was just being formed, Chernyaev said, and he would recommend me to Gorbachev to work on U.S.-Soviet issues and arms control, and also to help with speechwriting. Later that evening I talked with Lena about it, and even though I felt she had some doubts she said it was up to me to decide. Afterward she never questioned my decision—not in March, not in August, not in December.

The next day I called Chernyaev and said that I accepted the offer to join the president's staff. I also called Shevardnadze to congratulate him on his birthday and to tell him I was not yet ready to leave government service. I told him too that I had decided to join the president's staff.

"Well, Pavel," Shevardnadze said, "thanks for your congratulations, and thank you for all you have done for me. We worked well together, and I value you as a person. Whatever you do in the future and wherever you will be working, I hope we'll stay in touch, and I wish you good luck."

Chernyaev had told me that for some reason the process of organizing the presidential staff was very slow and that it would probably take some time to formalize my transfer from the foreign ministry to the president's office. In the meantime, I should continue in the foreign ministry, he said. He would talk to Bessmertnykh after getting final approval for my appointment from Gorbachev. That meant I would be going to Washington with Bessmertnykh at the end of January on a visit that was of critical importance for the immediate prospects of relations with the United States.

Gorbachev Appoints Bessmertnykh to the Foreign Ministry

Bessmertnykh's appointment had not been much of a surprise. His name had been mentioned in the press in early January as one of the strong possibilities. But other names were being mentioned too, including Yevgeny Primakov and Yuly Vorontsov. Gorbachev did not reveal his decision, but that was probably because he kept trying to persuade Shevardnadze to change his mind and stay on. In private he mentioned Bessmertnykh several times. "The Americans trust him," he said to Chernyaev and me after his telephone talk with Bush on January 7. It was clear that Gorbachev trusted Bessmertnykh too, as did Chernyaev. Other considerations probably influenced the decision, but trust was paramount. The appointment was met with a sigh of relief almost everywhere. Most people felt it was the best decision under the circumstances.

I knew Alexander Bessmertnykh well. By Soviet standards, his rise had been almost meteoric: from head of the foreign ministry's U.S. desk in 1985 to foreign minister and member of the country's top political leadership in 1991. In time of great change such things are not uncommon, and Bessmertnykh definitely was a foreign policy professional of high caliber.

As a policymaker, he was not in the same class as Shevardnadze, and he knew it, nor did he have the former minister's charisma and international respect. But he had his pluses too. His knowledge of international affairs was extensive and detailed; he knew just about everyone in Washington; and no one doubted his loyalty to Gorbachev, who singled him out from among other talented Soviet diplomats.

I welcomed his appointment too, even though I felt that Bessmertnykh was a man who would never have initiated the changes in our foreign policy that Gorbachev and Shevardnadze so boldly pursued—of course, with the support of and relying on the expertise of people like Bessmertnykh and Yuly Vorontsov, both graduates of Anatoly Dobrynin's "school of diplomacy"—the Soviet embassy in Washington. Was their support total or somewhat half-hearted? That I did not know. Bessmertnykh was, I thought, a highly skilled technician, and perhaps it was time for a technician to become foreign minister. If so, he was the best choice.

Events Adversely Affect U.S.-Soviet Relations

Bessmertnykh's visit to Washington in late January came at a time when relations with the United States, and with the West generally, seemed destined to go downhill. The events in Vilnius, and later in Riga, caused an uproar both in Europe and in the United States. The European Community (EC) reacted almost immediately by suspending or reconsidering a number of trade arrangements. The EC decision amounted to significant economic sanctions, and the U.S. administration was under heavy pressure to follow suit.

George Bush wrote a letter to Gorbachev expressing dismay and condemning the use of force. He also said he would like to continue cooperation with the Soviet Union and avoid economic sanctions, but that his position was difficult because the demand to punish the Soviet Union was bipartisan, and growing. The letter was quite cool, and I felt the only thing that constrained the administration was its need to have our cooperation on the Gulf.

The conflict in the Gulf was then, openly or more subtly, in the background of every foreign policy issue. On January 17 the United States had begun the air campaign against Iraq. Its effect was devastating, but Saddam Hussein did not immediately capitulate. This led many people, not only in the Soviet Union, to say that the U.S. plan for "blitzkrieg" had failed and that it was time to reconsider the entire approach to the conflict.

Gorbachev was under pressure to begin dissociating himself from the administration's policy and to play an equidistant role. Conservative Soviet newspapers were denouncing the U.S. air campaign as barbaric, leading to unjustified loss of life among civilians in Iraq. The administration was accused of trying to destroy Iraq and to change the overall balance in the Middle East instead of just expelling Saddam's forces from Kuwait. The conservatives and the military focused their attacks on Shevardnadze, who, they said, had tied us too closely to Washington's position. Their main objective, however, was to influence Gorbachev. He disregarded the more strident attacks, but he was not insensitive to the argument that he should be seen working for peace and for an early end to the hostilities.

Another sore spot in the U.S.-Soviet relationship was the increasingly explosive CFE issue of "naval infantry and coastal defense." The Soviet military wanted to exclude hundreds of tanks, artillery pieces, and armored personnel carriers from accounting under the treaty, arguing that naval infantry and coastal defense were not ground forces, according to its interpretation of the treaty. The argument was flimsy, and the Americans probably knew that many people on the Soviet side considered it untenable. The U.S. administration was insisting on including all those weapons, as well as about 1,700 armored personnel carriers attached to the strategic rocket forces protection units.

At one point in January or February, Defense Minister Yazov seemed on the verge of agreeing to the U.S. position. In a letter to the foreign minister, a copy of which I saw, he said he was willing to consider including all that hardware in the CFE ceiling. I don't know what was behind that willingness—perhaps some proddings from Gorbachev, who was on good personal terms with Yazov and had always been able to persuade him to go along with major arms control decisions. Initially, Gorbachev underestimated the importance of the "naval infantry" issue. In early January he told me he was sure it would "work itself out somehow" *(rassosetsya)*. If he meant that a compromise on that issue was possible, he turned out to be right. Eventually the Americans made significant concessions, but a lot of time was lost in the process.

In retrospect it is quite clear that accepting the U.S. position, which Yazov seemed ready to do, would have been preferable. But amazingly Yazov was overruled by the Chief of the General Staff, General Mikhail Moiseyev, whose influence was growing. He was heard several times saying that "the CFE is a bad treaty" and that no more concessions should be made to the West. That left Bessmertnykh with little room to maneuver and made his own position tenuous.

Officially, the United States and the Soviet Union were supposed to be preparing for a summit meeting in February, but relations seemed to be deteriorating and the best one could hope for was to halt that process. As Bessmertnykh and his team were going to Washington, the discussions on the plane centered on modest goals: how to work out an acceptable statement about postponing the summit for an indefinite time, and how to keep the administration from putting U.S.-Soviet relations in a deep freeze, given that it was under pressure and seemed to have many reasons to do so.

Gorbachev had written Bush a letter in which he tried to explain the situation in the Soviet Union and described his efforts to put it back on the track of peaceful, orderly evolution. He hinted in the letter—and Bessmertnykh did so even more strongly in his talk with Bush—that he would accept any outcome of the Baltic republics' process of self-determination, including independence, provided that it was done, as he put it, constitutionally rather than by an undemocratic shortcut. He said he hoped that a mechanism of negotiations could be established with the Baltic leaders, with whom he was ready to deal as elected and legitimate representatives of their people, and he asked Bush not to rush to judgment and not to apply any hasty sanctions. It was a good letter, but we had no way of knowing how it would play in Washington. Realistically, I thought our task—and the best we could hope to achieve—was to manage an inevitable cooling-down in the relationship.

Bessmertnykh and Baker Meet in Washington on the Gulf, the Baltics, and Other Issues

In Washington, Baker welcomed Bessmertnykh cordially. They were on a first-name basis, as Jim and Sasha, but Baker seemed worried. He did not seem to have much hope for putting U.S.-Soviet relations back on the track soon. More than other Americans, and Westerners generally, Baker appeared to appreciate the difficulty of Gorbachev's position. He knew that Gorbachev had to operate within a specific political and historical environment and that, unlike Yeltsin or even Shevardnadze, he could not set himself in opposition to many in his own government and to the Communist Party.

Those were real constraints on what Gorbachev could do, and he could easily break his neck if he tried to ignore them. But Baker was worried—and this became particularly clear to me during his visit to Moscow in March— that Gorbachev would allow his behavior to be governed by those constraints and those forces. He was also concerned about U.S.-Soviet cooperation on the Gulf: the longer the war continued, the greater the chances of a break-down. As a realist, Baker understood all that, but it was clear that the duration of the war was not something he could control.

On the Baltics, Baker told Bessmertnykh during their January talks in Washington that he was not sure how long Bush would be able to hold the relatively mild position of criticizing the use of force while refraining from economic sanctions. To be able to do so, Baker said, we have to see that you are working actively to rectify the situation, creating a mechanism for dialogue about self-determination in the Baltics, withdrawing the troops recently sent there and controlling those that remain. Until that was done, Baker said, a summit would probably be impossible. A statement on its postponement could be couched in diplomatic language and make no mention of the Baltic events, Baker said, but he made it quite clear that some improvement would have to take place before the U.S. administration would be ready to push again for the summit. Baker hinted strongly that, to avoid making Bessmertnykh's visit look like a failure, some signs of improvement would have to appear quickly, probably during the visit itself.

The two men discussed other issues briefly, almost as an afterthought. Bessmertnykh said Gorbachev's position of cooperating with the United States on the Gulf was being increasingly questioned but that he was determined to stick with it. One thing was clear, he said: we must avoid the impression that the Soviet Union is being used by the administration for its own purposes in the Gulf and that, once the war was over, the United States would take a tougher line against it. It must be made clear that both countries have been cooperating in earnest and would continue to do so. Bessmertnykh asked whether Baker would be willing to consider a U.S.-Soviet statement on the Gulf and another one on the overall Middle East settlement. Baker said that perhaps something could be worked out and asked Dennis Ross to look at our drafts.

When we returned to the embassy, Bessmertnykh's deputy Obukhov and Sergey Chetverikov, the Soviet chargé d'affaires, were eager to hear what Bessmertnykh thought of his tête-à-tête with Baker. The foreign minister answered briefly and without going into much detail. It was not as bad as we had thought, he said, but let's work on the specifics of the Middle East and arms control and let's get in touch with Moscow and see what else we could say to Baker on the Baltics. When the others left and we were alone, Bessmertnykh asked me to draft a cable with a detailed summary of his talk with Baker. He seemed to be a little nervous about it, because he did not want the hard-liners in Moscow to see him as just a messenger for U.S. demands on the Baltics, including particularly the reduction in our military presence there.

The Soviet Positions on the Baltics and on the Gulf and the Middle East

We decided to prepare a paper on the basis of Gorbachev's letter and his statement a few days earlier that would make clear Gorbachev's willingness to negotiate on the Baltics' self-determination. After some hesitation, Bessmertnykh also decided to appeal to Gorbachev for information that would demonstrate some scaling-down of our military presence in the Baltics. Bessmertnykh was also intrigued by Baker's apparent willingness to work on a Middle East statement, but he was not sure that anything substantive could be achieved.

In the afternoon, I worked on the draft of the cable to Moscow and tried to piece together something we called "the position of Soviet leadership concerning the Baltics" to be given to President Bush the next day. Of course, it had to be based on the stated positions and principles and could not break any new ground, but we felt that presenting those positions in a clear and compact form could be helpful. The text had to be cleared with Moscow, so I had to do it quickly. When the visit was over, I took that draft back to Moscow, and I still have it. Here is what I was able to put together:

> The position of the Soviet leadership concerning the Baltics:
> 1. The need to solve any problem through peaceful means. Any attempt to appeal to the armed forces in political struggles is inadmissible.

2. The use of force in the Baltics is not an expression of the president's policy. The events that occurred there were not the result of orders from above. Relations of civilian authorities with the military must be based exclusively on the laws of the U.S.S.R.

3. The constitutional right of the republics to secede from the U.S.S.R. is reaffirmed. The condition for this is that the will of the people must be expressed, through a referendum, and that the constitution and the relevant laws must be observed. The president has repudiated attempts by any "committee" or organization to claim power other than by lawful means.

4. Recognition of the legitimately elected parliaments and leaders of the Baltic republics and readiness to engage in a dialogue with them, including through the Council of the Federation.

5. The president states that he will do the utmost to prevent the repetition of anything like that which happened over the past weeks. He is confident that everything will be settled. This process has already been making substantial progress in Latvia and has begun in Estonia.

This, I believed, could be a helpful piece of paper. It went some way toward meeting Baker's insistence on a clear indication of Moscow's willingness to negotiate on self-determination for the Baltics and to establish a "mechanism" (a word Baker often used) for that. But I knew it would not have much effect without something about scaling down military presence in the Baltics.

That afternoon I also saw Dennis Ross and gave him our draft statements on the Gulf and the Middle East and talked briefly with him. My message to Dennis was: Don't create the impression you are pushing Bessmertnykh; his position in the Soviet leadership is still tenuous and too much pressure could be counterproductive.

I also spoke about the difficult position Gorbachev was in. The hard-liners were accusing him of watching passively while the country was falling apart. The nationalists in the republics, by radicalizing their demands, and the democrats in Moscow, by giving them unqualified support, made it even more difficult for him to steer a reasonable and balanced course, and I hinted it would be good if the people to whom they would have to listen told them that.

Ross responded readily that that was precisely what the U.S. administration was trying quietly to do, and he repeated Baker's words that specific information on the military presence would be helpful. I said we were working to get that, but that I could not be sure whether it would come in time for Bessmertnykh's meeting with Bush the next day.

The cable from Moscow came a few hours later in the evening, but it was unusable for our purposes. Written in the fuzzy language bureaucrats resort to sometimes out of need but also out of custom, it did not make clear whether any troop withdrawals were actually under way. Bessmertnykh was disappointed. "This is clearly not it," he said. He decided to have another try and quickly wrote a cable to Anatoly Kovalev, his first deputy, asking him to try to get clearer language from the defense and interior ministries. I went to bed late that night, and because of jet lag I did not get much sleep.

I came to the embassy early in the morning of January 28 and was told that another cable had come from Moscow. When I saw it I knew we had what we needed. In the meantime, a statement about postponement of the Moscow summit had been drafted that gave the reason for postponement as only that the START treaty was not yet ready; it did not mention Soviet domestic developments. When Baker tried to find some way to allude to that, Bessmertnykh told him that would badly embarrass Gorbachev domestically, and Baker did not insist.

Later on January 28, Bessmertnykh had a talk at the White House with George Bush. Like Baker, President Bush had known Bessmertnykh for a long time and probably found it easy to talk to him. In fact, Bush began by saying he was glad that Gorbachev had chosen Bessmertnykh to become foreign minister, and he recalled his talks with Gorbachev and thanked him for his cooperation on the Gulf. Bush also said he was not one of those who focused on problems and setbacks as soon as difficulties appeared in the relationship—he did not want to get sidetracked, nor did he want to interfere in the Soviet Union's internal affairs. But, he said, he hoped Gorbachev understood that the Baltics were a special case for the United States. Bush's introductory remarks were characteristically brief, and he said he was ready to listen to what Bessmertnykh had to say.

Bessmertnykh's remarks in response to Bush were in well-crafted English and, I thought, effective. Gorbachev, he said, still regarded U.S.-Soviet relations as of overriding importance and agreed that the two countries were cooperating well in the Gulf crisis. He also said Gorbachev understood that the events in the Baltics created problems for Western governments in continuing cooperation with the Soviet Union. He admitted that some of Moscow's actions had been unfortunate, but the important question, he said, was where we go from here. He then summarized the main points of Gorbachev's letter, which he had informally handed to Baker the day before.

Bessmertnykh also gave President Bush the paper on the Baltics we had put together and, based on the cable from Moscow, the information about the troop presence. Essentially, it said the army regiment from Pskov deployed in

Lithuania before the recent events "for guarding military conscription sta-tions" had now been withdrawn. On January 29 about 70 percent of the interior ministry troops deployed in January "for guarding vital installations" would be withdrawn from Vilnius. As of January 28, the cable said, there was not a single additional unit of the Soviet army in the Baltic republics; only the units permanently stationed in the Baltics were now there. Bessmertnykh said that he hoped the U.S.-Soviet relationship would weather the storm.

The United States Responds to the Soviet Position

Bush answered cautiously and sometimes deferred to Baker to ask additional questions and give clarifications. But the bottom line was that he still trusted Gorbachev although he did not know how long he would be able to hold on to the position of "not punishing" the Soviet Union. He did not want postponement of the summit to look like a slap in the face to Gorbachev, he said, and he would not rush to follow the Europeans in imposing economic sanctions. But without a clear sign that the aspirations for self-determination would not be thwarted by armed force, Bush said, he would have to do something in order not to be left isolated, and the relationship would be in danger. Another incident of the same kind, he added, and we would get into a hole from which we won't get out.

The Gulf and START were mentioned only in passing, and neither Baker nor Bessmertnykh mentioned the possibility of a joint statement on the Middle East. The conversation ended on a good note: Bush said he wished Gorbachev success in bringing the situation back to normal "and in all his efforts." They announced the postponement of the summit and said Baker and Bessmertnykh would continue talks on START and other issues.

Scoring Points

In the afternoon, Oleg Derkovsky, a former Washington embassy official and now a Middle East expert in Moscow, and I went to the State Department to work with Ross on the Gulf and Middle East statement. Ross said he wanted to say a few words to me privately. From what he said, I understood that Bush and his aides had analyzed the conversation with Bessmertnykh and had come to some conclusions.

The information and papers Bessmertnykh had given Bush and Baker, Ross indicated, were useful and would enable the administration to maintain its position for some time. How long that would be was not clear and depended entirely on the course of developments within the Soviet Union. But for the time being things seemed to be returning to normal — or something like it.

This became even clearer to me when we began to work on the statement with Derkovsky and a member of Ross's staff. Dennis said that although he was not prepared to discuss a separate statement on the Middle East he would be ready to consider "perhaps a paragraph" about it in the statement on the Gulf crisis. When Ross showed us the draft he had prepared on the basis of our two drafts, we found it quite acceptable as a basis for discussion.

Work on the statement went surprisingly well. Derkovsky and I were able to expand the "Middle East part" of the statement to three quite substantive paragraphs. Ross did not insist when we asked him to strike down a phrase about "the two sides' commitment to the use of force" in accordance with the U.N. Security Council resolutions; we were already being criticized enough at home for allegedly doing the bidding of the U.S. administration. We left a few phrases in brackets and agreed to consult with our ministers about them and meet if necessary later in the day.

I was amazed how much we had been able to achieve so quickly, and I said so to Bessmertnykh when I returned to the embassy. He agreed but said, "Let's wait for Dennis's call after he shows it to Baker." We did not have to wait long. Ross called with a few amendments and a general approval from Baker. I said I had a general approval from Bessmertnykh and wondered whether Dennis thought another meeting between us was necessary. He did not, and we agreed that it was up to the ministers to decide what they would do with our draft when they met the next day.

Bessmertnykh and I then worked on the cable to Moscow about the talk with the president and other events of the day. We gave it a positive twist, and there was good reason to do so. We felt that we now had breathing room during which something could be done to normalize the situation at home, and that the balanced position adopted by the administration could have a positive influence on some of the political forces within the Soviet Union and the European governments.

I was surprised that Bessmertnykh did not want to give Moscow a preview of the statement on the Gulf and the Middle East. In fact, he included in the cable a sentence to the effect that the possibility of such a statement was being discussed but that it was not likely that the Americans would accept our draft.

He seemed to be deliberately lowering expectations in order to produce a bigger splash when the statement was issued. That is precisely what happened.

The next day, it did not take the ministers much time to put the finishing touches on the statement. When it was issued—for some reason Bessmertnykh, when he talked to the press (in English), started to translate it back from the Russian text and went a couple of paragraphs before Vitaly Churkin realized what was happening and slipped the English text to him—the press immediately understood its meaning: the Soviet Union had returned to the Middle East as a full participant in the peace process; the United States was ready to push for a multilateral peace conference on the Middle East.

Many people, including the Israelis, were stunned by what they saw as a new departure in U.S. policy. Baker was accused of overstepping his authority, and Bush of allowing U.S. policy to be changed in an almost casual way. Later I was told by some of my American friends that our Middle East accomplishment had created big problems for the U.S. administration. They wondered why Bush and Baker did it and why they stuck to it despite sharp criticism from Congress and the problems it created with Israel. Did they misjudge the situation? Or did they want to help Gorbachev and did so incautiously? Or perhaps they wanted to hand a diplomatic success to Bessmertnykh, whom they liked, and thus strengthen his position in the Soviet hierarchy? There might have been a little of that, but basically I am convinced that the Americans never make "free gifts" and that the statement reflected a real shift in the U.S. position based on a serious assessment of the Middle East situation as it evolved under the influence of the Gulf crisis and other events. But for us it was a diplomatic coup, and back in Moscow I was congratulated by surprised colleagues.

More CFE and START Problems

While the Middle East statement was clearly a plus, I was worried about arms control. Bush mentioned the CFE problem in just one sentence, but the next day Baker made a point of emphasizing it. He said that it jeopardized the credibility of the arms control process, and when Bessmertnykh replied that he wasn't sure what could be done about it, Baker said firmly: "Then it's bad. We feel that we've been deceived. I will not be able to recommend that the treaty be sent for ratification unless this problem is resolved." There was also a clear link between that issue and START.

Baker said that he had told Bush that if work on that treaty were not finished by the end of February the situation in the Soviet Union might deteriorate later and "we would lose the treaty." Bush agreed. Bessmertnykh too agreed that everything must be done to complete START quickly, and Baker even suggested that Gorbachev should consider a short "nonsummit" at some halfway point—in Alaska, Siberia, or a European capital—just to sign the treaty. But that, I believed, could happen only if the CFE problem were out of the way.

I often thought later that some things might have turned out differently if the opportunity to settle the issues on CFE and to sign START had not been passed up during the weeks that followed. The final compromise on CFE took too much time to work out, and even accepting the U.S. position outright would not have done much harm to the Soviet Union's security, just as offering a reasonable compromise sooner should not have embarrassed the United States. But no one took the first step.

Gorbachev was too busy at home, threatened by strikes and demands for his resignation and maneuvering in search of a way out of a seemingly impossible situation. As for Bush and Baker, I felt that they increasingly tended to listen to those in the administration who did not trust Gorbachev and suspected him of planning a complete reversal of course. Even if they did not agree with them fully, they felt it would be prudent to wait and see. And they did.

In the meantime, according to the scenario known all too well from the history of START negotiations, further technical problems emerged, of the kind that only a few people on both sides understood. I was one of those people (only to some extent, of course), and when I was asked to explain "downloading" or "demonstrated range" I did so, but with a feeling of frustration: a great opportunity was being missed, and START seemed to become increasingly irrelevant, both politically and militarily. Of course, when I returned to Moscow from Washington at the end of January, I could only guess how things would turn out, and even though I was worried I still had some hope.

Gorbachev's Union Referendum

But February, always the bleakest and dreariest month in our latitudes, turned out to be a particularly cruel month for Mikhail Gorbachev. Fate seemed to be working against him, and of the many things happening at once both at home and abroad, few offered hope. Gorbachev believed at the time that his main task was to preserve the essential unity of the country, not to allow it to fall apart. Russia's declaration of sovereignty and of the preeminence of its laws over the laws of the Soviet Union made that task extremely difficult.

The ensuing "war of sovereignties" and "war of laws" created a situation of near-total chaos in the economy, particularly in the administration of finances. In September 1990 Baker had told Gorbachev he admired the fact that in such a situation Gorbachev did not want a confrontation with the republics' authorities or a crackdown. Indeed, by that time Gorbachev had already accepted the idea of a major redistribution of authority between the center and the republics in favor of the latter. But following the conflict over the "500 days" program, his relations with Yeltsin once again turned sour and the process of redistribution did not really begin. At the Congress of People's Deputies in December 1990, Gorbachev proposed a nationwide referendum on the question of preserving the Soviet Union as one country and, following the reaffirmation of unity, a redistribution of powers toward the republics that decided to stay and an orderly process of secession for those that chose to leave the Union.

It was a logical but risky strategy. The risk was not that two or three republics would decide to secede. Gorbachev had basically accepted that as a possibility and as a democratic and constitutional right of any republic. The risk was that Gorbachev's intentions would be misinterpreted, either deliberately or by mistake. That is what indeed happened, creating a paradoxical situation: in his fight for the Union, Gorbachev was not supported by his natural allies—the democratic forces and the newly emerging political elites. Instead, he got the support of the upper echelons of the party, the armed forces, and the KGB.

He also had the support of the "silent majority"—the people who on March 17 gave him a victory in all the republics in which the referendum was held, including Russia and Ukraine. But did it mean much? In politics, over the short term and medium term, things are decided by the politically active elements, and there the balance was different from the country as a whole. The democrats had decided that for Gorbachev the referendum was just a pretext and a prelude to execute a turn to the right, to preserve "the old system," not just "the old Union."

Yeltsin Calls for Gorbachev's Resignation

The radical democrats, particularly the Moscow and Leningrad intelligentsia, were moving further away from Gorbachev, rejecting every policy position he defended. Their choice was not just to work with Yeltsin, but to be led by him too. "Our support for Yeltsin has to be total and unqualified," said Sergey Stankevich, a young "new politician," who owed his rise to Gorbachev's perestroika and who was now deputy chairman of Moscow's city soviet. In fighting Gorbachev, the radicals were rapidly destroying what was left of the economy, calling for strikes and adopting social giveaway programs that no budget could withstand.

The radicals' first call for a political strike followed the January events in Lithuania. It did not get much support, particularly among the miners in the Donetsk and Kuzbas coal regions, which were of decisive importance both politically and economically.

The situation seemed to be gradually returning to normal, but on February 19 in a televised interview Yeltsin called for Gorbachev's resignation and the transfer of power in the country to the Council of the Federation. Why he did it on that particular day is still not clear to me. No one seemed to be sure at the time whether it was just tactics, to weaken Gorbachev and to arrest what the democrats perceived as his right-wing turn, or whether it reflected Yeltsin's strategic objective.

The suspicion that Gorbachev had changed and decided to abandon the democratic experiment was shared by quite a few people both in the country and abroad. I felt that it was also strong in the U.S. political establishment, including the Bush administration—which explained its cautiousness in dealing with Gorbachev and its unwillingness to move speedily ahead on START.

Nevertheless, it seemed to me that behind Yeltsin's tactics was not just the desire to correct Gorbachev's course, but also a striving for power, for becoming the country's top leader. The shortest way toward that goal was not to wait for the presidential election in 1995 but to squeeze Gorbachev out before that time. Hence the idea, put forward by Yeltsin's chief strategist Gennady Burbulis, for a Union without a president; hence the call for Gorbachev's resignation and the transfer of power to the Council of the Federation; hence the final stroke in December—creation of the Commonwealth of Independent States and the carving up of the country into several states.

Most people were shocked by Yeltsin's call for Gorbachev's resignation. The idea that a legitimately elected president could be pushed out of office was not yet firmly established in the minds of the populace. But neither was there any outcry or outpouring of support for the president or for the constitutional process. I believe that those who later plotted the coup against Gorbachev in August took note of that fact. Then, the danger to Gorbachev came from a different quarter, and the technique was different, but there was the same disregard for the constitution and the legally established authority.

Shevardnadze Speaks of Dangers

To my knowledge, the only person in the democratic camp who publicly, though mildly, disagreed with the call for Gorbachev's resignation was Eduard Shevardnadze. During the opening ceremony of his Foreign Policy Association, held the day after Yeltsin's television interview, Shevardnadze was asked by reporters what he thought of the call for Gorbachev's resignation. He answered, "This war of sovereignties, war of laws, and now the war of the presidents must be stopped. A compromise must be found."

I saw Shevardnadze a few times during the months of February and March. Tarasenko, who left the foreign ministry with him, asked me to interpret his interview with Diane Sawyer of ABC News. Shevardnadze did not sound optimistic at all. He said he still believed in the eventual victory of democracy but was worried about the near future. The danger of dictatorship still existed. When asked by Sawyer whether Gorbachev might lead that dictatorship, Shevardnadze said, "No. The Gorbachev I know is no dictator. If he were to do that, he would no longer be Mikhail Gorbachev." The answer was open to various interpretations, but Shevardnadze was clearly not burning all the bridges.

Shevardnadze wanted to warn Gorbachev, but as subsequent events made clear he did not know where and from whom the danger was coming. Asked by Sawyer to characterize Kryuchkov, Shevardnadze replied that he was trying to reshape the KGB. It was, he said, a difficult task, but Kryuchkov had been able to change a few things.

Less than two months before, Shevardnadze had criticized to me Kryuchkov's anti-Western rhetoric and his calls for the use of KGB against "illegal business activities." "That," he said, "smacks of the 1930s." But Shevardnadze's attitude to Kryuchkov was mixed. They had worked together two years earlier to extricate the Soviet Union from Afghanistan, and Shevardnadze's impression of him was then favorable. Like Gorbachev, Shevardnadze was not able to see in Kryuchkov the potential organizer and hands-on leader of a coup d'état. In the absence of such specifics, Shevardnadze's warnings to Gorbachev lost much of their value.

U.S.-Soviet Gulf Issues Continue

So, deserted by "the left" and forced into a mutually reluctant tactical dance with the conservatives, Mikhail Gorbachev was going through one of the most difficult periods in his life. On the international scene, things were not much easier for him. The conflict in the Gulf was moving ineluctably toward some conclusion. Its final shape was not yet clear, but an American victory and an Iraqi defeat seemed inevitable.

Many questions awaited an answer. Would there be a land war? Would the Soviet Union have any role to play in shaping the outcome? Would it strengthen or undermine Gorbachev? As the air war continued, his policy of cooperation with the United States came under increasing fire from the conservatives both in the party and in the military. It was also unclear how Muslims in the Soviet Union might react to possible complications. Yevgeny Primakov was actively lobbying Gorbachev for a modified policy that would allow him to play mediator and peacemaker.

Because the air war seemed to be going less successfully than many people expected, Primakov's ideas began to seem more plausible. Besides, he was behaving as a Gorbachev loyalist, refraining from open criticism of cooperation with the United States on the Gulf and willing to go to bat for the Soviet president. He also showed courage and a readiness to risk his life when he went to Baghdad, which was being bombed daily, to discuss with Saddam Hussein the terms of what amounted to capitulation and total withdrawal from Kuwait. The trick, Primakov believed, was to achieve those goals while not using words like "unconditional surrender" or, conversely, "saving Saddam's face." It could all be done in a way that suited everyone, he said.

Primakov was able to get Tariq Aziz, Saddam's foreign minister and the most realistic of the Iraqi leaders, to come to Moscow for talks with Gorbachev in February, just before the U.S. ground offensive. The Iraqis wanted the Moscow talks to look like negotiations, and whatever outcome they could achieve to look less like total defeat. Reading the records of Gorbachev's conversations with Aziz, I was amazed at how he was able to draw him closer and closer to accepting almost all the terms the United States had publicly insisted on.

Gradually but quite quickly, Aziz was shedding all the conditions and face-saving ploys that the Iraqis initially sought to attach to their withdrawal. Gorbachev went about his efforts with a kind of abandon I rarely saw. Perhaps he had taken on an impossible task, but he did try. Some of his talks with Aziz lasted until long after midnight, then he made telephone calls, including some to Bush. The ground offensive was imminent, he knew, and he wanted Bush to know how quickly the Iraqis were moving toward acceptance of unconditional withdrawal from Kuwait.

But Bush, I felt, had his own difficult political equation to solve. He had to decide what kind of victory he wanted and to ensure that it appeared to his country and to the world as his victory, not anyone else's. Still, he did not want to snub Gorbachev, whom he considered his friend and a friend of the United States. His political instincts, his feelings for Gorbachev, and the various strategic and geopolitical considerations were all at work when he talked to Gorbachev over the phone.

My own impression was that Bush had decided the conflict would have to be ended by a ground war and a clear U.S. victory. But I disagreed with those of my colleagues who considered Gorbachev's efforts useless. Simply waiting for whatever outcome would emerge was not an option for Gorbachev, either politically or psychologically. When the whole thing was over, it became clear that Gorbachev had been playing his own game and that everyone had had to reckon with his position.

On the night of February 22 and on February 23 Gorbachev had two telephone conversations with Bush. Between those two talks, Saddam made the final concession, agreeing to a total and unconditional withdrawal from Kuwait in accordance with the U.N. Security Council resolutions. All the U.S. demands, which Bush had put forward in a kind of escalation following every Iraqi concession, had now been accepted. Saddam Hussein, Gorbachev said to Bush, had raised the white flag. It would not have happened, he added, without the firmness displayed by the United States. But now there was a new situation, and he suggested diplomatically that Bush should reassess his plans. The important thing, he said, quoting the words of Egyptian President Hosni Mubarak, with whom he had just talked, was that the United States and the Soviet Union should continue to cooperate.

The Americans Go Ahead with the Gulf Land Offensive

Bush's answer was characteristically polite and nonaggressive, but it was clear that he had decided on a different scenario. He said Saddam was still setting conditions, particularly with regard to compensation for damages; he was setting Kuwaiti oilwells on fire, and he was calling the president of the United States a liar. Saddam's tactic, Bush said, was to draw us into negotiations and in the process to change the U.N. mandate (that is, the Security Council's set of demands). To put it mildly, Bush's arguments were less than totally convincing, and he probably felt so. There is perhaps just one difference between us, he said to Gorbachev. While you believe that Iraq has accepted unconditional withdrawal from Kuwait, I and my colleagues believe that is not so. But let us not allow anything to divide us, he added. Let us make sure that the United States and the Soviet Union continue to work together when this is over.

Gorbachev got the message: the land offensive could not be postponed. Although he made another effort, saying that perhaps what was needed was just a couple of days, he was under no illusion when the conversation was over. With him in the room wee Alexander Yakovlev, Chernyaev, Bessmertnykh, and Primakov. "They have decided," he told them after he put down the receiver. Only a few words were exchanged then. Gorbachev was clearly disappointed. All his efforts of the past weeks and days (and nights) seemed to have been in vain. But even among the men he trusted totally he did not show any emotion. There were no sharp words about the Americans, although under the circumstances I thought everyone would have understood a little outburst.

This was typical of Gorbachev. He acted and behaved on the assumption that you win some you lose some, that you fight until the end but once it's over you don't panic or rant or shed tears, but pick up whatever is left and go on. A few hours later the American ground offensive began, and this created a new situation. Gorbachev, always a realist, accepted that fact.

Gorbachev and Rajiv Gandhi Talk About Gulf Policy

During those final days of the Gulf crisis, Gorbachev had a meeting with an old friend, a man he always felt comfortable with. Rajiv Gandhi was in Moscow, not as prime minister but as a private citizen. He had been out of office for a little more than a year, but his successors seemed unable to make things work. India was going from one government crisis to another, which made inevitable another general election to clarify the political lineup and get a clear leader for the country.

Rajiv was confident he would win the election. "The only thing my opponents wanted," he said to Gorbachev, "was to push me out. But that is not a policy, so they began to squabble immediately afterward. They have nothing to offer the country, and they have no morals." He said he was glad to see Gorbachev in good shape physically and not submitting to frustration.

Gorbachev and Gandhi had lunch together with their wives. As always, Sonya seemed a little sad. Being the wife of an Indian politician was not what she had wanted in life, but it was obvious that there was a special bond between her and Rajiv, and also between them and their children.

Inevitably, Gorbachev and Gandhi discussed the Gulf War. Rajiv was suspicious of the Americans' intentions. He said Saddam Hussein had given the United States a golden opportunity to create a single-superpower world and that there was real danger that another attempt would be made to create a Pax Americana.

"Now that Saddam has accepted all the demands, what do the Americans want by starting the ground war?" Rajiv asked. "Do they want to destroy Iraq? Do they want to become sole masters of the Middle East? That would be a mistake."

Gorbachev agreed.

Gandhi also suggested cautiously that Security Council Resolution 678, authorizing the use of force to reverse the Iraqi occupation of Kuwait, might have given the United States too much leeway by enabling it to interpret the extent of appropriate force without consulting anyone.

Gorbachev did not respond to that suggestion, but he did seek to explain his position. From the outset, he said, our policy had two objectives. One was to make sure that aggression did not pay and to help end Iraq's occupation of Kuwait. It would be a tragedy if the end of the Cold War meant that regional aggressors had free rein—hence our solidarity with the United States to the extent that its actions were aimed at reversing Iraq's aggression. The other objective, however, was to prevent the destruction of Iraq, which we wanted to continue to exist as a significant factor in the Middle East. Its people should not have to pay an exorbitant price for the folly of their leader. The overriding objective, Gorbachev said, should continue to be peace in the Middle East. While the Arab-Israeli conflict continued, anything could happen in the region.

After the conversation between Gorbachev and Gandhi I had a feeling that Rajiv, having gone through a period of rejection by India's politicians and perhaps the people, had matured. He definitely had a future both in his country and in international affairs. He was confident that in the coming years India, despite its numerous problems, would be an increasingly important factor in Asia and in the world, and he undoubtedly wanted to lead India during those years.

No longer was he a reluctant leader, a prime minister more out of duty than out of the kind of passion that makes politicians tick. He had an agenda, I believed, and he would enjoy being on top once again. I accompanied Rajiv and Sonya downstairs to the cloakroom and we parted warmly. "See you later," Rajiv said. "See you soon."

Less than a month later Gandhi was assassinated during a campaign appearance in India. The editorial comment in the *New York Times* and other leading newspapers struck me as cold and somewhat condescending. He died a man not fully understood. I thought I understood him, and I grieved over his death. Gorbachev and Raisa, though having to worry about many things during that month of March, were shocked by the assassination, and both recalled Rajiv often, then and afterward.

Gorbachev's Ideological Evolution

Gorbachev made a cautious statement after the start of the American ground offensive. He expressed disappointment that the opportunities for peace had not been fully used, but he stopped far short of condemning the United States. He then went on a domestic political tour of Byelorussia. In Minsk he made a powerful speech condemning "Neo-Bolshevism," which had become his term for mindless radicalism and rejection of any compromise. Even if one understands some actions and tactics of the Bolsheviks in the context of their time, he said, this kind of radicalism and even extremism must have no place in a society that wants to be democratic.

Using the word "Bolshevik" with a negative connotation certainly was a bold departure for a leader of the Communist Party, and I believe many people in the party apparat never forgave Gorbachev for that. Similarly, when a few months later he said we should not idolize and make icons of Marx and Lenin, there was an outcry from the Communist fundamentalists.

Gorbachev did not make those statements lightly. Still, they did not satisfy the more radical democrats, who wanted Gorbachev to reject communism and the party totally and without qualification. But Gorbachev was not the kind of man who is always ready to make an ideological about-face. His philosophical evolution was slower than many people wanted. But it was honest, and it was not dictated by cynical political calculations.

Eleven
REPAIRING THE CRACKS
1991

Ending the War in the Gulf

While Gorbachev was away in Byelorussia, the ground war in the Gulf went
on. It was not much of a war. The Iraqis, as Tarasenko and I had predicted to
Baker in his plane several weeks before, were not putting up real resistance.
They declared that they accepted all the U.N. Security Council demands, and
their forces were fleeing from Kuwait.

Soviet diplomats in New York and elsewhere were working for an end to
the hostilities, now that the liberation of Kuwait was ensured. But the
intentions of the Bush administration were still unclear. Some of us thought
they wanted to execute a swift march on Baghdad and to install a government
to replace Saddam Hussein. If that were so, then any efforts of our diplomats
to secure a cease-fire were doomed to fail, and were in fact counterproductive
from the standpoint of our own interests. This is what one of our most senior
diplomats believed and what he argued in strong terms to Bessmertnykh.
"The fall of Baghdad," he wrote in a cable, "would be like the fall of Berlin at
the end of the Second World War. The aggressor, the war criminal, would be
finished off in his own lair. We should not be seen working to prevent that."

Bessmertnykh told me about that episode a little later, when it had become
clear that the Americans had decided on a different outcome. But during the
four days of the ground offensive, most of us did not regard such an outcome

as very likely. When Ambassador Matlock brought to Bessmertnykh a paper that outlined U.S. conditions for a cease-fire—conditions that were tough on the Iraqis but not outrageous—I for one was surprised.

"They have decided not to take Baghdad," Bessmertnykh said when Matlock left.

It was their decision, I thought, but also at least a partial vindication of Gorbachev's policy.

Afterward, Bush was severely criticized by many in the United States for failing to "go all the way" and for letting Saddam off the hook. Many wondered about his motives for deciding not to take Baghdad or to continue the hostilities long enough to provoke Saddam's downfall.

Some of my American contacts told me later that they thought Bush's decision had been prompted at least in part by a desire not to rub Gorbachev's nose in the dirt. I still don't know whether there is much to that theory. I tend to think the main reasons for that decision were squarely in the realm of "realpolitik." I thought that Bush and Baker, having played with the idea of encouraging turmoil in Iraq by supporting the Kurds and the Iraq Shiites, and perhaps with the idea of installing a friendly government in Baghdad, saw that they would get more than they bargained for: a messy long-term entanglement with totally unpredictable results.

As prudent and sober-minded men, they simply did not want to get America involved in an adventure of this kind. They also did not want Iraq to be destroyed or to fall apart, for that would have meant a dangerous relative strengthening of Iran and Turkey.

Bush, I felt, understood geopolitics well, having been prepared for that kind of decision-making by his previous career and his previous years in the White House. So he and Baker were prepared to take the criticism from Democrats and the media in the United States and from some people abroad. It was, after all, "their war," and they knew best when to end it. When Baker came to Moscow in mid-March, Shevardnadze, perhaps the United States' best friend in Moscow, told him he understood why the administration had ended the war that way. "You made a very prudent and sensible decision," he said to Baker during lunch in his Moscow apartment. "Anything different would have meant no end of trouble."

Pessimism About U.S.-Soviet Relations

Baker had come to Moscow against the backdrop of prevailing pessimism about the prospects of U.S.-Soviet relations. There were many pessimists on both sides. On our side, quite a few people were saying that the Americans were in the grip of euphoria following their military triumph in the Gulf, that they no longer needed cooperation with the Soviet Union and would now get tough with us. In the United States, some influential people were recommending suspending cooperation. They emphasized Gorbachev's shaky position in the face of economic troubles, strikes, and a continuing challenge from Yeltsin. Their advice was to wait and see what happened in the Soviet Union before deciding on the extent of further cooperation. The question hanging in the air was: Is Gorbachev the man to deal with?

I felt sad that this question was being asked. I was sure that from the Americans' own standpoint they would have no better partner in this country than Gorbachev—certainly no one more predictable or more earnest. But too much time was lost during the first months of Bush's presidency, and in the Soviet Union and elsewhere too many things happened afterward that skewed the big picture out of focus. Instead of working confidently to build a totally new relationship between the two countries, the leaders of the Soviet Union and the United States now had to walk a minefield of real and potential problems. They had to tread carefully and slowly, but the pace of the events continued to quicken.

Baker Talks with Bessmertnykh and Gorbachev in Moscow, Emphasizing Cooperation

Baker had good and detailed discussions with Bessmertnykh on the entire agenda of issues, including the Middle East and arms control. Regarding the Middle East, it was beginning to appear that all our efforts had not been in vain and that a new era of U.S.-Soviet cooperation in the region was in the offing. Baker was clearly in a hurry. The end of the Gulf War, he said, had created a new situation in the Middle East. All serious players there seemed more or less ready to talk peace. With some of them the Soviet Union had a traditionally good relationship and therefore some special leverage.

Baker outlined to Bessmertnykh the concept of a peace conference that was quite close to the idea of an international conference on the Middle East long supported by the Soviet Union. The administration had apparently abandoned the policy of squeezing the Soviet Union out of the Middle East, and that was a foreign policy success for us. In other times that alone would have been enough to make Baker's visit to Moscow a landmark.

But this time there were things that were overshadowing the Middle East. The main event of the visit was Baker's meeting with Gorbachev. As I was entering the ornate Catherine Hall of the Kremlin with the president, the question on my mind was: Will there be the same feeling of mutual trust that prevailed between them some time ago? Or have the events in the Baltics and the dramatic telephone conversations before the ground offensive in the Gulf began left an aftertaste of doubt and even mistrust that would now tinge the relationship? After the talk, I felt somewhat reassured, but without definitive answers to my questions.

Baker had obviously been listening to all kinds of people and getting different kinds of advice. Both in Moscow and in the United States there were people who felt that Gorbachev might use the positive outcome of the upcoming March 17 referendum on the future of the Soviet Union to start some kind of crackdown on the republics whose leaders had declared their intention to secede, and, more generally, that victory in the referendum would strengthen what was seen as Gorbachev's shift to the right.

Implicit in some of Baker's questions and remarks was a cautionary note and a plea to Gorbachev: Don't do that. "You are a man of great courage," he said, looking Gorbachev straight in the eye. "Your place in history is ensured by what you have initiated in this country and by the changes that have occurred in Europe and in the world over the past few years." But all of that, Baker went on, could be undermined if anything called into question Gorbachev's commitment to democracy and freedom in the Soviet Union. He suggested that there were now some doubts—though not, he seemed to imply, in the minds of Bush and himself—about that commitment.

Gorbachev was listening intently, taking notes. He answered, as always, in a discursive manner, describing the situation in the country as he saw it and insisting that he had made his choice irrevocably in favor of democracy and a totally new relationship between the center and the republics. But, he said, he was sure that the people of the Soviet Union wanted to stay together and that the referendum would bear that out. I thought Gorbachev made it quite clear that he was not planning any crackdown, and subsequent events demonstrated that he was against "emergency measures."

Whether Baker was impressed by Gorbachev's remarks I had no way of knowing. My impression always was that he wished Gorbachev well. "I hate to sound as if I were giving advice to the president of the Soviet Union," Baker said, "but if I were advising you I would say this: once you win your referendum on the 17th, tell the republics that refused to hold it [the referendum] that you are ready to discuss with them arrangements for their orderly withdrawal. And above all, focus on economic reform. Do something fast and radically."

Gorbachev made a note of this remark and nodded in apparent approval. Much of the conversation was about international issues. Gorbachev emphasized that he planned to continue to work together with the United States, and indeed wanted to emphasize that cooperation. This was not universally accepted by everyone in the Soviet Union, he indicated, and some people were challenging it in a harsh and aggressive way.

"They have now become more active," he said. "They are now attacking Eduard [Shevardnadze] in a vicious way but I know that they actually aim at me. Eduard's policy was our policy."

He referred specifically to an article by Georgy Korniyenko, deputy foreign minister under Gromyko and briefly under Shevardnadze, in the newspaper *Sovetskaya Rossia.* Korniyenko accused Shevardnadze of having been naive to rely on the goodwill of the Americans and to be ready to cooperate with the United States on the Gulf crisis. "Do you understand what you have wrought?" Korniyenko asked Shevardnadze, in a language and tone previously reserved for our "imperialist enemies." You have, he wrote, given a green light for the use of U.S. military force and for the United States to become a dominant power, and not just in the Middle East. You have also weakened our country's position in the world.

"I know how he tried to make the rapprochement between our two countries more difficult," Gorbachev said, referring to Korniyenko. "But there is more to it. Behind his criticism there are other people and other forces." He said we had to prove that working together with the United States benefited both sides. From that standpoint, the emerging cooperation in the Middle East was a good thing.

CFE-START *Issues Remain Deadlocked*

One issue that both Gorbachev and Bessmertnykh were unable to work out with Baker was CFE. Baker was firm: if the "naval infantry" problem were not resolved, he would be unable to send the treaty to Capitol Hill for ratification. Implicitly, START was also part of that equation. The issue worried me enormously.

A technical solution to the part of the problem that concerned armored personnel carriers seemed possible. And the Soviet military seemed ready to count some of the tanks and artillery pieces under the CFE treaty ceilings. But there still remained hundreds that could not be fitted into a compromise. And of course it was important for the administration to make sure that any agreement did not look like a compromise, that it had protected the integrity of the treaty, refusing to yield to the Soviet military.

The result was a stalemate that also extended to START and cast a shadow on the overall U.S.-Soviet relationship, which nevertheless looked better than could have been expected, given all the circumstances. Of course, arms control was not as important as in the past—Gorbachev told Baker that he no longer kept track of the details and was not much interested in bean-counting—but an obvious deadlock on arms control was indicative of a problem in the relationship that Baker's visit to Moscow had not solved.

Pro-Yeltsin and Anti-Gorbachev Demonstrations Follow Gorbachev's Unity Referendum Victory

I still believe that at the bottom of that problem was the Bush administration's caution and its conscious decision to wait and see how the mounting confrontation within the Soviet Union would resolve itself. The referendum, which was held on March 17 in nine republics accounting for more than 90 percent of the country's territory and population, ended in a clear victory for Gorbachev. More than 50 percent of the electorate supported the preservation of the Soviet Union as a single country.

Yeltsin had refused to come out in support of a "yes" answer. During the Congress of People's Deputies of the Russian Federation, which was to start on March 23, the Russian Communist Party's faction intended to challenge him and, his supporters suspected, oust him from his position of chairman of Russia's Supreme Soviet. Yeltsin had many followers in Moscow, and during the Congress they scheduled a mass rally on the day of its opening to strengthen his position.

By manipulating information and rumors of possible disorder during the planned demonstration, the hard-liners were able to get Gorbachev to agree to an order banning the rally from Manezhnaya Square, near the Kremlin, and police and army units cordoned off the square. As a result, the demonstration became not just pro-Yeltsin but clearly anti-Gorbachev. The confrontation in Moscow looked dangerous. With the demonstrators in an angry mood and armed men having orders not to let them enter the square, anything could happen.

I had lunch that day with two French diplomats. One of them was late, delayed by traffic jams caused by the gathering crowds or the troops. He had also been listening to the proceedings at the Congress broadcast over the radio. The mood was angry. A feeling of great alarm was in the air. My French colleagues were not at all enthusiastic about the tactics of the radicals, mentioning the names of some of them with obvious contempt, but most of all they were worried that the situation could get out of control, with dire consequences for Gorbachev and perhaps not only for him.

"What do you think will happen?" one of them asked me.

"It's extremely difficult to predict," I answered. "With this kind of confrontation and so many people in the streets, a small squabble or any accident could cause a chain reaction, and who knows what it could lead to? But if bloodshed is avoided today I still think that a slow movement toward some reconciliation could begin. There is still a chance for that. Gorbachev has won the referendum. Yeltsin will probably win this Congress. They must work together. If one looks at their positions on the issues, they have a lot in common. And there are quite a few people here who are against both of them. They must realize that and start working together."

There was no bloodshed on that day in Moscow, but my prediction of a slow reconciliation did not begin to come true immediately. Political and social confrontation has its own logic and its own inertia. Once it starts, it can't be easily stopped, even if the protagonists realize it is not to their advantage.

Yeltsin's call in February for Gorbachev's resignation was still reverberating in the country. A growing number of coal miners were going on strike, initially on economic issues. But the strike committees, dominated by Yeltsin's supporters, tagged on political demands, including a call for Gorbachev's resignation. Even when most of the strikers' demands were met, the strikes did not end. In early April the events seemed to be moving toward some kind of climax—what kind of climax was anybody's guess. The embassies in Moscow were frantically trying to get some clear indication of what might happen next. That was when former U.S. President Richard Nixon came to Moscow.

Nixon Talks with Gorbachev in Moscow

On April 2 Richard Nixon was received by Mikhail Gorbachev in the Kremlin. For me then, there was something enigmatic about their talk, and there still is. Former President Nixon began by saying that when he began his second term as U.S. president he was sixty years old—the same age as Gorbachev now. But just eighteen months later, he added, he had to leave.

"I hope this does not happen to you," Nixon said.

Gorbachev replied almost casually. "Well," he said, "we may have some special, 'Russian version' of events."

Was this a hint that he would be ready to resign under certain circumstances? The conventional wisdom of the time was that he wanted to hold on to his post at almost any price, but that was not the case. There was another similar hint toward the end of their conversation.

"I have met here with all kinds of people," Nixon said, "both those who support you and those who are against you. But, not to flatter you, I can say that no one on either side sees any real alternative to you."

Nixon then talked about attitudes in the United States on the issue of U.S.-Soviet relations. He began by recalling his own remark in a talk with Gorbachev five years earlier, that without U.S.-Soviet cooperation the future of the world and even its survival was inconceivable.

"I remember those words very well," Gorbachev responded, "and I believe that President Bush understands this. But I can't say the same about all who surround him."

Nixon agreed. "Frankly, that is true," he said. "You should have no doubt about his [Bush's] attitude. During the Gulf crisis many people in our country believed the Soviet Union was pursuing a devious policy there, but [President Bush] said publicly, and also in a telephone talk with me, that he believed the Soviet Union acted constructively. He trusts you."

Nixon said he wanted the Soviet Union to be a strong country, not just militarily, as it already was, but also politically and economically. "There are some in the United States," Nixon added, "who would welcome the disintegration of the Soviet Union. You may not believe me, but I disagree with that. The best relations are those of equality, when neither side has a substantial advantage over the other." Nixon then said that, despite Gorbachev's popularity in the United States, questions were being asked about his policies. A "strange coalition" of right-wing Republicans and liberal Democrats were saying that Gorbachev's actions in the Baltics and on the economy showed he was controlled by the hard-liners.

"The question today," Nixon said, "is are we dealing with the same Gorbachev, the man who changed his country and the world, or do we have a different Gorbachev, a Gorbachev who has moved to the right under pressure from the hard-liners and because the reformers have deserted him?"

Nixon had put this question to Shevardnadze, who responded that he had known Gorbachev for thirty years and was convinced that Gorbachev had not changed, that he was still the same Gorbachev.

Nixon gave Gorbachev one of his "meaningful" looks. "I shall report my conclusions to President Bush. I will also talk, off the record, to a bipartisan group of senators, and I want to be able to give them a clear answer."

Gorbachev gave Nixon more than ninety minutes of his time. "Six years ago, when we began what we called perestroika, we said that we wanted to be understood by the world," he said. "Today, this is as important as it was then." We have undertaken an effort to change this country, he added, and now that we have actually started to change the system in practical ways, the old ways and old forms of life in this country are exploding. That scares some people. They want to return to the past.

"And it's not just people in power, in the Party, the government, and the army, whose vested interests have been affected by the changes," Gorbachev went on. "It is also many ordinary people, those whose way of life and habits of several decades are being affected by this upheaval. During those decades many people here have lost their ability to show initiative, to think and act independently." Everyone was going through a painful transition, Gorbachev explained, and this was the price of radical change in a country like ours.

Gorbachev continued: "The allegations that I have reversed course are extremely superficial. If we do not check the disintegration of the economy, if we do not restore law and order, if we do not develop a new relationship with the republics, we shall have total chaos and its inevitable consequence: dictatorship. So we need some stabilization in the economy, in government, and in politics. We need a tactical maneuver in order to protect the democratic process in our country."

"I understand your dilemma," Nixon said. "Reforms without stability mean chaos, but stability without reform means stagnation. Some of your critics feel you have to listen increasingly to the hard-liners and therefore think too much about stability and retreat from reforms."

"They forget one thing," Gorbachev responded. "If I leave the political arena the ensuing reaction will stifle the democratic process, putting an end to all our democratic gains. There are reactionaries here who would be ready to do that. Our extreme left might provoke them. So we have to unite all sober-minded people, both the left and the healthy conservatives, in the interests of stabilizing the situation."

Nixon asked Gorbachev whether he believed that the alternative to him at the time was right-wing hard-liners, who were better organized and had a more solid base, rather than the left-wing radicals.

"The danger," Gorbachev replied, "comes from the increasing confrontation. The extreme left might provoke an even sharper conflict. We have to avoid that. I will not follow the advice of those who want me to crack down on the radicals. This country has to undertake radical reform, otherwise it cannot find a path to democratic development."

Nixon, it seemed, wanted to hear that. "So you are not with the hard-liners? It's just a tactical pause now, and you believe that the reforms are irreversible?"

Gorbachev agreed. "The answers to all our problems are in continuing the reforms, in moving ahead with democratic changes."

They talked about the republics, and Nixon, while emphasizing the special case of the Baltics, repeated that he was against the disintegration of the Soviet Union. Gorbachev said he intended to accelerate the Union treaty process and insist that the nine republics that had held the referendum and voted in favor of the Union sign the treaty in May. The treaty would give greatly expanded authority to the republics. In the meantime, Gorbachev said, he would like to request that his American friends not run ahead of the events.

Gorbachev spoke with great emphasis about the importance of relations with the United States. Even though some people here, he said, criticize us for trusting the United States too much, that is not the prevailing view in the country. The policy of improving relations with the United States has broad-based support. "I am sure," Gorbachev continued, "that we shall continue to cooperate well with President Bush. But it is even more important to make sure that cooperation continues after us. Not only now, with my present powers and authority, but in the future too I will use my influence to promote this."

To me this sounded like another hint that Gorbachev would not hold on to his post at any price, that in the interests of stability and to prevent civil conflict he would be ready to sacrifice his top position in the country. The striking coal-miners had demanded that. Yeltsin's demand for Gorbachev to resign the presidency and for transfer of power to the Council of the Federation had not been withdrawn. Would Gorbachev be ready to do it? I wondered.

The answer came three weeks later, when a statement signed by Gorbachev and the leaders of nine republics envisioned popular elections of the president of the country within six months after the signing of the Union treaty. That idea was probably already in Gorbachev's mind when he talked with Nixon.

Nixon did not respond to the hint. He concluded his talk with Gorbachev on a positive and almost obsequious note. "Mr. President," he said, "you have been awarded the Nobel Peace Prize, and you deserve it. You are leading a revolution that is distinguished by its predominantly peaceful nature. It would be tragic if political pressure led to a retreat from reforms. After talking to you I feel reassured. I am confident that President Gorbachev remains committed to reforms and intends to resume movement within the mainstream of the democratic process that he initiated."

A few days later came Nixon's surprise. When he returned to the United States he published a series of articles whose message was exactly the reverse of what he had said to Gorbachev. He wrote that Gorbachev was a Communist leader who had toyed with reforms but was now going full speed backward. Gorbachev, according to Nixon, was against a free market, against real democracy, against self-determination. It was so different from what I had heard him say that I could not believe my eyes.

I do not know how Gorbachev reacted when he learned of that, but Chernyaev, with whom I talked about it, was stunned by Nixon's lack of good faith. "Maybe I'm old-fashioned," he said, "but I still can't understand how anyone can be so two-faced. He knows we're not going to start a polemic with him. But why is he doing it?"

That was anybody's guess. "To put it mildly," I said, "Richard Nixon is known in the United States as a complicated man. He is not a square shooter."

I remembered 1974, when I first came to the United States. Nixon had just resigned. During his final moments in the White House, he could not fight back tears. He went without dignity, without honor, without being able to explain what he had done and why. In the 1980s, however, he made a comeback, becoming a kind of senior political commentator and even part-time adviser to the presidents. As my atheist grandmother liked to say, "inscrutable are the ways of the Lord."

"Everything Seems to Be Falling Apart"

The situation in my country that April was so tense that some people thought a denouement could come within weeks or even days. Gorbachev had scheduled a visit to Japan for mid-April, but people in the foreign ministry were openly asking, "Should he go when everything seems to be falling apart?" He did, and while he was away I had time to think about what was happening, and about my own situation.

A month earlier, during Baker's visit to Moscow, I had told Dennis Ross that I was going over from the foreign ministry to the president's office, in a matter of days, maybe a week. Then Chernyaev told me that, as a result of financial cutbacks, Valery Boldin, the president's chief of staff, was imposing a freeze on hiring new staff. "We'll work it out," Chernyaev said to me. "There's always an unfilled post somewhere."

But I felt he wasn't comfortable with the situation, and he never spoke warmly about Boldin. He was unhappy about some things that were happening around Gorbachev at the time, and about some people surrounding the president. "For a lot of them," Chernyaev said, "democracy is a nuisance. They would rather have it like in the old days. But Gorbachev is saying that he needs them, otherwise they will openly turn against him, and that may ruin everything. Also, he says they know how the system works and can keep the economy together."

With regard to Boldin, there was another reason for his being so close to Gorbachev: Gorbachev trusted him. Boldin had been working for him for a long time, and Gorbachev assumed his loyalty as a matter of course. He was a man who did not find it easy to drop people; he did not like to push people out. Instead, he would let them go when they decided to leave. As a result, the group of people with him in the spring and summer of 1991 was an odd mix.

Gorbachev believed that this was a reflection of the situation in the country. He could not just scrap the old system and its people and begin anew. His prime minister, Valentin Pavlov, was one of those who had made a career in the old system and knew it thoroughly. In contrast to what is now often said about him, he was a competent economist and manager. Even Stanislav Shatalin, whose economic concepts were quite different from Pavlov's, gave Pavlov "a B-minus" as an economic expert—a high mark from an opponent. But Pavlov was also cynical, impolitic, and given to making stupid pronouncements, like the one in February about an alleged conspiracy of Western bankers to inundate the Soviet Union with huge quantities of 50 and 100 ruble notes. He was said to have made some of those statements while not totally sober—another of his problems. He was more and more an embarrassment to Gorbachev. "With friends like this, who needs enemies?" was a frequent comment in Moscow.

Gorbachev needed to rethink the situation and to find a move that would change the position on the political chessboard. In early April, Alexander Yakovlev wrote him a long note in which he expressed concern about the way things were developing in the country, particularly about the increasing boldness of the reactionary right. He complained specifically about brazen personal attacks against him in some Stalinist publications, which surprised me since I did not regard him as being thin-skinned.

But his message to Gorbachev was clear and, I thought, quite right: the president's future was not with the forces and the people of the past. Yakovlev strongly suggested that the president find a way to dissociate himself from them, but he did not propose anything specific as to how to do it.

Reflections on Gorbachev and Yeltsin

To me, the problem, at least in the short term, seemed quite simple: Would Gorbachev be able to patch things up with Yeltsin? Some thought that was impossible, that there was too much bad blood between them. But it was the key to stabilizing the situation in the country. An end to confrontation between them could have a beneficial effect on just about every problem the Soviet Union was facing—economic, political, even diplomatic. My own position on that is even documented in the press.

On the eve of Gorbachev's departure for Japan, I published under an assumed name an article in the newspaper *Trud* that dealt ostensibly with the problem of the Kuril Islands—the territorial issue that had poisoned relations between the Soviet Union and Japan. I wrote about the danger of making that issue another bone of contention in the confrontation between the leaders of the Soviet Union and Russia. There were signs, I wrote, that they understood how dangerous that would be and that they were trying to avoid public polemic on the issue.

"What is necessary is an agreed Gorbachev-Yeltsin policy," I concluded, "and they should refuse to use this issue against each other. . . . Such a common position would also serve as an excellent example of reaching agreement and overcoming the antagonism between the two major political leaders in our country, which would be a gain for all of us. As the phrase goes, Well begun half done." The article was published on April 11.

Chernyaev finally told me that a slot had been found for me on the staff and that I could report to work any time after May 1. Bessmertnykh, however, wanted me to continue in the foreign ministry for a couple of weeks; he had a quick meeting scheduled with Baker in Kislovodsk and a trip to the Middle East in early May. That was to be my last assignment in the foreign ministry.

Bessmertnykh told me he regretted my leaving. We had a good rapport, and he said he would have offered me something quite interesting if I had decided to stay on. But I replied that I could not go back on my pledge, and he understood.

Gorbachev's "9 plus 1" Formula

The meeting between Baker and Bessmertnykh in Kislovodsk was held on April 24, the same day as a Central Committee plenum in Moscow at which, it was widely believed, the hard-liners would demand Gorbachev's resignation from the post of general secretary. When asked what I thought of it, I said that if the party was suicidal it should insist on the resignation, but that for Gorbachev it was not necessarily a bad thing. It was extremely difficult to predict what would happen.

On April 23, however, on the eve of the plenum, there was a dramatic meeting at Novo-Ogarevo between Gorbachev and the leaders of the nine republics that had held the Union referendum. The meeting, at which the "9 plus 1" statement was drafted and adopted, unexpectedly changed the situation. Gorbachev, it was said, pulled another rabbit out of his hat, leaving the hard-liners isolated and gaining for himself new allies, at least in tactical terms. The Novo-Ogarevo meeting reportedly began with some bitter exchanges between Gorbachev and other participants about who was to blame for the chaos in the country. Everyone soon agreed that something had to be done and that continuing the confrontation in rhetoric and action would lead nowhere.

Yeltsin had not renewed his call for Gorbachev's resignation for some time. Following the Russian Congress, which had changed the constitution of the Russian Federation, he was preparing to launch his own campaign to be elected the president of Russia in the first popular elections. It was therefore not to his advantage to appear too confrontational. Gorbachev saw an opening there. He also saw that he had to give something in return. The result was what was later called the "9 plus 1" statement, which launched the Novo-Ogarevo process. The statement was a belated attempt to complete the drafting of a Union treaty that would give the republics real sovereignty while preserving the Union as an entity under international law and avoiding division of the country's common armed forces, energy, and transportation systems. It also pledged that a new constitution would be adopted and that the election of the country's president would be held within six months.

I am still convinced the "9 plus 1" statement offered the best way out of a seemingly impossible situation. It contained something for everyone. Gorbachev's political magic seemed to have worked once again. The hard-liners' attempt to unseat him at the party plenum the next day failed, the coalminers' strikes fizzled out soon afterward, and the confrontation between the authorities of the Union and its largest republic, Russia, was gradually subsiding.

Offering something to everyone was Gorbachev's great strength, I believe. If only the "everyone" could take advantage of what was being offered! Even the party, which in its old capacity of the country's only ruler was clearly doomed, could have saved itself for some new role in democratic politics if it had followed Gorbachev's plea for reform and for an essentially social-democratic program. Even the top brass of the KGB and the military should have accepted Gorbachev's reform path, which at least offered them a chance to preserve their professional organizations while of course ceasing to be the country's invisible government. Less than four months later, in August, they showed that they were unable to accept that bargain. It was an act of utter folly, and it is incredible how much they were able to destroy with just one blow.

At the meeting with Baker in Kislovodsk, Bessmertnykh did not fail to alert the U.S. secretary of state to the importance of the "9 plus 1" statement, but it was probably too soon for the Americans to draw any far-reaching conclusions from it. The two men mostly discussed the mechanics of the Middle East peace process—the kind of diplomatic handiwork Bessmertnykh liked and was good at. When I went to the Middle East with him in early May, I saw proof of that again.

The Soviet Union was once again a player in the Middle East game, and even though the country was in dire straits, a good diplomat could take advantage of the opportunities that emerged. I was present at Bessmertnykh's meetings with King Hussein of Jordan, Israeli Prime Minister Itzhak Shamir, and Israeli Foreign Minister David Levy, and at his meeting with Baker in Cairo. Even though I had known and respected him as a professional for some time, I saw how a high office can sometimes make a person grow. During the Middle East trip, Bessmertnykh was already more than just a diplomat; he had the potential to become a major political figure within the country's newly emerging balance of forces. The three days in August changed that.

Later in May I formally joined the foreign policy development unit of Gorbachev's staff, a small group of experts working under Anatoly Chernyaev. The process of organizing the staff was still moving slowly. Chief of Staff

Boldin was emphasizing the branches that dealt with logistical and similar matters to the detriment of substantive units; another problem was the location of the staff offices.

An Image Problem for Gorbachev

Gorbachev had already moved to the Kremlin and rarely came to his office in the Central Committee, of which he was still general secretary. Most of his presidential staff, however, was still located in the sprawling complex of Central Committee buildings at Staraya Ploshchad. In addition to being inconvenient, this created an image problem. The democrats were criticizing Gorbachev severely for excessive loyalty to his party and letting its bureaucracy influence his decisions heavily. This was reflected, they said, even in the fact that his staff was still working in the Central Committee. "Where does one draw a line between the president and the general secretary?" they asked, and they had a point.

Chernyaev too was critical of the arrangement, and said both then and later that it was a mistake not to move the entire presidential staff quickly from Staraya Ploshchad. "We have to sever this umbilical cord," he said.

Boldin replied that it was impossible to do it any time soon. The building in the Kremlin to which the staff was to be relocated, and which was formerly occupied by the Council of Ministers military-industrial commission, was undergoing renovation. "It's so slow," Boldin complained. "It won't be over until the end of the year."

I saw in this whole thing a sign of a more profound problem, and that worried me. Still, I was determined to stick with President Gorbachev through the hard times.

"Do you really want an office in this building?" Chernyaev asked me. "Maybe we'll get something in the Kremlin soon. For a week or two you could continue to be based in the foreign ministry and come here as often as you need to," he said, referring to a small room adjoining his modest office.

I did not mind the arrangement, but a few days later Chernyaev said Boldin had offered us some space in the Kremlin that was totally unacceptable. "It's undignified," his secretary told me, "kind of a closet with a view of the Kremlin wall."

I moved reluctantly to Staraya Ploshchad. To me, my presence there had an air of unreality and temporariness. The corridors of the Central Committee building were somber, and a pall of the past seemed to be hanging over them. In the comfortable cafeteria I saw the faces of old-style bureaucrats and often read anger and discontent in their eyes. Some were openly attacking Gorbachev's "inability to crack down on those democrats."

The names of Yeltsin and Shevardnadze were most frequently mentioned in, to put it mildly, a negative context. Someone asked me, almost casually, "Is it true they still can't find the records of Shevardnadze's conversations in Wyoming and Houston?"

These people had an insatiable desire to create enemies, I thought. "No, it's not true," I answered. "Shevardnadze always made a point of conveying to Moscow the full record, not just some kind of synopsis. I ought to know."

The questioner reacted with distrust. "I have this information on good authority from the foreign ministry," he said smugly.

Gorbachev Seeks Participation in G-7 Meetings

Summer was beginning, but the pace of events was not slowing. Gorbachev believed that he absolutely had to do three things before his annual August vacation: complete the work on the Union treaty, conclude the START treaty with the United States and hold the summit with President Bush in Moscow, and participate in the Group of Seven meeting of leading Western industrialized countries in London. Even though all these tasks did not seem impossible, there were few optimists who thought he was likely to succeed in all of them.

Participating in the Group of Seven (G-7) meeting would have seemed quite improbable just a few months before. Before the previous summit, Gorbachev had written a letter to President Mitterrand of France, who hosted it. The letter was not a request to be invited, then or next time around, but it argued strongly that the Soviet Union wanted to be part of the world economy and would be changing its economic system to make it compatible with the free market economy of most of the world and particularly of the Western industrialized countries. "We want to play by the rules," Gorbachev often said.

Still, for obvious reasons the West had been reluctant to transform the Group of Seven into the Group of Eight, and inviting Gorbachev to London might appear to come close to doing so. Our information indicated that the United States and Japan were particularly skeptical, while the Europeans, particularly the Germans, took a more forthcoming attitude from the outset. Eventually, Gorbachev was invited to participate as a guest.

Gorbachev really put his heart into this new project. He did not seem to worry that he might appear to be fishing for an invitation. If he believed something was important he would forget about appearances. His main argument, set forth tirelessly to his Western partners, went like this: Following the end of the Cold War the world was faced with the threat posed by the rogue government of Saddam Hussein. The entire world took it seriously, and the Soviet Union and the West were on the same side of the barricades. The aggressor was rebuffed. There was a price, but the necessary dozens of billions of dollars were found, despite the economic and budget problems of the Western countries. Now the world was faced with another situation that was both potentially dangerous and full of promise: the Soviet Union had decided to create a democratic system and a market economy to replace the old totalitarian system. If it succeeded, the whole world, including the West, would gain enormously. If it failed, the cost in new instability and unpredictability would be staggering.

So, Gorbachev asked, should it be so very difficult to mobilize the financial resources to make the transition to a market economy in the Soviet Union less painful and less cataclysmic? Specifically, he had in mind a stabilization fund of several billion dollars to facilitate the transition to a convertible ruble, some easing of the terms of the Soviet Union's foreign debt, and—something he particularly stressed—Western governments' support for major investment projects and joint ventures with the Soviet Union to take advantage of the country's vast resources and technological potential in areas like space and formerly military-oriented industries, which were undergoing conversion to civilian production.

The Endgame on START and CFE

During those summer months of 1991 the Soviet Union and the United States finally played out the endgame on the START and CFE treaties. It was clear that the two were related and linked. Without a deal on CFE there would be no START treaty—period. Our military continued to sit tight on the remaining CFE issues. Having agreed to include in the treaty ceilings the weapons of the three naval infantry divisions, they argued strongly that the same approach must not apply to the armored personnel carriers assigned to the strategic nuclear forces protection units (they had a point there) and the weapons in the coastal defense units.

Gorbachev felt that he could not impose a solution on the military, that his relations with the army were strained enough. He wanted the top brass to come around to a more reasonable position. Once again he showed a preference for taking a patient approach. It can be said that neither the left nor the right liked that approach, but I am sure that with time it will become clear that that is the only approach that really works in our country.

Gorbachev sent Bessmertnykh and Chief of the Armed Forces General Staff Mikhail Moiseyev to Washington to try to work out the remaining START and CFE issues. They came close to clinching a deal on both, but not quite. Bush sent back a letter, followed up by a telephone call to Gorbachev. He too was a patient man, and did not react emotionally to the fact that the Soviet side had again failed to accept certain positions that he probably regarded as matters of principle. In fact, both in the letter and in the call, he gave Gorbachev a glowing account of Moiseyev's performance in Washington, calling him a real statesman, a man who he was sure would help find a solution.

On substance, however, Bush was quite firm. He asked Gorbachev to give one final political push to make sure that both CFE and START were completed soon. I felt he wanted those agreements badly. He made it clear that once we had a deal he would be coming to Moscow for his summit with Gorbachev on very short notice. It seemed to me that it had finally dawned on everyone that we were running out of time.

The final deal on CFE was close to what many would probably have suggested months before. The Soviet Union gave in on the three "naval infantry" divisions, and the United States gave in on the armored personnel carriers attached to the strategic rocket forces, which was a significant concession. As for the coastal defense, its armored personnel carriers were to be converted into light armored vehicles, not counted under treaty ceilings, and the other weapons were to be included in treaty limits.

While the two sides had been groping for that compromise, the START treaty was frozen, with the negotiators quietly bickering about something extremely esoteric called "downloading" and "demonstrated range." An American friend told me that only four or five people in the United States understood those issues. The number on the Soviet side was probably the same if not smaller. I am sure that more such issues could have been found to delay the treaty signing even further, but a political go-ahead was finally given in London when Gorbachev and Bush met there in mid-July at the Group of Seven summit.

Gorbachev, Yeltsin, and Tough Union Treaty Issues

At first, the Americans had not been enthusiastic about inviting Gorbachev to London. It was the Europeans, particularly the Germans, who pushed strongly for sending an invitation to him. Throughout the summer months of 1991 there was some maneuvering around certain formalities and protocol arrangements for Gorbachev's participation in the London meeting, but it became clear in May that he would be coming.

What Gorbachev wanted most of all—and of course not just for foreign policy reasons—was to come to London with the Union treaty signed or at least ready for signing. That took up the bulk of his time in June and July. His problem was that in wrestling for the treaty he did not have many allies among the leaders of the republics. His only real though sometimes capricious ally was Nursultan Nazarbayev, the president of Kazakhstan. Ukraine was reluctant to be actively involved because its Communist leaders were afraid of undermining their position in the December elections, which looked like a tough race between them and the nationalist opponents of the Union. The Ukrainian leader, Leonid Kravchuk, was therefore not among those who participated in the long and arduous negotiating sessions at Novo-Ogarevo. Yeltsin was there, but he did not make Gorbachev's life easier.

The president of the Russian republic, Boris Yeltsin, had his own agenda, and his positions on such issues as taxation (whether the Union would be able to levy federal taxes or would just be allocated fixed sums of money by the republics) were difficult for Gorbachev to accept. Another tough issue was whether the Union treaty would give Union laws priority over those of the republics. Anything else would have made the union arrangement totally unworkable, but during his period of confrontation with Gorbachev, Yeltsin had supported the Russian parliament's legislation that gave the republic's laws priority over those of the Union. It was now not easy for him to abandon that position, and he said he would defer to the parliament on that score.

It seemed to me from what I heard that this question could be solved and that Yeltsin was generally in the mood to sign the Union treaty. But he was a man of changing moods, and the fact that he did not actively push for the treaty and that the Party and government hard-liners were limiting Gorbachev's freedom of maneuver in their own way, made the treaty preparation process slow and arduous. It was becoming clear that Gorbachev would not have the treaty before the London summit. The domestic situation during that summer did not seem particularly tense, but that was a superficial impression. Tensions were simmering under the surface. The economy was not improving. The party and government apparat were not happy about Gorbachev's more cooperative relationship with Yeltsin, and they were even more unhappy about the emerging outlines of the Union treaty.

Political Tensions Create More Problems for Gorbachev

People like Anatoly Lukyanov, chairman of the country's Supreme Soviet, and Prime Minister Pavlov seemed to be maneuvering, creating problems for Gorbachev. The president was not unaware of that, but he thought he would be able to prevail, and in June he fended off an attempt in the Supreme Soviet to curtail some of his powers and to give greater executive authority to Pavlov's Cabinet of Ministers. This was later called an attempted "constitutional coup"—a coup that failed.

Gorbachev later said that each party plenum during the spring and summer of 1991 was an attempted coup. Each time—by persuasion, by threatening resignation publicly, or by careful maneuvering—he was able to ward off the threat. That probably made him overconfident, so that he did not pay sufficient attention to warnings of a real coup. One warning, based on a tip from Moscow's mayor Gavriil Popov, came from President Bush in a telephone conversation in June.

There was one thing, however, that made the value of all those warnings much less than it might seem. I don't know whether Bush pointed to the possible perpetrators of the coup in either that call or in other messages he might have sent to Gorbachev. If he had suspected KGB chairman Kryuchkov, he probably would not have given his warning in a telephone call, for the KGB was certainly listening.

My own feelings at that time were ambiguous. I worried about much that was happening—the continuing ethnic conflicts, the persisting mistrust between Gorbachev and the democratic forces, and the dangerous shenanigans of the hard-liners, who seemed increasingly desperate. But I felt that if Gorbachev succeeded in working out a Union treaty that would satisfy the leaders of Russia he would be home free, and that did not seem impossible.

Raisa Gorbachev, Author

One person who did have dark forebodings during that summer was Raisa Gorbachev. She sensed where the danger was coming from, even though her prescience did not go as far as pointing a finger at the eventual perpetrators of the August coup.

In June, Gorbachev asked me to review the English translation of a book Mrs. Gorbachev had written for publication in the fall. I read the manuscript and, to my surprise, rather liked it. The book, titled *I Hope*, described Raisa's life and contained some interesting information about herself and Gorbachev. Georgy Pryakhin, the writer who cooperated with her on the book, had tried too hard to embellish the text and make it more "literary." Still, it was a sincere book and, given the constraints of Raisa's position and traditions of Soviet society that she could not ignore, it was quite revealing.

When Gorbachev and Raisa asked me what I thought of the book I did not call it a masterpiece of Russian literature, but I did say it was a sincere and interesting book that would probably be quite successful. When the first draft of the translation came from London, I saw immediately that it would take a lot of work to clean it up. It had been done hastily and contained numerous omissions and mistakes.

In fairness it must be added that the text was not the easiest one to translate, and it took me many hours of painstaking work to set it right. I also needed to consult with Raisa on a number of points that, at least to me, did not seem immediately clear from the Russian text. We talked on the phone, and a couple of times we met to go through the manuscript and the translation of some sentences. Even though Raisa's understanding of spoken English was quite limited, she had a surprising ability to sense some fine points of the translation when she saw it in writing. My respect for her grew after each talk with her. She was not at all the aloof and didactic woman she often seemed to be on television. She was, I thought, an authentic person.

On a couple of occasions she talked to me not just about the book. During our last meeting to discuss the translation, I felt she was upset and disturbed about something. She told me she had just gone to the district party committee to pay her membership dues and was appalled by the atmosphere there. "When I talked to that party secretary there and watched his eyes," Raisa said, "I really felt he hated us. And, of course, it's not so much me that he hates. Those people feel that the kind of party in which they had made their careers will have to go away, and for them it's like a world that is slipping away from them. And many of them have no other career or occupation to go back to. They will never forgive Mikhail Sergeyevich."

I told her that most people I knew would not regret the passing of that "ancien régime," but I agreed that there was a large group of frustrated and vindictive people who were dangerous.

The Movement for Democratic Reform

Once again I thought about the missed opportunity of a couple of years earlier, the opportunity to divide the party into factions and to develop a movement for reform on the basis of the party's social democratic wing.

This was beginning to happen in the summer of 1991, but it was happening in our characteristically clumsy and circuitous way. In May, Eduard Shevardnadze had finally made a statement about the need to have a democratic reform party in the country, and I applauded him. But instead of just leaving the Communist Party and setting out, even though belatedly, to form his reform party, he allowed the Communist Party officials in the Central Committee to start an "investigation" into his remarks, which were deemed "inconsistent with the Party Statute." Of course they were inconsistent, and I would have much preferred that my former boss state his intentions clearly. He refused to cooperate with the "investigation," and only then left the Party.

I found it curious that all the democrats who were doing so failed to announce the real reason, which seemed valid and right to me: that we needed another party in the country, that a democratic system is impossible in a single-party state, a state where the whole society forms a kind of opposition to "them."

Finally, Shevardnadze, Yakovlev, Popov, and several other prominent reformers, both in and already out of the party, announced the formation of what they called a Movement for Democratic Reform, which, they said, was not a party and which would be a broad-based coalition to support continuing democratic change. My only problem with that was that I felt it was too late.

There was also the question of what Gorbachev thought about the new movement. Some people believed it was made-to-order for him and that he would eventually leave the Communist Party and rely on the movement for support. Others thought he resented the new movement, because it was inconsistent with his strategy of reforming the party, transforming it into a basically parliamentary, social-democratic organization. Gorbachev himself spoke ambiguously about the movement, perhaps intentionally so.

London Summit with Gorbachev, Bush, and Major

In London, where Gorbachev went in mid-July for the Group of Seven meeting and an official visit to the United Kingdom, he was asked by Prime Minister John Major to explain what he thought of the Movement for Democratic Reform and how he intended to position himself in relation to it. In answering, Gorbachev chose his words carefully. He indicated that he was in sympathy with the goals and purposes of the movement as stated by its founders, but that he would like to see a genuinely broad coalition that would not exclude members of the Communist Party. He said he was worried that smaller radical groups might begin to play too big a role in the movement's practical activities. "But there is no doubt in my mind," he told Major, "that a truly broad movement that would attract all kinds of reform-oriented people of various stripes is what we need."

The three days Gorbachev spent in London were so filled with meetings and discussions that I wondered how even Gorbachev could take in all of it, particularly given his extremely difficult schedule in Moscow: he was still working hard on the Union treaty, and the summit with Bush finally seemed set for early August.

Bessmertnykh had brought to London an interagency paper signed at the last moment in Moscow by Baklanov, Yazov, and others, which contained a proposed solution to the last remaining START issue: "demonstrated range of ballistic missiles." He called me at the hotel in the early morning of July 17 and asked me to come to the embassy quickly to translate something he would be showing to Baker within an hour. When I talked with him minutes later, he showed me the paper, saying, "It's very technical, but I know you still follow those things and I trust you to do it right." Thirty minutes later he had the typed text of the translation and rushed to meet with Baker. When he returned, I asked him how it looked. "Baker seemed to think it's okay," Bessmertnykh said, "but they have sent it to Washington to be examined by the experts."

Gorbachev and Bush met for a working lunch at the American embassy in

London. The question of whether the Soviet compromise proposal on range was acceptable to the U.S. side came toward the end of the discussion. Baker said that both he and Scowcroft found it acceptable but that it was still being studied by the experts in Washington. "It's always the bureaucracy!" Bush exclaimed. Nevertheless, both he and Gorbachev were already speaking about the Moscow summit as something certain, and a little later, during their one-on-one talk following the lunch, word came that Washington had approved the compromise. They could now announce the date of the summit.

Bush and Gorbachev Discuss the Future of the Soviet Union

That, however, was not the principal subject of discussion during the lunch at the embassy, which I still remember vividly. Most of it, and of the conversations Bush and Gorbachev had in Moscow during their summit, was about the future of the country that was then still called the Soviet Union. Bush said he was worried about possible misperceptions of the U.S. attitude, and of his own personal attitude, toward Gorbachev. You might have the wrong impression that I am vacillating as regards support for you, he said, and it worries me. "I know the Soviet Union is going through difficult times," I recall Bush saying. "But we have not vacillated, and we won't vacillate, in supporting your efforts."

I knew that Gorbachev believed Bush, so far as Bush himself was concerned. The trust was mutual. On several occasions Gorbachev said to Bush: "I think, Mr. President, you have had a chance to see that once we have given our word we have always kept it."

Bush agreed.

"Still," Gorbachev went on, "I wonder if you have decided definitively and irrevocably what kind of a Soviet Union you want to see? It sometimes seems to me that you haven't."

Gorbachev then told Bush about a meeting of the Soviet Union's Security Council two months before. He suggested that during that discussion there was no unanimity on the question of whether the United States was changing its attitude toward the Soviet Union. "Two members of our Security Council are present here," Gorbachev said, pointing to Bessmertnykh and Primakov, "and they will confirm that I was able to persuade the entire council that it is in our best interest to have a healthy and improving relationship with the United States. Frankly, not everyone in our country likes this conclusion. But it now has the support of most of our people."

"I want to tell you as my friend," Gorbachev said to Bush, "that I hope very much the answer to the question I put to you will be that the United States wants to see a dynamic, progressive, and secure Soviet Union. So far as we are concerned, we want to see a United States that is prosperous, strong, and secure, and that is our close partner."

Almost casually, Gorbachev then added, "We want this no less than you do. We want our two countries to be more dependent on each other."

A little more than a month later, after the coup, I was reminded of those words as I was lunching in the Kremlin cafeteria with a member of the president's staff whom I suspected of being a KGB man.

"Is it true that Gorbachev said during the summit in Moscow that we want to be dependent on the United States?" he asked me. "One of the papers wrote that, and it raised some eyebrows here."

What could I answer? Should I have said that taking anyone's words out of context was wrong? "It seems quite obvious to me," I replied, "that the more nations depend on each other the less the likelihood of conflict between them."

Bush told Gorbachev he would be concerned if there were still doubts about his policy. "Perhaps I am not articulate enough in explaining my policies if such questions arise at meetings of your Security Council," he said. He went on to say with some passion that he wanted to see a Soviet Union that was democratic, that had a market economy, and that had successfully resolved problems between the center and the republics. He praised U.S.-Soviet cooperation during the Gulf crisis and said he understood how difficult it had been for the Soviet Union to take that course, "given its historic ties to Iraq."

There was still some residual mistrust of the Soviet Union, Bush said, in Congress and among some sectors of public opinion (he did not mention the administration), but "I know how much has changed in your country and also what stunning changes you have allowed to happen in Eastern Europe." "Therefore," Bush concluded, "we are not gloating over your problems, we don't want economic catastrophe to happen in your country, and we know that the demise of the Soviet Union is not in our interests."

Bush made yet another important point during the luncheon talk in London with Gorbachev. He said Gorbachev had convinced him that the Soviet Union was firmly set on the path of reform. This was something Gorbachev definitely wanted to hear, not just from Bush but also from the other Group of Seven members, and he wanted them to act on that understanding.

At the end of that talk, Gorbachev casually mentioned that Gavriil Popov, the mayor of Moscow, had been to see him to discuss an interesting idea. "He wants to establish an American university in Moscow," Gorbachev told Bush. "Let us give our support to that idea."

Was the reference to Popov some kind of hint? Was Gorbachev suggesting that he and Popov had had a good talk and that more than just the project for an American university was discussed? Was the message behind his words "We're working together. Everything will be all right"? I still don't know. I never asked.

Gorbachev Discusses a Soviet Market Economy with Western Leaders

The reason for Gorbachev's presence in London was to discuss economic problems—more specifically, the West's assistance to the Soviet Union in its transition to a market economy. Two questions had to be answered. Has the Soviet leadership really decided to move toward a free market? And will the West help?

On the first question, the answer seemed to be contained in Bush's words to Gorbachev during the luncheon. But it was not at all clear to me that Western leaders had really recognized his commitment to market reforms. The questions some of them, particularly Japanese Prime Minister Kaifu, were asking Gorbachev at their afternoon meeting seemed like interrogation of a suspect or an attempt to micromanage the pace and specific modalities of the reforms. For example, when Gorbachev said that by the end of the year he planned to have 70 percent of the prices in the Soviet Union free from state controls, the rest to be regulated and gradually decontrolled later, Kaifu suggested that was not enough.

"We have to reckon with what our society can tolerate," Gorbachev answered. "The jump in prices would be very high anyway. We would like to go faster on price liberalization, but we have to be careful."

Some of the Group of Seven leaders were more constructive in their comments and questions than Kaifu, but it did not seem to me that a decision had been made to go all-out and help Gorbachev. What would have appeared to be a great victory for him just a year before—the fact that he was invited to attend the summit of leading Western industrialized countries—was beginning to look more like a defeat, in the absence of something specific from his Western counterparts.

Gorbachev sensed that. He was arguing passionately for a specific commitment and a clear effort to help make the Soviet Union a market economy. "What are our friends waiting for?" he asked. "We need a new kind and new level of cooperation, which would really integrate my country into the world economy. I really don't know when such a chance would come up again."

But his hosts seemed either not sure of his commitment to market reform or unwilling to commit any money to the project anyway, preferring to let the Soviet Union muddle through.

Gorbachev recognized that it was up to the Soviet Union itself to solve its problems. His requests were not exorbitant. He was not asking for huge handouts.

"One possible difference between us," Bush had said to him, "is if you think the only way we can support you is by a major injection of money. But you are not saying that. You say that what you want from us is a political impetus, and I agree with that."

"There also needs to be a mechanism for implementing whatever decisions are made," Gorbachev responded.

In the end the Group of Seven and Gorbachev agreed on something like a communiqué, which was read by John Major at the press conference that followed the meeting. It included a reference to visits by the finance ministers of the Group of Seven countries to Moscow to discuss possible ways of helping the Soviet Union, but the reference was vague and noncommittal. Both Major and Gorbachev put a good face on it, and it was true that the London summit was a major event symbolizing new relations between the West and the Soviet Union. But it appeared to be less than total success, and there was much discussion about why that was so.

Some thought Gorbachev had made a mistake in appointing Yevgeny Primakov to be the Soviet sherpa, the official in charge of preparations for the summit. Primakov, it was argued, was not popular in the West, and that would affect the outcome. Others believed the problem went much deeper. Gorbachev, they said, was not really committed to the profound and radical reform that would create a capitalist economy in the Soviet Union, and the Western leaders understood that. They had a telling signal from Grigory Yavlinsky, the radical economist who at the last moment refused to participate in Gorbachev's delegation to London, complaining that the reform plans Gorbachev was to outline there did not go far enough.

Like the liberal Russian intellectuals, Westerners had a soft spot for Yavlinsky, admiring his radicalism, his youth, and the fact that he spoke English. His economic programs were touted as the solution to the Soviet Union's problems. In private, however, Western leaders were often much more skeptical about him. When he went to the United States that summer to work on another of his programs, called "A Window of Opportunity," with Graham Allison of Harvard University and a team of U.S. and Soviet economists, Gorbachev's Western counterparts showed no particular enthusiasm about the project. When they saw the product, at least some of them were appalled because the new program called for huge injections of money into the Soviet economy. The situation was quite ironic: while the Western media were lionizing Yavlinsky, Western leaders were letting us know that they did not treat his program seriously.

Quite a few people, therefore, believed that regardless of the plans Gorbachev had brought to London, and regardless of who had been on his team there, the West did not want to throw money at the Soviet Union's problems—and had no money to throw anyway. There could be some truth to all those arguments, but the final answer is for historians to find. I believe they will conclude that Mikhail Gorbachev did his best in London.

Gorbachev Meets with Margaret Thatcher

On the last day of his stay in London, Margaret Thatcher came to see Gorbachev at the embassy. No longer prime minister, she was just an M.P., and everyone knew she was bitter about the way her own party had disposed of her the previous November. But she looked sharp and cheerful as she came to talk with her old friend. She said she had discussed the London summit with all the Group of Seven leaders and that they all agreed Gorbachev had handled it well and had positioned himself exactly right.

"They all recognize now," Thatcher said, "that the Soviet Union has firmly and irreversibly opted for reforms and that these reforms deserve the support of the West." That being so, Thatcher continued, she was disappointed that the Seven had not agreed on more specific and practical ways to give support. The important thing now, she told Gorbachev, was to seize on the Group of Seven leaders' unanimous statement of support and willingness to cooperate.

"Don't let go of them!" she told Gorbachev. "You should demand that they act on what they have said, that they put their money where their mouth is."

Margaret Thatcher said that she was optimistic about developments in the Soviet Union, an optimism that was shared by many U.S. businessmen with whom she had talked during her speaking tour of the United States in June. She also said she was encouraged by the young people she met on her recent trip to the Soviet Union. "This," she said, "is really a new generation. These are thinking people who are ready to act, to show initiative and take a risk."

Thatcher herself was in a combative mood that day. She said she intended to be active and to use her lectures, interviews, and contacts to persuade others that they should trust Mikhail Gorbachev and support the Soviet Union's transition to democracy and a free market.

In my opinion the talk with Thatcher was a good shot-in-the-arm for Gorbachev as he was returning to Moscow and to the daunting tasks he faced in the two weeks remaining until his vacation in August. They were very much on his mind in London and present in his talks with Western leaders, who seemed to understand what a Herculean effort was required of him. "So many things in your country are changing at the same time," John Major said to Gorbachev, "and any practical politician would understand how difficult it is to persuade people in such a situation."

Indeed, Gorbachev was trying to persuade. He was trying to persuade the huge apparat of the Communist Party that the time had come to accept the new democratic rules of the game; he was trying to persuade the radical democrats that abiding by those same rules and not rushing to gain total power and absolute control immediately would eventually produce more solid results for them and for the country; and he was trying to persuade the leaders and the nationalist parliaments in the republics that a redistribution of authority that would delegate a large portion of it to them from the center was better than crushing the center, because everyone could perish under the rubble.

Gorbachev Works on Union Treaty

During the final week of July, I was working with Chernyaev on briefing materials and speeches for Gorbachev's summit with Bush. Chernyaev sent them to Gorbachev, who was spending days and often nights with the leaders of the republics in Novo-Ogarevo. Gorbachev did not have much time for anything else, but he sometimes talked to Chernyaev, with whom he had a close personal rapport, on the phone. It was clear that every small advance toward completion of the draft Union treaty took a tremendous effort.

Negotiations with Yeltsin, Nazarbayev, and others seemed more difficult than talks with foreign leaders. The question of the federal tax was a particularly thorny issue. In London all Western leaders had recommended to Gorbachev that he firmly insist on such a tax. Jacques Delors, chairman of the European Community Commission, made an interesting point there. One thing absolutely necessary in a state, he said, was common armed forces financed by every citizen and every entity through a federal tax. Once you are able to insist on that, Mr. President, Delors told Gorbachev, you have won. And Gorbachev wanted to win, not so much for himself but because he believed his people needed the Union.

Gorbachev completed the final negotiating session with Yeltsin and Nazarbayev literally on the eve of Bush's arrival in Moscow. I was working with Chernyaev on the remaining summit papers when Grigory Revenko, Gorbachev's adviser on matters concerning the Union treaty, called to describe the details of Gorbachev's final effort at Novo-Ogarevo. Chernyaev, always more skeptical than many of us, said he was pleasantly surprised. "I really wondered if he would make it," he said. "It's now a totally different situation."

Neither he nor Gorbachev knew how dangerous the situation was. Maybe we were deceived by the recent and comparatively easy Central Committee plenum, where, despite some strident speeches by the hard-liners, Gorbachev was able to gain acceptance of the draft of a new party program, whose goals and substance were clearly social-democratic.

But Alexander Yakovlev was in a gloomy mood. "They will now approve almost anything in order to cling to the vestiges of power," he said a few days later about the conservatives. Clearly more worried than Gorbachev, Yakovlev was trying to warn him. But he too probably did not think the antireform people would strike so soon.

As for Gorbachev, he thought he had outmaneuvered the forces of the past. He now had his two treaties. Bush was coming to Moscow to sign START, and the signing of the Union treaty was scheduled for August 20 in St. George Hall at the Kremlin.

Bush, Gorbachev, and Yeltsin in Moscow

President Bush's visit, which began with an arrival ceremony in St. George Hall on July 30, was almost anticlimactic. We all felt good that the START treaty was finally to be signed after years of arduous negotiation, but somehow it was a less joyous occasion than the INF signing in Washington in December 1987. I was thinking of the time that had passed since then and recalling the opportunities missed and some naive hopes shattered.

I thought how much more the START treaty would have done politically for Gorbachev if it had been signed a year or eighteen months earlier. I recalled the letter Bush sent to Gorbachev with Henry Kissinger a week before his inauguration in January 1989. In that letter he said that even though his new team needed time to reflect on the range of U.S.-Soviet issues, particularly those relating to arms control, he was serious about moving the U.S.-Soviet relationship forward and wanted to raise the level of the dialogue beyond the details of arms control proposals.

It was now clear that the details of arms control had taken altogether too much time in the U.S.-Soviet relationship, and that instead of being an accelerator arms control was more often a drag. The outcome was a treaty that was much like what it would have been without the long months of reassessment and bargaining.

Although Bush and Gorbachev had detailed and in-depth discussions of bilateral and foreign policy issues, including the Middle East, Yugoslavia, and Afghanistan, the Soviet domestic policy overtones of the visit drew the most attention. The Gorbachev-Yeltsin relationship was closely watched, and during the Bush visit it was seen to be still far from perfect.

On the first day of the visit Yeltsin, apparently after some hesitation, decided not to come to the arrival ceremony at the Kremlin. Unlike Nazarbayev, who did attend the ceremony and who took part in the formal delegation-level talks that followed, Yeltsin probably did not want to be regarded as part of "Gorbachev's team." He was extremely sensitive about such things, and this sometimes created situations that amazed our American guests.

The day Gorbachev hosted a formal dinner for Bush in the Faceted Chamber of the Grand Kremlin Palace there was much speculation about whether Yeltsin would come. He did. As the Gorbachevs and the Bushes were receiving and greeting the guests, I could not help thinking that the guests were, to put it mildly, a mixed bunch. Labels—calling those people either the visible government or the invisible one, either the establishment or the opposition—did not really apply. Rather, the guests reflected the country's past, its present and its future, and some people had not yet decided where they belonged.

There was Anatoly Lukyanov, Gorbachev's old friend from his Moscow University days and now chairman of the Supreme Soviet; there was KGB Chairman Kryuchkov and Defense Minister Yazov. There were also Alexander Yakovlev and Eduard Shevardnadze, Gorbachev's co-architects of glasnost and the new thinking. There were government officials, intellectuals, members of the old and new establishments, artists, and new businessmen who would not have been allowed even to get close to the Kremlin's sanctum on such a day just a couple of years before.

I was surprised to see Mrs. Yeltsin, Naina, accompanied by Gavriil Popov, mayor of Moscow. The explanation came a few minutes later. When the last of the guests had shaken hands with the presidents and their wives, Boris Yeltsin appeared, smiling broadly and greeting the hosts. Everyone was clearly stunned by the maneuver.

Apparently, Yeltsin had decided not to be just one of the guests at the party. He wanted to enter the hall among the principals. But there was an element of compromise in his little ploy.

"Why did you entrust Popov with your wife, Boris Nikolayevich?" Gorbachev joked a little tensely.

"Oh, he is no longer a danger," Yeltsin replied. He then made a kind of grand entrance with the two couples into the Faceted Chamber, to the amazement of the other guests, who were already seated at their tables.

The Americans told me the next day that they were stunned and somewhat distressed by what had happened. Bush said much the same thing to Gorbachev too. The Americans were wondering how relations between the two men would evolve, and they were clearly worried.

Today we know that events in the months that followed resulted in a final split between Gorbachev and Yeltsin, and it is pointless to try to second-guess history. Still, I believe that, but for the August coup, things between Gorbachev and Yeltsin could have turned out differently. The relationship would probably have been patchy and sometimes acrimonious, but a truce would certainly have lasted much longer and might even have evolved into a kind of cooperation.

Well, it's over now. Or is it? The history of this country is full of ironies and paradoxes, some of them tragic, some funny, and some felicitous, and the paths of the two men might yet cross again—perhaps this time for the benefit of the country. [I still hoped so when I was writing this book in 1992. I decided not to delete these sentences, although the hope proved naive.]

Bush and Gorbachev Talk About the Soviet Domestic Scene and Prospects

That August, Bush and Gorbachev had long discussions about the situation and prospects of the Soviet Union. Gorbachev was in good spirits. There had been a difficult period earlier in the year, he told Bush, when he had to maneuver between the left and the right. (It was not a shift to the right, he insisted.) But the situation then was dramatic, and a maneuver was necessary in order to save what was most important and valuable: the policy of perestroika, the democratic process, and the movement toward a market economy. But now there was a new situation, Gorbachev told Bush, and the position of the conservatives and right-wingers had become weaker. We can now move faster, Gorbachev concluded.

Bush was clearly fascinated by Gorbachev's balancing act. He said that it sometimes seemed almost impossible to pull off and assured Gorbachev again that he would do nothing to make things more difficult for him. He made a point of saying privately to Gorbachev that he would be particularly cautious with regard to Ukraine, the Soviet Union's most complex and politically paradoxical republic, which he was due to visit after Moscow.

Ukraine had always been a republic with a bureaucracy that was both conservative and nationalistically minded, but what that bureaucracy cared most about was power, so its nationalism was subdued and never strayed far from the line imposed by central authorities. Now the situation was changing. As in all other republics, politically active groups were becoming more radical with every passing day, and in Ukraine radicalism meant pushing for sovereignty and independence.

Paradoxically, in the minds of most people two things coexisted. They wanted to be independent of Moscow, but they did not think of seceding from the Union. Hence the result of the March 17 referendum, in which a large majority approved both the sovereignty of the republic and the preservation of the Union. Nevertheless, with the general deterioration of the situation in the country the radicals were becoming increasingly vociferous and their pressure was more effective. The Communist Party bureaucracy was beginning to think that the only way they could stay in power was to make more concessions to the radical nationalists, who wanted total independence and secession. No one knew where that process would stop.

Bush was wary of creating the impression that he was interfering in the Soviet Union's internal affairs, and he said so to Gorbachev, first in Malta and now again in Moscow. His speech in the Ukrainian parliament, warning against mindless nationalism and calling on the Ukrainians to work out their relations with the center, was a shock to the radicals, who had expected some expression of support for the idea of self-determination and independence. It also caused problems for Bush among ethnic Ukrainians in the United States.

Clearly, Bush recognized that Ukraine, like the other republics, could solve its problems better by working together with Russia and other republics. Still, abandoning a neutral attitude in his Ukrainian parliament speech, and virtually coming out in support of Gorbachev and the Union, was not a step Bush could take lightly. To me, that and other signals during Bush's visit to the Soviet Union were a clear indication that, after some hesitation and perhaps soul-searching, he had finally decided to take a stand and begin doing something to actually support Mikhail Gorbachev at a very tough time for him. For Gorbachev, it was a big gain, but too late.

Premonitions of a Coup?

Perhaps my recollections of the Moscow summit are tinged with the knowledge of what happened less than three weeks after it. But I still can't escape the impression that a kind of heavy pall was hanging over it. I remember the morning Gorbachev and Bush spent in Novo-Ogarevo, in the same building where Gorbachev had just completed his discussion with Yeltsin and Nazar-bayev on the draft Union treaty. The day was sunny and nice, and the symbolism should have seemed just right, but somehow I had a heavy feeling, a kind of premonition, that I was trying to fight back.

I came to Novo-Ogarevo thirty minutes before Gorbachev was due to arrive. I changed into informal clothes and went out to the porch of the guesthouse. Standing there was Yury Plekhanov, chief of the KGB depart-ment in charge of protecting the top leaders. Though his responsibilities were administrative rather than operational, he was always in attendance whenever Gorbachev went abroad and during all other engagements I remember. That seemed strange to me. And there was something else: as a person he could not be more different from Gorbachev. He was glum, dull, and stolid, and as for his political views, which one could sometimes glimpse from his remarks, they were what was to be expected from a KGB man. Again I thought this reflected Gorbachev's larger problem. The KGB was an organization he had inherited and could not easily dismantle or openly fight. He had to work with those people and hope they would evolve, learning to live in a democratic society.

Did Plekhanov already know that in a few days he would have a special assignment from the coup-plotters: isolating Gorbachev at his summer house in the Crimea? Were Kryuchkov's plans all ready when he was shaking hands with Gorbachev and Bush at that Kremlin reception? What happened in their minds "between the acting of a dreadful thing and the first motion"?

Those who defend the coup-plotters say they acted for the good of the country as they understood it. But the results of their actions were exactly the opposite of what they might have intended. The fact that some of them meant well must not absolve them.

Provocation in Lithuania

All summits are alike—with banquets, handshakes, signing ceremonies, re-ceiving lines, reporters shouting questions—but each has a different feel to it, and a different aftertaste that colors the memories of it later. The Moscow summit in late July 1991 was the color of anxiety, and a feeling of darkness surrounded and closed in on the bright picture of the events. On July 31, when Gorbachev and Bush talked at Novo-Ogarevo, the darkness was suddenly up close and frightening, when the presidents and their foreign minister and secretary of state were sitting on the sunlit veranda of the guesthouse. They were talking about one of the regional issues when an American official brought a note to Baker, who read it, reread it, and looked at Bush, who did not need anything else to understand that his old friend had something important and probably bad to report.

"What is it, Jim?" I recall him asking. "It has just been reported by the AP"—Baker read the note in his dramatic voice—"that a Lithuanian customs post on the border with Byelorussia has been attacked by armed men, who killed a number of customs officials. There is nothing more for the time being."

Baker looked at Gorbachev. There was a stunned pause.

Gorbachev said to Chernyaev, "Anatoly, go call Kryuchkov to find out what happened."

Chernyaev left and returned a few minutes later with information from Kryuchkov about the start of the investigation.

It turned out later that some of the information Kryuchkov conveyed to Chernyaev had been inaccurate—he had said, for example, that four men were dead and a few wounded. The AP, not the KGB chief, had the figures right. Kryuchkov also said that there were initially three main versions of the reason for the killings the investigators were looking into. One was that the customs people had been killed by organized-crime figures; another was that there had been strained relations between the Byelorussian and the Lithuanian customs officials; another was that it could be "an internal Lithuanian thing."

The sense all of us had then, I believe, and the version I still regard as most likely, was that it was a cruel provocation in order to, at the very least, mar the summit and make Gorbachev look bad—helpless and embarrassed—on what ought to have been his day of triumph.

The investigation, as far as I know, has still not been completed and is in the hands of the government of independent Lithuania. The matter is, of course, extremely politicized, so I am not sure the whole truth will ever come out.

Signs of Trust in a Multipolar World

Whatever some people were saying at the time, the business of the summit was not a mere formality. The trust between Gorbachev and Bush was at that time greater than ever before, and I was struck by manifestations of that trust in the discussion of issues as diverse as the economy, arms control, strategic stability, and Yugoslavia.

On July 31 in Novo-Ogarevo, Gorbachev suggested to Bush a discussion of strategic stability, in the broader definition of that term. "The world is getting increasingly diverse and multipolar," he argued, "but in this world there needs to be a kind of axis, which our two countries could provide."

Bush agreed—not in so many words, but in the way he was willing to discuss with Gorbachev in a cooperative mode matters the United States would not have allowed the Soviet Union even to touch before.

The Middle East was one such matter. From the reports of Bessmertnykh and Baker at Novo-Ogarevo it was clear that the Soviet Union and the United States were moving toward real cooperation there. The Soviet influence was less than that of the United States, and limited to only a few of the parties, but whatever influence we had was used skillfully to move the process forward. The Americans agreed that the opening of the Middle East peace conference—a long-standing Soviet foreign policy aim long opposed by the United States—should be co-chaired by the presidents of the United States and the Soviet Union.

On Yugoslavia, Bessmertnykh and Baker had spent much time trying to work out the text of a joint statement. The United States, Bush admitted, was under pressure from the European Community. Germany was insisting that the principle of territorial integrity with regard to Yugoslavia should not be singled out and overemphasized. Bush did not hide his irritation. "The Germans are pulling out in front on Yugoslavia," he said. Eventually, the joint statement was issued, and territorial integrity was mentioned in it.

"Yazov Is Solid"

As I was riding with Gorbachev and Bush back to Moscow, I was thinking that if our country survived its crises there was a good chance it would develop a real partnership with the United States. Bush had indicated that he would be more willing than before to consider ways to help the Soviet Union economically and otherwise, but he was clearly worried about the country's domestic prospects. Sitting with Gorbachev in the back seat of the car, he asked an unusual question. "What do you think about Yazov, Mikhail? Do you trust him?"

"I do," Gorbachev answered. "He is a reasonable man. It is not easy to keep the military under control in such turbulent times, and he is helping me do it. He is respected by the officers. He is solid."

With the benefit of hindsight it is easy to criticize Gorbachev for placing his trust in Yazov. But I have always thought that whatever Yazov said later he never would have initiated the coup that followed a few weeks afterward. He was a reluctant last-minute addition to the list of conspirators. Was there a better man Gorbachev could have picked to run the armed forces at the time? Perhaps, but in my view almost any senior military official would have behaved much as Yazov did.

Summit Reflections

The Moscow portion of the summit was over with a farewell ceremony at the Grand Kremlin Palace. There were more reporters than officials present. Dennis Ross and Bob Zoellick were among the few in the line of U.S. officials in the ornate St. George Hall. We talked for a few minutes before the ceremony started. They asked me how I felt working in the office of the president. I replied that it was interesting but difficult in some respects.

"We Russians are not good managers," I said to Ross frankly. "We're just not good at organizing things." Stalin, I thought to myself, was the one exception, and he "organized" the country beyond recognition, making it work but breaking its back. It could not have gone on long in that condition. It was now looking for a better way, and there must be one.

As I was waiting for Gorbachev to appear, I thought that reflections on the history and future of this vast country—as mysterious to me as it was to anyone—were perhaps inevitable on such a day and in such a place. The walls of the Kremlin seemed to radiate something that inspired such thoughts, not particularly profound and certainly not very helpful in the day-to-day business, but inevitable.

There are always many things to do following summits: memorandums of conversations to be dictated, documents and papers to be put in order, and an initial analysis of what had happened to be done. I kept working for a few days, doing all this and reading the cables in Chernyaev's office. He and Tamara Alexandrova, his secretary, were preparing to go with Gorbachev to the Crimea—"to the South," the phrase went.

I had planned to go on vacation one or two days after they left. I was tired, and I needed a couple of weeks of rest—reading and just doing nothing, I thought. I had all the paperwork done for a short vacation, with a back-to-work date of August 21.

"August 21," I said to Chernyaev when he asked me when I planned to resume work. "But you will probably be in Moscow for the signing of the Union treaty on the 20th?"

"I sure will," he answered.

"Then I will be there too."

"Oh, yes, you probably should," he answered. "I don't know what kind of ceremony it's going to be, but perhaps they will speak to the press afterward, or something else might come up."

"I just want to be there for the occasion," I replied.

Lena and I had discussed the possibility of taking a week-long boat trip down the Volga, to Kazan or to Saratov, where Lena's sister had friends who were ready to offer us hospitality. Somehow, though, we decided against it. I don't even know who was more reluctant to go. "You get more tired than relax during such trips," one of us finally said, and we decided to stay in Moscow. Lena's vacation was to end on August 19, and she said she had much to do to spruce up the apartment and "get ready for the usual rat race."

"Strange Things Are Happening in Our Country"

I had a relaxed, vaguely worried, and hollow feeling during the two weeks preceding August 19. With hindsight it's easy to exaggerate or distort what all of us actually felt during those days, and I don't want to dramatize things. Life is dramatic enough without adding anything retrospectively. I got up every morning and did my usual ten minutes of exercises. I read a lot — *"L'Histoire Contemporaine"* by Anatole France, to brush up on my French, among other things — and I watched some old American movies on videotape.

Our days were quiet and surprisingly it was rather quiet — relatively so, of course — throughout the country. Even the ethnic conflicts and the political squabbles seemed to be in a subdued mode for the summer vacations. I thought developments would pick up the pace again after the Union treaty was signed, if only for the reason that not everyone would like the treaty and the prospect of some stabilization and real reforms it could usher in.

A couple of days before the signing ceremony, a statement of the Cabinet of Ministers was televised, with some faint praise of the draft treaty but also much criticism of it. To me, it seemed an astonishing document, but it did not make much of a splash and was not duly assessed even after the coup. Also on that same day, a television anchorman with ties to the "patriotic movement" began the evening news program something like this: "Strange things are happening in our country. We don't even know what our country will be called in a couple of days. The Union treaty has a different name for our country but who will sign it? And what about those who don't?"

Strange things were happening indeed. When we were watching the evening news program on Sunday, August 18, featuring an air show in Moscow, Gorbachev had already been isolated at his summer residence at Cape Foros in the Crimea.

Coup d'État

Lena got up early the next day to take our daughter to kindergarten and go to work for the first time after her vacation. I was half asleep, hearing vaguely the water running in the bathroom, the remote sounds of the radio, and the voice of my daughter, who was not eager to go to kindergarten and whimpered a little, as she always did in the morning.

Lena opened the door to our room and said, "Pavel, I'm late, and we have to run now. But turn on the television—they are reading some document from something called a Committee for the Emergency, saying that perestroika has run into a dead end."

"That's intriguing," I said, still half asleep. Lena and Liza were already gone.

I switched on the television and saw a symphony orchestra playing classical music. What Lena had just said suddenly became clear to me. A coup d'état—Gorbachev had been removed and the country had been put under new management.

"Keep a cool head," I said to myself as a violinist replaced the orchestra. I went to the kitchen, made myself a cup of instant coffee, and listened to the documents of the "State Committee for the Emergency" being read somberly by an announcer.

The first document read was Anatoly Lukyanov's statement containing an extremely critical assessment of the draft Union treaty. In it, a kind of prelude to the other documents read afterward, he said that the treaty was no good and should be substantially redrafted. If there ever was an act of political betrayal of a friend—and Gorbachev had considered Lukyanov his friend since their years at Moscow University—this definitely was one. Then they read a statement signed by Vice-President Gennady Yanayev, saying that because Gorbachev was ill and could not perform his duties, he, Yanayev, had assumed the duties of president as of August 19. The statement was dated August 18. Then followed the statement declaring the emergency "in some localities of the Soviet Union" and creating the "State Committee for the Emergency," and a "Statement of the Soviet Leadership" signed, for some reason, not by the entire "Committee for the Emergency" but only by Yanayev, Pavlov, and Baklanov.

I remember acutely the sick feeling I had listening to those texts, written in the inimitable bureaucratic style of the party officialdom. I knew what had happened, and why. The invisible government had seen that they could not get Gorbachev to come over to their side and had now struck to put an end to his democratic experiment. To me it was obvious that Gorbachev was not, and could not be, one of them, and that made the events of the day easier to bear. But where was Gorbachev, and was he physically safe? I did not know. Nor did I know what was going to happen.

On that first day of the coup, particularly during the dismal, foggy hours of the morning, I thought the chances of the coup-plotters to consolidate power and stay on top for, say, two or three years were good. People were tired of instability and frustrated about the material hardship the process of change brought. Many of them disliked Gorbachev, because he was linked to those hardships in their minds. They held him mostly responsible for the fact that changes were not easy and painless. As for the Moscow intelligentsia—and I had no doubt that the fate of the country would be decided in Moscow—they had not supported Gorbachev's prudent approach to reform, they were suspicious of him, and they would not, I believed, defend him or demand his reinstatement. About Yeltsin I knew nothing—where he was, what he was doing, and what attitude he would adopt. Another unknown factor was how cruel and brutal "the new leadership" was ready to be in imposing their rule. I didn't know, but I thought they could be pretty bad. So on that morning of August 19, the outlook was gloomy.

Today almost everyone in Moscow recalls doing something heroic during those three days in August. I am one of the few who do not claim to be heroes. But neither was I a coward. I made my decisions on the first morning and made no secret of my feelings about the coup-plotters. I told friends and even people I did not know too well that I would not work for "the new government" and that I was ready to spend the next few years working as a night watchman rather than do so. Lena gave me full support from the very beginning. She worked in the foreign ministry part-time, so she had returned home early, an hour or two after lunch.

"Do you understand what is happening?" I asked her.

"To some extent," she said. She told me how the coup was playing in the foreign ministry. "My boss is studying Lukyanov's statement," she said, "and berating the Union treaty. He has also told me he thinks you did a stupid thing going to work for Gorbachev. He says you should have stayed in the foreign ministry, that if you had done so you would have felt quite comfortable now."

Oddly enough, we both burst out laughing. Later she told me that quite a few people had been saying or suggesting the same thing to her during those days—some with apparent sympathy, others almost openly gloating.

I can only guess how I would have felt or behaved had I stayed in the foreign ministry, but in my position then the attitude of refusal to cooperate with the coup came naturally to me.

My wife and I discussed my future.

"It could get pretty bad," I said. "They could entrench themselves for a few years. I will need your support. We will survive. The apartment complex on the opposite side of the lake needs night watchmen, and my friend Sasha will always get me some translations and help to get an occasional interpreting job. It's well paid."

But we knew it would be tough. Above all, it would be tough psychologically, a kind of political exile for me, and tough also for Lena, in the uncomfortable position of being watched closely in a certain way. Could there be something worse? I tried not to think too far ahead at that time, but I now believe that the logic of their proposed "policy" would have inevitably led the coup-plotters to two things. First, they would have quickly come to reject the Gorbachev foreign policy and the new thinking. Second, sooner or later there would have been a crackdown against "internal enemies," including those associated closely with Gorbachev.

There are many vindictive people in our country, as in every country. Nobody knows what was on their minds then. By way of an example, in May of that year, three months before the coup, an article in *Literaturnaya Rossia*, the mouthpiece of the "patriots" and hard-liners, attacked Gorbachev's foreign policy and the treaties and agreements signed in the last several years. It called for hearings to investigate those agreements and went on to propose this: "Such hearings should identify the inequitable agreements that would be subject to immediate cancellation, and also identify the persons guilty of signing them, who should be brought to trial for the betrayal of national interests. . . . Only if we ourselves convict as criminals those who signed the inequitable treaties and agreements can we initiate the renegotiation of those deals." The article called for nonratification of a number of U.S.-Soviet treaties negotiated by the foreign ministry.

Once this process of reconsidering the Gorbachev-Shevardnadze foreign policy began in earnest, it could go far and, as they liked to say in Stalin's years, heads would roll. I knew that my mother, with those years and the drama of our family still alive in her memory, was worried about me, particularly because she was far away, visiting our friends in Czechoslovakia, and could not talk to me. She later told me about the agony she went through. She was afraid the old times were returning.

In the evening of August 19 Lena and I watched the television news. Liza had gone to bed crying because in their eagerness to control the television and rearrange its programs, the new bosses had ordered the cancellation of the nightly children's puppet show "Good Night to the Little Ones." We told Liza that some bad men had canceled the show but that her favorite puppets would certainly return soon, particularly "Piggie." In private we were less optimistic. But we learned from the news program that Yeltsin had not been arrested — still no one knows why — and that he was resisting the orders of the "Emergency Committee" and calling for a general strike.

The television showed tanks and armored personnel carriers on the streets of Moscow and barricades around "the White House," the building of Russia's Supreme Soviet. I did not want to watch the Emergency Committee's press conference, which they showed right after the news, but Lena made me watch. It was a squalid show, we agreed, revealing the coup-plotters' ineptness and suggesting that they might not succeed. But that hope was not enough to lift our spirits.

Lena went to bed while I sat in our living room staring blankly at the television, which was showing the ballet "Swan Lake." Finally, I switched it off and put on a videocassette tape that I took at random from my desk drawer. It was an old recording of "NFL Today" showing highlights from football matches of the 1987 season. When I lived in the United States, American football fascinated me. Now I was watching the tape drowsily with an eerie feeling. I could not concentrate, and perhaps that is what saved me from total depression that night.

Reaction in Moscow's Streets

The next day I wanted to see what was happening in Moscow. I went out, first to the food market near our neighborhood. All was quiet, some people were discussing the events, others went about their business as usual. A woman selling tomatoes was upbraiding Gorbachev. "Nothing has become better under him. It's good he's out," she said in a rasping voice.

"Oh yes, it'll get much better now," someone else retorted sarcastically.

A middle-aged woman, confident and well-dressed, interjected, "Well, Gorbachev—he's one of them. You'll see him reappear once they've put down the republics and the press."

I kept silent. Why argue with someone who obviously would not want to listen? She was like so many other women in Moscow—newly active politically, not particularly sophisticated, but convinced that they understood everything better than anyone else, and of course very radical. Why waste time telling her that Gorbachev would be crazy to negate everything he stood for: democracy, the air of freedom, his new foreign policy, and the Union treaty he had spent many hours, days, and nights hammering out?

No one recognized me at the market, or at least no one let me know if they did. But later, when I went to midtown Moscow, within fifteen minutes by subway from where I lived, a couple of women recognized me and came up to talk. Unlike the outlying areas of the city, the center of Moscow was not quiet at all. It was abuzz with people, with political talk, and with the smell of tanks and the military. The two women asked me what I was doing.

"Not much," I said. "But I expect to be unemployed for quite some time."

"So, you are not with them?" one of the women asked.

"Liza, how could you!" the other exclaimed.

"I am not one of them," I said, while thinking that my daughter's name was also Liza. What kind of future was in store for her?

A small group of people was beginning to assemble, peering at us. The women said goodbye to me and went on their way.

At home I watched television and listened to the radio, noticing fairly soon that the plotters did not have full control of the media. It was beginning to look a little more encouraging. When Lena came back from work I told her about my impression. "You know, they may not win after all," I said.

Lena was skeptical, but she frantically began to search the radio waves for information. She found the radio program "Echo of Moscow," which became our source of information during the next forty-eight hours. The more we listened the more I was beginning to think that the putsch, as Gorbachev later called it, was not succeeding. But once again, the main question was still unanswered: How ruthless were the plotters prepared to be, how much blood were they ready to draw?

The Coup Collapses

Another thing disturbed me greatly: all kinds of things were being said about Gorbachev. Near the Russian parliament, at the huge rally to protest the coup, Eduard Shevardnadze spoke, and even he had unpleasant things to say about his old friend. "Where's Gorbachev?" he asked. "Is he involved in this in some way? If not, he should be allowed to speak to the people and explain what is happening and why."

Then, and on a few occasions later, Shevardnadze was unsparing of Gorbachev. He still could not forgive him for his failure to speak out in defense of his foreign minister and, more important, in defense of his foreign policy. He could not forgive what he saw as Gorbachev's tactical mistakes and his failure to clearly dissociate himself from the hard-liners. He might have had a point in some though not all cases. But even if he had been 100 percent correct I would have felt uncomfortable with what he was saying and how he was saying it. Just as I disagreed with some of Gorbachev's remarks the previous January, I now disagreed with Shevardnadze's. That did not happen often, and I had a lot of respect for both men. And when it happened, it always hurt me to disagree with either of them. It was particularly distressing now.

On the night of August 20 there was first blood: three young men were killed by the armored personnel carriers moving toward "the White House." That blood was also the last—it was the beginning of the end of the coup. On the morning of August 21 I went to the Byelorussian railway station near the center of Moscow to meet my mother, who was returning from Czechoslovakia. She was glad to see me, having gone through hell worrying about me, and she did not know much about the present situation in Moscow. I told her it was still touch-and-go but that there was a good chance the plotters would fail.

We took the train to go to Monino, the Moscow suburb where my mother lived. We talked quietly about the developments and about the zigzags and reversals of Russian history and how that history had a way of affecting the lives of everyone in our family, and indeed in our whole country.

"If they win, " I said of the plotters, "it won't be easy for me. I am ready, and Lena supports me. But of course I will need your support too." I recalled also that it was not the first time my mother had had to prepare for possible hardships.

We also discussed something else: both of us were still members of the party. That spring and summer many people we knew had been leaving it, some because they saw an advantage in doing so, some for what they saw as reasons of principle. Mother had said she would leave only when Gorbachev did; she really trusted him. We now decided that we would quit the party if the coup-plotters succeeded. It certainly would not be the easy and fashionable thing to do then, unlike a few months earlier, but we both felt it would be right to do so.

By the time I returned home from Monino at about 5 o'clock in the evening it was almost all over. Lena told me it had been announced that Gorbachev was alive and well and that a plane had left Moscow with a delegation led by the Russian Vice-President Alexander Rutskoy to take Gorbachev back to Moscow. The television was showing the meeting of the Russian parliament, and it was clear that the media were no longer controlled by the coup-plotters or their sympathizers. The rest is well-known. Within a few hours Gorbachev was back in Moscow and the coup-plotters were arrested.

Why the Coup Failed

The putsch collapsed quickly, before its organizers even had time to try to implement whatever they wanted to do in the country. Why did they lose? Some believe it was because they failed to arrest Yeltsin. Others say the hope was that Yeltsin could be persuaded to cooperate with the coup-plotters, because of his animosity toward Gorbachev. That, of course, was highly unlikely. Of all the leaders of the republics, Yeltsin was the one who had come to hate the old establishment—unlike, for example, Leonid Kravchuk in Ukraine, whose television interview on August 19 had shown that he was quite ready to respect and cooperate with the new "central authorities." In the interview, Kravchuk said, "What had to happen has now happened," and had not the slightest objection against the coup.

Another theory explaining the coup-plotters' quick failure was that they were not ruthless enough. However, they had been prepared to give orders to special troops to storm "the White House" on the night of August 20, but the unit to which that mission was assigned refused to obey. Gorbachev later said that those soldiers were among the heroes who thwarted the coup.

One explanation for the coup's collapse was shared both by Prime Minister Pavlov, one of the participants, and by Alexander Yakovlev. Both said that the Emergency Committee's most stupid mistake was deploying troops and tanks in Moscow. Without that, the resistance would have been much less focused and the overall impression much more business as usual, and of course there would not have been the deaths of three young men on the night of August 20, which horrified the country, the world, and probably even the plotters themselves.

Another reason for the coup's failure was that Gorbachev doomed the coup on August 18 when he refused to submit to the blackmail of the delegation sent by the organizers of the coup, which included his own chief of staff, Valery Boldin. As a result it was clear from the start that the "new authorities" lacked any legitimacy. No one believed them, and because the years of the democratic experiment had not been in vain there were already people who were prepared to resist them. Most of those people had already become Gorbachev's opponents on many issues, but they defended him in August 1991 because that meant defending themselves. They were part of the democratic experiment, a unique initiative in the history of Russia that Gorbachev had launched a few years before. The "invisible government" was not part of that experiment. On August 21 the experiment resumed, and its continuation was stormy.

Gorbachev Returns to a Different Country

At the press conference the next day, Gorbachev said he had returned to a different country and was now a different man. As I was interpreting that press conference I was fighting back a feeling that Gorbachev was not yet in command. I was happy he was there, and glad to be doing my work again. My friends in Washington told me later that they had been wondering about me.

"Boy, were we glad when we heard your voice on CNN translating that press conference!" Margaret Tutwiler said to me in September.

In Washington, like everywhere else, they were watching Gorbachev and listening to his every word. And some of those words showed that he was unaware of one fundamental change that had occurred over the previous days, a change in people's attitude toward the party.

Already on August 22 crowds began to gather outside the Central Committee building, and it was clear that storm clouds were also gathering. But it seemed that Gorbachev had not been told about that, and did not realize even that almost the entire party leadership, both in Moscow and in most of the regions, had betrayed him and supported the coup.

"The Party is over," I told an English-speaking member of Gorbachev's staff on that day.

But when a question was asked about the Party at the press conference, Gorbachev launched into a defense of it and said he still hoped to reform it.

I never allow my mind to be deflected when I interpret, but this time, even as I was speaking into the microphone, I thought, "This will cost him dearly." Indeed, the next day there was a lot of talk that Gorbachev had understood nothing, and the radical democrats, who had a justifiable feeling of triumph, could not forgive Gorbachev for trying to stay with the party after all that had happened.

In the afternoon of August 23 I was in Chernyaev's office in the Central Committee building, discussing the events of the last few days. Much had happened, and we knew we had little time for analysis, so fast were the developments. Chernyaev said that the three days at Foros had been worse for him than even his most dangerous moments at the front during the Second World War. "There at least you are in control of what you do," he said, recalling his years in the front-line reconnaissance unit. "But at Foros we were completely cut off and our every step was watched. It was utter helplessness, especially at first."

We agreed that something totally new was beginning, and we worried about Gorbachev.

The television was showing the meeting of the Russian parliament attended by Gorbachev. What a humiliating experience that must have been for him! He was insulted and shouted at, and Yeltsin literally forced him to read out a piece of paper purported to contain the record of the meeting of the Cabinet of Ministers on August 19. Jeers and even some catcalls accompanied the reading. We were stunned.

"How can they do this to him?" Chernyaev wondered. He was always amazed at the brazenness of people. "And how can he continue as president after this?" he added quietly, almost as an afterthought.

Chernyaev, Unsung Hero

Of all the people on Gorbachev's staff, Chernyaev was probably the most committed and personally loyal to him—which does not mean he always agreed with Gorbachev's decisions and his judgment, both before and after the coup. He disliked "the men of the invisible government," and at a certain point he had believed their influence was growing too much and that they were reasserting control again. January 1991 was a terrible month for Chernyaev. After the massacre in Vilnius he thought of resigning and even wrote a letter of resignation to Gorbachev.

Tamara Alexandrova, Chernyaev's longtime secretary, later told me she had refused to type the letter and send it to Gorbachev.

"This is not the time to run away from Mikhail Sergeyevich," she had said.

And I am sure she was right. She based her judgment not on politics but on the concept of loyalty, which she intuitively understood better than most people I knew. Eventually, Chernyaev changed his mind and came to be even closer to Gorbachev than before. Again, he sometimes disagreed with Gorbachev, and I believe he was often right, but the bond between them was strong.

I admired Chernyaev for his courage and common sense, and also for another quality I believed quite a few people close to Gorbachev lacked: he never did anything just to show off, to demonstrate how smart he was, "smarter than the boss," to give himself credit for what was done right and dissociate himself from what was wrong. Chernyaev soldiered on, intelligently and inconspicuously, doing many good things behind the scenes and not asking for applause from the fickle audience. To me, he is an unsung hero who deserves to be better known.

"The Radicals Want Gorbachev Out"

As we were watching the live television coverage of the Supreme Soviet session, with the deputies continuing to humiliate Gorbachev, an announcement came over the Central Committee's public address system. "By order of the Mayor of Moscow approved by the president of the Soviet Union," a man's voice said, "this building will be sealed today. Those now in the buiding should leave immediately. You will be allowed to take out your personal belongings, and the police will ensure your safety."

It sounded ominous, and as we learned later from those who left the building after the announcement, there was a lot of unpleasantness. The building was surrounded by an angry crowd, quite a few people were drunk, all the entrances were blocked, and as employees, secretaries, and others were leaving they were jeered and roughed-up by the crowd.

Chernyaev was in no hurry and did not want to leave surreptitiously. "I can stand up to anyone," he said to the security guard who told us we must leave by a hidden exit from an adjoining building, which was not blocked by the crowd. I know he would have reacted properly to any attempt to humiliate him, but the security men insisted, and he reluctantly agreed. He and I went out of the Central Committee building, never to return to it again.

The next day Chernyaev was given an office in the Kremlin, one that had been used by Vadim Bakatin and before that by Lev Smirnov, the powerful deputy prime minister responsible for the defense industry. It was huge, pompous, and not very convenient for day-to-day work.

The four months we had spent there were full of anxiety and uneasiness. I never felt at home there. There was something hostile in the environment, and other people were already planning how to get there. Soon they would evict us, but I also felt that the environment itself was trying to eject us. There was an air of inevitability about what happened four months later.

When I came back home on that day I said to Lena, "The radicals want Gorbachev out. I think they don't know yet how to do it. After all, they were calling for his return to power just a couple of days ago. But they hate him, and they will not rest until he is out."

"Perhaps he should go," my wife said. "He has been through a lot lately. Can he take more?"

"Leaving now would be abandoning the country in grave trouble," I answered. "I know he won't do it."

Thirteen

PICKING UP THE PIECES
September–November 1991

Gorbachev Takes New Steps to Protect the Union

The next day, I reported to work at our new office in the Kremlin. Gorbachev was to receive the new U.S. ambassador, Robert Strauss, who was coming to present his credentials. But that was by far not the most important thing happening that day in the Kremlin. When Gorbachev arrived at his office in the morning, a group of his close associates were waiting: Yakovlev, Bakatin, Primakov, Chernyaev, Vadim Medvedev, and a few others. Their faces were grim; they knew things were not going well for Gorbachev. He had to act quickly to dissociate himself from the Communist Party—his party—which had betrayed him and his cause. They had to open Gorbachev's eyes to what the party hierarchy had done during the coup.

By the end of the day, Gorbachev issued a statement renouncing his position as general secretary and calling for dissolution of the Central Committee. This is something he ought to have done right after his return to Moscow, but he needed a push from someone like Yakovlev, Primakov, or perhaps Shevardnadze. But they had not been at the airport when Gorbachev returned.

When Gorbachev received Ambassador Strauss, no high officials from the foreign ministry were present. He had just dismissed Bessmertnykh, "for passivity during the coup," as he put it. (Bessmertnykh had refused to join

Primakov and Bakatin, two fellow members of the Security Council, in condemning the coup and preferred to wait it out.) Gorbachev now knew that most of the ministry's top brass had been ready to work for the coup-plotters. Only one ambassador—Boris Pankin in Prague—clearly dissociated himself from "the new government"; some spoke openly in support of it, and most were neutral at best. So I understood Gorbachev: he felt the diplomats had failed him. They ought to have spoken out. After all, in foreign policy his accomplishments were clear, and many ambassadors owed their careers to him and to the new thinking. Nikolay Uspensky, who was briefly Gorbachev's interpreter and was appointed ambassador to Sweden by him, told the press on August 19 that Gorbachev's ouster was understandable and that the "new authorities" had acted properly.

Things like that pained Gorbachev greatly. What really surprised me was that Shevardnadze tended to justify the diplomats and showed some understanding of Bessmertnykh's behavior during the coup. The only explanation I have for this is that Shevardnadze was then still at odds with Gorbachev, thinking he had not done enough to prevent the coup. "He should not have gone on vacation," Shevardnadze said. I remember how the Italian foreign minister commented that Shevardnadze's remark was naive, but later Gorbachev himself said he should have been more vigilant.

Ukrainians Declare Independence

Gorbachev told Strauss that the coup had dealt a heavy blow to the Union but that he believed integrational tendencies would reemerge and that he wanted to resume work quickly on a new version of the Union treaty. "Yeltsin too thinks we should sign the treaty without delay," he said to Strauss. "And we now think that all the republics in which people voted for the Union in the March referendum should sign at the same time, including Ukraine."

The next day the Ukrainian parliament, dominated by the same Communist nomenklatura (the old Communist establishment) who had been ready and willing to accept the coup, voted for the Declaration of Independence. It was an amazing about-face. Leonid Kravchuk, for many years the Ukrainian Communist Party's chief ideologist, now became the chief proponent of independence. No one knew yet what independence meant, particularly in economic terms, but one thing was clear: the Ukrainian party bosses, who were able to cling to power, would not want to sign the Union treaty. They set a referendum for December 1 to confirm the parliament's decision. That was a time bomb that would blow up under Gorbachev and that the Russian radicals quickly decided they could use for their own purposes.

Gorbachev, however, refused to abandon his cause. He believed passionately in the inherent unity of the country and felt that, despite everything that had happened, a way had to be found to rebind the republics into some kind of union—at least a "soft" union, as he soon began to call it.

Could that be done? I still believe that it was not impossible. A great deal hinged on Yeltsin's position. At first Yeltsin did not want to "lose" Ukraine. After its parliament voted for independence Yeltsin's office even issued a statement saying that if Ukraine were to leave the union the borders between the two republics would have to be renegotiated. This was a thinly veiled hint that Russia would claim the Crimea, which had been "given" to Ukraine in 1954 by Khrushchev. Because most of the Crimea's population was Russian, Yeltsin's statement was understandable, but it was clumsy and untimely and only accelerated Ukraine's drive for total independence.

Post-Coup Union Strategy

As Gorbachev continued, against all odds, his efforts to build a new basis for a union treaty that would give the republics political and economic freedom while retaining common structures, such as the army and the energy and transportation systems, Britain's John Major came to Moscow en route to China. Gorbachev knew, of course, that in the period preceding his meeting with the G-7 leaders in July, Major had not been "on his side." In fact, like Japan, Britain had been reluctant to make any tangible commitment to supporting economic reform in the Soviet Union. But Gorbachev bore no grudge against Major. He and Major were comfortable with each other, and their meetings in Moscow went well.

The first meeting was what one would expect, but it was quite different from previous such meetings in that just about the only thing they discussed was the situation in the Soviet Union. Major was obviously eager to hear Gorbachev's assessment and to see whether he felt confident enough under the pressure of extremely rapid developments.

Gorbachev told Major that the coup had created a situation of enormous chaos and disintegration from which it would be difficult to recover, but that it was not hopeless. We are working hard to put things back on track, he said, and I am meeting with Yeltsin and the leaders of other republics to develop a common strategy before the extraordinary Congress of People's Deputies. The Congress was due to begin in a day or two, and it was not yet clear what might happen there. A common platform shared by Gorbachev and the leaders of the republics would have been a great plus for him, but I was not at all sure whether he could pull it off.

Yeltsin was very much in the saddle, and a veritable cult of Yeltsin was developing among the people and the democratic intelligentsia. Would he want to cooperate with Gorbachev, who appeared politically weak, particularly after the Ukrainian Declaration? As Major was questioning Gorbachev, I saw that he too had his doubts. But Gorbachev spoke with confidence. Most people do not want the country to break up, he said, and reintegrational tendencies were coming on strong again. The politicians would have to respond to what the people wanted. "Wait until the evening," he said to Major. "I would like to see you again to tell you how we are doing with the republics' leaders."

The Congress Adopts Gorbachev's Union Approach

The second meeting with Major took place late, certainly after 9:00 P.M., perhaps at 10:00 P.M. Gorbachev looked tired but pleased. "We have worked out a common strategy," he said. "Tomorrow, Nazarbayev will open the Congress with a statement signed by me and the leaders of eleven republics calling for the early conclusion of a new Union treaty based on the principles of a common economic area, common armed forces, and guarantees of individual rights and freedoms through the territory of the Union."

The statement also called for a transitional period before the treaty took effect, a period during which the Congress, which was too conservative for the new times, would be suspended. This was bound to make the deputies unhappy. Gorbachev told Major what his tactic would be the next day: instead of opening a debate on the statement, he would call for a break right after Nazarbayev's speech, in order to give the deputies time to digest the joint statement, and to apply some pressure on the most influential deputies.

It was a good strategy, and it would work, but on the eve of the Congress that still remained to be seen. Nevertheless, Major was obviously impressed with what Gorbachev had just told him. "I wish you good luck," he said. "You are facing a formidable task, and I am amazed at the energy and vigor with which you are handling it. I will be very pleased to report it to my G-7 colleagues."

My own impression was that Major left the meeting reassured and eager to hope that chaos in the vast Soviet Union could be avoided. This was, after all, what the West wanted very much, even though the West did not do enough to ensure this outcome.

What Gorbachev had achieved before the Congress was indeed impressive. The fact that Ukrainian leaders found it possible to support the statement worked out under Gorbachev's auspices meant there was still hope of drawing that republic into some kind of a union. Later, when Kravchuk was under pressure from his radical opponents in the presidential elections, and when he saw that Yeltsin did not really want a union, things changed dramatically. But in early September almost all republics, except of course the Baltic states, declared their support for some kind of a Union treaty. Perhaps Gorbachev overestimated the importance of that fact and later did not maneuver deftly enough, with a full understanding of Yeltsin's and Kravchuk's own agenda.

Still, the "10 plus 1 Declaration," as it later came to be called, was a great achievement. It contained a paragraph in which I had a hand. Several days earlier I had written a note to Chernyaev, which he passed to Gorbachev saying he was in full agreement with it. In that note I said that the republics wanted international recognition more than anything else, but that none of them was yet capable of deploying a full-scale diplomatic presence in other countries. That being the case, I argued, "the center" should act preemptively and call for recognition of the republics under international law while retaining for the Union the permanent membership, and the veto power, in the U.N. Security Council. This two-tier system would satisfy the republics' craving for international recognition but leave the question of diplomatic representation in other countries to be addressed later, hopefully in quieter and less emotional times.

The declaration Nazarbayev read contained the following paragraph: "We request that the Congress of People's Deputies support the application of the republics to the United Nations requesting their recognition as subjects of international law and consideration of the question of their membership in the organization." This, I still feel, would have been a proper and practical approach, and we had information that the U.S. administration considered it quite favorably during the ensuing months. But, like many other reasonable things, this was not to happen. In revolutionary times simple solutions are preferred to reasonable ones, and the logic of power takes precedence over any other logic.

The Congress of People's Deputies was a tumultuous and unpleasant affair. It was full of hard-liners, conservatives, and all kinds of people who bore a grudge against Mikhail Gorbachev. They raised hell and did their best to thwart him, but amazingly he was able to have all the principal points of the declaration passed by the Congress. The Congress adopted the concept of a transitional period leading up to a new Union treaty and in effect the creation of a new state, and it agreed to adjourn for the duration of that period.

Changes in Gorbachev's Team

Now that Gorbachev had succeeded in getting his approach approved in principle, the question was whether the leaders of the republics really wanted to work to get it implemented and whether Gorbachev himself had a team of people who would really help him achieve his goals. The answer to both questions turned out to be no. This became obvious in October and November as Gorbachev fought on in increasing isolation.

Right after the coup, Gorbachev sought to bring back to work with him the committed reformers who were with him at the beginning of perestroika or who worked with him later but turned away in late 1990 or in 1991. The group included Shevardnadze; Alexander Yakovlev; the liberal editor of the *Moscow News*, Yegor Yakovlev; the mayors of Moscow and Leningrad, Gavriil Popov and Anatoly Sobchak; Vadim Bakatin; and economist Grigory Yavlinsky, chief author of the "500 days" economic program.

Of all these people, I had the highest regard for Eduard Shevardnadze. Of course, I knew him best. Some others, particularly Popov and Sobchak, did not impress me a great deal. Too often they confused democracy with populism, and although they were not as ruthless as Yeltsin, they always took his side in any dispute with Gorbachev. I found the way they switched positions and delighted in taking cheap shots against Gorbachev quite cynical. Nevertheless, I understood why Gorbachev wanted them to be members of the Political Consultative Council—a kind of kitchen cabinet he formed to advise him on strategy and tactics during the transitional period.

The arrangement did not work out well. The group was not as smart and as expert in political intrigue and infighting and, more important, not as fiercely loyal to their boss as people around Yeltsin, and they just watched as Yeltsin's team was taking advantage of Gorbachev's good faith and, some would say, gullibility. Most of these people believed that Gorbachev had at some point betrayed them by not giving them enough support. In reality, though, I think Gorbachev had more reason to feel betrayed, or at least let down by his friends. As for his foes, they betrayed and deceived him viciously and with a vengeance.

"I don't know of any happy reformers," Gorbachev said a few months later in an interview. Trying to guide a country like ours through major reforms without civil war or nationwide upheaval may be a losing proposition in the first place. Doing so while preserving old friendships is definitely impossible.

The Gorbachev-Shevardnadze Relationship

Gorbachev's friendship with Shevardnadze went through stormy tests in 1991. It happened before the eyes of the whole world. In September everyone was asking why Gorbachev had not offered Shevardnadze the post of foreign minister. The ministry's staff was eager to see him in his old office at Smolenskaya Square again. A delegation led by the head of the first European department, Anatoly Glukhov, a bright and popular guy whom Shevardnadze liked, was sent to Shevardnadze to talk to him about it. Shevardnadze said Gorbachev had not asked him to become foreign minister but indicated that he would consider such a proposal.

My friends in the ministry believed that Gorbachev was missing a great opportunity. "What happened?" one of them asked me. "We did all we could, and Eduard was ready. There is no way that Pankin will be able to assert himself and restore morale in the ministry."

It was too late to argue then, so I did not point out to him what had happened just a couple of weeks earlier.

Shevardnadze's remarks at a rally on August 20, questioning Gorbachev's position, had hurt Gorbachev, but he was always able to rise above any hard feelings, at least once. So right after the coup he offered Shevardnadze membership in a revamped Security Council. Shevardnadze played hard-to-get, saying he did not quite understand the idea behind that body, and that was one of the reasons the whole thing was quickly dropped. I doubt that after such a snub it was easy for Gorbachev to risk repeating the same experience, so he offered the job to Boris Pankin, who accepted, perhaps without quite understanding the magnitude of the task before him.

Post-Coup Meetings with James Baker

Pankin was the foreign minister when U.S. Secretary of State Baker came to Moscow in mid-September. My impression from the meetings with Baker I attended was that the Americans were somewhat confused. They had not yet come to any definite conclusions following the coup. They were not sure how relations between Gorbachev and Yeltsin would work out.

Baker was mostly listening. He also wanted to encourage rapid and radical economic reforms, and there was some hope for that. Gorbachev had at his side Grigory Yavlinsky, who took part in the Kremlin meeting Gorbachev had with Baker. As always, Yavlinsky was confident and articulate. He explained to Baker how a more radical economic policy would be implemented on the basis of an agreement among the republics that he was then drafting. Baker was impressed by the decisiveness and expertise of people like Yavlinsky. They seemed to be in command, he said, and the country seemed to be ready for painful economic medicine to be administered quickly.

Behind Gorbachev's Back

But politics intervened. Cooperation between Gorbachev and Yeltsin soon began to unravel, and four months were lost. When prices were finally decontrolled after the dissolution of the Soviet Union, it was done in a situation of total chaos. Prices skyrocketed. The people had to pay for the politician's failures. Looking back, I am amazed how little of what later happened one could predict in September 1991. James Baker was asking questions and heard what seemed to be answers. There was, of course, the underlying tension because of the continuing mystery about relations between the two principal political figures in the country, but the concept of a transitional period leading up to a new Union, perhaps a confederation, and a market economy seemed acceptable to just about everyone.

My feeling at the time was that the issue of what kind of union would eventually emerge should not be forced and that the focus should be on hammering out an economic agreement between the republics. I knew this was Chernyaev's view. Chernyaev was close to Gorbachev but not a member of the Political Consultative Council. I felt that his intuition about the danger of focusing on the Union treaty was right.

Yeltsin pledged his cooperation to Gorbachev, and his people were working with Gorbachev's experts on the new draft. But this was a trap. There were endless delays, and soon it became clear that Yeltsin's people were manipulating the process. Nevertheless, no one in Gorbachev's inner circle alerted him to that fact. I believe that Yakovlev, Shevardnadze, Bakatin, and others were simply not cynical enough to see what was happening not only behind Gorbachev's back but also behind theirs. A new ruthless breed of Russian political animals were at work, and they would soon sideline the entire group that started perestroika and brought democracy to the Soviet Union.

August and the ensuing months were a trying time for most of us. I think only those who were smelling power and rushing ahead to grab it felt good about what was happening. Others, in varying degrees, were torn apart by inner conflicts or by the drama of what increasingly appeared to be the collapse of their country and the ideas they believed in.

There were a few suicides that captured everyone's attention. The Americans were particularly fascinated—if that is the right word to use about something like this—by the suicide of Marshal Akhromeyev. They asked me and others about it. Baker asked Alexander Yakovlev, "Why do you think Akhromeyev took his life?" I don't know how much Yakovlev knew then, and I don't know much even now. Anyway, Yakovlev replied that it was a personal tragedy. Akhromeyev, he said, profoundly believed in the ideology of communism and in the indivisibility of the Soviet Union, and when he saw how quickly both began to unravel following the coup, he just broke down.

Later Gorbachev told me that Akhromeyev had written him a letter before taking his life and he was convinced that Akhromeyev was not one of the plotters. He had been on vacation when the coup began, and he wrote in his letter to Gorbachev that he had rushed back to Moscow believing that Gorbachev was indeed incapacitated and that he should be in the Kremlin at a time like that. Apparently, he did cooperate with the "Emergency Committee." How true his explanation in the letter was we will never know, but the suicide showed how he felt afterward.

Gorbachev never spoke badly about the marshal. Basically, Akhromeyev was a loyalist. He was not a cynical man, and, having seen him on numerous occasions and worked with him, I can say that he was making an honest effort to understand what was happening and to move with the times. I think I understand why the Americans respected him. But revolutionary times are cruel, particularly to people who are basically decent.

A Disarmament Initiative from President Bush

Baker's departure from Moscow was quickly followed by a major disarmament initiative from President Bush. The U.S. embassy's deputy chief of mission, Jim Collins, called me early on September 28 to say he had an urgent message from Washington that he would like to convey through Chernyaev to Gorbachev. (By that time the Americans had begun to deal more and more with the president's office, bypassing the demoralized foreign ministry.) It was an arms control initiative, he said, but as Chernyaev and I were reading the paper Collins brought to the Kremlin less than an hour later, we understood that it was more than just arms control—it was really disarmament. Whole categories of weapons, particularly tactical nuclear weapons, were to be destroyed or radically reduced.

My first thought was that the U.S. government had concluded that the prospect of major upheaval in the Soviet Union was real and decided that the fewer nuclear weapons such a country had in the restive republics, the better. But, be that as it may, the initiative was based on reciprocity—the United States was ready to dispense with a major portion of its own nuclear arsenal—and I quickly saw that it was a major breakthrough.

Having translated the U.S. paper, I sent it to the foreign and defense ministries, and Chernyaev took it to Gorbachev, who asked Chernyaev to call a meeting of defense and foreign ministry officials for an initial assessment of the U.S. proposals. We got on the phone. Defense Minister Marshal Yevgeny Shaposhnikov was not immediately available, and Deputy Foreign Minister Obukhov was ill. Within twenty minutes we had in Chernyaev's office in the Kremlin General Vladimir Lobov, the new chief of the General Staff; General Fyodor Ladygin, the defense ministry official in charge of arms control talks; and Victor Karpov, the foreign ministry's veteran disarmament negotiator. Marshal Shaposhnikov was on the way, we were told.

The two generals were not particularly enthusiastic about the U.S. proposals. As was their habit on other occasions, they started to pick out aspects that reflected the long-standing U.S. positions, particularly on strategic arms and space defense, that were not acceptable to the Soviet Union. Even the proposals on tactical nuclear arms, which were obviously fair, did not look good to them. Lobov said that on the face of it, it looked as though the Americans were calling for destruction of both nuclear artillery shells and artillery pieces on the Soviet side but not on the U.S. side. I replied that even though that particular part of the proposal was awkwardly phrased I thought his interpretation was wrong. General Ladygin said that if the U.S. proposals regarding strategic arms and space defense were accepted "strategic parity as we know it" would no longer exist.

Finally, Chernyaev lost patience. "Tell me," he said, apparently not to anyone in particular, "do you think these U.S. proposals are intended to lead us into some kind of trap, or are they an earnest attempt to start a process of reducing nuclear arms?"

I knew what he himself thought, and he knew what my view was. There was a moment of awkward silence.

Then Karpov spoke: "I believe it's the second thing."

I had seen Karpov in different situations and had not always been proud of him, but this time I was. The generals did not try to overrule his simple statement. "We'll have to study it all very carefully," Lobov said.

"Fair enough," Chernyaev answered. "Please prepare a quick assessment with foreign ministry experts, and your suggestions for our response."

Five minutes after the group left, Marshal Shaposhnikov entered Chernyaev's office. A naturally jovial man, he was smiling and took a minute to chat with me. Like Alexander Rutskoy, vice-president of Russia, he was a graduate of the Gagarin Air Force Academy, located in Monino, where I grew up, and we had some mutual friends. Shaposhnikov had not yet seen the U.S. proposal. I gave him the paper, and he glanced through it in what seemed less than a minute. From his reaction I saw that he was a quick study.

"Well, it's okay," he said. "As for tactical weapons, it's practically all acceptable. On strategic arms it's mostly old stuff, but there are some new things—and we must take a fresh look at the whole subject." I had never heard a military man speak like that. I was encouraged.

Later that day Gorbachev and George Bush spoke on the phone. Chernyaev and I had prepared some talking points for Gorbachev, based on the first assessment of the U.S. proposals. The conversation was warm, although Gorbachev's reaction at first appeared to me—and maybe to President Bush on the other end of the line—to be a bit on the cautious side. Perhaps Gorbachev did not want to overcommit himself or create the impression that he was making a decision before the military had a chance to consider the U.S. initiative. But he welcomed the spirit of the Bush initiative and promised an appropriate response soon.

Something occurred toward the end of the talk that had not happened before. Bush's voice seemed a little hesitant as he was saying "Mikhail, on questions regarding nuclear weapons we shall deal with the center and with you, but as a courtesy I wanted to inform Boris Yeltsin too. He is absent from Moscow, and our people seem to have a problem reaching him, but I hope you don't mind it."

Indeed, Yeltsin had just left Moscow to take a vacation in the south. There had always been something a little mysterious about Yeltsin's absences. Only the people closest to him saw him during such vacations, and a battle for Yeltsin's "soul" was probably in progress then. Afterward there was a great change in the Russian president's behavior toward Gorbachev, so it became clear who had won that battle. But that was later. The telephone talk between Gorbachev and Bush ended on a note of mutual trust.

Shaposhnikov and Lobov were both present during Gorbachev's talk with Bush. As all of us waited in the office for the call, Gorbachev briefly discussed the Bush initiative with them, then suddenly started to talk about his visit to the theater the day before. He had seen a play based on Thornton Wilder's novel *The Ides of March*. "It's been so stressful," he said, "that Raisa and I simply needed a change. We really enjoyed it." Gorbachev then spoke with admiration about Mikhail Ulyanov in the role of Caesar.

None of us had seen the play. It was a hit that was drawing huge crowds, but I had read the novel. The historical analogy—the theme of betrayal—was all too obvious, but Gorbachev did not belabor it. He just discussed the story and the acting. Then the call came. After it, Gorbachev rose from his desk and shook hands with the generals. "I will appoint a commission under [Ivan] Silayev, with both of you on it, to prepare a good response to this initiative," he said. "Goodbye. And go see that play whenever you have the time."

Gorbachev's Book on the August Coup

I still have not seen *The Ides of March* at the Vakhtangov Theater. And other than submitting some suggestions as to our response, I was not involved in working out Gorbachev's disarmament initiative, which was unveiled a few days later, because by then I was in London where Harper Collins was rushing to publish Gorbachev's book about the August coup. The book, based entirely on Gorbachev's own notes and the records of his conversations with Soviet and foreign leaders, had been hastily put together, and was not a "staff-written" book.

Gorbachev always disliked the rhetorical tricks of speechwriters. Whenever someone inserted what looked like a clever metaphor or a punch line in drafts of his speeches, he always deleted it sooner or later. His speeches and books are therefore rather dry—all substance and no flash. I have always wondered why. Gorbachev liked a funny phrase or a joke here and there in his talks, but he had a quite different attitude toward the written word. That's why many were disappointed not to find what they had expected—anecdotes, revelations, or anything sensational—in *The August Coup*.

Gorbachev asked me to review the translation of that book, and when I saw the first draft I saw how necessary it was. I spent four days weeding out inaccuracies and mistakes and making last-minute changes based on Gorbachev's final editing of the text. In the rush to publish the book quickly, as Gorbachev had requested, Harper Collins apparently neglected to pass on some of those changes to the French publisher. This resulted in a flap a few weeks afterward, when both editions were published. The French edition included the phrase "Mitterrand wanted to call me" (at Foros, when the coup was over), the result of a typist's error. She had misread Gorbachev's handwriting. It should have been "I wanted to call my mother." I still have that page from Gorbachev's handwritten notes, and the two words in Russian are easy to confuse. Anyway, the mistake was found and corrected, but for some reason the wrong sentence appeared in the French translation.

The French press, always eager for a scandal, made much of it, saying, "Gorbachev complained that Mitterrand never called him at Cape Foros." The whole thing was of course not worth a straw, but even the Soviet press made a big thing out of it. *Pravda* even published a feature article by its Paris correspondent with insulting remarks about Chernyaev, who wrote a letter to the editor to set the record straight. But *Pravda* was approaching its agony, and we persuaded Chernyaev to drop the whole thing.

Reaction in London

My four days in London in early October were quite full. In addition to working on the translation, I spent some time with the officials at the Soviet embassy, most of whom I knew well. They were eager to hear the latest news from Moscow, of course, but they were even more anxious to tell me what was worrying them. The office of the ambassador was still occupied by Leonid Zamyatin, whose behavior during the coup my friends described to me in graphic detail.

On August 19, right after the news of the coup came from Moscow, Zamyatin called a meeting of embassy staff and other Soviet officials. He started off by saying "What had to happen has now happened." Gorbachev, he said, had made too many mistakes, and it could not go on like this. He told the diplomats they should give "propaganda backing" to the State Committee for the Emergency. He did not hesitate to say similar things to the British press. The younger diplomats openly disagreed, but Zamyatin stuck to his guns until August 21, and of course made a quick about-face that day. Like a few other ambassadors, he was recalled to Moscow to explain, but to the surprise of the embassy staff, he returned apparently unscathed and was given time to wrap up his business, pack, and say goodbye to his British hosts. The British government, though, refused to talk to him.

"Pavel, this is a disgrace," my colleagues at the embassy told me. "Look, he is taking his time, he may stay another month or two, for all we know. In the meantime, great damage is being done to our relations with this country. Something has to be done."

There was not much I could do, but I was concerned. Zamyatin invited me to his office for a talk and it was a profoundly depressing conversation. Apparently he had persuaded himself that he had behaved properly during the coup—not worse, and perhaps even better, than most of the other ambassadors. "The situation was so confusing," Zamyatin complained. "I gave that foolish interview, but you know the British press—it blew it all out of proportion."

I contradicted Zamyatin on one point. The situation on August 19 was not really confusing, I said, but very clear.

Still Zamyatin took his time to work on me. His plan was clear; he wanted to drag his final weeks in London out as long as possible, to create the impression that he was not leaving under a cloud. The old propaganda chief of the Brezhnev government was playing out the endgame as best he could.

The day after I came to London I went to the Foreign Office to talk to a high-ranking official dealing with relations with the Soviet Union. The embassy arranged that meeting for me, and I found it quite revealing. The official mentioned Zamyatin almost in passing ("Frankly, we are very surprised that he is still here. Mr. Hurd mentioned it to Mr. Pankin in New York but I am afraid he phrased it too mildly. It's not good for our relations") and I answered that as far as I knew the matter was settled—in principle. But most of our conversation was about the situation in the Soviet Union.

The British official minced no words. "We are watching the situation very closely," he said. "On the one hand, the republics seem to be moving toward signing an economic agreement, and that is good. On the other hand, Ukraine seems increasingly inclined to go it alone politically. If it confirms its political independence on December 1, as seems increasingly likely, Russia may not want to stay in such an abridged Union, and twelve fully independent states would probably come into being." Britain would for the time being continue to deal with the center, he continued, but within six or seven weeks it would have to rethink its position. December 1—the date of the Ukrainian plebiscite to confirm the Declaration of Independence—would be a watershed, he said, and he asked me what I thought about that.

I replied that the situation was indeed complex and that much depended on the position the West would take. "Do you want to help our country disintegrate? Then, of course, you may consider December 1 the watershed, or in fact the green light. But is it really in your interest to see twelve independent states? And are you sure that the Ukrainians' vote for the Union on March 17 no longer means anything? December 1 should not be the end of the process but a beginning—before independence is recognized, things like the army, borders, and human rights would have to be addressed. Is it not in your interest to see them resolved?" I argued forcefully.

My British host listened with apparent interest, but he did not seem impressed. He repeated that Britain would have to reconsider its position after December 1. His mind was all made up.

Intelligence Activities Discussed in London

The British official brought up another subject—an interesting one, and one that is discussed only with an administration you expect will stay in charge for some time at least. The subject was the activities of the two countries' intelligence services. My host began by saying that the British government viewed the activities of Soviet foreign intelligence on British soil as having gone beyond reasonable limits. Of course, he admitted, British intelligence was also active in the Soviet Union, but now that the Cold War had ended we should discuss how intelligence activities might be changed: they should become less hostile and keep within reasonable bounds.

"Look at our relations with other countries," he said, and after a pause added, "let us say, France or Israel. We do have some intelligence people there, but we do not engage in hostile activities, or aggressive recruitment. We should begin discussing these things. If your people have any ideas about it, they will find us receptive."

I responded only by saying that I personally would be in favor of discussing any problem. To myself I thought the idea should be tried, although even then I doubted that such things can be decided through formal talks. They might be helpful, but change can be effective only if it results from a slow evolution, a kind of cultural shift that can take generations to become complete.

I had always been skeptical about the obsession and fascination with foreign intelligence of many people raised in the Cold War years. Much of the work intelligence services do is against each other. The hard facts they are able to produce as a result of covert activities are often difficult if not impossible to interpret, or they can be developed just as well by studying open sources. The game of mirrors and dirty tricks is draining, corrupting, and ultimately morally wrong. I know that some essentially good people were and still are involved in it, but there is little in their work that I would call a saving grace.

Alexander Yakovlev once told me how Kryuchkov always tried to exaggerate to Gorbachev the effectiveness of foreign intelligence, saying that billions of dollars had been saved thanks to the political, economic, and technological information provided by his people. Perhaps that is what a spy chief ought to believe and say, but I have always believed that the only justification for engaging in what they do is that the others are also doing it. So my British host's suggestion had some appeal for me. Whether it was ever made, officially or otherwise, to the Russian government that soon replaced ours in Moscow, I do not know. But my host obviously wanted me to take it to the very top, and I did.

I also talked with an old friend of mine, a U.S. diplomat stationed in London whom I knew at the time of the INF talks and then later in Moscow. I told him about my discussion of the Union issues at the Foreign Office, and he was not surprised. He himself would like to see the Union preserved, he said, and this was generally the preference of all Western countries. There are two basic reasons for this, he explained. "Number one, if there is a common state, we'll feel much more comfortable about your nuclear weapons and the military in general. And secondly, we would prefer to deal with the center so far as economic and financial assistance is concerned." He continued: "We want to help you because your democracy will not survive if the economy collapses. And we feel we could do it better through some kind of center."

My friend confirmed my impression that there was some drift in the British position, but he said it was happening more at the expert level than at the political level. Answering a question I put to him bluntly, he told me the U.S. government did not necessarily regard December 1 as a watershed. At least, he said, Secretary Baker and his close associates, some of whom he knew well, were counseling a cautious approach.

The Economic Agreement and Foreign Debt

In Moscow I told Gorbachev in some detail about my impressions. He did not comment a great deal, but subsequent events showed that he took note of at least some of the points I made. He seemed concerned about the situation in the country, but he did not regard it as hopeless. "Slowly and with great effort," he said, "we are putting the situation back on track. Once the republics sign the economic agreement—and I am sure almost all of them will—other things will begin to fall into place. They must stick together. It's not because I want it, it's because they need it."

That was true, but many people I talked to were much less optimistic about the ability of the republics' leaders to understand what was necessary and to act accordingly.

Yavlinsky, who came to see Chernyaev from time to time, was increasingly frustrated. The economic agreement his team had prepared was ready for signing, but the leaders of the republics were still maneuvering, engaged in political games. Their experts were dragging their feet on the various annexes to the agreement, detailing the mechanisms of cooperation in various fields. Behind every tree, they saw the "hated center." And fighting the center seemed much more important to them than the welfare of the people, who were increasingly affected by the disintegration of the economy.

Another issue that became political, to Yavlinsky's growing frustration, was the Soviet Union's foreign debt. The country was nearly bankrupt, but the West was willing to consider easing the terms of debt repayment. In the new political situation, however, this had to be coordinated with the republics, and their leaders immediately saw the potential for politicking and demagoguery inherent in this issue. Ukraine and Uzbekistan said they had their own ideas about how to divide the debt. Yavlinsky complained about the economic illiteracy of many of the republics' representatives, and he definitely had a point there. As for politicking, I felt he had been guilty of it himself. He had not always been a predictable and loyal partner for Gorbachev; he was more interested in having his way on every issue than in moving ahead prudently and doing what was possible at a given moment. He wanted to be proven right, just for the satisfaction of it. But there is no doubt that Yavlinsky is smart, and he may well have a political future.

Yeltsin Plays the Waiting Game and Gorbachev's Future Is Uncertain

In late October, as the nights grew longer and the weather worsened, the mood in the Kremlin grew darker. It was becoming increasingly clear that Yeltsin wanted total control, and there was little if any room for Gorbachev in his plans. Even though the republics, including Ukraine, signed the economic agreement and the Russian leaders were going through the motions of drafting another version of the Union treaty, Gorbachev looked weaker with every passing day.

Yeltsin returned from his vacation in an aggressive mood. His advisers had persuaded him that he was in danger of losing the power and authority he had gained in August. He began issuing decrees that put "under Russia's jurisdiction" various branches of government and the economy.

Gorbachev was in no position to resist Yeltsin. He concentrated on saving what he felt could still be saved by completing a treaty that would preserve under common jurisdiction at least some indispensable areas, such as the army (particularly the strategic forces, while allowing the republics some military forces of their own), coordination of foreign policy—while allowing the republics to become subjects of international law—and common energy and transportation systems. Yeltsin and his people pretended that they agreed with this, but they were actually playing a waiting game, to see what could be done after December 1.

In mid-October two academics, whom Gorbachev knew even though they were not particularly close to him, wrote a memo to him describing their view of the situation and suggesting he consider resigning. They said that "the new politicians," who owed their existence to Gorbachev's perestroika, were cynically abusing him and the country and that he should say so. "If you go now, denouncing the game that they are playing, and wait on the sidelines," they wrote, "we are ready to help you develop the policies and tactics that would enable you to continue in politics and to return when the time comes."

I was appalled when I saw the memo. Although I agreed with the analysis, I thought the advice was exactly wrong. What could be more unlike Gorbachev than quitting before the game was over? Such a step would have left him open to the accusation that he did not discharge his duty and was responsible for the collapse of the country.

Gorbachev, so far as I know, read the memo but refused to take the advice. To me, it was more proof that the quality of advice he was receiving was mediocre at best. Apparently, few if any of his advisers were recommending what seemed the most sensible course to me: getting the republics to reaffirm the concept of the transitional period and focusing on getting the economic agreement implemented while letting the Union treaty wait a while. Tactically, he also would have done well to announce early that he would not seek the office of the president of the Union. Finally, he should have said early and clearly that he was not against the independence of any republic and was ready to discuss a special status for Ukraine once it reaffirmed its independence on December 1. Eventually, Gorbachev did all those things, but it was too late. In fairness, I don't know whether it would have helped if he had acted earlier.

Yeltsin Takes Aggressive Steps

The real problem, though, was Yeltsin's eagerness to get to the Kremlin—and to be the only man there.

In the second half of October we in Chernyaev's office were working, among other things, on a draft of Gorbachev's speech at the opening of the Conference on the Middle East in Madrid. By any measure just a year before, the fact that the Soviet Union was co-sponsoring and co-chairing the conference—its major foreign policy goal for years—would have been considered a great success.

But other things were on people's minds. The Middle East—a political focal point for decades and a permanent crisis around which political and diplomatic careers were made or broken—seemed insignificant compared with the crisis that was shaking the Soviet Union. Foreign policy goals, I thought, are almost always achieved when they become nearly or totally irrelevant.

On his return from vacation, Yeltsin acted aggressively to deprive Gorbachev of much of his residual power. Some of his decrees could perhaps be justified by the need to have a major redistribution of authority within a new Union, but most could not. Yeltsin and his people felt no need to provide any explanation or justification. They just went ahead and left it to Gorbachev's people to wonder and to try to answer questions from reporters.

Finally, at the Congress of Russia's People's Deputies in late October, Yeltsin made a speech that left no doubt he had chosen to push radically forward without consulting with the other republics or with the center. His speech still included some ritualistic references to Russia's readiness to work with others for a new Union, but no one was deceived. Not in Moscow and not, as we saw a few days later, abroad. Yeltsin let it be known that he was the chief policymaker in the Soviet Union, and he clearly relished it. The bottom line of the speech was: Russia can go it alone, it won't mind going it alone, and whatever remained of Gorbachev's powers could just as well be disregarded.

On the eve of Gorbachev's departure for Madrid we sat down together with some of my colleagues in Chernyaev's office to discuss the developments. Yeltsin's speech and his promise to decontrol quickly almost all prices had caused another round of panic buying in Moscow shops. People in the streets seemed concerned and depressed. Our mood was similar.

"This is the end," one of my colleagues said. "He is ready to destroy the country."

I disagreed somewhat. Perhaps, I said, it is inevitable that fifteen independent republics should emerge in place of the Soviet Union. After all, once you've said the republics are sovereign—and even Stalin's constitution said so, what could prevent them from taking the next step? But did Yeltsin know what to do with the army and all those other things that cannot be easily dismembered? I asked. I thought he didn't, and therefore I said that there might still be a chance to create some kind of process that would put the developments—even if they were inevitable—on a more reasonable track.

Apparently, Gorbachev thought it could still be done. Judging by some of Alexander Yakovlev's private remarks and the cables he sent from Washington, where he went a couple of weeks later, he shared that view.

An Era Ending Too Rapidly

Gorbachev had meetings with U.S. President George Bush in Madrid, which turned out to be their last meetings as presidents. They talked twice—at lunch in the Soviet embassy on November 30 and at a small private dinner hosted by King Juan Carlos, at which the Spanish prime minister, Felipe Gonzales, was also present. As I interpreted their conversations I thought that no one could predict the course the developments might take within the next weeks or months, but an era was definitely coming to a close, an era that turned out to be much shorter than would be required for the transition from the Cold War to a new relationship to be smooth.

Bush, and particularly Baker, were clearly concerned about Yeltsin's speech, and even more, about some other things they were hearing from Moscow. Baker indicated that the American embassy had made representations about some aspects of Yeltsin's speech even before it was made public. Apparently, the American embassy had some good sources in the Russian president's camp. Underlying the remarks and questions of both Bush and Baker was a single theme: "We don't really understand what is happening in your country. Do you?"

Gorbachev's answers were, as usual, extensive and quite detailed, amounting to an expression of his remaining hopes, not those of a man who had conceded defeat. Those hopes were based on the fact that work on the draft Union treaty was continuing and that the republics needed one another, at least economically. Gorbachev took the position of someone who would fight to the end because he believed that the people both of his country and of the world needed a Soviet Union that remained together in some form. I saw that Gorbachev still had the sympathy of Bush and Baker, but I also saw something else.

Right after their meeting, Gorbachev and Bush held a press conference at the Soviet embassy. I did not have to interpret it, so I stood on the podium, a few yards away from the two presidents, ready to help if there was any conversation between them or some technical problem. As they were answering questions from the reporters, I watched the audience. As usual, the first row was occupied by U.S. and Soviet officials.

I looked at the Americans, some of them people I knew well and regarded as friends, trying to interpret for myself the expressions on their faces. That was not difficult. As they watched Gorbachev, their expressions were skeptical, cold, and indifferent. "To them, he is already a goner," I thought. I wished I was wrong, but there could be no mistake about it. They had all the information the U.S. government could gather; they worked for an administration that was sympathetic to Gorbachev even though it had not done enough to help him; they were, I thought, basically good people. But they had now concluded that Mikhail Gorbachev belonged to the past. Could it be that I was reading too much into their faces? I looked again. I was sure I was not.

A day after the official opening of the Conference on the Middle East in Madrid, Gorbachev and Bush were invited to the king's palace for a private dinner. The talk, which was surprisingly frank, focused on the Soviet Union. Felipe Gonzales was the most emphatic in arguing that some kind of unity had to be preserved in our vast country. "Fragmentation is dangerous," he insisted, "and once it starts it cannot be stopped. It won't end in Russia. Europe will be the victim too. Europe needs these two pillars—the European Community in the West and the Soviet Union in the East."

Gonzales was one of the most impressive foreign leaders I met—well-informed, articulate, and passionate in defending what he believed in. Later I learned that in his private talks with Gorbachev he encouraged him to persevere—not to be content with just an economic agreement between the republics but to go for the Union treaty. Gonzales, like Gorbachev, believed in policies rather than politics, was issue-oriented, and had a clear position on every problem. One could disagree with him, but his belief that issues matter and that government must not let things drift was admirable. I felt that he was thinking and defining his positions more clearly than others.

At the time of the August coup, Gonzales did not hesitate to speak out against the plotters. He also telephoned Bush, who was said to be uncertain about what to say and who worried that a firm denunciation of "the new authorities" might jeopardize the gains of the past few years and rekindle the Cold War. France's Mitterrand had similar doubts, but not Gonzales. One might argue that it was easier for him to take a clear stand because he was not, after all, the leader of a nuclear superpower. But the argument could be reversed: the leader of a modest European country could have easily kept silent or confined himself to some perfunctory statement, as some actually did.

King Juan Carlos too was outspoken at that dinner. He said he was appalled by Yeltsin's speech. "What about dignity?" he asked rhetorically. "Whatever the power struggle, one should think about how one's speech would look to the outside world. The Soviet Union still exists, so how can he speak as if it already didn't?"

Behind the emotions of our Spanish hosts was, of course, the reality of their own country. "The demonstration effect" of the disintegration of the Soviet Union was clearly a factor in the unraveling of Yugoslavia, then gaining momentum, and who could say which country would be next? Spain too was a multiethnic society, and the king and Gonzales spoke with concern and disgust about extreme nationalism.

The king, whose position is supposed to be mostly ceremonial, clearly cared about his country. I recalled the day in 1981 when a group of military officers attempted a coup in Spain. Madrid was the venue of a CSCE follow-up meeting, and I was interpreting there. For several hours the situation was uncertain; the military seized the parliament building and held the deputies captive. A colleague of mine and I were in my hotel room watching television and waiting for any kind of news to clarify things. Finally, long past midnight, it was announced that the king would speak to the nation. As he appeared on the television screen, his face was tense, but he spoke in a firm voice. "The Crown, as a symbol of the nation's permanence, will not tolerate this attempt to stop the democratic process," he said, and his statement was of key importance in defeating the coup. In October 1991, as I translated the comments of the king, who spoke good English, I could not help but think of historical analogies and similarities—and also, of the differences.

That evening Bush seemed pensive and sometimes confused. He was asking Gorbachev questions about recent developments, about Yeltsin, and particularly about Ukraine. "Do you think Kravchuk will win the elections? Our people have some doubts about that," he added before Gorbachev had time to answer.

"Oh yes, he will," Gorbachev said without adding anything.

"And do you think that after that he will join you in some kind of Union or association?" Bush asked.

"Of that I am not sure," Gorbachev responded quickly. "But I know one thing. Whatever happens in the near future, Russia and Ukraine eventually will be together. Those two nations are branches of the same tree. No one will be able to tear them apart."

Gonzales agreed. He knew a great deal about Ukraine, Kazakhstan, and other republics.

The conversation veered toward the election that Bush was already thinking about. "I dread the next year," Bush said. "The election year is tough—all the issues become so distorted. I really don't know how we are going to get through it," he continued, in what seemed like an overstatement to me. His problems, and the problems of his country, were not even remotely comparable to those of Mikhail Gorbachev and the Soviet Union.

The next day Gorbachev was going back to face all those problems, but he made a stopover in France, at Mitterrand's persistent request, for a meeting at Latche, in the south of France, from where the French president came. I was not present during those talks, but on the margins of that meeting I had the same impression I had in Madrid, that an era was ending and that it was ending too rapidly for anyone's good. The diplomats from the Soviet embassy, many of whom I knew well, seemed confused and uncertain about their future; the press seemed hostile or indifferent. Some Soviet reporters had clearly changed their orientation, which in and of itself was not terrible—but they did it clumsily.

At the press conference the most hostile question was asked by a Soviet reporter whom some people on our team remembered as a zealous Communist propagandist only a few years before. Both Gorbachev and Mitterrand seemed rather tired as they were answering, and Mitterrand did not seem particularly supportive of Gorbachev. As we were going to the airport, Chernyaev told me that the French president had seemed much more forthcoming and supportive during the talks than he was at the press conference, but that made the contrast even more disconcerting. "His friends are writing him off," Chernyaev said as the bus sped through the sunlit rolling hills of southern France.

Fourteen
THE FINAL WEEKS
November-December 1991

Gorbachev Pushes Ahead on the Union Treaty

On the flight back to Moscow, Gorbachev invited a few people to lunch with him in the small compartment that served as an in-flight conference room. There was Chernyaev, Gorbachev's press secrertary Andrey Grachev, and Grachev's predecessor Vitaly Ignatenko, recently appointed director-general of TASS, and also myself and Vitaly Gussenkov, a longtime aide in Gorbachev's office.

The conversation was rambling and not clearly focused, but the bottom line was that Gorbachev had no intention of calling it quits. He was impressed that all the foreign leaders he had talked to were worried about the possible disintegration of the Soviet Union. "They understand it better than those guys back home," he said. "They want at least some predictability, and they know they won't get it if the country falls apart."

The question, of course, was how to halt or manage a process that had already gone quite far. Gorbachev had one answer: to push ahead with the Union treaty process while supporting Yeltsin's determination to pursue a radical economic reform. That seemed to be the correct course—even the skeptical Chernyaev did not disagree.

One person on the plane who seemed pessimistic about the chances for success was Raisa Gorbachev. She was not saying much, but it was clear she had grave concerns on her mind.

As the days became shorter and the weather more and more gloomy in November—always a rather cheerless month in Moscow—there were two episodes in the middle of the month that seemed to offer hope. On November 14 Gorbachev and the leaders of several republics—including Russia, Byelorussia, and Kazakhstan, but not Ukraine—agreed on a text for the Union treaty. Gorbachev, Yeltsin, and others held a press conference at Novo-Ogarevo, right after a long and dramatic session of the State Council. They all seemed exhausted and psychologically drained. As Gorbachev recalled later, the session had included his walkout to protest the other participants' intransigence and unwillingness to compromise, an appeal from the others for him to return, and finally agreement on the text. The participants agreed to initial it in a few days, after discussion of some "fine print" details at the expert level. This might have been another mistake by Gorbachev—not insisting on initialing the text promptly.

But to almost everyone's surprise, Gorbachev did look like a winner in the late evening of November 14, as Yeltsin and others spoke into the microphones on live television repeating the phrase "The Union will exist. There will be a Union." Watching the live broadcast with my colleagues, I felt that they, like me, were surprised Gorbachev had pulled it off.

The next day, I talked with a co-worker about it. It seemed that the Union treaty had a chance, but what about Ukraine? The polls indicated that the vote for independence would be overwhelming. We believed that Gorbachev and Yeltsin should make a statement that they accepted Ukrainian independence but that in their view it was not tantamount to outright secession and did not rule out association with the Union. They could offer to sign a defense treaty with Ukraine first—which in addition to the economic agreement Ukraine had already signed could have created a strong bond while allowing it to go ahead with acquiring the trappings of an independent country.

Later Gorbachev indicated that he had a basically similar plan, but two things were needed for it to succeed: Gorbachev's clear statement of support for Ukrainian independence, which he was reluctant to make, probably for fear of being accused of provoking a landslide "yes" vote, and Yeltsin's willingness to work with Gorbachev and accept him as president at least for a transitional period, which could be rather short. That second condition was lacking, but in mid-November that was not yet fully clear.

Shevardnadze Reappointed as Foreign Minister

The other event that supported the impression that Gorbachev might have a chance to pull the country through the crisis was Shevardnadze's return to the post of foreign minister. I was in my slotlike room adjoining Chernyaev's huge and inconvenient office when Tamara Alexandrova, our secretary, looked in and said I was being summoned to Gorbachev's office. No meetings with foreigners had been scheduled, as far as I knew, so I was curious about what the sudden call could mean.

Gorbachev's secretary let me in immediately. I saw the president sitting at his desk and, in two chairs on the other side of the desk, Shevardnadze and Pankin. They were silent when I entered. Whatever discussion there had been between them was apparently now over. Gorbachev's secretary later told me it had lasted more than two hours.

Gorbachev asked me to call the office of John Major and request an urgent talk with the British prime minister. "Tell them it's not on any issue of bilateral relations or an international problem," he said, "but that there is something I want to talk to him about before making an important decision."

I thought I knew what Gorbachev wanted to discuss with Major and was glad that it was happening. When I contacted 10 Downing Street, I was told that the prime minister was at a meeting out of his office and that they did not know when they could talk to him. I suspected that Major's office was reluctant to commit their boss to a telephone discussion of some sticky issue—such as, for example, the apportionment of the Soviet Union's foreign debt. Negotiations between a G-7 delegation and a Soviet delegation including representatives from the republics were then under way in Moscow and seemed to be going nowhere.

I repeated Gorbachev's request with some emphasis, including his wording about an important decision that he must make soon, and I said I would call again within half an hour. I then returned to Gorbachev's office and told him about my conversation. "I think that was the best I could achieve now," I said, "but you probably will be talking with Major in thirty minutes." I turned out to be right, and when I called back I was told that the prime minister would be on the line in a minute or two.

With Shevardnadze and Pankin still in the room, Gorbachev told Major what it was all about. "John, I need your help on a rather urgent matter. Yesterday at the State Council we decided to move rapidly toward a new

Union and to begin setting up new government departments even before the Union treaty is signed. We'll have a combined ministry of foreign affairs and foreign trade. And all of us, including Boris Yeltsin, agree that Eduard Shevardnadze should be the new foreign minister. I have offered Boris Pankin the post of state counselor on foreign affairs, but he tells me he would prefer to work as ambassador to a European country. The post of ambassador to Great Britain is now vacant, and I think he would be a good ambassador to your country. So I need your consent to this appointment before I can make an announcement. I know there are some formalities to be taken care of in such cases, but I need your agreement today."

Major was clearly pleased to hear all this. He said he welcomed Shevardnadze's appointment and that he would be glad to see Pankin in London. He had to see the Queen about consent to receive the ambassador, and he would be seeing her in the evening but would try to have an answer even sooner, and he was sure the answer would be positive. "We'll let you know through our embassy in Moscow as soon as we can," Major said. In a minute the conversation was over. Everything was set.

I went out of Gorbachev's office, and Shevardnadze and Pankin left a few minutes later. I was glad to see Shevardnadze on Gorbachev's team again. Given what had happened over the last months, I was not sure there could ever be the old warmth between them. The appointment was a political deal for both of them, but I thought it was a good one. By striking it, both of them were expressing the hope that a Union—and a common foreign policy—could be preserved. Later Tarasenko told me in private discussions that they were "giving themselves perhaps a year," knowing that developments were moving on inexorably and that the best that could be done was to carry out an orderly transition to something different—they did not know what. He may have been saying that with the benefit of hindsight, but anyway their guess was wrong, and the time allotted by history, or by the power hungry people waiting for their chance, was much less than that.

The U.S. Stance on Ukrainian Independence

The final collapse began on November 25. At the meeting of the State Council on that day Yeltsin refused to initial the draft Union treaty. Speaking to the press, Gorbachev tried to put the best possible face on it, and it was true that Yeltsin had agreed to a resolution that contained approval of the text and recommended it for discussion in the republics' parliaments. But the message of his refusal to initial the text was unmistakable, and it was not lost on either the media or the Western governments. It became clear it was extremely unlikely that the treaty would be signed in 1991; it was also clear that Gorbachev would not be getting any help from Yeltsin after the Ukrainian referendum. By working together they could have established a more or less orderly process, but Yeltsin turned his back on Gorbachev. Perhaps he thought that he had saved him in August and that once was enough, maybe more than enough.

A couple of days later I was watching the news on CNN when it was almost routinely announced that a policy meeting had taken place at the White House in Washington to discuss the U.S. stance on Ukrainian independence. It was reported that the decision was not to recognize it immediately after the referendum but to "move toward recognition quickly," within a few weeks. I told Chernyaev and my colleagues about the news. "Whatever the details of the decision made by Bush," I said, "this announcement is a real blow." Everyone agreed.

Later, in a telephone conversation with Gorbachev after December 1, Bush sought to explain himself. He sounded defensive. He said he hoped a quick recognition of "the Ukrainians' aspirations for independence" would make them feel more comfortable working with Gorbachev and perhaps becoming involved in the Union treaty process. The explanation sounded lame to me, and Gorbachev did not even bother to argue with it.

Clearly, there were many avenues available to the administration if it really wanted to encourage the Ukrainian leaders to work with Gorbachev. But the administration did not have such a policy. Did it have any policy? In a moment of frankness a friend at the U.S. embassy told me what had happened at that White House policy meeting in late November. The two cases were presented—one for quick recognition, the other for a wait-and-see attitude.

"Bush, as usual, cut it down the middle," my friend said, "and that allowed the proponents of recognition to present the decision to the media the way they wanted to. And it's all a matter of perceptions."

I asked him whether he thought the presence of Russia's foreign minister Andrey Kozyrev in Washington at that time had anything to do with the administration's decision, and he said he did not think so. I was not so sure. Then, and particularly later, Kozyrev had a habit of making contemptuous remarks about Gorbachev in conversations with his foreign counterparts, some of whom then passed on those remarks to Gorbachev or his people. I found Kozyrev's behavior inexplicable and unprofessional, and later there were many occasions when I doubted his professionalism even more. Russia deserved a better foreign minister.

Yeltsin Loyalists Execute Their Game Plan

In December 1991 Kozyrev, whom I had known as a rather nondescript though clearly career-minded mid-ranking official, was among the small group of Yeltsin loyalists and confidants who were planning and executing the final blows: the killing off of the Soviet Union and of Gorbachev's Union treaty. In hindsight it may look almost easy, but in reality it wasn't. Too many things had to be done in a precise and carefully planned fashion, and one has to admit that Gennady Burbulis, Sergey Shakhrai, and Andrey Kozyrev did it perfectly. It cost the country and its people dearly, and it was the last "perfect thing" they were able to do. But no one can deny that they executed their game plan with almost German precision, a rare thing in the history of Russia.

During the week between December 1 and December 9 Yeltsin talked with Gorbachev a few times, and also with Shevardnadze. I think he was still hesitating at that time, unlike his lieutenants. It is not easy, after all, to do what the leaders of Russia, Ukraine, and Byelorussia finally did on December 8. Like many other people, I was not able to predict what they would do, but at one point I came close. That was in a conversation we had in our office on Friday, December 6, on the eve of the Yeltsin-Kravchuk-Shushkevich Minsk summit.

One of my colleagues, normally a pessimist, said perhaps something good might come out of the Minsk summit, if only because for the first time in months Ukraine was involved in any kind of discussion with other republics. I disagreed, though normally I took a more optimistic view than he did. "The thing about the three of them," I said, "is that for reasons of their own each hates or dislikes Gorbachev. And I think this will be the guiding factor at their meeting. This will determine their decision."

Few people had expected the unraveling to happen as quickly as it did. I remember Gorbachev and Shevardnadze dining with Bob Strauss, the U.S. ambassador, a few days before the Minsk meeting. The dinner was at Gorbachev's official country retreat, a large house within the Novo-Ogarevo compound, that used to belong to a millionaire Russian merchant. The atmosphere in those days was gloomy, and the news from Ukraine was not good: Kravchuk had just declared himself to be commander-in-chief of all forces located in Ukraine, and both he and his nationalist opponents insisted that the vote for independence had confirmed Ukraine's secession.

Gorbachev and Shevardnadze, and the Americans who were present (Ambassador Strauss and Dwayne Andreas, a leading U.S. businessman and an old friend of both Gorbachev and Strauss) were with their wives, but the conversation was far from light and the ladies did nothing to sweeten it. In fact, from some of their remarks, particularly those of Mrs. Shevardnadze, Nanuli, I perceived that their mood was gloomier than that of their husbands and that they felt everything might end very quickly. But Gorbachev and Shevardnadze seemed determined to try to save what could still be saved.

Strauss, in the few months he had spent in Moscow, had made up his mind about the country in which he was ambassador and about the U.S. interests there. From what he was saying it was clear that he regarded the collapse of the Soviet Union as not at all desirable from the standpoint of those interests. It is difficult to say what his prognosis was at that time, but it was probably far from what actually happened a few days later. Strauss was leaving for the United States, and he told Gorbachev and Shevardnadze he was thinking of ways to help them to keep the country together. "Too many people in the United States just don't understand how important it is to avoid chaos here," he said. From some of his comments in the United States a few days later, it was clear how much he disliked the surprise sprung by Yeltsin and others not just on Gorbachev but, it seemed, also on him.

Memory, even recent memory, is selective, but what I remember well is that of the many feelings I experienced on the morning of December 9—when I heard on television the news of the "Minsk agreement to dissolve the Soviet Union," creating the Commonwealth of Independent States (CIS)—surprise and astonishment were the least intense. I had known that Yeltsin and his associates would do something to dispose of Gorbachev, and now they had done it. I was somewhat surprised by the way Yeltsin and his people, assisted by Leonid Kravchuk and Stanislav Shushkevich, did it—not stopping at "abolishing" a country to get rid of its president. It amounted to a coup and was of course illegal, but, as became clear within a few days, they had evaluated the balance of forces precisely and cynically.

An hour later I was discussing what was clearly a new situation with my colleagues in the Kremlin. There was a feeling of shock and bitterness about the unfolding drama. The country was being divided like some inherited estate, and the heirs were acting quickly and heavy-handedly, without lawyers or accountants, in an almost medieval way. But those were, of course, our emotions. There remained the question of what could or should be done in this situation.

The Minsk Agreement and Its Aftermath

The question of Gorbachev's resignation now became a serious one. This was not the first time the possibility was discussed, and just a few days earlier, I had been asked about it by a British diplomat, in the presence of others. I knew what Gorbachev thought then, and I replied that he had firmly decided not to leave the ship. But the Minsk agreement obviously changed the situation dramatically. Gorbachev called a meeting of his Political Consultative Council and caucused with a group of leading experts on constitutional law. One person who was close to him during those days told me that Gorbachev's immediate impulse was to resign—"The hell with it all!" But the way Yeltsin, Kravchuck, and Shushkevich did what they did was so blatantly illegal that immediate resignation by Gorbachev could have been seen as giving the stamp of approval to their actions. It might have seemed as though Gorbachev had just been waiting for a pretext to step down.

There was tension in the corridors of the Kremlin, but no panic or hysteria. People behaved with dignity despite the bitterness most felt. The various views expressed by members of Gorbachev's staff boiled down to perhaps three positions: one, that he should call the whole thing illegal and fight on; two, that he should try to cooperate with the leaders of the republics and institute an orderly process of transition, and perhaps even see where he could fit in it; three, that he should just resign, slam the door. I came down somewhere between those three positions. But above all, I said to Chernyaev when he asked what I thought—and he was always ready to ask for an opinion, regardless of the difference in rank or position—Gorbachev should play it cool. If his patience snaps and he loses his nerve, I said, that will be remembered for years to come.

"Of course what those guys did is illegal, and he should say so," I said to Chernyaev. "They are not even seeking ratification or some kind of consent from their own parliaments. That is the least that must be demanded very firmly, and I think they would have to go to the parliaments. But there should be no doubt about it: the parliaments will ratify it. People are tired, and they will say that a Commonwealth—any kind of association—is better than nothing. Of course, the commonwealth strategy will eventually fail, but don't say so now. And Gorbachev should not look for a position in the commonwealth for himself. It's just undignified to seek anything from those people. As for the resignation—well, he should think about stepping down. But resignation is not the right word. You resign an office that exists. But once the process of creating the Commonwealth has been completed there will be no such office, and no need to resign. There is one thing that must be done before stepping down—whatever you call it. He must make sure the nuclear weapons question is handled properly. He is still commander-in-chief, and it is his responsibility to the country and to the world to see to it that the matter is resolved responsibly and safely, beyond any reasonable doubt. Once this is taken care of, he should go."

Gorbachev did not settle on a course of action immediately. I don't blame him. I do not know what advice he got from his consultative council, and anyway I do not believe their analysis was very incisive or their recommendations very clear. Ultimately he himself had to decide, as always during his years in power. Given the emotions and the turmoil, it was not easy to decide.

Another factor was complicating the situation: The Commonwealth agreement itself was a jerry-built structure, a shell that was almost totally empty and that had only one purpose: to jettison Mikhail Gorbachev. Even that clear goal was complicated by the obvious fact that the perpetrators of the "December coup" had not devised the mechanics of achieving it. At a reception in the U.S. embassy in the evening of December 9, I talked to a U.S. official with whom we always had candid discussions.

"We were in touch with Kozyrev today," he said. "We asked him about Gorbachev, and whether he would still be president when Baker comes to Moscow in about a week. Kozyrev said he did not know."

They did not know many things. Although they talked and behaved confidently they had no idea what they were setting up. A few days later Burbulis went to Brussels to ask for help. Like a student in search of material for a term paper, he asked the officials there for documents on the establishment of the European Community and the mechanics of its functioning. Nor had they any plan for the military aspects of the Commonwealth. As for the status of Russians and other ethnic groups who would overnight become foreigners in countries that were no longer their own, a few months later Yeltsin himself would admit in an interview that they had not given enough thought to that matter when they were "creating the Commonwealth." But they acted confidently, like real winners, during those first days!

A young man I knew fleetingly during one of Shevardnadze's visits abroad, then a low-ranking official in a remote Soviet embassy and now Kozyrev's aide at the Russian foreign ministry, was strutting around at the U.S. embassy reception on December 9. He was condescending as he talked to me. The Russian foreign ministry, he made clear, was preparing to take over Smolenskaya Square.

"Watch out," I said. "You are swallowing more than you can digest. Gorbachev and people like me will not sink in these waters, but you are doing something that will haunt you for years."

We parted without outward animosity, and a few weeks later I saw him at a reception at another embassy. He was quite down. "It's chaos at Smolenskaya," he said. "There is no policy, morale is low, and no one knows when things will settle down."

Gorbachev's first formal statement about the Minsk agreement, issued on December 10, was mercifully brief, nonconfrontational, and left various options open to him. Still, "fighting on" was not really an option, particularly after the three leaders understood that they needed some semblance of legitimacy and put the Minsk agreement before their Supreme Soviets for approval. The parliaments' approval was not really in doubt, but the process made very clear how cheap Yeltsin had sold out everything to Kravchuk in Minsk.

The Ukrainian parliament tagged on to the agreements "amendments" that made the articles on coordination of foreign policy, common defense, free travel, and citizens' rights totally meaningless. When members of the Russian parliament asked Yeltsin about it, he answered that the amendments were "purely editorial."

Everyone probably knew this was not true, but the Russian parliament approved the Minsk agreement overwhelmingly. People were tired of political fights and uncertainty, and they thought something was better than nothing at all. The top military officials thought the same. There was a lot of bad blood between them and Gorbachev, and a hope—of which Yeltsin would quickly disabuse them—that the Russian president would take better care of their needs.

I believe it was after the Russian parliament's decision to approve the Minsk agreement that Gorbachev decided not to resist the process that had taken on its own momentum. He still hoped the process could be made a little more constructive. As I saw from Gorbachev's talks with foreign leaders, that was also their hope. They were looking into the unknown, and they were far less enthusiastic about it than some of their subsequent statements might suggest.

Bush Sends Baker to Moscow

The prospect of many new and totally independent countries—unformed, immature, their elites distasteful or unreliable, and their problems countless— was frightening to the Western leaders steeped in the politics of consensus, evolution, and predictability. George Bush sent Baker to Moscow to find out what was happening. The Russian leaders wanted him to see a celebration of their victory and perhaps to join in it. They were close to triumph—just a few stitches remained, like getting the inevitable consent from Kazakhstan's President Nazarbayev, who despite his bitterness at having been left out of the picture had nowhere else to go.

The Soviet bureaucracy was rapidly beginning to pledge total and undivided allegiance to Yeltsin. The ambassadors abroad had begun to do it even before Minsk, some in subtly diplomatic ways, others rather crudely. Few of them were rewarded for the quick about-face. The top officials of the military and the police did it on the eve of Baker's arrival. Kozyrev said triumphantly to reporters: "Watch the composition of the Russian delegation tomorrow when President Yeltsin will be meeting with Mr. Baker." The delegation included Marshal Shaposhnikov, the Soviet minister of defense, who was offered the position of commander-in-chief of CIS strategic forces, which soon became meaningless, and Minister of Internal Affairs Victor Barannikov.

The turn had been completed and both Gorbachev and Baker knew that when they were meeting in the Catherine Hall of the Kremlin. Some questions remained, but it was clear that this was their last meeting. Shevardnadze and Yakovlev were with Gorbachev, two men who had been with him at the beginning of the road. The grand hall, ornate and majestic, was brightly lit as always, but I had a feeling that darkness surrounded it. It was the twilight of those three men, and also of Chernyaev, who was inconspicuously present. A large chunk of my life was also ending. I had no regrets, and I felt some quiet pride about the things I had done with those men, but it was a sad day.

A Rumor and a Warning

A couple of days before Baker's arrival I had a troubling conversation with a member of Gorbachev's staff, a well-connected and well-informed former

Central Committee official who, incidentally, later worked for Yeltsin's administration. He buttonholed me in the Kremlin corridor and, after a few routine words, said: "I think we should be concerned about Gorbachev's future. I know that efforts are afoot to fabricate a case against him. There is a team searching frantically for 'compromising material,' and the coup-plotters will quite likely change their stories to help frame him."

He was silent for a moment. I thought what he was saying was plausible. In times of trouble people look for a scapegoat, and the new authorities could well be tempted to make Gorbachev one. There were too many precedents for this in Russia's history to ignore this warning.

"Baker is coming here soon," the man went on. "Why don't you talk to your American friends? They could stop it."

I did not answer immediately. I was not at all sure "they could stop it." But should they know about what was going on? The Americans, I thought, were probably aware of these rumors, but this warning seemed more than a rumor, and after some thinking I decided to pass the information on to Baker through Strobe Talbott, a *Time* magazine reporter whom I knew and trusted. He had come to Moscow to observe the rapidly evolving developments, hoping also to interview Gorbachev for the magazine and for the book he was writing.

Talbott had good contacts in the administration, and my message went through quickly. Its essence was that Gorbachev could become a private citizen soon, that he would like to help in the transition from Union to Commonwealth but was not looking for a role in its institutions. The key words were that it should be made clear to Yeltsin that he must not get involved in attempts to fabricate a criminal case against Gorbachev.

Baker took the message seriously, as indicated by the fact that he raised the matter in a one-on-one conversation with Yeltsin. He later told me that he thought I had acted properly. Whether or not the rumors that prompted me to act were true—and I have no way of knowing—I have no regrets about what I did.

Later I permitted Talbott to describe the episode in his book *At the Highest Levels*, co-authored by Michael Beschloss, but unfortunately the book suggested that I had been prompted to act by Gorbachev, that he virtually asked the Americans for protection but did so indirectly to preserve "deniability." Nothing could be further from the truth or more out of character for Gorbachev. He has courage, and he deals openly. James Baker, who described this episode accurately in his book *The Politics of Diplomacy*, is, as he told me, of the same view.

Baker's Last Talk with President Gorbachev

Gorbachev knew that Baker was trying hard "not to get involved in internal affairs"—indeed, Baker said that from the start of their conversation. Gorbachev did not spend much time explaining what had just happened.

"We now have a new reality facing both you and us," he said to Baker. "I want to do my best to make sure that the Commonwealth process does not lead to an even greater disintegration of the country. There is a real danger of that." He continued, speaking to Baker, "As an experienced man, you must understand that an agreement like the one signed in Minsk is easy to conclude but impossible to live by. It's too general."

Baker agreed. "It's just a shell."

Gorbachev went on to say that he was willing to help make the Commonwealth more meaningful and viable and to cooperate in setting proper succession procedures to legitimize it. He had no bitter words for those who were pushing him out. "I wish them good luck even though I don't believe they will succeed. But I want them to at least half succeed—for if they don't, everything we have achieved will be jeopardized."

This worried Baker too, judging by what he said. As someone who appreciated decency and fair play, he was also concerned about the way Gorbachev and his associates were being treated. "You have been our partners and, more important, our friends for many years now. You remain our friends and perhaps, as I said to the press, will remain our partners. Whether that happens is your country's internal affair." (Those words might sound strange today, but at the time Baker may still have hoped that some common international representation of the Commonwealth could be arranged, perhaps by inheriting the Soviet Union's permanent membership in the U.N. Security Council. U.S. diplomats were informally suggesting this until almost the very end.) Baker added, "Whatever happens, you are our friends. And it makes us very sad when we see, as we do on this visit, that you are being treated with disrespect. I'll tell you very frankly: we are against it."

Baker wanted Gorbachev's advice about how the United States should behave during the transitional period. Yeltsin had led Baker to understand that the transition might take until mid-January, but he was not clear about what to expect at the end of the transition. "We were told today that the Commonwealth will be similar to the British Commonwealth, with one exception: the defense component. There would be a common defense made up of all armed forces, with the exception of ground troops. But how can there be a common defense if they plan to have ten fully independent foreign policies? And who will give instructions to the commander-in-chief of the common armed forces?"

Baker was well informed, as always. He knew that the country was being torn apart, not just dissolved, and he knew what that could mean. He recalled how the U.S. Congress had demanded that the administration take a tougher line with the Soviet Union on the Baltics and how the administration had resisted, arguing, among other things, that quick independence could lead to massive violations of the rights of Russians there. "And today we see what is happening there. And we see what is happening in Chechen-Ingushetia, and in the Dniester area, and in Yugoslavia, and that it could be even worse here."

Baker also worried that while the political tug-of-war about the Commonwealth continued, nothing was being done to pull the economy out of the crisis and precious time was being wasted.

Gorbachev agreed. "We have to end this political schizophrenia," he said.

I knew Gorbachev had made up his mind. He would step down even if all the issues he cared about were not handled right. The country could not afford continued political confrontation. Baker was of the same view, but it was his clear preference that the process take orderly and legitimate forms and that a viable Commonwealth emerge as a result. He said as much to Gorbachev, but as so often happened during the Bush-Gorbachev years, the Americans were not able to articulate their preference to all the political forces involved.

Shevardnadze on the Way Out

In fact, the day after Baker left, Yeltsin and Kozyrev acted as though they believed they had the U.S. administration's go-ahead for a quick destruction of the remaining Union structures—specifically the foreign ministry headed by Shevardnadze. Yeltsin issued a decree appropriating to Russia all properties of the foreign ministry in Russia and abroad. Union foreign ministry personnel were being transferred to the Russian ministry. That made Shevardnadze redundant and he understood that and did not want to fight. He held a meeting with his associates in the morning, asked them to thank the staff on his behalf for their cooperation, and left the building at Smolenskaya Square, never to return.

Shevardnadze, with his keen sense of decency and propriety, was perhaps the most unhappy about how things developed in December. He knew that all the rhetoric about the historical inevitability of independence and the need to destroy "the imperial center" was just a screen to obscure the one goal that united "the creators of the Commonwealth": to solve their immediate political problems by removing Gorbachev. "As soon as it's over, Yeltsin will try to establish a new center. He just needs to get you out of the way," Shevardnadze told Gorbachev right after the conversation with Baker.

Shevardnadze's implication, as he confirmed to me later, was that Yeltsin would try to interpret the Minsk agreement as something specific and viable that would bring the republics together rather than separating them, but that he would not succeed. Subsequent events would soon be proving him right: the Commonwealth was dying almost before it was born—it was rarely even mentioned. But in the new scheme of things, Yeltsin was someone Shevardnadze had to deal with as the leader of Georgia that he again became.

The Denouement

What followed was the denouement, the final days and hours, some of which it still hurts me to remember. I recall Chernyaev asking what I intended to do, and my answer that I was surprised at the question. "You can't think I would do anything other than leave government," I answered.

In fact, I had just had a call from the foreign ministry offering me employment after the liquidation of the office of the president of the Soviet Union. "We feel it is our moral duty to offer it to those of our people who left to join the president's office," I was told. The caller was the recently appointed deputy foreign minister in charge of personnel. "Of course," he said, "we are being taken over, so I don't know what is going to happen to myself in a day or two. But we just feel we have to make this offer."

I politely refused. The entire government bureaucracy would soon flock over to the new bosses and wait for their fate to be determined by people like Kozyrev. I understood them, but it was not for me.

Gorbachev was making preparations for stepping down. Basically, it was a question of when and how. During those shortest December days in Moscow, American reporter Ted Koppel of ABC was allowed to film the Kremlin from the inside and to talk with Gorbachev and people who were with him until the end. He talked with Gorbachev about what he had set out to do and why he had not succeeded, at least for now, about his feelings, and about the meaning of life. It was not terribly profound—such conversations rarely are—but it was sincere. I interpreted at those interviews, and I felt Gorbachev was taking the final blows much more courageously than many of the people around him.

Before the last filming session I talked briefly with Yegor Yakovlev, whom Gorbachev had appointed chairman of the radio and television company just a few months before. Yakovlev, a Communist liberal reformer for decades, had been through a lot in his lifetime, but this session was obviously difficult for him.

He asked me what I intended to do after Gorbachev's resignation, and I said I did not know yet. "But I know I just can't go over to work for the new boss, like the staff of the Kremlin cafeteria," I said, and saw I had touched a raw nerve.

He did not try to hide it. "That is my problem," he said, but he did not finish the sentence because the interview was beginning.

During the interview, Gorbachev noticed how depressed Yakovlev was—he seemed to be on the verge of tears—and said, "Well, Yegor, keep your chin up. Everything is only just beginning." He often repeated the phrase afterward, and I think it was that conviction more than anything else that gave him strength in his final weeks as president and during the months that followed.

In those days it seemed that the most important thing for Yeltsin and his team was to humiliate Gorbachev as much as they could. The day after Gorbachev's resignation speech, Yeltsin, Ruslan Khasbulatov, and Gennady Burbulis—the winners and the heirs—came to the Kremlin to take over Gorbachev's office. Between them they drank a bottle of whiskey there—an act of multiple symbolism—and inspected the adjoining rooms. Gorbachev was ordered to vacate his city apartment and country house within days. Rumors were being spread about some compromising material the new government had on Gorbachev from the accused members of the State Committee for the Emergency. The government-orchestrated campaign of harassment against Gorbachev was rolling full steam ahead, but the object of that campaign seemed unperturbed—he was above it. I saw Gorbachev almost every day that December, and more than ever admired his courage. Given the history of this country and the fate of many of its leaders, it was amazing how well he was bearing up.

Now that Gorbachev had reconciled himself to the fact that his project for a new Union had been rejected by the political elite that emerged from perestroika, he had two priorities: one was to make sure the transition to the Commonwealth took place "within a legal constitutional framework," the other concerned nuclear weapons—the nuclear button had to be transferred in a way that was safe and reliable.

"Nothing can be done constitutionally in revolutionary times," I remember Chernyaev saying sometime in mid-December. I had to agree with him. Gorbachev tried to give the Commonwealth some legitimacy by calling for a final meeting of the U.S.S.R. Supreme Soviet that would, as he put it, record formally the end of the Soviet Union and the beginning of something new. He had some support, even from people who had disagreed with him on many issues, like Anatoly Sobchak, one of the few radical democrats who cared about legality and legitimacy. But people like him were already a minority among the new leaders. Few had bona fide democratic credentials, most were former members of the Communist Party apparat, and all seemed to feel instinctively that when an opportunity presents itself power should be grabbed quickly and without regard for legalistic niceties.

When Gorbachev called for a constitutional transitional process, the media, increasingly subservient to Yeltsin and other new leaders, had no difficulty representing it as an attempt to play for time and cling to power. "Those people find me difficult," Gorbachev said of the new leaders to his foreign guests. He met a few foreign emissaries in those final days in the Kremlin, but their visits with him looked more and more like courtesy calls. It seemed that the world too did not particularly care how legitimate the process of transition was. It was almost begging "Make it quick."

Yakovlev and Chernyaev worked with Gorbachev on his letter to the leaders of the eleven republics who were to meet in Alma-Ata to ratify the new composition of the Commonwealth. No longer was it a purely Slavic organization that Yeltsin, Kravchuk, and Shushkevich originally set up. Even though a few people would probably have preferred it to be limited to those three republics, such an outcome was not politically acceptable for Russia. Kravchuk, reluctantly, had to go along. But he was in a strong position to reject anything that seemed to bind Ukraine into something resembling a union. Therefore Gorbachev's sensible suggestions had no chance for approval or even a sympathetic hearing.

I thought there were two proposals he could make with at least some chance of being accepted: about common citizenship and common representation in the U.N. Security Council. But they were both rejected at Alma-Ata, the first by Kravchuk, despite Yeltsin's timid attempt to suggest it, and the second by Yeltsin himself, who regarded Russia's seat on the Security Council as the most cherished prize from this championship fight.

Like most Russians, Yeltsin was, I believe, inwardly dubious about the breakup of the country. In his heart, he probably agreed with Nazarbayev, who said almost plaintively: "But we are still together, are we not?" Yet by conceding to Kravchuk on almost every important point, and by grabbing the Security Council seat, Yeltsin made the breakup inevitable. He returned from Alma-Ata an apparent winner, and he was ready to talk with Gorbachev about the terms of surrender. Gorbachev, realistically, saw it and accepted it.

The Nuclear Button Transfer

Gorbachev had been thinking a great deal about the nuclear button problem. After Minsk, the initial statements of the three leaders, particularly some remarks by Kravchuk, concerning joint control of the button by the leaders of the republics that had nuclear weapons were incredible—they were both politically silly and technically not feasible. Gorbachev did point this out, but I believe that representations by Baker and other Western leaders played a bigger role in the final determination on the issue.

Whatever Gorbachev thought and knew of Yeltsin, he decided that the only way to resolve the issue was to transfer the button to him. Any other decision would have created enormous political or technical problems. Given Yeltsin's well-known personal character traits, transfer of the button to him was the subject of much discussion during those days, both in the Kremlin and elsewhere.

I remember an American reporter saying to me that the world had trusted Gorbachev as a man not given to rash decisions or reckless actions and therefore did not worry about the nuclear button. There was a clear hint in that remark. I had already been thinking about how the issue would be handled, and had concluded there was only one way to go about it. "Well," I said to him, "it is essential that there be single control of the button, that it remains in Moscow, and that all the existing multiple layers of protection and nuclear safety remain in place. That means Yeltsin will have the button."

In his final telephone conversations with Western leaders, Gorbachev insisted that there should be no worry about the nuclear button. But he said he would be transferring it to Yeltsin only in his talk with Bush, two or three hours before his resignation speech. Without too much enthusiasm, Bush welcomed the certainty.

Gorbachev and Yeltsin discussed the procedure for transfer of nuclear weapons control and agreed it would take place in Gorbachev's office right after Gorbachev's television address to the nation announcing that he was stepping down. Yeltsin, however, was incensed at the content of Gorbachev's speech and refused to come. Gorbachev, in turn, rejected the demand that he come to "neutral ground." So right after the speech and Gorbachev's interview on CNN, which I translated, I saw Marshal Shaposhnikov enter Gorbachev's office. Gorbachev would hand over "the button" to him.

Shaposhnikov left the office a few minutes later with two men in civilian clothes—the code operators, whose faces were very familiar to me. They had accompanied Gorbachev on all his trips abroad and certainly had a gift for being inconspicuous. I remembered them sitting in the front section of the presidential plane, almost always silent and with an oddly inexpressive yet dignified look. Amazingly, I had never wondered what they were. Had I thought they were members of the plane crew or of the security detail? I can't say. The question never arose, and one has to give them credit for that.

Reflections on the End of the Soviet Union

My final days in the Kremlin were so busy that I had little time to think about the momentous significance of what was happening. There was a lot of talk in the media and among the "leading lights" of the Moscow intelligentsia about "the end of the last empire." I had always been critical of a great deal in my country, but I had never thought of it as an empire. There was something indecent in how the satraps and propagandists of the old regime were now stigmatizing the country, not the regime.

If an empire had to disappear, why was it dismantled so clumsily, and, people would soon start asking, why was Russia again coming out a loser, a truncated territory with dubious contours, without Kharkov, Odessa, Minsk, the Crimea, and the steppes of southern Siberia—all traditionally Russian lands that now belonged to others? Almost every state that emerged from "the empire" was a mini-empire itself, multiethnic, with disputed borders, and in some cases without any historical roots.

I was sure we would have been much better off in some form of union, so my final hours in the Kremlin were filled with anxiety and great concern, tempered only by the workload. I was translating letters from foreign leaders to Gorbachev, and drafting his letters to Reagan, Thatcher, Bush, Major, and others. I was interpreting his telephone conversations, which he later described in some detail in his book about the events of December 1991.

Two of those conversations I remember well; of the dozens I interpreted, they were unique. One was with John Major; the other, with George Bush. Major called on December 23. We did not know yet when Gorbachev would make his final statement, but it was clear that he would be stepping down within days, maybe hours. The administrators were already reassigning the Kremlin offices to Yeltsin's people, and it was said that Chernyaev's office would go to Burbulis. There could be no more graphic symbol of the fact that power in Moscow was passing into the hands of a different breed of people.

Chernyaev was working with Gorbachev and Yakovlev on the text of the final statement. Gorbachev's letters to foreign leaders were sent out on December 25. Comparing them with my drafts, I saw that Gorbachev had not changed much, that he had just made the text even leaner and less sentimental. I was working on one of those drafts when Gorbachev's secretary called me asking to come by right away. The time was about 6:00 P.M. The security post near the entrance to Gorbachev's office was manned by a larger than usual group of people, and Yeltsin's guards were there too. One did not seem to know me and asked for an I.D. Let him pass, his colleague said to him, and I entered the reception room. Gorbachev's office was on the left, and on the right was the so-called Walnut Room, in which Gorbachev sometimes, but rarely, received foreign guests. More often it was used for private discussions with Soviet officials and small groups.

As I was waiting in the reception room I saw food being taken into the Walnut Room. A table at which there were three men—Mikhail Gorbachev, Alexander Yakovlev, and Boris Yeltsin—was laid. Their conversation, as Gorbachev said to Major later, had begun at noon. When the call from London came, I told Major's secretary that Gorbachev would be on the line shortly. Gorbachev was already emerging from the caucus room. As he shook hands and said something to me, I noticed there was a whiff of liquor on his breath—the three men had obviously sprinkled their dinner with vodka.

Discussing the Transition

On the telephone with Major, Gorbachev told him he was in the midst of discussing the transition and the future with Yeltsin and Yakovlev. He was, however, in no hurry to rejoin them. He talked with Major for almost half an hour, telling him he intended to announce his resignation "in a day or two." He was choosing his words carefully, perhaps partly because he did not want any slips of the tongue caused by the drinks he had had. But there was, I believe, also another reason: the understanding that in those final hours of the Soviet Union and of its president every word was of momentous importance.

"Yeltsin and I both understand our responsibility in this transition," Gorbachev told Major, "and all of us are responsible for ensuring that in this time of turmoil all that we initiated in the country and the world is not lost." Gorbachev was still not prepared to resign himself to the partitioning of the country. "Whatever happens afterward," he said, "this, for the time being, is still one country. Politically, it is being divided, but it should not be torn apart even more." He pleaded with Major to help Russia. "Above all, let us help Yeltsin. I want to help him here, and you should help Russia from over there. Russia will be on the cutting edge of the economic reform, and it will bear the brunt of its hardships. So, once again, let us help Yeltsin."

Major's voice, at the other end of the line, was not much different from usual—warm and yet a little formal. His sentences were so well-rounded and precise as to have an air of superficial formality. But there could be no mistake that Major was deeply moved as he spoke with Gorbachev; he just never crossed the line beyond which he might sound sentimental. He said that he would like to see Gorbachev as soon as things settled down and that he was always welcome in Britain. Mulroney, Bush, and others offered similar invitations, and there was talk in Moscow that Gorbachev might leave the country for a period of time; veiled threats of prosecuting him were already being made. "I might come on a visit one day," Gorbachev invariably replied, "but now my place is here in Russia. Everything will be decided here."

The next day, which turned out to be the day before Gorbachev's last day as president, American newsman Ted Koppel interviewed me for a television documentary about the end of the Soviet Union. On camera and off, we talked about many things—Gorbachev, Ukraine, the CIS, my work in the president's office, and so on. Koppel wondered at the size of the cubicle that passed for my office—it seemed barely adequate to him, "given the importance of all those issues you handle"—and inspected the books and dictionaries I kept there. I was ready to move out.

Koppel asked me whether I agreed with the characterization of what was happening as a coup d'état. I replied that I might, but that Gorbachev had specifically rejected such a characterization. "I would describe it this way," I said, on camera. "This is something that's being done by democratically elected people but in a less than democratic and fair way."

A couple of days later Koppel's documentary was shown on our television, with that remark included. A friend of mine, after watching it, said to me, only half-jokingly and perhaps quite seriously: "I think you should ask the Americans for some kind of protection." Indeed, there was a lot of fear in Moscow during those days, but for some reason I felt free from it. I had a feeling of emptiness, perhaps similar to what Gorbachev described to a reporter who asked him what he felt about having to leave the post of president: "No country, no president. True, we have many presidents now. So losing one is not a big thing. But you've lost the country, and this is much more important."

Gorbachev's Last Telephone Call to Bush

Gorbachev seemed determined to bow out with dignity, but we all felt how difficult his final steps were. On the last day, December 25, the corridors of the Kremlin were hushed, even more quiet than usual. There was an air of waiting. I asked Chernyaev about a telephone talk with President Bush. The Americans had indicated that Bush expected a call from Gorbachev whenever it was convenient to him. "Well, I guess, today is the day," Chernyaev said, and after checking with Gorbachev he asked me to call the U.S. embassy about arranging the call.

It was Christmas Day, and the American embassy was closed. The answering machine gave the telephone number of the marine on duty—in case of emergency involving an American citizen. I did not want to ask for help at the foreign ministry—now the foreign ministry of the Russian Federation, Kozyrev's domain. What should I do?

Finally, I found in one of my address books Jim Collins's home telephone. Jim, the embassy's deputy chief of mission, had become a good friend in the months we worked together. I wished him a merry Christmas and told him what my business was. He gave me the number of the State Department operations desk—"They will put you through wherever the president is"—and promised to help if there was a problem. I then asked the Moscow operator to connect me with that number in Washington. It was early morning there.

The operations desk officer told me President Bush was at Camp David for the Christmas season and that he was asleep, but that I could talk to someone on duty there. A minute or two later I talked to a marine officer at Camp David, who gave his name and answered my questions in a clipped military manner. Yes, the president was asleep, but he would definitely want to talk to President Gorbachev. Yes, it could be at any time convenient to Mr. Gorbachev after 8:00 A.M., eastern standard time. Yes, he would wait for my call to specify the time of the conversation.

Gorbachev's television address announcing his stepping down was scheduled for 9:00 P.M. Moscow time. He decided to talk to George Bush just before then, at 7:00 P.M. As the time approached, there seemed to be more tension, a kind of electricity in the air. I was in Gorbachev's reception room at 6:45. He had allowed a U.S. television team to film his final telephone talk with Bush, and they were busy installing their equipment.

It felt a little unreal—while the president was putting the final touches on the text of his address and the decree passing to Yeltsin control of the Soviet Union's nuclear weapons, American television technicians were coming and going busily, checking their wires and microphones. Who could have thought that this—all of this—were possible just a year ago?

But there was no time for this kind of wondering, analyzing, or waxing sentimental. I was checking the line with Washington. My American colleague was at the other end, greeting me before what I knew was the last such talk not only for Gorbachev but also for me. The right thing to do in such situations—there aren't too many "such situations" in one's life, though—is to keep going in the normal mode, as if it's the usual.

There was no trembling of the fingers in the Kremlin on that day. The American television group recorded the conversation, and Gorbachev has since published most of it in his book about the events of December 1991. So it is in the public domain, and what was said then is not, at least in my opinion, as important as the implications and the connotations. I could not get my mind off those as I interpreted the talk. The two men were saying more or less what could reasonably be expected of them under the circumstances. They were speaking calmly and to the point.

Gorbachev was emphasizing that even in this new situation everything possible must be done to make sure that the cause of democracy in his country was not lost and that the international achievements of the past years were preserved. Bush was telling Gorbachev how much he appreciated what his Soviet counterpart had been able to do.

But I could not help wondering what was going through the minds of those two men. Was Gorbachev perhaps thinking that Bush could have done more for him? Was Bush trying to rationalize some of his decisions, saying to himself that he had done his best and that whatever happened to Gorbachev and to his country was beyond his control or his ability to influence things?

Then and later I often tried to rethink that telephone call, and my conclusion always was that something like those thoughts must have crossed their minds but that both probably pushed them back.

Whatever one's assessment of Gorbachev and Bush, neither could be accused of simplistic thinking. The complexity of everything in the world is something they understand better than most people I know. Gorbachev has a way of taking a large view. He knew that the first attempt to move the country toward normalcy, morality, and natural evolution was perhaps bound to be only partly succcessful. "Democracy, freedom of choice, political and intellectual freedom, social justice and the rule of law are great goals," he had said to a group of reporters a week before, "they just cannot be achieved overnight." So how could he blame Bush for getting burned in the process? But some of us did blame the Americans.

I remember someone saying that Bush's policies had the curious effect of having Mikhail Gorbachev out and Saddam Hussein in. The person who said it probably understood that his remark was unfair. Whatever one thought of George Bush, he could not be blamed for failing to recognize Gorbachev's role and importance. He talked to Gorbachev the man of history, and Gorbachev was a man he respected in a very human and personal way. That much was unmistakable.

Somehow I was thinking all that and was still able to concentrate on what the two men were saying to each other. Professionally, I would not recommend getting distracted that way, but this was not an ordinary day, and not an ordinary talk for everyone involved. It went well, considering.

The Final Statement

Finally, the moment some dreaded and many had been waiting for approached. A few minutes before nine o'clock the room from which Gorbachev was to speak to the people on live television was filled with associates, reporters, technicians, security guards, and some others who happened to be there—most of the faces were familiar to me. We were speaking in hushed voices while Gorbachev shuffled some papers, taking a final look at the text of his speech and exchanging remarks with the technicians.

Once again, when he began to speak, I found myself doing several things at once: listening to his speech, watching the people, and thinking about the years past and what was happening. It was a good speech. Gorbachev spoke without rancor or bitterness, but also without any sweet good wishes to his successors, and Yeltsin was said to have been enraged by it—understandably, I believe. It was, on balance, a wise speech, and I am sure it will be read for many years hence.

As I watched the faces of those present, I saw that many were moved; some had tears in their eyes. I could not tell what they were thinking, but I guessed that most were admiring of Gorbachev at that moment. I knew some of them well, and they were all together now for the last time. Tomorrow they would go their own ways: Anatoly Chernyaev and Georgy Shakhnazarov, who would soon join Gorbachev at his Foundation; Andrey Grachev, his press secretary, who would politely refuse the invitation; Vladimir Shevchenko, his chief of protocol, who would soon become chief of protocol for Yeltsin. Perhaps someone was watching me too, wondering where I would be a couple of weeks later.

Down but Not Out

Two weeks later I got back from the personnel department my "labor record book," a curious Soviet document that officially records one's employment during one's entire lifetime. It said: "Discharged from his post due to the abolition (liquidation) of the office of the President of the U.S.S.R." As simple as that. The office and the country were in their final minutes.

I thought, was Gorbachev an honorable failure? That was, after all, not the worst thing one could be in life. Was he a prophet with no honor in his own country? Many people thought so, and said so. Henry Kissinger, who was not believed to be a great admirer of Mikhail Gorbachev, was the first foreigner who saw Gorbachev at his Foundation a few days after he stepped down. He recalled that biblical phrase and added that history was working faster in the twentieth century and that "the lead time for prophets has now shrunk."

Gorbachev was not an easy man to fit into definitions and pat phrases. I had seen him in different situations, in different moods and states. I saw him supremely confident and happy, and I saw him puzzled, saddened, upset. I saw him down, but not out. In his final months I saw how his opponents tried to humiliate him and worked to destroy him politically. And there were of course times when I believed he was not doing well for himself and hence for the country. He had made mistakes, and he had character flaws that it would soon become fashionable to enumerate. I knew that, but I never agreed that they were decisive in what finally occurred.

Gorbachev had done his best, and it was a great deal. As I watched him conclude his address—and as the year when I was close to him, the year between the two Decembers, 1990 and 1991, flashed through my mind I thought: It had been a tough year, and perhaps unwinnable for Gorbachev. So often he had looked helpless and bound to lose. And he did lose. In the end they had him out. But it took two powerful blows—a coup in August and then the breakup of the country—to seal Gorbachev's fate politically. But, I thought as I shook his hand saying goodbye to Mikhail Gorbachev, the country would survive, and his cause—moving toward democracy, the rule of law, and human rights—would continue. Perhaps he was right—everything was only just beginning.

Afterword (1996)

I finished writing this book in 1992. It took some time to find a publisher, because public interest toward Russia and the former Soviet Union was waning in 1993. After the events of October 1993, when Boris Yeltsin dismissed the Russian parliament and then ordered its building shelled, Americans saw Russia no longer as an exciting, promising democracy but, rather, as a forbidding, even threatening country. The time of glasnost and perestroika seemed ancient history.

When Penn State Press decided to publish the book, I reread the manuscript and was somewhat surprised to see that there was very little I wanted or needed to change or add. It is, after all, a personal memoir, and first impressions and initial recollections often have more insight than subsequent second-guessing. It goes without saying that I stand by the factual account of the events described in this book. As for analysis and evaluations, some things have become clearer than they were then, but the bottom line is the same.

I feel now, as I did then, that in the late 1980s the West and the Soviet Union had a unique opportunity to build new international relations and to ensure a relatively manageable transition from a bipolar world based on the superpower confrontation to a multipolar world of the future. To succeed, the East and the West needed to cooperate not only on arms control and regional issues but also in helping the Soviet Union to modernize its political and economic systems. That did not happen, and I am not blaming anyone for it. Events moved too fast for anyone to be able to adjust to this idea and to control them.

It must be clear to my readers that I disagree with the conspiracy theories—now current in the former Soviet Union, and sometimes supported by remarks from irresponsible or ill-informed people in the West—that the United States is to blame, or to take credit, for the demise of the Soviet Union. Seeking the dissolution of the Soviet Union into fifteen independent states would have been a reckless policy for the United States to pursue.

The record shows that the U.S. administration, far from wanting it, was worried about such a prospect. And rightly so. It is not tantamount to calling for the restoration of the Soviet Union to say that its breakup has had numerous negative consequences both for the people of the former Soviet republics and for the world.

The breakup of the Soviet Union was, in my view, part of a larger failure.

Gorbachev and his small group of supporters in the Soviet leadership had set out to achieve revolutionary changes—both in the country itself and in its relationship with the outside world—by using evolutionary methods. This presupposed a profound change in Soviet/Russian political culture and mentality. In fact, the task Gorbachev took on can be described not so much as an economic or even political reform but as a normalization of Soviet consciousness.

By the time Gorbachev assumed power, Soviet society was saddled not only with a basically Stalinist political and economic system but also with a Stalinist culture and ethos. In foreign policy, it was based on the assumption that the country was uniquely different from the West. Whereas good relations wtih the West were regarded as desirable, and no one thought seriously of promoting a "world revolution," good relations could, in extremis, be sacrificed—and world peace put at risk—to protect the "uniqueness" of the Soviet Union and the "loyalty" of its East European satellites. In the final analysis, the interests of the system came first.

Therefore, when Gorbachev embraced the idea of global interdependence and of the Soviet Union being part of an interdependent global whole, and when that concept was approved by the Communist Party hierarchy, it was a decisive break with the past that had far-reaching and, at the time, unappreciated consequences.

Former Secretary of State George Shultz made a fascinating remark at a conference at Princeton University in February 1993. The press, he said, missed the story of Gorbachev's U.N. address in December 1988 because it was captivated by the "hard news" of Soviet troop withdrawals from Eastern Europe. "But the first half of the speech," Shultz went on to say, "was philosophical, and if anybody declared the end of the Cold War, he did in that speech. It was over. And the press walked by that." Shultz chided the press, but he may also have been referring to almost the entire U.S. foreign policy establishment.

More than most of its other members, Shultz seemed to be aware of the impending change in the global balance, of the movement away from the certitudes of U.S.-Soviet preeminence. I remember how, in April 1987, he showed Gorbachev a chart reflecting projected changes in different countries' and regions' share of the global gross national product. By the year 2010 the share of the United States and of the Soviet Union would shrink, while that of China, India, Brazil, and the European Community would increase significantly. "We must be ready for this new world, Mr. General Secretary," Shultz said. Gorbachev agreed.

I believe it is this understanding, among other things, that prompted Mikhail Gorbachev, Eduard Shevardnadze, and their supporters to break with the past so dramatically in foreign policy. This break was voluntary. It did not result from the U.S. arms buildup of the early 1980s, which could have been met with a counter-buildup or a policy of "waiting out Reagan" and hoping for a better deal with his successor. There were more than a few proponents of those alternatives among, respectively, conservatives and liberals in the Soviet elite.

Gorbachev rejected these alternatives. He was committed to dialogue with available counterparts and disliked "waiting games." He never rejected or resented a negotiating partner because of his or her ideology. Although his foreign policy had solid popular support, he was careful to build consensus for it within the Soviet leadership. This sometimes resulted in delays in the decision-making process, but it enabled him to secure documented support of even conservative political and military leaders for his major foreign policy decisions.

Still, the question is being asked: Were we naive in making too many concessions to the West and in expecting a favorable response from the Western leaders?

It is for historians to study the details of the Soviet concessions, now often criticized by people who had ample opportunity to challenge or try to change those decisions at the time. The documentary record is available, and I am confident it will demonstrate that almost all the concessions were necessary, because the initial Soviet positions, adopted before Gorbachev, were either not negotiable or contained issues or initiatives that were extraneous to the negotiations.

As for the response of the Western leaders, Gorbachev has said repeatedly that it was generally positive and helpful to him. The full story, in my opinion, is more complicated. Conspiracy theories aside, it can be argued that the response was not always forthcoming enough. We now know a lot more about the differences within the U.S. government that made it difficult—though they should not have made it impossible—to develop a more positive response. At some point in 1991 the perception of "Gorbachev making all the concessions" became a negative factor for him domestically and contributed to the atmosphere in which a coup against him was attempted in August 1991.

Nevertheless, the list of Gorbachev's foreign policy accomplishments is quite impressive. They put an end to the isolation of the Soviet Union, created a basis for new relations with the United States and Europe, set in motion the process of nuclear disarmament, and made possible an honorable withdrawal from Afghanistan, resumption of the peace process in the Middle East, and lasting normalization in our relations with China. They also set the stage for a peaceful exercise of free choice by the peoples of Germany and Eastern Europe—the ultimate "proof of Gorbachev's sincerity" that both our domestic radicals and the West had been demanding.

By rights, Eduard Shevardnadze must share much of the credit for these accomplishments. For many people, therefore, his break with Gorbachev in December 1990 remains a perplexing mystery. Some of that story will probably continue to remain unclear, based as it is on factors like "personal chemistry"—it cannot always remain perfect—and fatigue. But I think I now understand more about the underlying reasons for his decision.

In my opinion, Shevardnadze at some point misjudged his old friend Gorbachev. He felt that, faced with a threat to the country's political unity and territorial integrity, Gorbachev would not be able to avoid the use of force. This, after all, is what Shevardnadze himself had to do a few months later in Georgia, when, as the country's head of state, he authorized the use of force to try to prevent the secession of Abkhazia.

The story of Shevardnadze's return to Georgia and his leadership there is too long and complicated to recount here. I shall make only one point: I believe that things might have turned out differently—a lot better—for him and his country Georgia had he stayed on with Gorbachev in 1991 despite his disappointments and problems. Compared with what happened afterward, those appear almost trifling.

Since 1992, Russian politics have been dominated by Boris Yeltsin. There is relatively little about him in my book—almost nothing about his foreign policy role and thinking. This is not just because I did not know Yeltsin and never worked for him. In the period I am describing in the book, Yeltsin took little interest in foreign policy, and even less interest in theoretical concepts such as "new thinking." Yeltsin's main political strength is his unfailing instinct for power. In 1988–91 his road to power went through populist politics. He had a gut feeling for what the people wanted, and the people supported Gorbachev's foreign policy. There was therefore little that Yeltsin could do or say on foreign policy issues with a clear political benefit for himself.

Nevertheless, he did occasionally use those issues for two purposes: to show himself as a more consistent and decisive leader than Gorbachev, and to seek status in the international arena. Essentially, this meant that he was trying to "out-Gorbachev Gorbachev," sometimes coming close to irrevocable concessions on such issues as the territorial dispute with Japan. When, as the leader of independent Russia, Yeltsin took up foreign affairs, with zeal and zest, he was at first eager to show that his policy was more consistently pro-Western than Gorbachev's. His foreign minister Andrey Kozyrev often said that there had been little "real new thinking" under Gorbachev and that only the "new, democratic Russia" was capable of becoming a dependable partner to the "civilized countries" of the West.

The motivation behind this was probably twofold: first, to have Yeltsin's international status confirmed by those who "really matter," that is, Western leaders; second, to clinch Western financial support for his program of economic reform through shock therapy.

An interesting aspect of Yeltsin's foreign policy in 1992 was its ideological aspect. In a memorable address to the U.S. Congress in June of that year he said: "The Communist idol has collapsed and will never rise again." The ideological rhetoric was in sharp contrast to the concept of "de-ideologizing" relations among states, espoused by Gorbachev and Shevardnadze. Yeltsin's anticommunism may have been sincere, but it was also part of an effort to secure large-scale financial support from the West, which never materialized in the quantities expected.

Yeltsin made no visible effort to create a base of domestic support for his foreign policy, and it quickly became apparent that such support was quite fragile and therefore difficult to sustain. It was also quite susceptible to foreign and domestic pressures. One example is the 1992 deal to sell rockets to India for commercial launches; the policy was changed several times, and the assurances given India were eventually rescinded following appeals from President Clinton.

A perception rapidly developed in Russia and abroad that Moscow was mostly following the lead of the United States and that it could therefore be taken for granted. Hence, a change toward a more balanced foreign policy was inevitable. The change began in the latter part of 1992, one of its first signs being the postponement of Yeltsin's visit to Japan. The problem, which is still with us today, was that the change (in some respects, a necessary "course correction") occurred at least partly and at least apparently for the wrong reasons, as a result of pressure from chauvinists such as Vladimir Zhirinovsky, and it often went too far.

I was watching Yeltsin's meetings with foreign leaders as a spectator, not an insider. My impression was that most of his Western counterparts initially liked Yeltsin, both politically and personally, and one reason was that his policy in some areas, particularly arms control issues such as START and the elimination of chemical weapons, showed continuity with Gorbachev's policies. He was, of course, also regarded as the guarantor of Russia's overall democratic and market-oriented course. But Yeltsin was not a stable and predictable partner, and that, coupled with the West's own errors of judgment and missteps, helped produce such disasters as Yugoslavia.

Although Germany must probably take most of the blame for rushing to recognize the former Yugoslav republics as fully independent states, the record shows that Moscow too acted hastily, both in the matter of recognition and then in agreeing to a premature economic embargo against Serbia, which only made the crisis worse. Clearly, the impulse behind Yeltsin's decisions on Yugoslavia was at least in part the desire to act unlike Gorbachev—more decisively, accentuated by a rather sympathetic attitude toward separatism.

As I watched the unraveling of Yugoslavia, I had to admit with dismay that all major powers, including the United States, Germany, and Russia, acted not so much for the sake of peace but more in order to test their strength in a new regional balance of forces and to advance their perceived interests. They gave no real support to the Vance-Owen plan, a deal that, though imperfect, would have been a lot better than what followed its virtual rejection. The results of the big powers' clumsy and often incomprehensible policies are there for all to see. Not only Yugoslavia but also the credibility of major powers and international organizations are a shambles.

The change in Russia's foreign policy that became increasingly evident throughout 1993 and 1994 came not only for the wrong reasons but also too late to change the perception of Russia as a kind of junior partner to the West. This perception is now shared by virtually the entire Russian political establishment, many members of which are insisting on an even more "independent" and essentially anti-Western policy. It is bizarre to watch some of the formerly "Western-oriented" democrats join in this chorus. I believe this is a trap, not only for them but also for Russia and for the West, which by some of its actions has been helping this nationalistic tendency gain momentum.

Nevertheless, most Russians, when asked in public opinion polls about the specific foreign policy actions taken in the years of perestroika—such as the withdrawal from Afghanistan, arms control treaties, and allowing German unification and the changes in Eastern Europe—have continued to give them full support. The anti-Western tendency also seems to be less pronounced among the general public than among the elites. This is an encouraging sign of the people's common sense and good judgment. Still, it would be wrong to take it for granted.

It might be interesting to speculate how international relations would have evolved if the Soviet Union and the Gorbachev-Shevardnadze foreign policy had survived in some form. Hypothetically, the world could have moved toward an essentially cooperative search for a new world order. Given the inevitable economic troubles the Soviet Union would have experienced, its international role would have become more modest, but it would still be a credible partner to the United States and other countries in an increasingly multipolar world. The role of the two "post-superpowers" would still be an important factor, though perhaps one of gradually diminishing importance. There would have been a real possibility of defusing some post–Cold War conflicts, even the one in Yugoslavia.

In contrast, what we see now looks more like "world disorder"—a phrase both used and abused repeatedly, but one that has a grain of truth in it. Conflicts and crises have become virtually unmanageable; and it is increasingly difficult to exert positive influence on them from outside. The upshot is a reduced role not only for Russia but also, ironically, for the "sole remaining superpower"—the United States—and for Europe.

Indeed, the only recent real success in U.S. foreign policy seems to have been in Haiti, where the United States was facing an essentially regional crisis and acting as a regional power. There has also been considerable progress in the Middle East peace process, but that was set in motion when the United States still had in the Soviet Union a real partner with modest but not negligible influence in the region. Although no such partner is available now, the process still has momentum.

The foreign policies of most countries seem to lack clear goals, and the transition to a new global structure is proceeding in the mode of drift. Most distressing is the fact that people have not benefited from a real and tangible "peace dividend." Even though military spending in a number of countries has been somewhat reduced, the trend seems to be waning or even reversing itself; the military/security/intelligence establishment continues to be bloated and is looking for new applications. With the increasingly nationalistic, narrow-minded tendencies gaining ground in the politics and policies of most countries, those new applications may well be another edition of the old ones, slightly retouched for greater plausibility.

And yet it is not true that the only real benefit from the end of the Cold War was the lifting of the global nuclear threat. For most regions, it would be wrong to say that the negative consequences have outweighed the positive ones. From South Africa to the Middle East, from Northern Ireland to Central Europe, from Latin America to Southeast Asia, things are a lot better today than they were ten years ago. Conflicts are being defused, and many potential conflicts have not erupted in the absence of outside support that fueled such conflicts during the Cold War. More than in other areas, in foreign policy the defeat of perestroika was far from absolute. Its legacy survives.

It is well-known what has been happening to this book's main protagonists, so just a few words will suffice.

I have already mentioned Shevardnadze. Georgia's current ordeal is his ordeal. For this and other reasons, it would be wrong for me to comment on some of his specific steps.

Gorbachev has not become a nonperson in his own country, which is a great achievement in itself, but he has become a kind of scapegoat for the Communist hard-liners, the radicals, and the current authorities, all of whom must explain their failures. He is also a scapegoat for many ordinary people, whose early hopes have been dashed. Yet when he meets with the people both in Moscow and in the provinces, he is received well. People listen to him and speak their mind. That they are free to do so is another of his achievements.

His opinions and views are shared by some people and rejected by others. I have found myself in agreement with some but far from all of them. Gorbachev has made mistakes. One, which I hoped he would avoid, was to run for president in the 1996 elections. I, as well as most of those who remained with him after 1991, tried to dissuade him from that, but he said he could not stay on the sidelines and watch as the Russian people were offered "a choice between two evils."

It is true that there was a need for a "third force" in the campaign. Many people were not happy with either President Yeltsin or Communist Party leader Gennady Zyuganov. But Gorbachev, his rapport with the people ruptured and still not restored, was in no position to lead a third force. Besides, Yeltsin and Zyuganov were the only people with the money and the organization to conduct a proper campaign. The issue in the election was therefore formulated in stark terms: Do the people want to continue to move away from the past or do they want to turn back the clock? With the question framed this way, a majority, as Gorbachev had predicted, chose Yeltsin—despite the economic chaos, the war in Chechnya, the mounting crime, and the corruption that has become a way of life.

It is to Yeltsin's credit that he did not heed the advice of those in his entourage who wanted to postpone or cancel the election. The elections, free though by any objective standards less than fully fair, were held as scheduled, thus becoming more and more a part of Russian life—and for this, as

Gorbachev has said, much if not all may be forgiven Yeltsin. But for years to come the course of Russian history will be marked not only by the arduous continuation of the democratic process but also by Yeltsin's character flaws, which are, to use a fashionable phrase, "larger than life."

The failure of Gorbachev's ill-advised campaign did not leave him a bitter man blaming the people for not being worthy of their former leader. He took it all graciously, with the dignity that he so often showed under stress and pressure and that is so sadly lacking in Russian politics.

I continue to work with Gorbachev and to enjoy my friendship with him and his family. So does Anatoly Chernyaev. Since Gorbachev stepped down, they have disagreed on a few issues. On some of the big ones, I believe that Gorbachev was right more often than he was wrong, but on some others I wish he had listened to Chernyaev's advice. Anyway, the important thing is that, unlike some others, Chernyaev has never deserted Gorbachev.

With Alexander Yakovlev, Gorbachev had to part company when Yakovlev decided in 1993 to go to work for Yeltsin. Yakovlev worked for him in various capacities, including chief of radio and television, and was not particularly successful in any of them. Yakovlev's inability to succeed in practical matters always was his main problem.

Some people close to Gorbachev in his final months in office, such as Georgy Shakhnazarov and Vadim Medvedev, now work with him at the Gorbachev Foundation, a think tank Gorbachev set up in 1992. Others have gone their separate ways. Yevgeny Primakov was chief of foreign intelligence, a position to which Gorbachev appointed him in the fall of 1991, until early 1996, and then, following the unceremonius dismissal of Andrey Kozyrev, was appointed minister of foreign affairs. Vitaly Ignatenko, Gorbachev's press secretary in 1990 and 1991, is still director of the ITAR-TASS news agency. He too was appointed by Gorbachev—and in 1995 he became deputy prime minister in Victor Chernomyrdin's government. Andrey Grachev, Gorbachev's last press secretary, is an independent journalist.

Some of the diplomats mentioned in the book, such as Victor Karpov and Yuly Kvitsinsky, are retired and not particularly visible. Others, like Oleg Grinevsky and Alexey Obukhov, are ambassadors in Scandinavian countries. They may be complaining about some things, but probably not about the workload.

Alexander Bessmertnykh heads the Foreign Policy Association, which he inherited from Shevardnadze. Teimuraz Stepanov spent two difficult years in Georgia working as Shevardnadze's assistant. Eventually the pressure was too much for him, and his family in Moscow insisted that he return. He once said to me that in Georgia he had felt like a minor actor in a horror movie. He is currently a leading journalist for the newspaper *Izvestia*.

Sergey Tarasenko too felt it was his duty to try to help Shevardnadze in Georgia, but he returned to Moscow when the war in Abkahzia started, saying war was not his business. He is currently employed by a think tank in Moscow. Kozyrev's foreign ministry had no place for this remarkable man.

Valentin Falin, Gorbachev's opponent on the issue of German unity, has been increasingly vocal in expressing his disagreement with Gorbachev's policies. He lives in the united Germany.

I live in Moscow, fifteen minutes by subway from the city center.

Key People in the Book

Abalkin, Leonid	Soviet economist; Deputy Chairman of the Council of Ministers, 1989–90
Akhromeyev, Sergey	Marshal of the Soviet Union; Chief of the General Staff, 1984–88; adviser to Gorbachev, 1989–91
Andropov, Yury	General Secretary of the Communist Party Central Committee, 1982–84
Aziz, Tariq	Deputy Prime Minister of Iraq
Bakatin, Vadim	Minister of Internal Affairs, 1989–90; member of the U.S.S.R. Security Council, 1991; Chairman of the KGB, September–December 1991
Baker, James A.	U. S. Secretary of State, 1989–92
Baklanov, Oleg	Secretary of the Communist Party Central Committee, 1988–91; member of the coup-plotters' "Emergency Committee," August 1991
Bessmertnykh, Alexander	Deputy Foreign Minister of the U.S.S.R., 1986–90; Ambassador to the United States, 1990; Minister of Foreign Affairs, January–August 1991
Boldin, Valery	Head of the Central Committee's General Department; Gorbachev's Chief of Staff, 1990–91; member of the "Emergency Committee"
Burbulis, Gennady	Yeltsin's close associate
Bush, George	President of the United States, 1989–93
Chernenko, Konstantin	General Secretary of the CPSU Central Committee, 1984–85
Chernyaev, Anatoly	Gorbachev's assistant and close associate, 1986–91
Dobrynin, Anatoly	Ambassador to the United States, 1961–86; head of the Central Committee's International Department, 1986–89; adviser to Gorbachev, 1990–91
Dubinin, Yury	Ambassador to the United States, 1986–89
Falin, Valentin	Head of the Central Committee's International Department, 1989–91
Gandhi, Rajiv	Prime Minister of India, 1984–90

Gorbachev, Mikhail   General Secretary of the Communist Party Central Committee, 1985–91; Chairman of the U.S.S.R. Supreme Soviet, 1988–90; President of the Soviet Union, 1990–91

Grachev, Andrey   Deputy head of the Central Committee's International Department; press spokesman for Gorbachev, September–December 1991

Grinevsky, Oleg   Head of the Soviet delegation at the Stockholm Conference, 1984–86; head of the Soviet delegation at the CFE talks, 1988–90

Gromyko, Andrey   Foreign Minister of the Soviet Union, 1956–85; Chairman of the Presidium of the U.S.S.R. Supreme Soviet, 1985–88

Ignatenko, Vitaly   Gorbachev's spokesman, 1990–91

Karpov, Victor   Head of the Soviet delegation at the START talks; Deputy Foreign Minister for Arms Control

Kissinger, Henry A.   Former U.S. Secretary of State

Kohl, Helmut   Federal Chancellor of Germany

Korniyenko, Georgy   First Deputy Foreign Minister of the U.S.S.R. until 1986; deputy head of the Central Committee's International Department, 1986–88

Kovalev, Anatoly   First Deputy Foreign Minister of the U.S.S.R., 1986–91

Kozyrev, Andrey   Soviet Foreign Ministry official until 1990; Minister of Foreign Affairs of Russia, 1990–96

Kravchuk, Leonid   Chairman of the Ukrainian Supreme Soviet, 1990–91; President of Ukraine, 1991–94

Kryuchkov, Vladimir   Chairman of the KGB, 1988–91; member of the "Emergency Committee"

Kvitsinsky, Yuly   Head of the Soviet delegation at INF talks, 1981–83; later Ambassador to Germany; Deputy Foreign Minister, 1990–91

Landsbergis, Vitautas   Chairman of the Supreme Soviet of Lithuania, 1990–93

Ligachev, Yegor   Member of the Politburo, Secretary of the Communist Party Central Committee, 1985–90

Lukyanov, Anatoly   Secretary of the Communist Party Central Committee, 1986–89; Deputy Chairman of the

	U.S.S.R. Supreme Soviet, 1989–90; Chairman of the U.S.S.R. Supreme Soviet, 1990–91
Maslyukov, Yury	Deputy Chairman of the Council of Ministers, 1987–90
Matlock, Jack F.	U.S. Ambassador to the Soviet Union, 1987–91
Medvedev, Vadim	Member of the Politburo, Secretary of the Communist Party Central Committee
Mitterrand, François	President of France
Mulroney, Brian	Prime Minister of Canada
Nazarbayev, Nursultan	First Secretary of the Central Committee of the Communist Party of Kazakhstan, 1989–91; President of Kazakhstan since 1991
Nitze, Paul	Head of the U.S. delegation at INF talks, 1981–83; arms control adviser to Presidents Reagan and Bush
Obukhov, Alexey	Head of the U.S.A. and Canada Department of the U.S.S.R. Foreign Ministry, later Deputy Foreign Minister of the U.S.S.R.
Pankin, Boris	Soviet Ambassador to Sweden until 1990; Ambassador to Czechoslovakia, 1990–91; Minister of Foreign Affairs of the U.S.S.R., September–November 1991
Pavlov, Valentin	Chairman of the Cabinet of Ministers of the U.S.S.R., January–August 1991; member of the "Emergency Committee"
Popov, Gavriil	Mayor of Moscow, 1989–91
Primakov, Yevgeny	Adviser to Gorbachev; Chairman of the Council of the Union of the U.S.S.R. Supreme Soviet, 1989–90; member of the Presidential Council and later of the U.S.S.R. Security Council, 1990–91
Reagan, Ronald	President of the United States, 1981–89
Ross, Dennis	Head of the State Department Policy Planning Bureau; close associate of James Baker
Ryzhkov, Nikolay	Chairman of the U.S.S.R. Council of Ministers, 1985–90
Sakharov, Andrey	Soviet nuclear physicist and leader of the human rights and democracy movement

Scowcroft, Brent	National Security Adviser to President Bush
Shakhnazarov, Georgy	Gorbachev's assistant and close associate, 1985–91
Shaposhnikov, Yevgeny	Minister of Defense of the U.S.S.R., August–December 1991
Shatalin, Stanislav	Soviet economist, member of Gorbachev's Presidential Council, 1990
Shevardnadze, Eduard	Minister of Foreign Affairs of the U.S.S.R., June 1985–January 1991, November–December 1991
Shultz, George	U.S. Secretary of State, 1982–88
Shushkevich, Stanislav	Chairman of the Supreme Soviet of Byelorussia
Stepanov, Teimuraz	Shevardnadze's assistant and close associate
Strauss, Robert	U.S. Ambassador to the U.S.S.R., 1991
Sukhodrev, Victor	Soviet foreign ministry official and longtime interpreter for Soviet leaders
Tarasenko, Sergey	Shevardnadze's assistant and close associate
Thatcher, Margaret	British Prime Minister until November 1990
Tutwiler, Margaret	U.S. State Department spokeswoman
Vorontsov, Yuly	First Deputy Foreign Minister of the U.S.S.R., 1986–91, and concurrently head of the Soviet delegation at START talks, 1987; Ambassador to Afghanistan, 1988–89; Ambassador to the United Nations, 1990–91
Yakovlev, Alexander	Member of the Politburo and Secretary of the Central Committee until 1990, later member of Gorbachev's Presidential Council
Yakovlev, Yegor	Editor of the newspaper *Moscow News*
Yavlinsky, Grigory	Economist, author of the 500 Days economic reform program
Yazov, Dmitry	Marshal of the Soviet Union; U.S.S.R. Minister of Defense, 1986–91; member of the "Emergency Committee"
Yeltsin, Boris	First Secretary of Moscow Committee of the Communist Party, 1985–87; Chairman of the Supreme Soviet of the Russian Federation, 1990–91; President of Russia since 1991

Index